Runways & Racers
Sports car races held on military airfields in America 1952-1954

Other great books from Veloce –

www.velocebooks.com

First published in May 2011 by Veloce Publishing Limited, Veloce House, Parkway Farm Business Park, Middle Farm Way, Poundbury, Dorchester, Dorset, DT1 3AR, England.
Fax 01305 250479/e-mail info@veloce.co.uk/web www.veloce.co.uk or www.velocebooks.com.

ISBN: 978-1-845842-55-0 UPC: 6-36847-04255-4

© Terry O'Neil and Veloce Publishing 2011. All rights reserved. With the exception of quoting brief passages for the purpose of review, no part of this publication may be recorded, reproduced or transmitted by any means, including photocopying, without the written permission of Veloce Publishing Ltd. Throughout this book logos, model names and designations, etc, have been used for the purposes of identification, illustration and decoration. Such names are the property of the trademark holder as this is not an official publication.
Readers with ideas for automotive books, or books on other transport or related hobby subjects, are invited to write to the editorial director of Veloce Publishing at the above address.
British Library Cataloguing in Publication Data – A catalogue record for this book is available from the British Library.
Typesetting, design and page make-up all by Veloce Publishing Ltd on Apple Mac. Printed in India by Imprint Digital Ltd.

Runways & Racers

Sports car races held on military airfields in America 1952-1954

Terry O'Neil

VELOCE PUBLISHING
THE PUBLISHER OF FINE AUTOMOTIVE BOOKS

Contents

Acknowledgements	5
Data sources	6
Foreword	7
Preface	8
Introduction	10
1 The beginning of the SCCA/SAC era	14
2 SCCA National/SAC races 1952	19
3 SCCA National/SAC races 1953	26
4 1953 Statistical Review	57
5 SCCA national & regional races at other military bases 1953	74
6 1953 Statistical Review	87
7 Other motor clubs using military bases	96
8 1953 Statistical Review	112
9 SCCA National/SAC base races 1954	122
10 1954 Statistical Review	155
11 SCCA national and regional races at non-SAC military bases 1954	175
12 1954 Statistical Review	186
13 1954 – end of the SCCA/SAC era	194
14 SCCA Championship standings	200
Index	205

Acknowledgements

Whilst I readily have to acknowledge that no-one person can have every piece of information available to them, I am still stunned by the realisation of just how many people have contributed towards this book in one way or another.

Extracting accurate information for events that took place over 50 years ago was always going to be challenging, though little did I know just how difficult it would be. Memories have become blurred, and photographs faded, but that is all part of the challenge in the quest to arrive at something nearing the truth.

In writing this book various people have freely given their time to assist me. Luckily, I had help and encouragement from knowledgeable enthusiasts David Seielstad, Michael Lynch, Gary Horstkorta, and Willem Oosthoek, to guide me along the way. Michael Eaton selflessly opened up the David Ash Archives to provide material, and Bruce Perry was able to provide a number of programmes and other material from his own collection for this book. Photographs came from numerous sources, though, in particular, I would like to thank Mark Steigerwald, from the IMRRC at Watkins Glen, together with Ron Kellogg, Pete Lyons, Michael Eaton, Stacey Hopkins, Doug Chadwick, and Rex McAfee for their assistance. Without such people my task would have proved impossible.

A special 'thank you' goes to Jim Sitz, noted motor racing historian and historical consultant for *Vintage Motorsport* and *Road & Track* magazines. Jim readily agreed to proof-read and suggest additional input to the contents of this book. It is he who sorted out some of my 'facts' (known commonly as damn lies!), and has tried to ensure that I did not rewrite history.

I am grateful to Mark Steigerwald and Bill Green, at the International Motor Racing Research Centre at Watkins Glen, for accepting and answering my frequent calls for assistance in finding specific material. Through their assistance it has been possible to access the wonderful archives for which they act as custodians. I am also grateful to Dean Butler, for being able to access the remarkable collection of literature in his library.

It would be remiss not to mention the assistance that I received from the Offutt Air Force Base, and from Patt Buell, historian of the SCCA, Nebraska region.

The Library of Congress, together with public libraries throughout America, have enthusiastically responded to requests for access to local newspapers, a valuable source for background information on venues and race participants. I appreciate the rapid feedback of information from the libraries at a time when I know they are under financial and staff-level pressure. It is a credit to the staff that they were able to help so efficiently.

I must not, of course, forget my wife, Pam, who has continually encouraged and chivvied me to greater efforts at those moments when my inspiration flagged. It is to Pam that I dedicate this book.

Data sources

The following list details those sources from which information has been extracted and analysed for forming background information, race information, results, and, where possible, chassis numbers.

Autosport 1952-1954
National Speed Sport News 1952-1954
Road & Track 1952-1954
Speed Age 1952-1954
Sports Car 1952-1954
Valve Noise 1953
Albany Sunday Herald 1953
American Statesman 1954
Arizona Republic 1953
Atchison Globe 1954
Austin American 1954
Champaign-Urbana Courier 1954
Charleston Daily Mail 1954
Columbus Evening Republican 1954
Department of the Air Force, Offutt Air Force Base
Fort Worth Star-Telegraph 1953-54
International Motor Research Centre, Watkins Glen
Journal and Star 1954
Kansas City Times 1954
Kerrville Times 1953
Library of Congress, Washington
Marion Star 1953
Nevada State Journal 1953
New York Times 1953-54
Omaha World Herald 1953-54
Phoenix Gazette 1953
Reno Evening News 1953
Reno Evening Gazette 1953
Springfield Republican 1954
Springfield Union 1954
Tampa Tribune 1953-54
The Daily Register 1954
The News-Gazette Champaign 1954
Time magazine 1953
Washington Post 1954
Waukesha Daily Freeman 1954

Foreword

By 1953, sports car racing in America had established itself as an emerging sport and a rival to traditional oval track racing. Racing on public roads was as exciting as it was dangerous, and it was the excitement that helped encourage many individuals, the majority with limited income, to enter into race competition. The dangers involved were a lesser consideration to some drivers; however, an increasing amount of fatalities had made the race organisers nervous of putting on such events, and state authorities throughout America were increasingly scathing when they did occur. As a consequence alternative venues had to be found, and in one of those rare moments of opportunity, the right circumstances occurred to take sports car racing in an alternative direction in a sustainable manner.

Throughout history decisions have been taken that immediately impacted on organisations or individuals, though only in the course of time has it been possible to evaluate the longer term effects, beneficial or otherwise. The signing of an agreement between the Sports Car Club of America and Strategic Air Command to hold motor races at SAC bases was just such a moment in time, when an immediate impact was felt on sports car racing in America.

The fascination of why and how an agreement was reached between the SCCA and Strategic Air Command has always occupied my mind. To allow a relatively short yet important stage in the development of sports car racing in America to go unrecorded would be an injustice – both to the people and organisations involved in arranging the deal, and to the many people who supported it.

With that thought in mind I set about to discover as much information about the subject as I could find, and put pen to paper. That I have managed in my own fashion to do so brings much pleasure and satisfaction, and I humbly hope that I have done justice to the story. I have learnt a great deal about the subject as facts came to hand, and I would hope that this book brings a sense of enlightenment and enjoyment to those who read it.

Terry O'Neil

Preface

During the postwar years up to the mid-1950s, sports car racing in America underwent major changes in both its administration and its venues. It was a truly transitional period for the sport, changing from its traditional road racing venues towards the end of the 1940s and into the 1950s, to private enclosed tracks and airports by the mid-1950s. While it can be argued that these changes were forced upon the race organisers by parties outside motorsport, it nevertheless represented genuine progress in terms of organisation for what was then an amateur sport, and safety for the competitors and spectators alike.

Typically, motor sport organisation was in the hands of a few larger motor clubs such as the California Sports Car Club, the American Automobile Association, the Four Cylinder Club of America, the Road Racing Register, NASCAR, and the Sports Car Club of America. In addition, there was a host of single marque clubs, race promoters, plus a few individuals that shouldered the responsibility of doing the work, together with the inherent risk involved. It was not unusual for the events to be co-hosted and sponsored by parties such as the local chamber of commerce or local businesses.

This book predominantly concentrates on the activities of one of these organisers, the Sports Car Club of America, which liased with Strategic Air Command and between them organised a number of races that counted towards the SCCA national championships. Mention is made of other races organised by the SCCA regions and held at military sites where details are available, together with events organised by motor clubs other than the SCCA. As with most other things in life, nothing was clearly defined when it came to organising race events, with some venues having more than one organising body involved. In such cases I have endeavoured to include all of the organising bodies by name.

To confuse the issue, when the SCCA organised its national championships, events other than road races were included – for example, hillclimbs and speed trials. However, these other events have been excluded from this book, which concentrates purely on the road/track racing activities of the day.

In 1950 there was no clear definition as to what constituted either a national or regional event, other than the fact that in a few instances a regional club name had been mentioned as being involved at some point in the event's organisation. It matters little, as no national championship was held that year. The national championship came into existence in 1951 as the SCCA was growing in size and stature, with nearly 30 regional clubs being formed throughout America. However, the title was tenuous at best, due to the manner in which the championships were organised.

In 1951 the national championship was awarded to the driver who scored most points in national events, no matter how many cars that driver ran in different classes. They were all added together, so for someone rich enough to own and race a variety of cars in different classes it was fairly easy to pile up points against someone with only one car at their disposal. The drivers were ranked according to the points accumulated, with one national champion, and the system remained that way until the end of 1953. The system also handicapped the drivers on the West Coast, as there was initially only Pebble Beach that counted towards the national championships, and there were few people who could afford the time and money to keep travelling East in the hope of picking up points.

In 1954 the points system was changed. The national races continued to be taken into account. However, there were national champions for each of the 15 classes within the races. Points were accumulated in these national races, of which there were between 15 and 20 each year. The first six positions in each class gained points: first place 1000 points, second place 750 points, third place 500 points, fourth place 300 points, fifth place 150 points, and sixth place 75 points. The classes, based on engine capacity, basically followed international convention, and certain classes were broken into production and modified sections.

In postwar America sports car racing was not, in real terms, a sport for the masses. Ask a man on the street about motor racing and his mind would focus on oval racing, for there appeared to be a race oval at nearly every town in America, where events would take place on a weekly basis. Consequently media attention was focused on this, as the magazine *National Speed Sport News* will bear testament to, with other types of races gaining only limited coverage, even in motoring magazines. In fact, it was as likely to have mention of the sports car races in the social columns of the local papers as it was to have a report of the event in the sports pages.

The need to keep accurate records was not a prerequisite for the organisers of the races, and as a result in some instances there is no record of how many cars either started or finished in a race. Also, bearing in mind that late entries to the races were common, these would not appear in the published event programme, so it is not unusual to find a result for a car and driver who does not appear as an entrant. A 'flagged off' policy was adopted in some races, and overall positions were not published at those events. It has therefore been impossible to assemble a 100 per cent accurate record, either in terms of race entries or race results. I might add that newspapers were notorious for the mis-spelling of names, but where I have been unable to verify the spelling from other sources I have used it as presented.

NOTE ON THE RESULTS TABLES

Despite intensive research by the author, information on some of the races featured in this book was very hard to find. Blank records in a table indicate known entrants about which no data was available at the time of writing. These will be expanded on where possible in any future editions. Blue headers show the race number, race distance, which classes it was for, the number of starters, the race winner's time, and the average speed (where known). Yellow columns show entrant information in the following order: car number, car make and model, chassis number, driver name, and position.

The result tables reflect the absence of some data for several reasons. Where a 'flagged off' policy was being used in an event anyone outside of the top three per class were not listed as finishing the race, albeit in reality they did. Class placing was considered more important than the overall result where there were a number of classes in the same race, and usually no more than the top five cars were listed in the overall placings.

Introduction

Sports car racing conducted on public roads in the United States of America has its roots in the early 1900s, and continued concurrent with track racing up to 1941 when America entered World War II. It was in the 1930s that a group of enthusiasts formed the Automobile Racing Club of America. Amongst their number were the members of a wealthy landed family, the Colliers. In 1930 they lived on a vast country estate in Westchester County, New York. Called 'Overlook,' it was located near the town of Pocantico Hills on the eastern shores of the Hudson River, within easy driving distance of New York City. Barron Gift Collier, founder of the Barron Collier Company, made a substantial fortune at the turn of the 20th century with a virtual monopoly in subway and tram advertising. Keen to diversify and expand his empire, he purchased 1.3 million acres of land in Florida in 1911 and established Collier County. To help with his plans to develop the area, Barron Collier constructed the 368-mile highway (known as Alligator Alley today) to link Florida's western coast with Miami.

The family's link with Florida was to become even stronger, as it decided to relocate to Florida after World War II. Back in 1930, the three Collier sons – Barron Jnr, Miles, and Sam – were all still in education, with Barron Junior at Yale University, and Miles and Sam at St Paul's Preparatory School. Despite this, the young men all had an interest in motor racing, with European drivers being high on their list of heroes. With friend Tom Dewart, they designed a road racing circuit using the service roads within the family estate. They started racing using home-made karts, though quickly graduated to jalopies and hot rods.

During this time Barron Junior had met and become engaged to a young lady by the name of Barbara Mav, and it was she who presented Barron Junior with a MG-J2 as an engagement present. Barron Junior married Barbara on 24 November 1933, and it was around this time that the Collier brothers and their friends formed the Automobile Racing Club of America, representing very much a minor sector of motor sport in America at that time.

In 1934 Sam and Miles travelled to Great Britain, where Miles bought a used Riley Brooklands car. After purchasing the car, the brothers went to Abingdon to visit the MG factory, where they met Cecil Kimber to talk about importing MGs into America. Their negotiations were successful, and it was agreed that a small number of the J2 model would be shipped to New York. They also arranged for the purchase of an MG L-type for Barron Junior. Returning to America, Miles and Sam formed an MG sales company, Motor Sports Inc, and arranged for fellow racer George Rand to store their cars. By now Sam and Miles were at Yale, so many of the MG car sales were either to fellow racers or by word of mouth. They would never sell more than 15 cars in a year.

Nothing much in ARCA changed in the period leading up to 1940. The club was run on an informal basis, this being reflected in both the quality and location of their events, many in northeast America. Tragedy struck the Collier family in 1939, when Barron Gift Collier died, leaving Barron Junior to sell off the Collier's New York businesses.

10

The most significant venue that the club managed to attend before America entered World War II was in the grounds of the New York World's Fair at Flushing Meadows, where the race was run on closed spectator streets around various nations' pavilions. The race took place on 6 October 1940, and while it brought publicity to the club and hopes that it had at last attained recognition, it turned out to be its last race meeting due to the onset of the war.

In December 1941 the ARCA president, George Rand, officially suspended the racing activities of the club following America's entry into the war. The final letter to each member, dated December 9 1941, began: "Dear member: The purpose for which the Automobile Racing Club of America has existed suddenly ceased to have any significance as of five minutes past one o'clock on last Sunday afternoon." Each Collier brother served their country during the war, and all survived the experience. After the war the brothers decided to settle in the Palm Beach area of Florida, where they could focus on the family's business interests in that state.

It was not until 1944 that thoughts of motor enthusiasts again turned to forming a club. On February 26 1944, a group of seven motor enthusiasts from the Boston area met at the home of Chapin Wallour to discuss the possibilities, and by the end of the meeting they had decided to go ahead and form the new club. This they called the Sports Car Club of America (SCCA). Officials were appointed immediately, these being Theodore Robertson as president, Chapin Wallour as vice president, and Everett Dickinson as secretary and treasurer. The other four attendees were John Duby, Arnold Engborg, George Schulz, and Robert Townsend. It would appear that none of these people had any association with the Automobile Racing Club of America. Bearing in mind that the fate of ARCA was unknown at that time, the SCCA constitution that was drawn up did not include within it the remit to organise sports car racing.

Article two of the constitution stated: "The purpose of the club shall be to foster the preservation and operation of sports cars, to act as an authentic source of information thereupon, and to provide events for those cars and their owners." Further to that, the SCCA in its first newsletter stated: "The necessity for the existence of a sports car club in this country has become increasingly obvious during the last few years. The existing car clubs have concerned themselves entirely with the preservation of veteran motor cars, a worthy objective. There are among us, however, those whose interests vary somewhat from this concept. The vintage sports car has now become sufficiently rare as to warrant an organisation devoted wholeheartedly to its care and preservation. In view of this condition, the Sports Car Club of America has been founded." (*Sportswagon*, March 1944)

After the end of the war when petrol rationing had been lifted, competitive speed trials were organised by the SCCA, but the drivers and the public had to wait until 1948 before sports car racing was restarted in America. When it did commence it was under the guise of the new organisation, the Sports Car Club of America. It became evident that the ARCA would not be revived, and the new club gained many members of the defunct Automobile Racing Club of America within its ranks who were keen to see racing back into the event calendar. As a consequence, a few races were introduced over the next two years. These were well supported by the membership, with many of the competitors driving to the events, racing, then driving back home in the same car they would use day-to-day. Considering that the sport was purely amateur, it was to become very popular with certain sections of the public in the early 1950s, with reasonably large attendance at the SCCA public road race venues in Florida, California, and the northeastern states.

The SCCA was not the only organisation to recognise the upsurge of interest in sports cars. On the West Coast of America, southern California in particular, sports cars were becoming more prominent due to the efforts of Roger Barlow, who through his contacts in the film industry had a ready-made market for his imported sports cars. As Barlow was interested in motor sport, in 1947 he and two other enthusiasts, John von Neumann and Taylor Lucas, decided to form a motor club to provide competitive events for other interested parties. Their club would become the California Sports Car Club, and would prove to be the dominant club in California for a number of years to come, remaining bitter rivals with the Sports Car Club of America in the early 1950s. Whilst the SCCA was busy with its events in the eastern states, the CSCC held its first event at Palm Springs in 1950.

Other clubs sprang up. For example, the Four Cylinder Club of America founded by John Foster, supposedly for people expressing interest but unable to afford to race. The MG Car Club of Northern California was also formed. Kjell Qvale, a car importer and race enthusiast, was the driving force behind this venture, and it was he who organised what was possibly the first of the road races in California, at Buchanan Field, in November 1949. Another important club was the Motor Sport Club of America (more commonly referred to as the Jewish Motor Club) with Bob Grier as its president. In places where such clubs existed and flourished, the SCCA found it necessary in the early 1950s to form an alliance with them in order to put on some of the events. It was not always an agreeable alliance; many an argument raged between the SCCA and the CSCC, as they found themselves fierce competitors even on the few occasions they were forced to co-operate with one another.

Watkins Glen was the first venue to be used for competitive road racing by the SCCA, when the Watkins Glen Grand Prix was run on 2 October 1948. Much to the delight of race organiser Cameron Argetsinger, Sam and Miles Collier turned up to join the SCCA and enter the race, each bringing with them a finely tuned MG-TC. Slowly but surely, over the next few years new venues appeared with the SCCA organising events at Bridgehampton, Elkhart Lake and Pebble Beach, all attracting a high level of competitors and large crowds to watch them. Sam and Miles were keen supporters of the SCCA and attended both Bridgehampton and Watkins Glen in 1949, with Miles winning the Grand Prix at Watkins Glen in his Riley, now sporting a 3.9-litre Mercury Flathead V8 engine. Despite the Colliers residing around Palm Beach and some of the well-heeled members having a winter residence in Florida, nothing had been forthcoming as a suitable venue to expand the circuit network to that part of America. In an attempt to rectify matters, a 'Florida Grand Prix' for sports cars was arranged to take place on 27 February 1949 at Broward County Speedway which was a one-mile paved oval. While it did not compare with the circuits already in use, it did serve to get a finger-hold in that part of America. The race was supported by some of the more prominent SCCA members, with Sam Collier, George Rand, and Bob Gegen all taking part, with the race being won by Tom Demetry driving an MG TC.

However, following a spate of accidents, trouble for the SCCA came to a head following the races held at Watkins Glen in September 1952, where seven-year-old Frank Fazzari was tragically killed while sitting on the curb on Franklin Street. Twelve other people were injured in the same incident, including the dead boy's brother, James, when the left-side rear wheel knock-off hub of Fred Wacker's Allard brushed against a crowd of spectators. This was not the first fatality to occur since public road racing had been re-introduced, and a feeling of acute unease surrounded the SCCA officials, particularly with regards their public liability insurance. The consequences of this latest accident changed the way that races were to be organised in future, and saw the end of racing on public roads; not immediately, but over the next twelve months in the eastern states of America, following a disastrous meeting at Bridgehampton. Legislation was proposed in the New York state assembly to prohibit racing activity on all public roads in New York state following the accident at Watkins Glen, following a similar move already taken in Pennsylvania. Change was imperative, and had to be immediately instigated. With a history of accidents, insurance payments for any further road race would have been prohibitive to the organisers, and without that public liability insurance, townships would no longer agree to their public roads being closed off for racing. The proposed new laws settled this dilemma.

To add to its concern, the SCCA also reluctantly published some financial reports showing that it was losing money at these public road racing venues, as there was no way to control spectator admission, and crowd control and communications were both difficult and expensive to maintain.

Earlier than the 1952 meeting at Watkins Glen, the club organisers feared that steps would be taken to prevent future road races. Anxious to preserve sports car racing, some individuals had taken it upon themselves to look to the future, with the resulting introduction of a paved road course at Thompson Raceway. This, though, was only a small first step towards what would eventually take the place of the public road venues, but it proved possibly the most important accomplishment of 1952 for the long-term future of the sport. This groundbreaking project would serve as a model for future development of race facilities throughout America in years to come.

Three distinct areas of activity existed for sports car racing in America during 1950. On the west coast it was California, whilst on the east coast there was Florida, and further north, an area concentrated around New York state, New Jersey and Wisconsin. As the sport was predominantly amateur it was rare for any drivers to race in any but their own locality, such was the expense and time involved in getting from one side of America to the other side.

A national championship was introduced for certain events run by the SCCA for the 1951 season. These events included racing and hill climbs, but for the purposes of this book hill climb results have been excluded from the result tables. However, when mentioning the championship at the season's end, points awarded for non-racing events have been taken into account.

1952 was to see a significant increase in activity in sports car racing. Popularity in California was intense due to the California Sports Car Club organising major events at places such as Palm Springs and Torrey Pines, and with SCCA regions springing up throughout America, smaller first time events were also being organised.

A truly national championship for SCCA members to participate in was still not viable, but a motor sport magazine, *Motor Sports World*, introduced a 'Golden Steering Wheel Award' that would be competed for in two divisions: over 1500cc and under 1500cc. As the award was announced half way through the season, four of the eight planned races counted retrospectively. It was decided that points would be allocated on a FIA Grand Prix basis to the top five finishers in each division, depending on their finishing positions. The eight events chosen for the award of points were Palm Springs, Pebble Beach, Golden Gate, Bridgehampton, Torrey Pines, Elkhart Lake, Reno, and Watkins Glen. It should be noted that of these eight events, the ones held at Palm Springs and Torrey Pines were not organised or sanctioned by the SCCA.

During the period from late October 1952 until early November

1954, a number of air force bases, naval air stations, and National Guard bases were used for motor racing, mainly by the Sports Car Club of America, but occasionally by smaller clubs as well. The majority of SCCA national races were held in conjunction with Strategic Air Command, whilst the remainder of the national and SCCA regional races were organised in conjunction with the local AFB or NAS commander. In addition to these active bases, a number of former air force bases were also used within the same timescale for local races. It is this area of motor racing, from autumn 1952 to the end of 1954, that is examined within the pages of this book.

Locations

01 Paine AFB, Everett, WA 1953
02 Stead AFB, Reno, NV 1953
03 Moffett Field NAS, San Francisco, CA 1953
04 Luke AFB, Glendale, CA 1953
05 March AFB, Riverside, CA 1953-1954
06 Reeve Field NAVSTA, Terminal Island, CA 1953
07 Offutt AFB, Omaha, NE 1953-1954
08 Fort Worth NGB, Newark, TX 1953-1954
09 Bergstrom AFB, Austin, TX 1953-1954
10 Chanute AFB, Rantoul, IL 1953-1954
11 Stout Field NGB, Indianapolis IN 1953
12 Atterbury AFB, Columbus, IN 1953-1954
13 Lockbourne AFB, Columbus, OH 1953-1954
14 Westover AFB, Chicopee, MA 1954
15 Floyd Bennett Field NAS, New York, NY 1953
16 Suffolk ADC, Westhampton, NY 1954
17 Andrews AFB, Nr Washington, MD 1954
18 Hunter AFB, Savannah, GA 1954
19 Turner AFB, Albany, GA 1952-1953
20 MacDill AFB, Tampa, FL 1953-1954

Map showing locations where races took place on military installations. (Terry O'Neil Collection)

1

The beginning of the SCCA/SAC era

The 26th of October 1952 may not be a date that many people would hold as being special, although in the world of sports car racing in America it proved significant, as it was the day that, in true Hollywood fashion, a marriage of convenience took place between two parties. As with many events in history, the significance was not recognised at the time of the event, but only in the years that followed.

The 26th of October heralded the start of a two-year joint venture between the Sports Car Club of America and Strategic Air Command, whereby sports car racing was held on operational air force bases under the control of SAC in America. The consequence of this was the expansion of the SCCA's racing programme, using other military sites for regional activities. It was a short but memorable time, and an exciting transitional period for racing, going from the postwar years of temporary courses on public roads to the privately owned courses that followed.

The joint programme of races organised between the Sports Car Club of America and the Strategic Air Command came to fruition as a consequence of both parties identifying a specific need. The SCCA had come under pressure due to an increasing number of fatalities and serious accidents happening on the temporary road circuits. The fatalities were of both drivers and spectators, and a growing voice of opinion was concerned with the safety aspects of the sport. So great was the opposition to racing on public roads that it was to bring about the demise of this form of motor sport in America over the next year. The SCCA president, Fred Wacker, saw air force bases as an opportunity to channel the enthusiasm of the participants in a different direction, and at the same time provide a safer environment for both drivers and spectators. (It also possibly saved the SCCA from extinction.)

The commanding general of the SAC, General Curtis E LeMay, had also identified a need, and that was to raise money. The American government funded the running of the SAC at tremendous cost. It was little wonder: at any given moment of the day or night, long range bombers were drilling through the skies at altitudes of six to eight miles on simulated bombing missions, as part of the on-going training that the aircrews received. As a result of the already over-burdened budget, LeMay was experiencing difficulties in agreeing funding with Congress, as well as suffering from declining re-enlistment rates, the latter put down to the competitive labour market in the expanding civil airline industry, and poor accommodation at the bases.

Le May's idea was to utilise the SAC bases to raise revenue, and looking at the facilities they offered, he concluded that they would be suitable for sports car racing. Using the legal basis of Public Law 150, the Air Force Organisation Act of 1950, section 101(a), he approached the chief of staff and the secretary of the air force and put forward his plan. If nothing else, it proved that LeMay was a salesman, as he had to show that the races would improve SAC's "welfare, preparedness and effectiveness," at no extra cost to the government. He obtained the consent needed for this idea on the basis of using 'volunteer' labour, and it was left to him to approach the SCCA with a proposition that would benefit both parties. The SAC calculated that by allowing the SCCA to organise races at its air bases, it could take the profit of each

General Curtis E LeMay, Strategic Air Command. (Terry O'Neil Collection)

Strategic Air Command badge. (Terry O'Neil Collection)

event and plough it into the Strategic Air Command Airmen's Living Improvement Fund. These unlikely, though coincidental, circumstances formed the basis of a practical agreement being drawn up that would suit both parties.

Unsurprisingly, the story begins away from the runways of the air force bases, with road races taking place in the townships of America. The success of these early races also led to their downfall.

The backdrop to the initial meeting between the SCCA and the SAC was one of a slow climate of change in America. World War II had, in relative terms, not long finished, and the growing social middle class was clinging to the values of thrift, conformity, and dedication, learned during that difficult period. Foreign cars were rare, sports cars even rarer, and their owners looked upon as being elitist. Anyone who engaged in street racing was regarded as sinister at best, lawless at worst, and those who chose to race would join a motor club such as the SCCA. In its own right the SCCA was elitist, as it blackballed candidates, discriminated against Jews, and certainly had no black members. Many of the SCCA members were part of the wealthy society that spent as much money on a sports car as the average middle class American could afford to spend on a house, and were looked upon by the conservative middle class as being particularly anti-social, if not anti-American!

So, when a wealthy Chicago sports car racer killed a young boy at Watkins Glen, the SCCA knew it was in serious trouble. Nobody wanted to be associated with the SCCA activities, and insurance became a major issue. It was somewhat fortuitous that circumstances would drive the Sports Car Club of America, and Strategic Air Command, into each other's arms.

A few months prior to the meeting at Elkhart Lake and the tragedy at Watkins Glen, LeMay had ordered his PR manager, Reade Tilley, to write to Fred Wacker suggesting a meeting to discuss the idea of the SCCA using SAC bases for its race events in future. At that precise time there was no pressure mounting on Wacker to reply to Tilley's letter, so it lay in the pending file. Eventually Wacker replied, and with the blessing of the other SCCA officials arranged a meeting with LeMay. Talks for the SCCA/SAC joint programme began at Glenview Air Station near Chicago in late summer of 1952. Fred Wacker drove himself to the meeting while Curtis LeMay arrived in a four-engine bomber, and he had a team of legal aids with him for good measure. Frank discussions between both parties resulted in an agreement being reached, with genuine mutual enthusiasm for the project – it was clear that both parties had pressing needs. Curious to find out how the organisation of road races evolved, LeMay and Tilley went to the Elkhart Lake meeting, where they were not impressed with what they saw. LeMay was stunned by the lack of organisation, and soon realised that there was a great deal of work to be done. His worst fears were confirmed about the dysfunctional organisation when he heard of the accident at Watkins Glen in September.

General Curtis E LeMay was born in Columbus, Ohio in 1906. He achieved a successful career in the air force, and was credited with creating an effective (if not controversial) systematic strategic bombing campaign with B-29s in the Pacific theatre of World War II. In October 1948 he was appointed commander, and made responsible for reorganising the Strategic Air Command as a military arm for conducting nuclear war. Through his experience of World War II he remained a staunch believer in the power of strategic bombing. Politically he would be described as 'far right,' and was characterised by his opponents as a belligerent warmonger and something of a loose cannon. His determination and focus on the job in hand was well defined in the saying "To err is human, to forgive is divine – neither of which is current SAC policy."

One facet of his command that LeMay had quickly developed was identifying the needs of his men in Strategic Air Command, and to trying to fulfil those needs whilst getting the best effort of those men under his charge. However, this strategy required a great deal of money – money that Congress had seen fit to deny him due to increased spending on nuclear-age hardware. That money had to be found from somewhere, and as a consequence it was the personnel budget that suffered.

In the early 1950s recruiting and retention of airmen within the SAC was an ongoing problem, a major factor being their poor living conditions. LeMay figured that if the airmen and their wives were kept happy, retention and efficiency of personnel would naturally improve. Two areas within the SAC were identified as being priorities for this improvement. Firstly, there was the problem of living accommodation for both single and married airmen, and secondly, there was a lack of recreational facilities for the personnel. These were both major issues and were affecting morale. LeMays first job was to motivate the airmen, which he did by introducing a new programme of spot promotions: a policy aimed at boosting morale by awarding promotion and extra pay to the top 15 per cent of aircrews in Strategic Air Command, based on efficiency. The incentive was for the aircrew to remain in the top 15 per cent, because if they dropped out, promotion was lost along with the extra pay. It was amazing how this encouraged the wives to get their men to work on time!

Having instigated the spot promotion programme, something that was unique to Strategic Air Command, it was time to tackle the housing and recreational problems. Most single airmen lived in open-bay barracks that allowed little or no privacy. LeMay felt that in an elite operation such as the SAC, the men should be in rooms rather than open-bays, and hoped to provide a degree of privacy and dignity by building barrack rooms that would house just two people. It was left to the army engineers to fulfil this task, and eventually all the SAC barracks would be provided with the same kind of accommodation.

Housing for the married men demanded a different approach. Historically there had always been a staggering shortfall of family accommodation, and it was acknowledged that each SAC base needed several hundred units to meet their needs. The change began with the formation of the SAC Housing Association. This organisation was based on the idea that the airmen would contribute money as capital, and each man would get his money back, though without interest, when he retired or left the Command. With the money collected, the association would buy prefabricated houses at the bases and rent them to the airmen. To get this radical idea passed through Congress a new law had to be introduced, the Wherry Housing Act, which entailed leasing the government land to building contractors, who built the houses, then leased them back to the military.

Having reached the stage of improved accommodation, it was at this point LeMay realised his desperate need for money to furnish the housing – hence the Airman's Living Improvement Fund came into being. LeMay reasoned that if the SCCA raced at the bases then the profits raised could go to the Airman's Living Improvement Fund to help provide extra comforts for the airmen.

LeMay also came up with the idea of creating hobby shops at the bases so that airmen could utilise their recreational time constructively. The first hobby shop was built at Offutt where LeMay was based, and following its success local SAC base commanders were encouraged to open hobby shops at bases throughout America.

LeMay's interest in sports cars emanated from his friendship with car enthusiast General Francis Griswold, commander of the British third air force in the early 1950s. Through him, LeMay became friends with Sydney Allard. It was through this contact with Sydney Allard, and his support given to the Allard Team at Le Mans in 1953, that LeMay had the opportunity to do a deal whereby he and two other officers could purchase the Le Mans cars. These were the trio of Allards fitted with Cadillac engines used at Le Mans, which suffered from engine trouble prior to the start of the race. Though not known at the time, LeMay

FRED G. WACKER, Jr.
R. E. Chicago Region

Fred G Wacker Jr, President of the Sports Car Club of America. (Terry O'Neil Collection)

SCCA logo. (Courtesy SCCA Nebraska Region)

used an SAC bomber to fly the broken motors from France to Omaha and back again to be refitted in the cars. LeMay made good use of the hobby shop at Offutt, as he and the two other officers that purchased the Allard JRs – Colonels Dave Schilling and Reade Tilley – formed an SAC race team and used the hobby shop to work on the cars.

Le May's logic behind the purchase of the cars was to prove that his men could hold their own against established SCCA drivers. LeMay was refused permission to race his car by the chief of staff, as it was considered too dangerous for a man of his position, but it didn't stop him working on the car in the hobby shop and testing the car on the runways of Offutt air base. Fred Wacker drove LeMay's car at the Offutt event, and Roy Scott from Texas was appointed by LeMay to race the car for him at other events.

Fredrick G Wacker became president of the Sports Car Club of America in 1951. Born in Chicago on 10 July 1918, Fred Wacker was the founder of the Chicago region of the SCCA in late 1948. He was an enthusiastic amateur driver, and a regular sportscar competitor from 1949 to 1955, first with MGs and Healeys, then with Allards. His biggest success came in the 1950 Sebring six-hour race, where he won with co-driver Frank Burrell in an Allard-Cadillac. Frank Burrell was an engineer at Cadillac, but got into trouble with General Motors for unofficially helping Cunningham with the C-1 racer, causing Cunningham to switch to Chrysler engines. Wacker also drove for the Cunningham team at Le Mans piloting a Cunningham C2-R Chrysler with George Rand, but failed to finish the 24-hour race. He also made several appearances for Gordini in European Grand Prix racing during 1953.

From Fred Wacker's perspective, the needs of the SCCA, and the benefits that would be accrued from fulfilling these needs, were quite clear. Simply, the SCCA needed somewhere to race in safety. He knew that sports car racing had the drawing power to attract crowds in numbers beyond the organisational manpower available to the SCCA. Part of the proposed agreement with SAC would see volunteers from the air force bases carrying out the majority of the manual tasks, including crowd direction and control. This would significantly improve the poor crowd safety record the SCCA had acquired over the past few years. The second benefit would be for the safety of the drivers. The sports cars featured little, if any, safety equipment such as roll bars or fire extinguishers, and drivers were without fireproof driving suits. Technical inspection of the cars was basic, with just tyres, brakes, and steering checked over. Given such basic safety standards, broad runways, large clear run-off areas on the bends, and no hazards such as trees and buildings would contribute to greater driver safety for all concerned. It also meant that there was no expenditure for upkeep of permanent facilities in different parts of the country. On the other hand, the drivers found the racing less demanding of their skills, with miles of long, straight, flat concrete, and a few sharp corners to negate.

With the realisation that the proposed plan was the best on offer, the joint SCCA/SAC draft agreement received general approval within the ranks of the SCCA – though there were still some dissenting voices. Opinions were expressed along the line of 'this would not be real road racing,' (which of course it was not) and that 'sloppy driving habits will creep in, endangering other drivers,' together with 'excursions from the course will not carry the penalty they deserve.' On the positive side, driver safety and spectator safety would be greatly enhanced, giving greater satisfaction to all parties involved.

The safety lobby won the day, the Watkins Glen accident being the final straw for many members, and an agreement was drawn up between the SCCA and the SAC for the race at Turner AFB to commence as a trial run in late October. While the deliberations of the SCCA membership were taking place, LeMay's lobbying efforts had paid off, and on 29 November, air force headquarters at the Pentagon issued a letter of approval for major commands to stage car races under guidance adapted from the Turner event. There followed a seven-race package for 1953 that would count towards the SCCA national championship.

A set of basic rules governing the running of the races was established between the two parties at the Glenview meeting. They would be held at a weekend or a holiday so there would be no interference with the normal operations at the base, and airmen would be available as volunteers on free time to assist with the race programme. Stringent rules to ensure safety of both participants and spectators would be enforced. Ample insurance would be provided to cover the United States government against any contingency. No expense to the government would be involved – any money needed prior to the race for the provision of publicity or advertising would be provided by special entertainment sponsored by the airmen, or from the advance sale of tickets. The air base would make its runways available, and certain volunteer personnel would be provided for crowd control and safety measures. The Sports Car Club of America, on the other hand, would assume all responsibility for the conduct of the race.

According to Curtis LeMay, he would arrange that on the weekend of the races the planes would be airborne, and it wouldn't cost the government anything, as it had to do a certain number of routine flights anyway. It was all a matter of scheduling.

During the period of co-operation between the SAC and the SCCA a number of other races were arranged on a regional basis between the SCCA and active air force, naval, and National Guard establishments, but by their very nature, these were low key events. Although not under SAC control, these bases had a similar agreement with the SCCA that a percentage of profits from the event should be allocated to the Airmen's Living Improvement Fund.

With both parties being satisfied that this was the right way forward, they set a date of 26 October in the SCCA 1952 race schedule for an event to be held at Turner air force base in Georgia, as an experiment. Turner AFB was chosen in particular by LeMay, as the commanding officer, Thayer S Olds had already approached LeMay with the idea of holding a race there. It was agreed that should this innovative trial run be successful, then a futher programme of events would be scheduled to run at air force bases during the 1953 season.

Spin-offs were not at the fore when agreements were made, but undoubtedly there was a positive spin-off, as inevitably the local population around the designated AFBs would benefit economically from these races.

SCCA national/SAC races 1952

Turner AFB, Albany, Georgia, 26.10.1952

"Driving strategy, rather than top speed, extended the Cunningham victory streak at the well planned sports car races at Turner AFB." (Speed Age)

Sunday 26 of October had arrived, and a hot and sunny day had dawned on the outskirts of Albany, bringing with it a new era for sports car racing. Turner AFB – located four miles east of Albany, surrounded by pecan groves, farms and plantations – played host to the SCCA for a significant race meeting.

Turner was established during World War II, deactivated in 1946, then reactivated in 1947. Following the start of the Cold War, a part of Strategic Air Command was installed at Turner AFB in March 1951, and remained there until 1957. The inaugural SCCA/SAC race meeting held at the Turner air force base, home station of the 40th Air Division and the 508th Strategic Fighter Wing, was advertised as the Sowega National Sports Car Races. A great deal of planning and hard work was put in by the SAC personnel to ensure that the meeting was a success, especially as prominent members of the SAC and the National Safety Council were in attendance to witness the event.

General Curtis LeMay, Commanding General of the Strategic Air Command, accompanied by his wife, drove his Allard from Offutt AFB, Omaha, to be in attendance. In support of the races, he entered his

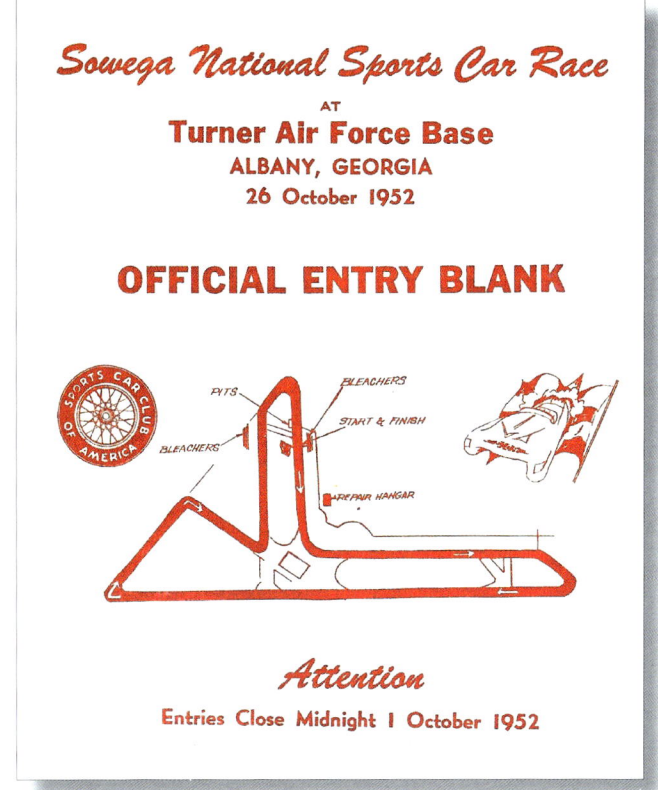

An Official Entry Blank for the inaugural SAC/SCCA event at Turner AFB. (Courtesy Bruce Perry Collection)

Track layout at Turner AFB. (Terry O'Neil Collection)

straight, the track width was 150ft, which would enable four cars to pass each other easily. 1000ft escape roads were located at each of the six turns on the circuit for those who were tardy on their brake pedal, and the spectators were kept 300ft away from the outside of the track behind snow fences. Whilst on the one hand it ensured their safety, on the other hand they were a little remote from the action. No spectators were allowed on the inside of the track – that area was for officials, pit crew and journalists. The competitors were well catered for, as they had the unaccustomed luxury of having an aircraft hanger in which they could carry out pre-race repairs and engine tuning while being sheltered from the heat of the sun. Members of the press appeared satisfied, as they had the luxury of a large press box, an adequately furnished press conference room, and raised portable stands at every curve for the photographers.

The SAC had advertised the SCCA national event aggressively, spending $23,000 on the promotional campaign, and it had paid off. Air force personnel had travelled to the meeting held at Elkhart Lake to observe and find out how things were done on race day, but the volunteer airmen were in for a surprise at Turner AFB. Nothing can prepare you having to cope with a crowd of 60,000 people, but they were praised for their efforts, as the logistics of parking cars, selling tickets, and attending to spectators who arrived aboard aircraft, all in a short period of time, could not be practised before the day.

25 cars from classes six, seven and eight lined up for the start of the first event, the Keenan Sowega Trophy race: a 12-lap, 54-mile contest on a sunbaked track. The field was predominantly made up of MG derivatives, with very strong competition in the form of two OSCA 1350cc cars, a Bandini, and a Glockler Porsche. The remainder of the field was less competitive, and would be battling for class wins as opposed to the overall win.

Military precision was the order of the day, as Curtis LeMay was given the honour of starting this first race. As the flag dropped, James Simpson, a gentleman farmer from Illinois, took an immediate lead as he sped away from the line at double the pace of the other cars, apart from the other OSCA of Al Garthwaite. The two OSCAs opened up a considerable gap over the 12 laps, the only other car to even vaguely challenge for second position being the modified MG TD driven by Bob Salzgaber. Chuck Hassan won the contest for class seven cars in his Bandini, and George Schrafft took the honours in class eight driving a Crosley.

Racing was not the only item on the agenda for the day. Southern hospitality was on offer to the drivers and guests, with a number of buffet lunches and barbecues dotted around the pit area to occupy the non-racing time.

The second race of the day was the 54-mile M W Tift Pioneer car for Roy Scott of Dallas to drive in the M W Tift Pioneer Trophy race. Major General Joseph Atkinson, former Commanding General of the second air force, and Brigadier General Fay Upthegrove, ex-Deputy Commanding General of the second air force, were other ranking visitors. Mr Ned Dearborn, president of the National Safety Council, and Arthur Godfrey of radio and TV fame, were also guests of Curtis LeMay. Ned Dearborn ended up as a working guest, as he served as honorary safety director for the races. Fred Wacker was representing the SCCA, and Captain George Huntoon represented both the SCCA and the SAC. He acted as race chairman, also finding time to enter two of the races in a C-type Jaguar belonging to Max Hoffman, Jaguar importer for the United States.

The track, laid out on the maze of runways, measured 4.5 miles in length, the main straight being 1.75 miles long. At strategic points, but well back from any danger, the course was outlined with yellow marker barrels. In view of the high speeds that could be attained on the long

Never slow to take advantage of publicity, LeMay invited Joe Lunn, national soap box champion, to attend as a special guest for the Sowega National Sports Car Races. (Courtesy Dean Butler)

Trophy race for cars with an engine capacity over 1500cc. 16 cars lined up for the start of the race, amongst them nine Jaguars, three Allards, all with Cadillac engines, and two Ferraris.

George Huntoon, driving a Jaguar C-type, was an easy winner of the event ahead of the Allard J2 of Jack Ensley and Curtis LeMay's Allard K2 driven by Roy Scott. These cars gave a fair indication of what was achievable, as the organisers had arranged speed traps along the 1.75 miles straightway. The Allard K2 was clocked at 130mph down the

LeMay standing next to his Allard, having driven from Omaha to Turner AFB for the races. Roy Scott drove the Allard in the races. (Courtesy Dean Butler)

straight, but the 150mph that Huntoon was getting from the C-type Jaguar gave him an advantage. The pace proved too much for some cars, with five of the starters covering less than seven of the 12 laps.

The result of the main race of the meeting, the Strategic Air Power Race, was to be decided on a time factor, as it was set to be four hours long, and would prove to be a test for both cars and drivers. A large field of an assortment of 51 cars took to the starting grid for this arduous race. Briggs Cunningham had sent a strong team of cars and drivers, hoping to continue his impressive run of results. John Fitch and Briggs Cunningham were in C4R models while Phil Walters was in the C4RK model. They would be up against an equally strong presence of Ferraris. Jim Kimberly was there with his 225S, as was Bill Spear, while Marshall

The start grid for the main event, the Strategic Air Power Race. (Courtesy Dean Butler)

Lewis, who was Kimberly's mechanic, had Kimberly's 340AM. Lunken, having won his class in the previous race, entered his Ferrari 166MM, while Charles Brown was in his 340AM model. SCCA president Fred Wacker was in his Cadillac-powered Allard, and was supported by Carroll Shelby and Jack Ensley. The C-type Jaguar of George Huntoon, together with the OSCAs driven by Benett, Garthwaite, and Simpson, were also expected to do well. Much further down the grid were the smaller capacity Crosley, MGs, and Morris representatives who would be contesting the class awards.

The 1pm start to the race was a noisy and smoky affair, but as the cars came into clear air it became apparent that Marshall Lewis had taken the lead as they swept through the second bend. Not being satisfied with just leading the race, he extended his advantage over the remaining cars as he roared up the 1.75-mile straight at over 150mph, averaging more than 100mph for the first completed lap. At that point Lewis was clearly driving the quickest car in the race. As things settled down Lewis continued to lead, but by now he was being stalked by the Cunningham driven by John Fitch, and Fred Wacker in his highly tuned Allard J2. Some distance behind was the C-type Jaguar of George Huntoon, battling to stave off the advances of Spear's Ferrari and the other two Cunningham cars. As the fuel loads decreased, the straight line speed of the cars increased, with Fitch recording 168mph through the speed trap and Lewis 168.5mph (though it should be noted that there was a prevailing wind of 15mph when these readings were taken). It could well account for some of the frighteningly quick times recorded by most of the cars at that point in the race.

Pit stops played an important part in the outcome of the race. Lewis was obliged to stop more frequently than Fitch, and it was not too long before the latter took the lead. Fitch then retained the lead for the next two hours, trailed by Lewis until the three-hour mark, when Fitch came in the pits to refuel. He came out again just behind Lewis, and the two cars vied for position for the next few laps, until Lewis had to pit for new tyres. That final pit stop was the deciding factor in the race, as Fitch built up a 30-second lead over Lewis that he was not about to relinquish.

Fitch averaged 85.7mph and covered 342 miles during the four-hour race, winning by a scant 32.3 seconds from Marshall Lewis. Fred Wacker finished in third position, well ahead of George Huntoon in the Jaguar C-type. While things were going well for the front runners, life was more demanding at the rear of the field, with desperate times calling for desperate measures. Ludington pushed his car down the last stretch to cross the finish line to qualify, while Hassan pushed his Bandini all of four miles to pass the finish line and qualify in third place in class seven. Class winners were John Fitch, George Huntoon, Bill Spear – who finished fifth overall, four laps adrift of Fitch – Benett in the OSCA, nine laps down on the leader, Schrafft in a Crosley, and Hamlett in a Morris. A tired but elated John Fitch was awarded the Sowega Air Power Trophy by Thayer S Olds, Commanding Officer of the 40th Air Division. When asked the reason for his success, Fitch said that he put it down to strategy. He saw the Ferraris as the biggest threat, but reckoned (correctly) that they would have to stop more often for fuel and tyres.

The race was a triumph for the Cunningham team, but had no bearing on the outcome of the SCCA driver's championship, as that had already been tied up by Sherwood Johnston prior to this event, in which he finished ninth overall.

Briggs Cunningham was a firm supporter of the SCCA together with the values that the club stood for. Although in no way related to the SCCA/SAC agreements, the strong presence of the Cunningham team at these races stirred a patriotic fervour amongst the crowds, something much needed in those troubled times, and the importance of the team and what it symbolised should not be understated. To have an American-built car challenging, and winning, against the much-vaunted foreign opposition such as Ferrari gave impetus to sports car racing throughout America.

The whole event at Turner AFB had turned out to be a remarkable success, and Ned Dearborn, president of the National Safety Council, was not slow in congratulating all concerned. " I have never seen anything comparable to the safety measures taken by this meet to ensure safe crowd control and I want to compliment everyone who had a part in it." (Quote taken from *Sports Car* magazine)

The published financial results for the event justified the planning and hard work that went into the race meeting. The financial results* were as follows:

Income		Expenditure	
Ticket sales	$70,570.35	Insurance	$3334.94
Programme sales	$2699.25	SCCA	$2932.05
Concessions	$4703.06	Promotion	$23,975.16
Miscellaneous	$465.00	Miscellaneous	$431.74
Total income	$78,437.66	Total expenses	$30,673.89

Net profit $47,763.77

The total net profit was donated to the Airman's Living Improvement Fund. Of the sum, $11,500 was spent on a new pavilion, and the balance of the money went on furniture and equipment for day rooms and barracks.

*As published in *Sports Car* magazine.

1952 Statistical Review

Turner AFB 26 October 1952

Keenan Sowega Trophy 12 laps	Race distance 54 miles	Class Under 500cc	Starters 25
Race winner's time 43min 50.4sec		Average speed 73.9mph	

91	OSCA MT4 1350	1123	Simpson J	1oa	1cl 6M
84	OSCA MT4 1100	1114	Garthwaite A	2oa	2cl 6M
85	MG TD		Salzgaber R	3oa	3cl 6M
120	Bandini Crosley		Hassan C	4oa	1cl 7
104	MG TC		Samuelson R	5oa	4cl 6M
111	Palm Beach Crosley		Schrafft G	6oa	1cl 8
90	Glockler Porsche		Lloyd W	7oa	5cl 6M
81	MG TC		Banes W	8oa	6cl 6M
44	Simca 8 Comp		Brundage J	9oa	7cl 6M
103	Cisitalia 202MM Spyder		Ceresole P	10oa	8cl 6M
89	Jowett Jupiter R1		Pace A	11oa	1cl 6 S
79	MG TD		McRae D	12oa	2cl 6 S
92	MG TD		Kuhn R	13oa	3cl 6 S
82	MG TC		Gardner R	14oa	9cl 6M
106	MG TD		Woods A	15oa	4cl 6 S
78	MG TD		MacArthur J	16oa	5cl 6 S
88	MG TD		Steel R	17oa	6cl 6 S
73	MG TD		McCall R	18oa	7cl 6 S
121	Crosley		Dodds W	19oa	2cl 8
109	Siata 300BC Spyder		Ludington F	20oa	3cl 8
117	Morris Minor		King D	21oa	2cl 7
118	Morris Minor		Hamlett J	22oa	3cl 7
119	Morris Minor		Willis J	23oa	4cl 7
83	Jowett Jupiter		Manley D	Dnf L3	
112	Crosley LM		Von Kreidner E	Dnf L3	

Programme cover for the Sowega SAC/SCCA event. (Courtesy Bruce Perry Collection)

M W Tift Pioneer Trophy 12 laps	Race distance 54 miles	Class over 1500cc	Starters 16
Race winner's time 39mins 30.6secs		Average speed 82.00mph	

100	Jaguar C-Type		Huntoon G	1oa	1cl 3M
9	Allard J2X Cadillac		Ensley J	2oa	1cl 2
7	Allard K2 Cadillac	XKC 009	Scott R	3oa	2cl 2
11	Allard J2 Cadillac		Shelby C	4oa	3cl 2
35	Jaguar XK120 Special		Johnston S	5oa	1cl 3
29	Jaguar XK120		Wallace C	6oa	2cl 3

38	Jaguar XK120		Urbas J	7oa	3cl 3	
4	Jaguar XK120		Tilley R	8oa	4cl 3	
24	Jaguar XK120		King B	9oa	5cl 3	
55	Ferrari 166 MM	0054 M	Lunken E	10oa	1cl 4	
36	Allard J2 Mercury		Brundage J	11oa	4cl 2	
10	Ferrari 340 AM	0118 A	Brown C	12oa	2cl 3M	
20	Jaguar XK120		Pace T	13oa	6cl 3	
23	Jaguar C-Type	XKC 013	Blackwood R	14oa	3cl 3M	
21	Jaguar XK120		Rainwater L	15oa	7cl 3	
62	Simca-Ford		Scholl L	16oa dnf		

Strategic Air Power race 76 laps	Race distance 342 miles	Class Unrestricted	Starters 51
Race winner's time 4 hours		Average speed 85.7mph	

2	Cunningham C4R		Fitch J	1oa	1cl 2
5	Ferrari 340AM	0204 A	Lewis M	2oa	2cl 2
8	Allard J2 Cadillac	J1577	Wacker F	3oa	3cl 2
100	Jaguar C-Type	XKC 009	Huntoon G	4oa	1cl 3
60	Ferrari 225S	0218 ET	Spear W	5oa	1cl 4
3	Cunningham C4RK	5218R	Walters P	6oa	4cl 2
1	Cunningham C4R		Cunningham B	7oa	5cl 2
6	Ferrari 225S	0220 ED	Kimberly J	8oa	2cl 4
35	Jaguar XK120 Special		Johnston S	9oa	2cl 3
98	OSCA MT4 1350	1121	Benett C	10oa	1cl 6
25	Jaguar XK120		Blackwood R K	11oa	3cl 3
11	Allard J2 Cadillac		Shelby C	12oa	6cl 2
29	Jaguar XK120		Spitler S	13oa	4cl 3
91	OSCA MT4 1350	1123	Simpson J & Colby C	14oa	2cl 6
90	Glockler Porsche		Lloyd W	15oa	3cl 6
26	Nash Healey		Naughton D	16oa	5cl 3
36	Allard J2 Mercury		Brundage J	17oa	6cl 3
56	Frazer-Nash Mk II LM	421/100/124	Yung R & Tobin E	18oa	3cl 4

21	Jaguar XK120		Rainwater L	19oa	7cl 3
93	MG TD		Allen F	20oa	4cl 6
87	MG TD		Richman H	21oa	5cl 6
111	Palm Beach Crosley		Schrafft G	22oa	1cl 8
81	MG TC		Banes W	23oa	6cl 6
55	Ferrari 166 MM	0054 M	Lunken E & Clark B	24oa	4cl 4
92	MG TD		Kuhn R	25oa	7cl 6
121	Crosley		Dodds W	26oa	2cl 8
27	Nash Healey		O'Hare F	27oa	8cl 3
118	Morris Minor		Hamlett J	28oa	1cl 7
119	Morris Minor		Willis J	29oa	2cl 7
120	Bandini Crosley		Hassan C	30oa	3cl 7
109	Siata 300BC Spyder		Ludington F	31oa	3cl 8
9	Allard J2 Cadillac		Ensley J	Dnf	
10	Ferrari 340 AM	0118 A	Brown C	Dnf	
24	Jaguar XK120		King B	Dnf	
37	Jaguar XK120		Cheatham R	Dnf	
4	Jaguar XK120		Tiller T	Dnf	
22	Jaguar XK120		Wing R	Dnf	
99	Jaguar XK120		Stiles P	Dnf	
77	Jaguar XK120		Bentley J	Dnf	
23	Jaguar C-Type	XKC 013	Blackwood R A	Dnf	
103	Cisitalia 202MM Spyder		Ceresole P	Dnf	
17	OSCA MT4 1100	1112	Makins R	Dnf	
79	MG TD		McRae D	Dnf	
75	MG TD		McCall R	Dnf	
57	Ferrari 166MM		Simpson J	Dnf	
74	Porsche 356	0010 M	Wrego E	Dnf	
44	Simca 8 Comp		Brundage H	Dnf	
85	MG TD		Salzgaber R	Dnf	
84	OSCA MT4 1100	1114	Garthwaite A	Dnf	
117	Morris Minor		King B & Creel C	Dnf	
112	Crosley LM		Von Kreidner E	Dnf	

3

SCCA national/SAC races 1953

MacDill AFB, Tampa, Florida, 21.2.1953

"The last half-hour duel between Hill and Fitch had the crowd standing on the bleacher seats, screaming."
(Speed Age)

The success of the joint SCCA/SAC race programme at Turner AFB left both parties with little doubt that they had found a winning formula. Air force headquarters at the Pentagon issued a letter of approval for major commands to stage motor races, under guidelines adapted from the Turner event. With little hesitation, the SCCA set forward a proposed timetable of jointly arranged races that would count towards the SCCA national championships for 1953. These would be held at seven different SAC air force bases throughout America, bringing new audiences to sports car racing on a grand scale. In addition to the seven SAC/SCCA national races, there would be national events held at Paine AFB in Washington State, and one at Moffett naval air station in California. A regional event was also arranged, to be held at Chanute AFB.

The first of the new programme of events was scheduled to take place at MacDill AFB, located eight miles south of Tampa, Florida, on the tip of the Interbay peninsula. It was sponsored by the Tampa Bay chamber of commerce. When the race programme was being put together for MacDill, the SCCA officials planned to cause a certain amount of discomfort for one of its former officials, Alec Ullmann.

Ullmann had initiated the racing at Sebring in 1950 under the auspices of the SCCA, but early in 1952 he had broken away from the SCCA, as his views on the future of the sport did not coincide with the opinions of the remainder of the SCCA officials.

The Sebring race was run again in 1952, though this time the 12-hour race was under the sanction of the American Automobile Association. The SCCA struck back by introducing a 12-hour race at Vero Beach, for the weekend prior to the date for Sebring, hoping to disrupt Ullmann's plans. This time Vero Beach had not been considered, as the race at MacDill was only two weeks prior to the race at Sebring. The SCCA decided to run a six-hour race as the main event of the programme, in direct competition to the Sebring endurance race, again hoping it would attract the top teams of cars and drivers. Just for good measure, it named the event the Florida National Sports Car Races, and re-introduced the Sam Collier Memorial Trophy (originally awarded at Sebring) for the handicap winner of the six-hour race, in an attempt to affect the credibility of the Sebring race.

The MacDill course measured 4.2 miles, encompassing ten right- and five left-hand corners, together with a straightaway of 1.35 miles, laid out over the runways, taxiways, and parking ramp of the huge B-47 Stratojet bomber base. The format used at Turner AFB was adopted here, namely, having a wide track, ample run-off areas at each corner, and keeping the crowd at least 150ft from the cars on the outside of the track. Volunteer airmen executed the duties ascribed to them: crowd control, selling tickets, and organising the car parking. It turned out

Track layout at MacDill AFB. (Terry O'Neil Collection)

to be an exceptional piece of planning, as a massive crowd of 90,000 people turned up throughout the day. It would appear that, once again, the SAC had been successful with its mass advertising campaign, and the public responded well.

The day dawned bright and warm, which was perfect for those spectators who were there to witness the beginning of the programme. Due to the six-hour race taking up the majority of the time available it was an early start (8.30am) for the first race, featuring production sports cars for the new classes CP and FP (class CP – over 2700 but under 3500cc, class FP – over 1300 but under 1600cc). The SCCA decided to adopt the 'flagging off' system of scoring for this event and the next, the 50-mile race, for which a mixture of Jaguar XK120s and MGs lined up. The course was tricky, but the long straight soon separated the classes. Ernie Erickson took an early lead followed closely by Lup Rainwater, and these two exchanged the lead for several laps before Rainwater had to make a tyre change. At this point Erickson regained the lead, and held it until the end of the race. Rainwater fought back well to regain second position, finishing ahead of Andy Rosenberger, all three drivers piloting Jaguar XK120s. In class FP a real duel had developed for the first three places, and the drivers finished just seconds apart. Bob Fergus was first in his MG TC, Bill Fleming second in a TD, and Bob Gardner finished in third place driving his TC model.

The second event of the day started at 9.45am, and was a 50-mile race for novice drivers in all classes of modified sports cars. Participants in class C drove Jaguars, Allards, and Cunninghams; class F was Porsche and MG; class G an assortment of small Italian cars, Siata, Cisitalia and OSCA; and class H, Bandini. 36 cars took part in the race, leaving the start line in a cloud of dust. Fred Warner took an early lead in his Cadillac-powered Allard, followed by Phil Stiles in a production Cunningham C-3 coupe. For the first few laps, Warner and Stiles were closely challenged by Bob Blackwood driving a Jaguar C-type, and Coby Whitmore in his Jaguar-powered Whitmore-Fitch Special, until Warner's car developed minor mechanical problems and he decided to retire, leaving the Cunningham in the lead. A few laps later Stiles, who worked in promotion and advertising for Cunningham, spun off the track at the hairpin bend, and was unable to get back into the race. Blackwood's Jaguar C-type inherited the lead, followed by Coby Whitmore, and they finished the race in that order. Classes F and G were both tight finishes, Haycraft's Porsche finishing fifth overall, first in class F, while Rees Makins in an 1100cc OSCA took the honours in class G.

At 11.45am the feature event of the day got under way. 65 cars lined up for a Le Mans-type start for the six-hour Sam Collier Memorial Handicap Trophy race. The organisers had managed to attract some of the most potent cars running on the East Coast of America. Briggs Cunningham brought along a team of his cars, with John Fitch and Phil Waters driving Cunninghams, and Briggs driving a 1500cc OSCA. Ferraris was represented by Jim Kimberly's 225S, Bill Spear's 340 Mexico, Moran's 212 Export model, and Lunken's 166MM. Matched against them were six Jaguar C-types, five Allards, plus numerous Jaguar XK120 production models. Smaller engined cars included Porsche, OSCA, Siata, Crosley and MG models, all of which were in contention for the handicap prize.

As the flag dropped the sprint to the cars began, doors slammed, engines roared into life and Phil Walters and John Fitch in the Cunninghams were first away, followed closely by Bill Spear's Ferrari. That was no mean feat by Spear, as he was somewhat heavier than other drivers, and the Le Mans start was not his favoured option. Meanwhile SCCA president Fred Wacker, who had drawn pole position, couldn't get his Allard started until the last car flashed by. His day was to get worse, as he retired the car with engine trouble after fewer than 20 laps. Walters set the pace and was clocked at 132mph along the straight early in the race. Whereas at Turner AFB there had been a prevailing wind, here there was a head wind of 20mph, which reflected in the times recorded by the speed traps. At the end of 18 laps Walters was still leading, with Fitch running second, Sherwood Johnston in Art Feuerbacher's Jaguar third, Fred Warner fourth, and Jim Kimberly fifth. Soon after this point Walters ran into trouble, as the transmission on the Cunningham locked up and he was forced to retire, leaving Fitch in control of the race. Further down the field James Simpson had moved his OSCA up into eighth spot, and the Coby Whitmore Special was ninth.

At the three-hour mark John Fitch was still leading, with Sherwood Johnston's Jaguar C-type second, Jim Kimberly up into third place, and Bill Spear fourth. Many of the heavier cars were making pit stops for fuel and tyre changes, and at the same time some of the cars had driver changes. Of the leading contenders Phil Hill had taken over Bill Spear's Ferrari and George Huntoon had taken over from Jim Kimberly. In the meantime, John Fitch had retained the driving seat in the Cunningham, but as the fourth hour approached Hill began closing in on Fitch, taking six seconds a lap out of his slender lead. The inevitable happened; Hill caught Fitch on the main straight, going past the huge crowd side-by-side at over 130mph. At the end of the straight Hill's hard work paid off, and he passed the Cunningham to take the lead. Meanwhile, George Huntoon in Kimberly's Ferrari was dropping back, suddenly finding that the brakes were rapidly fading. One of the smaller capacity cars was making steady progress through the field – Briggs Cunningham, driving an OSCA, had been barely noticed until the pit stops began taking effect on the larger cars' race positions. He had reached seventh and was comfortably holding some of them off.

Phil Hill led the field with less than one hour to go, when the left front wheel of his Ferrari broke on the hairpin bend at the beginning of the long straight. Using all of his considerable skills, Hill managed to guide the car into the pits driving on the brake drum! This gave Fitch just enough time to pass the Ferrari and the dual started again. Hill was pressing hard, and recorded a speed of 140mph through the speed trap, closing the gap to the Cunningham when another wheel broke at the same hairpin as before, causing Hill to repeat his manoeuvre into the pits. This second unforeseen pit stop allowed Fitch to pull out a

Briggs Cunningham was a regular entrant with his team of cars during 1953. Phil Walters was a regular driver for the team, seen here at Floyd Bennett field. (Ozzie Lyons, courtesy Pete Lyons Collection)

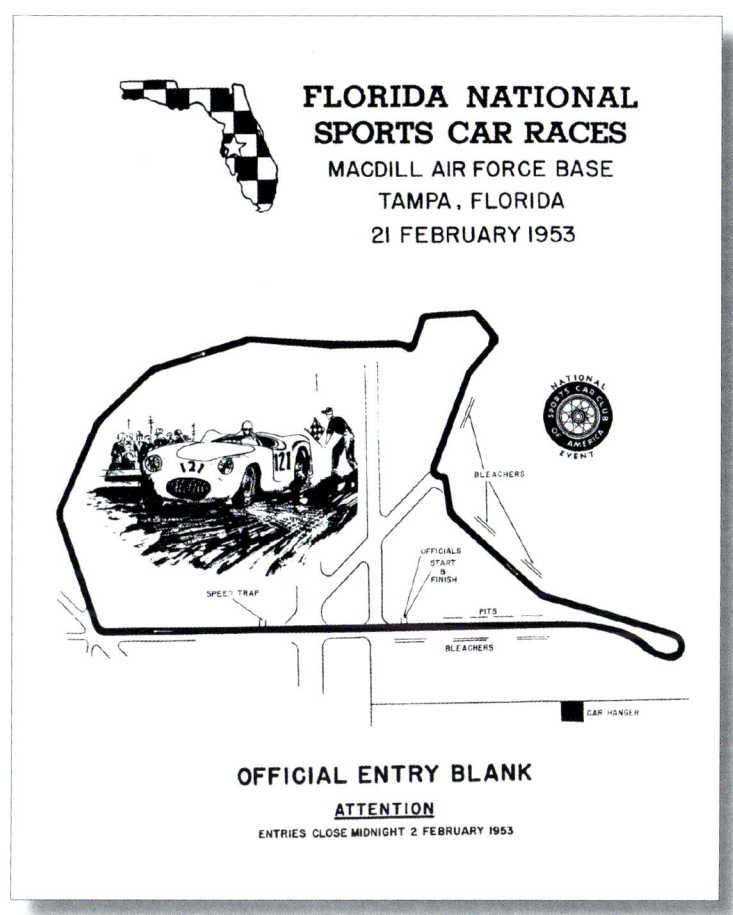

An Official Entry Blank for the event at MacDill AFB. (Courtesy Phil Charlwood)

were announced by the master of ceremonies, TV star Dave Garroway, at the victory dinner held that same evening. General Curtis LeMay presented the Sam Collier Memorial Trophy to Briggs Cunningham after the dinner, and Brigadier General Henry K Mooney, Commanding General of the 6th Air Division at MacDill, offered his congratulations to both Briggs Cunningham and John Fitch for their efforts.

The published financial results for the event show that, despite an increase in spectator numbers compared to the Turner AFB event, overall revenue was $7000 less, and because of having to pay federal tax, expenditure was $10,000 more. Consequently, the net profit was below that taken at Turner AFB. Nevertheless, $30,746.00 was a significant contribution to the Airman's Living Improvement Fund. The fund managers decided that $3260 should be given to the Air Force Aid Society, and the remainder spent on mechanical window fan ventilation, this providing some relief from summer heat for 850 airmen.

The financial results* were as follows:

Income		Expenditure	
Ticket sales	$55,579.25	Insurance	$3839.99
Programmes	$9347.60	SCCA	$5337.77
Concessions	$4815.49	Promotion	$19,505.55
Miscellaneous	$2047.03	Federal tax	$11,135.60
Total income	$71,177.14	Total expenditure	$40,431.14

Net Profit $30,746.00

* As published in *Sports Car* magazine.

considerable lead, but Hill fought back gamely to secure second place on distance covered. George Huntoon, well in control over his nigh brakeless Ferrari, finished in third place, ahead of the C-type Jaguar of Sherwood Johnston in fourth position, Gegen fifth, and Carson in sixth place, with Fred Warner seventh in his Allard. Since this was really a handicap race, the Sam Collier Memorial Trophy was awarded to Briggs Cunningham by using a pre-determined formula adopted by the SCCA, for driving his 1500cc OSCA a distance of 113 laps at an average speed of 77mph. Second on the handicap basis was the Ferrari 225S of Kimberly and Huntoon, and third, the 1100cc OSCA of Rees Makins and Frank Bott. One of the more unusual cars to be seen in this race was that driven by Phil Stiles. He was in charge of a Cunningham C3 Vignale-bodied car, which, at first glance, could have been mistaken for a Ferrari. The car failed to finish the race, and to the author's knowledge was never raced again.

Results based on distance covered and on the handicap formula

Bergstrom AFB, Austin, Texas, 12.4.1953

"It was going like a bomb ... BOOM!" – Fred Wacker's description of his car's demise. (Sports Car)

Bergstrom AFB, located south east of Austin, Texas, was the venue for the second joint SAC/SCCA race of the year. Unlike the event held at MacDill, the elements conspired against the organisers. In the early morning of 12 April, possibly the heaviest rainstorm hit that part of Texas, and it continued until nearly 9.00am. It was more than enough to test the skills of the volunteer airmen, doing their very best to guide the crowds through the deluge of water.

It was a wonder that anyone turned up so early to stand in the wet, just hoping that racing would take place. They must have known something the organisers didn't know, as come 9.00am the rain stopped,

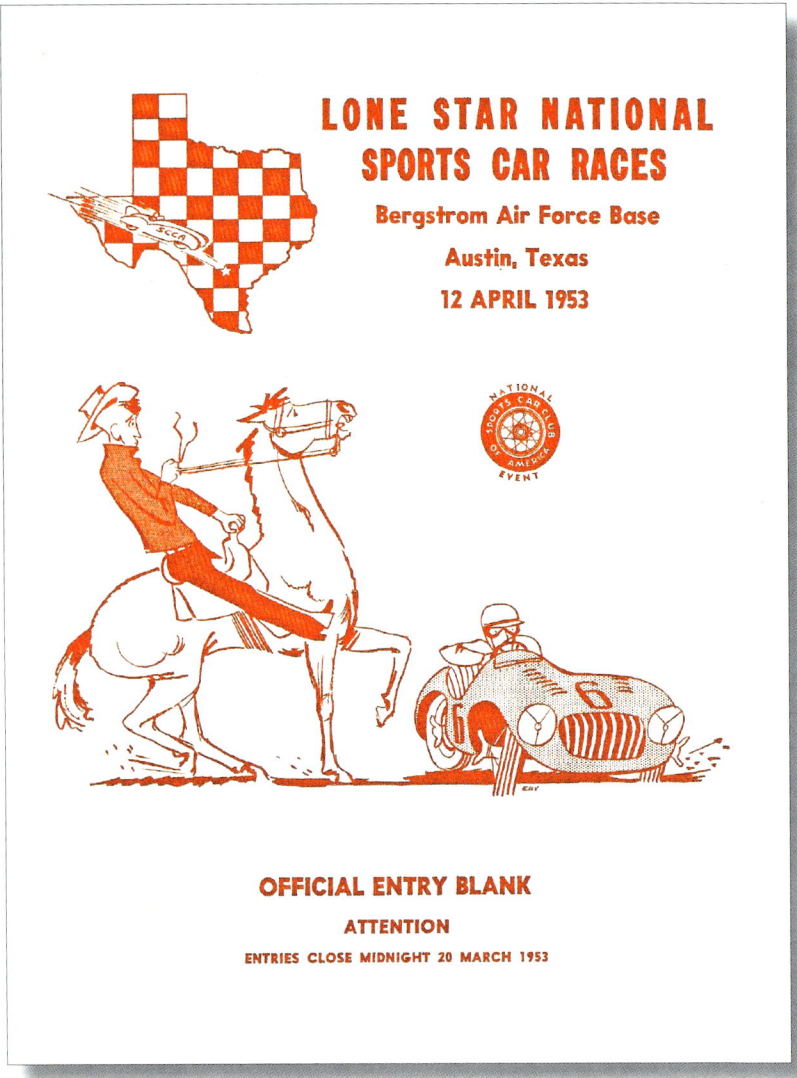

The Official Entry Blank for the event at Bergstrom AFB. (Courtesy Bruce Perry Collection)

Despite the wet and cold start to the day, between 35,000 and 40,000 people turned up, which was not as many as anticipated by the local newspaper editor, who thought nearer 100,000 people might arrive for what was publicised as the greatest sports event in Texas history. Under the circumstances, though, it was a healthy attendance figure that ensured that the coffers of the Airmen's Living Improvement Fund and the Air Force Aid Society would be enlarged. While 80 per cent of the profits would go to these organisations, the other 20 per cent would go to local Austin charities, because officials from Bergstrom AFB wanted to express their appreciation for Austin's hospitality.

The circuit, built on the paved runways, measured 4.48 miles with six right-hand and four left-hand turns. There were four straightaways, the longest being some 6000ft long, on which speed traps were set. These speed traps were manned by a group of volunteers led by Major Ed Craig from Elgin AFB. Long run-off areas were set at each acute bend, and spectators were situated well back from the cars in temporary grandstands to the outside of the track. For the comfort and convenience of the competitors, an aircraft hanger was set aside for their use. They were truly grateful for it, as without this facility it is doubtful if the cars could have been made ready for racing, so appalling was the weather. "Bergstrom's course will be one of the fastest we've had," stated Terry Field, director of national events for the SCCA, "but it will be extremely safe – well supplied with escape roads." He made this observation before assessing the weather!

the skies brightened, and the sun and the brisk wind began to dry the sodden surroundings. The organisers' relief was more than apparent at the lunch interval, as the base had arranged for an unusual air display to take place to demonstrate the skills of the airmen. Four helicopters from the Fort Sill Base put on a square dance routine to music played over the public address system. Even then the weather had the last say, as due to the rain making the ground so soft, one of the grandstands collapsed just before the start of the first race, resulting in a few minor injuries and a delay of the races by 90 minutes. This did at least allow more time for the track to dry out, much to the satisfaction of the competitors involved in the first race.

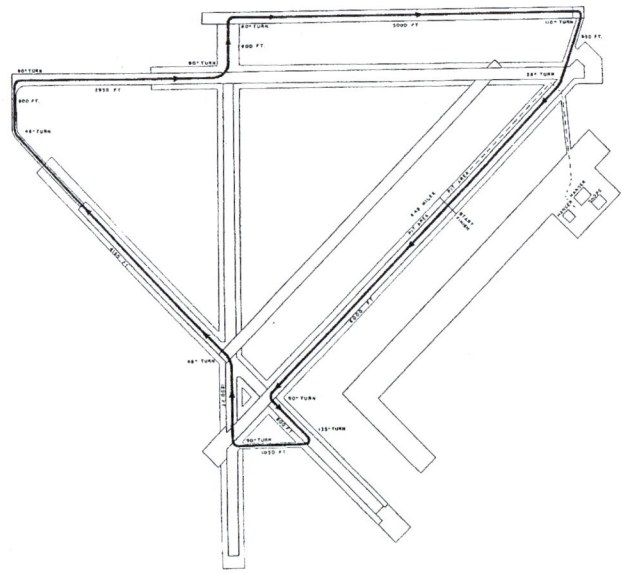

Track layout at Bergstrom AFB. (Terry O'Neil Collection)

However, the weather hadn't been to blame when George Moffett had an accident the previous day during practice. He had spun his new OSCA 1500, and in an attempt to avoid a passing car had the misfortune to hit a landing-light base made of concrete, overturning the car as a result. George was taken to Brackenridge hospital in Austin having sustained a broken leg, broken shoulder, dislocated arm and numerous cuts. Moffett's injuries could have been considerably more serious had his safety belt not held him in.

As for the car, it didn't look too good either. It was taken to the hanger for close inspection to see what structural and mechanical damage had been sustained. Fortunately there was no mechanical damage so the co-driver of the car, Bob Said, decided to try and get the car running again for race day. Six volunteers from the air base machine shop joined the OSCA pit crew together with some of the other competitors, and laboured all night to rectify the body damage and running gear the best they could. At 8.30am on race day, the car, sporting a new coat of red paint with the words 'BAFB Special' emblazoned across the bonnet, was presented for technical inspection and was given clearance to race. It said a great deal about the sportsmanship, comradeship, and determination shown by all those concerned in achieving a successful conclusion

Jack McAfee attends to his Ferrari during the lunch interval at Bergstrom AFB. In the background, four helicopters from the base perform a square dance routine to help keep the crowds entertained. (Courtesy Jack McAfee Collection)

to this unlikely project. On their behalf, Bob Said was awarded the Sportsmanship Trophy presented by the Shell Oil Company.

With the base commander, Colonel Ben Lichy, and race officials being satisfied that all damage to the grandstand had been rectified, and that the spectators were safely relocated, the first event of the day was started, albeit 90 minutes behind schedule. It was a 50-mile race for production sports cars of all classes. A small number of entrants braved the elements, with the Jaguar XK120s expected to be vying for the overall win. There were also several interesting class battles taking place, especially in class F where the Porsches driven by Brocken and Richter were trying to keep the MGs at bay on the drying track. Rainwater and Newcomer, both driving Jaguars, swapped the lead until lap nine when Rainwater fell off the pace. It stayed this way to the finish, with another Jaguar, driven by Harold Fenner, in third. Brocken, an industrial designer from Milwaukee, maintained his lead in class F and finished fourth overall, ahead of the MGs. Local interest centred round Colonel Ray Williams from the Bergstrom AFB. He was driving a MG TD, and finished seventh after driving a trouble-free race, hitting a best top speed of 83mph through the speed trap. The only lady driver entered in the races, Stella Chaney Brown, a fashion consultant, finished in a commendable ninth position.

The second race of the day, 75 miles for modified sports cars, all classes, saw Bill Spear in his Ferrari 340 Mexico take an early lead, never to be headed. At the end of the first lap Roy Scott driving LeMay's Allard was in second place, followed by Fred Wacker's Allard and Jim Kimberly in his Ferrari 340AM. On the fourth lap Scott retired with engine

Jack McAfee's Ferrari 340AM on its way to sixth place in the 200-mile main event. (Courtesy Jack McAfee Collection)

trouble, his place being taken by Jack Ensley in his Allard, followed by Walt Gray in another Allard. The C-type Jaguars were not proving competitive in the early stages of the race, and languished behind the front runners, being harassed by a bunch of XK120s and the rebuilt OSCA driven by Bob Said.

At the halfway stage Spear held a lead of 17 seconds over Fred Wacker and Jim Kimberly, the latter drivers shadowing each other the whole time. Further down the field, the C-type Jaguars of Dale Duncan and Charles Wallace had improved their positions and were catching the Allard driven by Ensley. Among the smaller cars the OSCAs were leading class F, and the tiny Nardi, driven by Paul Gougelman, surprised everyone by holding the MGs at bay. Positions remained unchanged for the last laps, Spear winning comfortably, Wacker winning class B, Bob Said winning class F, Makins class G, and Gougelman class H.

Race three was for production and modified cars under 1500cc. The race was dominated by the latter, with the rebuilt OSCA driven by Bob Said leading from the start, together with Ed Trego's Glockler Porsche driven by John von Neumann. They exchanged the lead at least a dozen times within the first 15 laps, but from thereon Said began drawing away gradually, accumulating a 14-second lead by lap 23. He crossed the finish line just 12 seconds ahead of Von Neumann, with Rees Makins third in another OSCA ahead of Fred Hill's MG TC. The first production car home was the Porsche 356 Super driven by Richter for fifth, closely followed by the highly impressive class HM Nardi driven by Paul Gougleman.

The main race of the meeting was the 200-mile event for modified and production sports cars over 1500cc. There was a diversity of cars rarely seen on this scale in this part of America, the crowd appreciating the chance to witness a selection of top drivers fighting for honours in Ferraris, Allards, and Jaguars, together with a Ford Special brought over from Mexico. Unfortunately Bill Spear, winner of the second race, was unable to take to the start grid due to his Ferrari 340 Mexico suffering from mechanical troubles. Despite the length of the race Kimberly set a quick pace from the outset, being timed through the speed trap at 137mph on the second lap. If his plan was to break the opposition it had an immediate effect, as Fred Wacker in his Allard retired on lap four with a blown engine. As Wacker said later, "It was going like a bomb ... BOOM!" Phil Hill had moved up into second position with the Jaguar C-type, entered by Alex Thompson, with Masten Gregory in third place in a similar car. The rapid pace was beginning to thin out the field.

On lap 18 Sherwood Johnston joined the list of retirements, his Jaguar C-type, entered by Art Feuerbacher, suffering from gearbox problems, while further down the field Chuck Leighton was experiencing cooling problems in the inappropriately-named Jaguar XK120 Silverstone, also entered by Feuerbacher. The car was one of three built for the Le Mans race in 1951, as the Jaguar factory was unsure that the C-type would be ready in time, and was one of two lightened XK120s acquired that same year by Charles Hornberg, the Jaguar representative for America. It had a special one-piece body similar to the standard XK120 in appearance only, being made of magnesium alloy and fixed to a fairly standard XK120 chassis via a tubular framework. One of the Silverstone examples had been raced unsuccessfully by Hornberg in 1951, but it is unclear which of the two cars was sold to Art Feuerbacher. The XK120 Silverstone finally retired with over-heating problems on lap 23.

Phil Hill was still in contention with Kimberly, but after maintaining the same pace as the leading cars for the first half of the race Gregory began slipping back towards the following pack of drivers, and out of contention for the major prize. So it was left to Kimberly and Hill to fight it out to the end of the race. They were neck-and-neck on the 40th lap at 142mph through the speed trap, but the Chicago driver inched ahead after that and led for the closing laps of the race, although Hill kept no further than three seconds behind. Gregory maintained third place in the Jaguar C-type ahead of Jack Ensley in his big Cadillac-powered Allard, while Frank Larson grabbed fifth place in another Jaguar C-type ahead of Jack McAfee's Ferrari.

The whole event was deemed a tremendous success, a fact reflected by the financial statistics. Despite the bad weather early in the morning on race day, ticket sales were better than at the previous meeting held at MacDill AFB. $58,353.42 was taken at the gate, and after expenses the net profit turned out to be in excess of $24,000.00. Twenty per cent of the net profit was given to a variety of local charities, the remainder being used to purchase furniture for the newly assembled barracks at Bergstrom AFB.

The financial results* were as follows:

Income		Expenditure	
Ticket sales	$58,353.42	Insurance	$2766.00
Programmes	$2943.91	SCCA	$6375.21
Concessions	$5737.41	Promotion	$16,515.24
Miscellaneous	$329.40	Federal tax	$9,401.68
		State tax	$4852.48
		Miscellaneous	$3116.17
Total income	$67,363.84	Total expenditure	$43,026.78
Net profit	$24,337.06		

*As published in *Sports Car* magazine

One week after the races held at Bergstrom, *Time* magazine published what appears to be a rather innocuous account of the proceeding at Bergstrom AFB. The report gave a brief outline of the main race and how the money raised by the event would be used for the benefit of the airmen at the base. It resulted in two letters being published in *Time* magazine, purporting to come from dissatisfied airmen at Turner AFB. To receive two letters appears to be more than a co-incidence, especially when both were complaints aimed at Curtis LeMay, implying that no money had been spent on airmen's creature comforts at Turner. It was not surprising that neither letter had the name of the sender published.

"The amount of time spent working on the project by all ranks was not 'off duty' time by any means ... Now, six months afterward, the money is still in the bank (we hope) with no definite project in mind for the improving of airmen's living conditions…The 'Big Cigar' (LeMay) has lost a lot of respect of his men here because of this." Airman's name withheld (*Time* magazine)

"The article about the sports car race held at Bergstrom AFB was a shock and a joke to many airmen stationed at Turner AFB. Turner was the first base to sponsor such a race. The sole advantage gained was General LeMay's prestige. We at Turner AFB feel bitter toward the project and can guarantee, when Turner has another race the airmen will not support it. Turner made $35,000 from the race. It is believed that the proceeds may have been for the use of airmen's living conditions, but Turner has not proven it to us." Airman's name withheld (*Time* magazine)

In response, Thayer Olds, commanding officer at Turner AFB, admitted there had been a delay due to "existing regulations or public laws prohibiting the expenditure of non-appropriated funds." He also added that a committee of officers at Turner had decided that the funds should be used for construction of a picnic pavilion and certain improvements in the hobby shop, and work on these projects was imminent.

"Re the two letters from Turner AFB airmen, appearing in *Time's* issue of 11th May, complaining about the delay in expending funds provided by a sports car race. I feel that an injustice has been done to a most worthwhile project. General LeMay granted permission for the race to be held at Turner AFB's request. He didn't direct it. Subsequent to the race a committee of airmen and a hearing committee of officers from each unit on the base was formed to decide what, in the way of living improvements, should be purchased with the money made on the race. This committee has made six proposals, but it was discovered that existing regulations or public laws prohibited the expenditure of non-appropriated funds for the projects selected due to the fact that Turner is considered a permanent installation. This has resulted in delay. The fund is now in the bank and plans are well advanced for construction of a picnic pavilion, which conforms with regulations. The balance of the fund will be used to make certain improvements in the hobby shop." TS Olds, Colonel USAF (*Time* magazine)

Contrived or otherwise, a seed of discontent had been sown and publicly aired by members of a SAC Base.

Offutt AFB, Omaha, Nebraska, 5.7.1953

"A relative newcomer to sports car racing, Gregory, fresh from a win in the feature event at Golden Gate, promptly did it again, and he did it in a style that will not be forgotten for some time." (**Sports Car**)

Following on from the Bergstrom race, more national events were held at Pebble Beach in April, Golden Gate San Francisco in May, and Bridgehampton, also in May. Not too much of a pattern was emerging towards the SCCA championship, as honours had been spread over the first few events, and no points were awarded at Bridgehampton as the race was stopped after only nine laps due to a fatal accident.

The sixth SCCA national sports car event of 1953 was held at Offutt AFB, a 4000-acre site near to the town of Bellevue, headquarters of the Strategic Air Command, and home to General Curtis LeMay as well as the headquarters of 3902D air base wing. The nerve centre of the SAC looked deceptively innocuous, with pastel-shaded rooms for the enlisted men and an administration block that appeared bland but bristled with security personnel once inside the doors. No wonder, really, for if war was declared, it was here that hard decisions would have to be taken.

Preparation for this showcase event began in April under the control of general race chairman Lieutenant Colonel Reade Tilley, who also helped look after LeMay's Allard. A meeting was convened between base commander A J Beck, Reade Tilley, Ned Dearborn and T K Field to agree the proposed layout for the course. Also at that meeting, a commitment was made by Strategic Air Command for necessary improvements to be implemented to the runway drainage system at a cost of $41,900.

Nothing had been left to chance. Facilities for both drivers and spectators were excellent, the hospitality wonderful, and the circuit turned out to be probably the finest airport circuit in the whole of America, for this, the first SCCA national event to be held in the mid-west.

The course was precisely three miles in length, with a main straight of 5700ft ending in a hairpin corner with a 125ft radius that led onto

An Official Entry Blank for the event at Offutt AFB. (Courtesy Bruce Perry Collection)

An advertising envelope used by the race organisers of the event at Offutt AFB. (Courtesy SCCA Nebraska Region)

another straight 2900ft in length. This shorter straight led into a complex of three bends, the first of 160 degrees followed by two 90 degree bends, and a third sweeping one with a gradient. This unusual feature had been introduced by placing parking ramps between a main runway and access roads. Any driver failing to negotiate this complex was offered the only escape road in the world with a roof over it – a ¼-mile-long hanger with its doors left wide open! There followed two more 90 degree bends and another sweeping corner, again on a gradient, which led back to the main straight. The pits were located on the inside of the track just after the bend that led onto the main straightway.

Safety for spectators, as at previous races, was of paramount importance to the organisers, and the attention given to this aspect was every bit as good as that given to the race track. Ned Dearborn, president of the National Safety Council, was again named as safety director for the event, and it was his responsibility to ensure that the 22,000 bleacher seats were correctly installed along the main straightway. Subsequent to the initial race at Turner AFB in which he was involved, Ned Dearborn said "What I saw at those races convinced me that nothing was being left undone to make the races as safe as is humanly possible. In fact, the racers and the people handling the races seemed to me to be more safety-minded than many of the drivers I had seen on the public highways."

Crowd control was the finest so far, with no spectators allowed on the inside of the track. Estimates of crowd size vary, with over 50,000 being the predicted number, though figures of 45,000 to over 60,000 were reported in several magazine and newspaper reports. None of these figures corresponded to ticket sales income, as tickets were advertised at a price of $2.00 each. Advertising for the event was spread far and wide, with the *Omaha World Herald* giving good pre-race coverage, though some of the hype was inaccurate. In addition to the newspaper coverage, Strategic Air Command drummed up interest with a parade through Omaha and Council Bluffs on the Friday preceding the races, featuring sports cars, antique cars, and, of course, pretty girls.

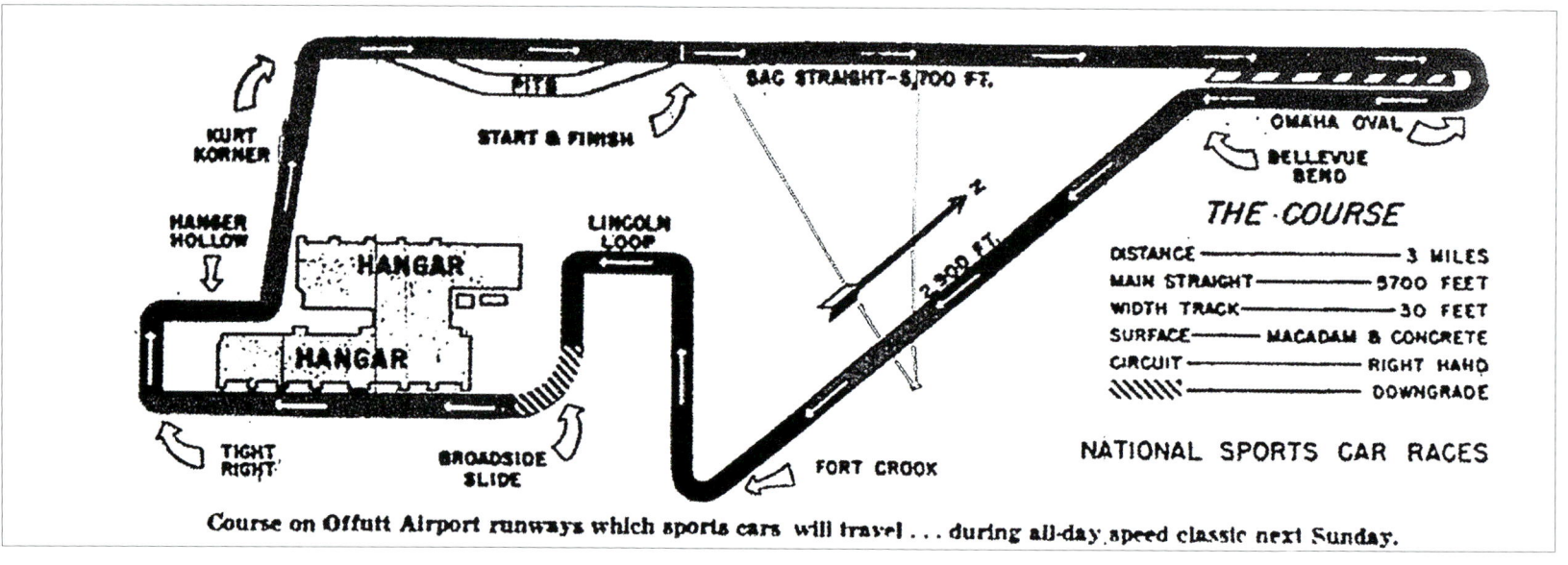

Track layout at Offutt AFB. (Terry O'Neil Collection)

Curtis LeMay and Phil Walters sitting in LeMay's Allard at Offutt AFB. (Courtesy SCCA Nebraska Region)

It was unfortunate that, of all places, there was concern over the methods used to promote ticket sales to the general public from Offutt AFB. They went on sale in late May, and it would appear that one over-enthusiastic officer had exerted undue pressure on a transport company to take a number of ticket books. This action was reported to the Omaha chamber of commerce, which in turn reported it back to Offutt AFB. Reade Tilley quickly dealt with what was described as a misunderstanding in the marketing of tickets, and put forward a simple guideline to those responsible for sales. "Regardless of what methods of promotion used, the air force, Offutt and SAC must not be in the position of applying pressure."

Undaunted by the threat of possible thundery showers, the large crowd began arriving at 7.30am, well in time for the first of the day's four races. The first began promptly at 9.00am, with General Curtis LeMay given the job of starting the 22 class C and F production cars on their 51-mile journey. The Jaguars soon established their own race, being far quicker than the MGs and Porsches. Andy Rosenberger took an early lead, but was overtaken on the third lap by Tom Newcomer from Kansas. Despite being challenged by Rosenberger, Newcomer held on to take the chequered flag after the 17 laps had been completed. The crowd had expected to see Rosenberger cross the line in second spot, but Rosenberger's Jaguar blew a tyre and left the course, leaving Rosenberger with a long walk back to the pits. Roger Wing was promoted into second position, with Ernie Erickson in third place. Phil Moore, driving his Porsche 356, won class F, and did well to finish in fourth place overall, behind the Jaguars.

*McGrade's MG TD ran in the first race of the day, and finished third in Class F.
(Sandy Downs, courtesy SCCA Nebraska Region)*

The second race of the day was for modified sports cars in all classes. The 75-mile event would give ample opportunity for the entrants to sort out their cars, ahead of the 200-mile feature race of the day starting at 3.00pm. Due to the diversity of the machinery competing, internal races evolved. Jack Ensley took the early lead in his Allard J2-Cadillac, followed closely by a pack of Ferraris, Jaguars, and Allards. It soon developed into a duel between Warner, Shelby, and McAfee, as Ensley dropped off the pace, whilst further down the field, the smaller cars in class FM were led by Benett, Salzgaber, and Makins. The leading positions were maintained until the 19th lap when mechanical troubles forced both Warner and McAfee out of the running. This allowed Shelby to coast to victory at an average speed of 75.694mph. Finishing second overall was James Hall of Houston in his Allard, while third place was clinched by Frank Larson driving a C-type Jaguar. William Lloyd won class DM in a Ferrari, while Benett's MG took the honours in class FM. Class HM was won by Charles Brown in a 750cc Siata Spyder.

The lunch interval gave a limited amount of time to those drivers making adjustments to their class F, G, and H modified cars, before they were out again with the under 1500cc production machinery for the third race of the day, a 100 mile event.

James Simpson in his new OSCA MT4 took an early lead, followed by Benett, Makins and Salzgaber. Simpson managed to hold on to his lead for the whole of the race, while during the early stages a lively duel for second position developed between Benett and Salzgaber. Simpson finished one lap ahead of second-place Benett, who limped over the finish line with his MG firing on only two cylinders, with Salzgaber a

*A distance shot of the pit area to the inside of the track shows Tom Newcomer's Jaguar, on the right of the picture, behind Kimberly's Ferrari 340AM and Ferrari 225S.
(Sandy Downs, courtesy SCCA Nebraska Region)*

few car lengths behind him. Simpson's victory followed his success at Turner AFB in 1952, and he was again proving difficult to compete against. The class F honours went to Bill Fleming driving his Porsche 356 and Bob Samuelson scored a first in the class H modified with his Siata 750cc. It proved to be a frustrating day for the only lady driver in the race, Stella Chaney Brown. After completing 25 laps, her MG developed engine trouble. She remarked " I couldn't do more than 80mph. I had to quit. I'd be back in the race if someone would lend me a car."

The 200-mile feature race produced a high quality field of 33 entrants, with particular interest centring on the entry of Curtis LeMay. His Allard JR Cadillac had been placed in the experienced hands of SCCA president Fred Wacker, a shrewd and diplomatic choice of driver! Against him were seven other Allards, Ferraris of various engine displacements, and C-type Jaguars. Pre race favourites were Kimberly, Shelby and Gregory. Kimberly was in confident mood, having given an interview to the *Omaha World Herald,* in which he said "I highly enjoy sports car racing. SCCA racing as an amateur sport is comparable to sailing. The most difficult thing I had to learn as a sports car racer was to back off when things get rough."

As the starter's flag dropped, Warner's Allard stalled on the line, holding back a line of traffic, while Kimberly had a clean start and

Fred Wacker was the nominated driver for LeMay's new Allard JR in the 200-mile feature race.
(Sandy Downs, courtesy SCCA Nebraska Region)

Another distance shot, this of the main race, shows just how remote the crowd was from the action.
(Sandy Downs, courtesy SCCA Nebraska Region)

Carroll Shelby and Jack McAfee drove the Ferrari to a second place finish in the feature race.
(Sandy Downs, courtesy SCCA Nebraska Region)

completed the first lap in the lead, with Duncan's Allard on his tail. Lap two saw Duncan take the lead, but by lap three the lead had changed again. Gregory in his C-type Jaguar had gone to the front, and was building a comfortable cushion between him and the second place car. As the race developed into a pattern Shelby advanced through the field in his Ferrari – the car Ascari had driven in the 1952 Pan-Americana road race, and now owned by A V Dayton – and secured second position on lap nine, pushing Warner back to third place.

By the 25th lap Gregory had lapped the remainder of the field up to fourth position. At this point in the race reliability was fairly high, with Ensley was the only major casualty so far. Walt Gray disappeared on lap 40 with a broken rear axle, and the leading cars started to pit. Shelby pitted to take on new rear tyres, and Jack McAfee took over as driver. The previous night's party had taken its toll on Shelby, who was suffering from a monumental hangover. As the pressure to catch Gregory increased, so did the number of failures. Warner retired on lap 46 and Kimberly on lap 64. Further down the field the pace was also beginning to tell on the cars, with many spending as much time in the pits as on the track. Masten Gregory remained unchallenged at the front coming home an easy winner ahead of the Shelby/McAfee Ferrari and the C-type Jaguar owned by Larson and driven by John Urbas, proving that his recent victory at Golden Gate was not just a one-off. Fred Wacker did not disappoint Curtis LeMay or the crowd,

finishing in fifth position, first in class BM. Tom Newcomer won class C production, and Marshall Lewis in Jim Kimberly's other Ferrari won class DM.

Awards were presented at a victory banquet served at the officers' club on Sunday evening. As a gesture of appreciation, the mechanics of the winning cars were presented a plaque by the Wynn Oil Company.

The event at Offutt proved to be the largest source of revenue for the SAC to date, with over $56,000 going to the Airmen's Living Improvement Fund. Requests were approved for the purchase of bedding equipment, lamps, and pool tables.

The financial results* were as follows

Income		Expenditure	
Ticket sales	$59,926.10	Insurance	$5008.60
Programmes	$9898.75	SCCA	$3511.72
Concessions	$7512.61	Promotion	$11,214.46
Miscellaneous	$835.26	Miscellaneous	$3900.04
Total income	$78,172.72	Total expenses	$24,634.82

Net profit $56,537.90

*As printed in *Sports Car* magazine.

Lockbourne AFB, Columbus, Ohio, 9.8.1953

"The airmen (who had volunteered to help) did a lot of shining. Jim Kimberly owes a medal to the two boys who religiously polished his red Ferrari after practically every practice lap." – Alix Lafontant (Sports Car)

A national meeting was held at Paine AFB in Washington state, one day before the meeting at Lockbourne AFB. The vast distance between the two venues precluded any clashes of interest, with just a few of the top drivers opting to make the long journey to Washington. National championship points gained there would make little or no difference to the general picture that was emerging.

The fourth SCCA/SAC race meeting of the 1953 season was staged on the wide runways of Lockbourne air force base, near Columbus, Ohio, home to the 801st Air Division. This AFB provided "the eyes of the air force," with its' fleet of RB-47 Stratojets. Honouring the state's 150th anniversary, the event was labelled the Ohio Sesqui-centennial National Sports Car Races. As with each of the previous SCCA/SAC events, all proceeds went to the Airmen's Living Improvement Fund for the local Base. The event was sponsored by the Columbus chamber of commerce, and was run under the sanction of the SCCA.

The course was designed to be basically rectangular in shape with a series of curves and bends to one end. The main straightway on which the start/finish line was situated measured some 6800ft, and the one

An Official Entry Blank for the event at Lockbourne AFB. (Courtesy Bruce Perry Collection)

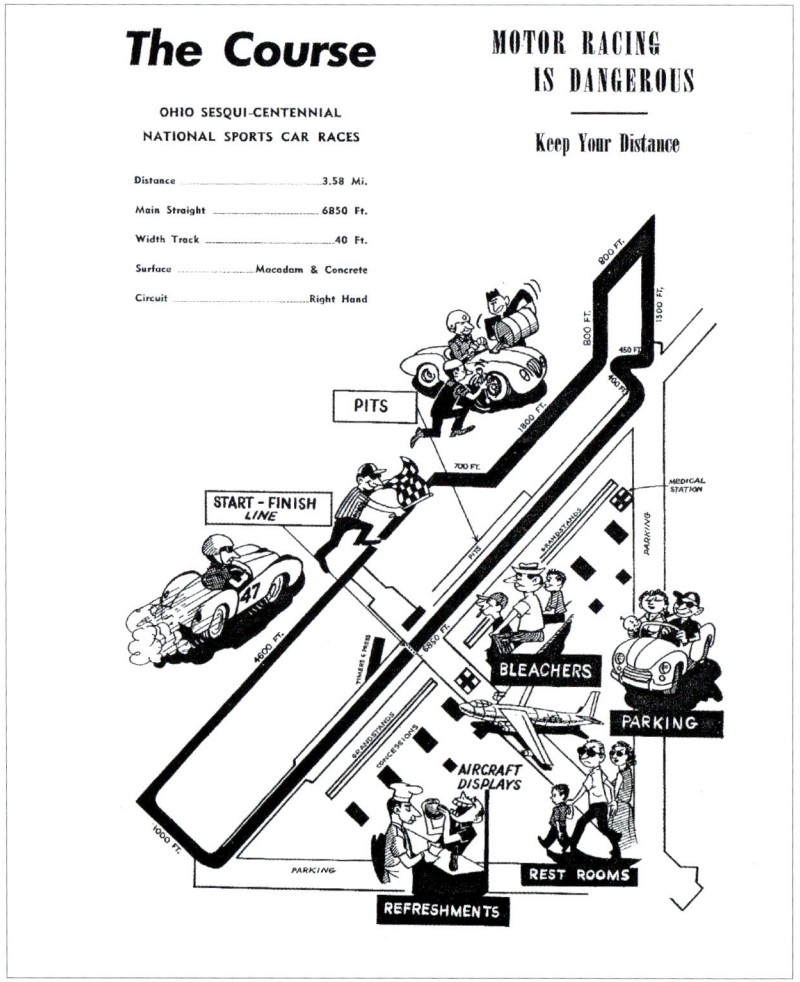

Track layout at Lockbourne AFB. (Terry O'Neil Collection)

running parallel to it was some 4600ft. Overall distance for the track was 3.58 miles on the newly reinforced tarmac and concrete surfaces of the runways and taxi strips, with the pits situated on the inside of the track halfway down the main straightway. Colonel Lewis E Lyle, base commander, was optimistic that it would prove to be the quickest track used by the SCCA.

As was now normal, the SAC publicity machine sprung into action and generated a great deal of column inches in the local papers. It was mooted, quite optimistically, that over 100,000 spectators would turn up for the event. Indeed, one day after the races the *Marion Star* newspaper stated "More than 100,000 racing enthusiasts – a record crowd – were on hand to watch as Fred Wacker swept to a victory in the feature race at Lockbourne AFB." This was also echoed in the *Columbus Dispatch*, which said that "record breaking was the theme of the all-day event. A 100,000-plus crowd, number of foreign sports cars entered and speeds recorded on the 3.5-mile track shattered previous marks." If this was the case, a lot of spectators found their way into the air base free of charge, as ticket sales revenue was just over $51,000. It is doubtful if anyone really knew (or cared) how many people attended; suffice it to say that the crowds looked impressively large and nearly overwhelmed the organisational structure put in place by the SAC.

Over 150 cars were entered for the various races, giving the officials and scrutineers a busy time. In the first race of the day for class F production cars, 46 lined up awaiting the green flag. Apart from a Singer 1500 SM and a Simca 8, they were all either MGs or Porsche derivatives. It was not surprising that the various Porsche models had the edge over the MGs, and at the end of the 50-mile event Bernie Kerner crossed the finish line ahead of Charles Moore and Denny Cornett, all driving Porsche 356 Super models. The first MG was the reliable and very rapid TC model of sports car dealer Robert Fergus, ahead of

Lt Irvin Hoff entered his Porsche 356 America in the first race, finishing 5th in class F3. (Courtesy Doug Chadwick)

Don Marsh in an MG TC, and Charles Stoll driving his MG TD Mk II. Although mainly enjoyable, not everyone came away from the race feeling satisfied. Lieutenant Robert Kuhn had recently sold his Siata and bought an MG TD. His mediocre performance in the car brought about a succinct message from his pit crew as he circulated – SELL IT.

The second race of the day was for cars from classes FM, GM, and HM, and attracted 37 entrants. Taking the lead right at the start was James Simpson in his OSCA MT4, a lead he maintained throughout the race. The true duel was for second and third positions. Max Goldman in the ex-Proctor Porsche battled hard with Proctor in his recently acquired Glockler Porsche. Despite the fan belts breaking on Proctor's car, he held on by a few seconds from Goldman, with fourth spot going to Benett in his modified MG Special. Rees Makins finished fifth overall, and first in class GM, while Paul Gougleman drove his Nardi to a class HM win. Simpson's win earned him more valuable points towards the driver's championship, and people began to wonder if a driver of a small car might take the title this year.

The third race was an all Jaguar affair, split into three separate classes depending on the specification of the car. Thirty cars were on the start line, with Ryberg and Wyllie dominating from the first lap. Wyllie led on the first, but Ryberg took over the lead and held it comfortably to finish first overall. Wyllie finished second, and Kerr in third place, both driving modified cars. The first standard production Jaguar was that of Roger Wing, finishing fourth overall. Isabelle Heskall was awarded the Shell Sportsmanship Trophy for her courtesy and consideration towards quicker drivers in this race.

Richard Yares' Siata 300BC 750 Spyder is ready to go through technical inspection. (Courtesy Doug Chadwick)

Hood mascots to be removed prior to racing! Maybe this is what inspired Roger Wing to a first in class finish in the third race? (Courtesy Doug Chadwick)

The fourth race was the big race of the day, with the much-anticipated battle for championship points between Spear and Kimberly in Ferraris and Gregory and Wallace in C-type Jaguars. An impressive array of 38 cars appeared on the start grid for the 100-mile race. As the flag dropped, Spear's Ferrari 340 Mexico, meticulously prepared by Alfred Momo, eased away from the rest of the field with Gregory, Kimberly and Warner in close pursuit. Wallace, driving the Feuerbacher Jaguar C-type, and Johnston, driving Spear's Ferrari 225S, were conducting their own battle, while at the same time hanging on to the leading pack. It was not a happy venture for Curtis LeMay, as his Allard, driven by Reade Tilley, went out on the first lap with mechanical troubles that could not be cured on the day. Spear could not be caught up by the other drivers, and went on to win the race about one minute ahead of Gregory in the C-type Jaguar, with Kimberly taking third place and Johnston in fourth.

Gregory had amassed a large points tally over the past few races with wins at Golden Gate and Offutt, so Spear was pleased to have come back to some form in this race at Lockbourne.

Further down the field Koster had driven his Maserati A6GCS with much gusto to end up class EM winner and eighth overall, while Boynton's Frazer-Nash ended second in class EM. In the unrestricted class, Whitmore finished first in his Jaguar Special.

The fifth race was a handicap affair, based on performances in the day's other races. The smaller, slower cars left first, some 17.45 minutes ahead of Bill Spear's Ferrari, in a staggered start procedure, and the object was to have them all run the same distance and finish at the same time. Thus Warner and Gregory, having fast cars and on previous performance, receiving a small handicap, while Spear was 'scratch' and had to start last. For a while it looked as if Spear was going to capture

Something has the attention of everyone in the picture – and it's not Whitmore's Jaguar Special. Could it be that Lockbourne AFB was putting on some entertainment? (Courtesy Doug Chadwick)

Abandoned Jaguar! Masten Gregory's C-type Jaguar is parked up prior to the races. (Courtesy Doug Chadwick)

a second win for the day in the 75-mile dash, but Warner in the Allard finished first with Spear's Ferrari a close second, and Fergus' MG TC a creditable third.

Lockbourne proved to be successful again in raising much needed money for the Airmen's Living Improvement Fund, with over $45,000 available to purchase anything from furniture to carpets and curtains.

The financial results* were as follows:

Income		Expenditure	
Ticket sales	$51,837.69	Insurance	$5089.00
Programmes	$10,052.36	SCCA	$3314.78
Concessions	$4302.48	Columbus chamber commerce	$2702.17
Base fund drive	$8352.00	Promotion	$7900.49
Miscellaneous	$220.59	Federal tax	$6000.00
Contribution AFAS	$4140.00		
Total income	$74,765.12	Total expenditure	$29,147.44

Net profit $45,617.68

*As printed in *Sports Car*.

The reliability of Spear's Ferrari 340 Mexico played a huge part in Spear winning the SCCA Drivers Championship in 1953. His win at Lockbourne AFB earned him valuable points towards this achievement. (Ozzie Lyons, courtesy Pete Lyons Collection)

Koster's Maserati A6 GCS finished first in class E in the feature event of the meeting. In the background is the Porsche 356 Super belonging to John Bentley. (Courtesy Doug Chadwick)

Stead AFB, Reno, Nevada, 17/18.10.1953

"Though the filthy weather cut deeply into the expected crowd, more than 33 cars faced the starter's flag at the beginning of the two and a half hour handicap race."
– Alfred Coppel (Sports Car)

Following on from the Lockbourne event, over two months elapsed before the next SCCA/SAC race took place. In the meantime, three other national events had been held, those being at Moffett Field NAS on the west coast, and Janesville and Thompson Raceway on the eastern side of America. At those meetings Spear did best, accumulating 1050 points, while Benett, Kimberly, Stroppe, and Cunningham each gained 1000 points towards their national championship bid.

Early in the spring of 1953, when the San Francisco region was formulating its programme for the year, Reno was pencilled in as a prospective race venue. Talks involving the SCCA had been ongoing with the Stead AFB officials, and approval had been gained from both the SAC and the USAF to hold races at the base, home of the SAC Survival School, situated some 12 miles north of Reno. With final approval from the SCCA, the venue was not only confirmed, but also added to the programme of national events for 1953. Technically it constituted the second running of the Reno road races, although the first event was held around the streets of Reno in 1951.

The races were run under the sanction of the SCCA, and jointly sponsored by the Reno chamber of commerce and the San Francisco region of the SCCA. Tactical control of the races was handed over to

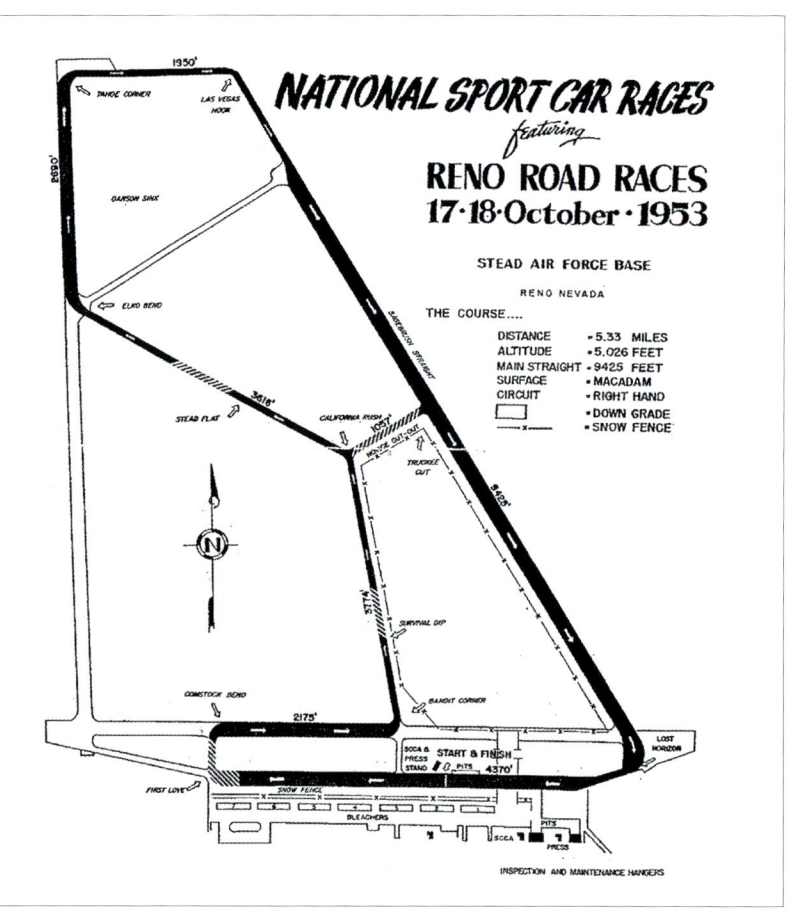

An Official Entry Blank for the event at Stead AFB.
(Courtesy Bruce Perry Collection)

Track layout for the two courses used at Stead AFB.
(Terry O'Neil Collection)

Colonel D G Stampados, who was assigned to the organising committee. All profits derived from the races went to the Airmen's Recreational Facilities Fund, the monies spent on furnishing squadron day rooms and providing athletics equipment for airmen at the base.

Two courses were mapped out over the runways and taxi stripes of the base, one being 2.84 miles in length with six turns, which was used for the ten-lap races, and a 5.33-mile course involving eight turns and an enormous straightway of 9450ft. This was easily the longest straightway used for SCCA racing, and was also the highest, being just over 5000ft above sea level. The extended course was used just for the main event, the two-and-a-half-hour long Reno road race. 8000 bleacher seats were erected along the start/finish straight, but the vast majority remained empty over the weekend.

The *Reno Evening News* reported that a new timing device would be in operation for the races. "Timing in the straightway to obtain speed will be by a crystal-controlled 100 kilocycle oscillator accurate to two-parts per million. The device was designed by University of California." There was also mention of a movie production team being present, Columbia Pictures filming the races for *The Little Giant* starring Mickey Rooney.

It was reported in the *Nevada State Journal* that practice runs were set up on 4 October for local drivers to familiarise themselves with the track layout. However, they were cancelled at the last moment due to the repainting of guidelines on the runways.

Ask anyone from Nevada about October, they will tell you that in a dry, crisp atmosphere, with precipitation never exceeding 6in for the month, temperatures are between 42 degrees low at night and 70 degrees high during the day. Not this weekend! The weather conditions were bad for the Saturday races, and even worse when Sunday dawned. Biting cold winds gathered momentum over the Sierra peaks, and swept across the open expanse of the airfield on Saturday. To add to everyone's misery, there was freezing rain on Sunday.

Two events were planned for Saturday: first the Sagebrush race, a ten-lap event for novices held on the short course. A fair few of the entrants had travelled from a warm and sunny California and possibly wondered what they were doing, sitting on a runway at high altitude with a freezing wind blowing. As the green flag fell, the MGs of Chatfield (actually Barlow's old Simca, reworked) and Qvale sped off with Helm in a Porsche Special and Taylor in his Simca. Initially, Taylor's car was going well, but began to struggle after a few laps with carburetion trouble due to the altitude, and Chatfield's car also went out with mechanical failure, leaving Qvale in the lead. Qvale remained out front and took the chequered flag ahead of Taylor's spluttering Simca and Helm's Porsche Special, with Mack's MG close behind in fourth place. One competitor who did not have to brave the weather was Bob Wallace. He had a new motor shipped in for his MG TC. With mechanics waiting to install the engine, it arrived safely, only for it to roll off the truck and hit the cement with a sickening thud, signalling the end of his weekend before he had turned a wheel.

The second and final event of the day was entitled "The Biggest Little Race," for novice drivers with cars over 1500cc, and was run for ten laps over the 2.84 miles course. Fourteen cars lined up, and it was Joe Cochrane's Allard that took an immediate lead, closely followed by the Allard LM driven by Carl Block and the 1932 Ford Special of Max Balchowsky. The order remained the same for five laps then the Ford Special retired, allowing Tom Henderson's Jaguar to move up into third place. These three cars maintained their positions until they reached the chequered flag. With a biting wind and the threat of rain the few brave spectators and competitors dissipated swiftly hoping that a new day would bring better weather.

Sunday dawned and there was definitely a feel of winter in the air. It was wet, windy and cold and left the spectators disappointed. It was therefore no surprise that spectators were thin on the ground and bleachers left empty, and also accounts for why programmes are so scarce, for many of those that were issued became sodden and thrown away.

The Airman's Cup for MGs and the Survival Race for Jaguars ran concurrently over the short course, but so hard was the rain it was difficult to monitor the progress of the cars. Plumes of spray obscured all but the front runners ,and sight of the end of the pit straight was lost in the curtain of rain. It turned out to be a good race for the local drivers, Ray Seher and Harry Banta. As Al Torres dropped the green flag, Weiss managed the best start and took the lead. His advantage was not to last for too long, however, as his Jaguar had several excursions off the track that took him to the back of the field, leaving Seher's Jaguar in the lead. Try as he might, Weiss couldn't make up enough ground to catch Seher, but finished the race in a well-earned second place. Harry Banta was the best (bravest) of the MG drivers, finishing seventh overall and first in class.

Next up came the Comstock Trophy, a ten-lap race for Formula Three cars and the winners of the novice races. There were grave doubts as to the wisdom of starting the race, but it went ahead despite the heavy rain and poor visibility. Cochrane's Allard took an immediate lead over the rest of the field and maintained it to the end of the sixth lap, at which point the race was terminated. The visibility was so poor that the officials were having extreme difficulty identifying the cars. Cochrane was declared the race winner, followed by the Jaguars of Byrd and Ramsey. Quite incredibly, the F3 cars kept going in the appalling conditions without getting waterlogged, with Trimble finishing ahead of Swift and Steiner, all of them driving Coopers.

After a break of 40 minutes to allow the rain to subside, 33 slightly apprehensive drivers lined up for the gruelling two-and-a-half-hour Reno Road Race – a time-distance handicap for all classes run on the 5.33-mile circuit.

Eager to gain championship points, the main West Coast contenders were all there, but with the exception of Masten Gregory there was a noticeable absence of top East Coast contenders, such as Spear and Kimberly. The officials decided that a conventional grid start in order of decreasing engine displacement would be employed due to the wet conditions, instead of a Le Mans type start. Minutes later a few of the drivers would regret that decision as Phil Hill, sitting on the front row, stalled his engine and jammed the entire left-hand lane of the grid as the flag fell. Sterling Edwards in his new Ferrari 340AM took the lead closely followed by Gregory, Dickey and Block. Edwards had been waiting for his Ferrari since July, his original car being sold to Bill Spear. After his failure to start, Hill eventually fired up the Ferrari and set off in pursuit of the field as it disappeared into the distance.

The first significant retirement was that of Masten Gregory's C-type Jaguar, Gregory experiencing trouble with the rear end of the car on the ninth lap. His retirement allowed Hill into second place after cutting his way through the remainder of the field, followed by the Kurtis-Cadillac of George Sawyer and the OSCA of Bill David. By the halfway mark Sawyer's Kurtis was out of the race, promoting Bill David's OSCA to third position, followed by Carl Block's Allard LM, Coppel in an OSCA, MacDougall in a 2-litre Ferrari, and Von Neumann in a Porsche 356 America.

The two-hour mark saw the demise of a few other cars – the Kurtis of Rhode, Dickey's Allard, and Pinkerton's Jaguar – while Block had to pit on lap 27, and in so doing, lost a place to Coppel's OSCA. Most of the Jaguars were struggling due to water in the brakes, and in general it was a poor showing from the marque.

Within the final 30 minutes there were no changes of significance, so it was Edwards who took the chequered flag ahead of Phil Hill, followed by an outstanding performance from Bill David in an OSCA 1350 and Al Coppel in an OSCA 1100. After the race, Hill said of Edwards "He just out-dragged me to the finish line."

It had been agreed that an Index of Performance award would be given, and this went to Harry Eyerly in his Crosley, just ahead of Pete Lovely in his Giaur, with Al Coppel's OSCA 1100 in third place. Twenty-four of the 33 starters finished the race, an unusually high percentage, possibly due to the low temperature and wet conditions, which prompted caution and slower than normal lap times.

On the Sunday evening, trophies were awarded to the winners at the victory dinner dance at the Riverside Hotel, by master of ceremonies Aldo Ray, an increasingly popular Hollywood star. In addition to the regular trophies, a 'tough luck' award was given to Chuck Leson of Oakland by the SCCA. Leson, who was considered to have an excellent chance in the Reno Road Race, allowed his mechanic to drive in the novice event. During the race the engine was damaged, and in spite of frenzied attempts to make repairs on Saturday night, they were unable to put the car back into shape for the big race, leaving Leson without a drive.

There were no figures published by the SCCA or the SAC to indicate how much money had been raised for the Airmen's Recreational Facility Fund. Suffice it to say that, although the attendance was extremely low over the two days due to the weather, it was fortuitous that the organisers had thought to take out a rain insurance policy to cover the event. This at least provided them with a profit for their hard work over the weekend.

Turner AFB, Albany, Georgia, 25.10.1953

"The greatest sports car event ever to take place in the USA featured an exciting Ferrari-Cunningham battle in the 252-mile main race." – Ruth Sands Bentley (Autosport)

A week after the Reno event, attention turned to the remote city of Albany in South West Georgia. The race event held at Turner AFB was a significant landmark for the SCCA for a number of reasons. Importantly, it was the first event staged by the SCCA that gained sanction by the Federation International de L'Automobile, the international governing body for automobile races. Secondly, the event celebrated a year's activities between the SCCA and Strategic Air Command. It was also the first event where a lap of over 100mph was recorded under race conditions. On the wide-open space of the airfield runways William Spear achieved this feat in his Ferrari 340MM while racing in the Strategic Air Power Trophy race.

Just as significant was the fact that Porsche entered its factory sponsored cars in a race in the United States for the first time, en route to compete in the Carrera Panamericana in Mexico. These cars were in the hands of Karl Kling and Baron Hushke von Hanstein, the first German race drivers in the United States since World War II. They made the front page in the *Albany Sunday Herald*, alongside the grave news that on the eve of the races, tragedy struck, when John Negley from Pennsylvania was killed on a practice run. His Allard J2 LM went out of control, skidded, struck an immovable object off the course, and rolled several times. The accident was later attributed to a wheel breaking. In 12 months of SCCA/SAC racing, this unfortunate accident was the first racing fatality recorded at an SAC base.

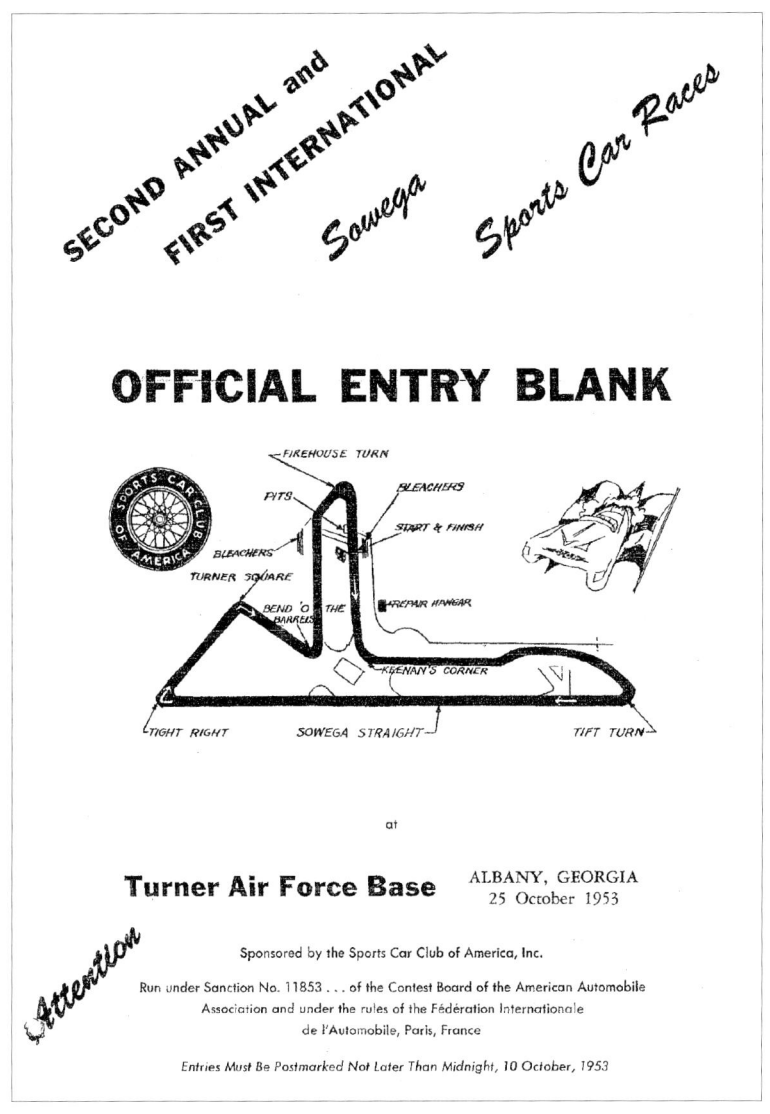

An Official Entry Blank for the event held at Turner AFB. (Courtesy Bruce Perry Collection)

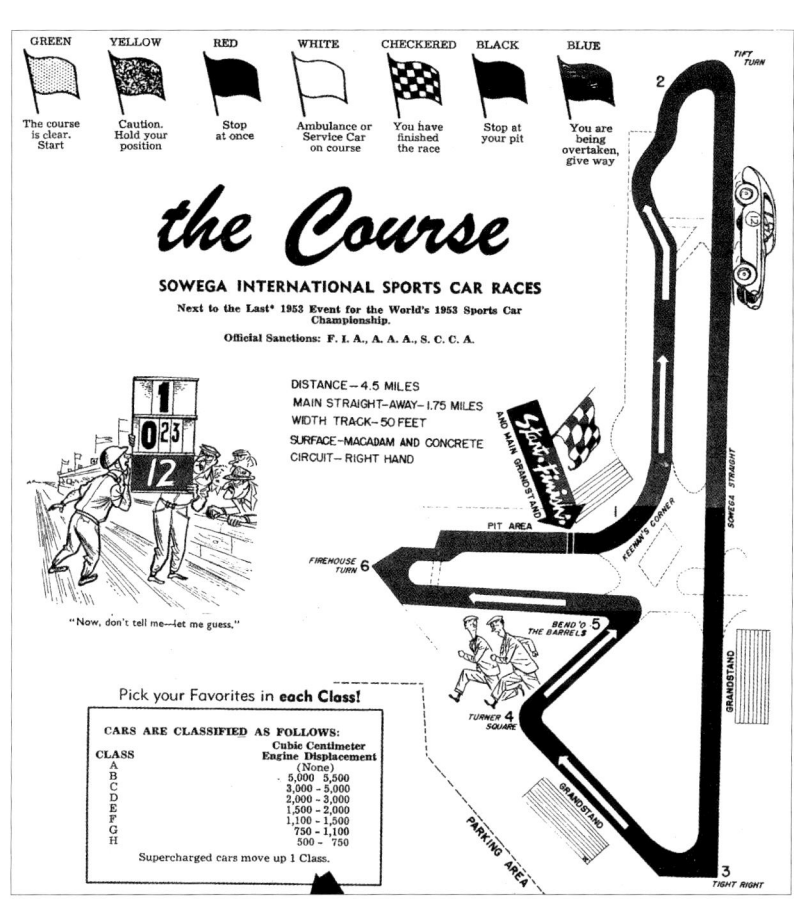

Track layout at Turner AFB. (Terry O'Neil Collection)

With the exception of a little bend just before Tift Turn, the course for the Second Annual Sowega Sports Car Races remained the same as in 1952, with eight turns and a 1.75-mile long, 50ft-wide main concrete straightway. The pits were situated to the inside of the track, while the base personnel had erected bleachers at strategic points around the

Technical inspection of the vehicles was a prerequisite of entry to the races. The Jowett Jupiter and the Porsche 356 Speedster belonging to Tex Hopkins is next in line. (Courtesy Stacey Hopkins Collection)

49

Practise grid line-up for the King George Cup race, with Huntoon's C-type Jaguar on the front row alongside the Ferrari 225S of Bill Lloyd. (Courtesy Stacey Hopkins Collection)

Walt Hansgen's Jaguar Special finished 6th overall in the King George Cup race. (Courtesy Stacey Hopkins Collection)

course. It proved to be very quick, with the Cunninghams, Allards and Ferraris attaining speeds of over 150mph through the speed traps along the main straightway.

The *Albany Herald* reported that "The Turner races might outclass the famous Le Mans annual classic." Well, a little hype did nobody any harm! A large number of entries for the races had been received, attracting drivers from all parts of America, partly because the national championships were reaching a climax for the season and the top contenders were keen to add to their points tally. Due to the number of entries rolling in, the event was advertised as "the first American race featuring over a million dollars' worth of cars on the track."

The first race of the cool but sunny day was the King George Cup, attracting 47 starters with modified cars from all classes, many of which were also entered for the feature event later in the day. As a rehearsal for the main event, it was a great spectacle for the crowds, which had gathered for an 8.30am start. The larger capacity Allards, Cunninghams and Ferraris soon weaved their way through the smaller capacity back markers in the field. Fitch and Walters, both in Cunninghams, were battling for

the lead, while Briggs Cunningham (in the third Cunningham) was being pressed for third place by Scott in Curtis LeMay's Allard. Fitch held the lead until the 11th lap, then Walters edged into first place for one lap, before Fitch regained the lead. Walters, driving the C5R model that had run at Le Mans earlier in the year, had to pit on lap 16 to change a flat tyre, costing him dearly, and Cunningham moved into second place with Scott in third, these being the positions they finished

Rare photo of a Morris Minor-MG, driven by F Leddington in the King George Cup race. It created more interest with the spectators than the lap-scorers, as the car retired early in the race. (Courtesy Stacey Hopkins Collection)

in one lap later. Further down the field Bob Keller won class FM in an OSCA belonging to Briggs Cunningham, ahead of Makins and Moffett in similar cars, while Candy Poole just held off the attentions of George Schrafft to win class HM. There were a number of retirements in the race due to various mishaps, none more scary than for Paul Ceresole, who was driving the Jaguar Special belonging to Sherwood Johnston. The fan belt snapped and broke a fan blade while at speed, and the disintegrating pieces not only punctured his radiator but also pierced a hole in Briggs Cunningham's car.

The second race, run over 75 miles, attracted 29 starters, the majority of them either Porsche or MG derivatives. It turned out to be a race within a race, as the Porsche contingent far outpaced the MGs, which were left to do their own battle. Out front Dr Richard Thompson had taken the lead on the first lap after being drawn to start in 14th position on the grid. It proved to be a lead he would not relinquish, despite being challenged from time to time by Goldman and Cornett, who were conducting their own battle while trying to keep Curtiss out of the picture. Meanwhile the MG battle revolved around Bob Fergus in his well-used and successful MG TC, and Ralph Durbin in the later model MG TD. Despite Durbin's best efforts he failed to overtake Fergus, who stayed in front to win his class. In doing so Fergus maintained his proud record of never finishing outside of the top two positions in his class with this car.

Race three was for the Jaguar contingent, amounting to eight standard XK120s and 12 XK120M models. Although everyone expected the XK120M to out-pace the standard model, Jack Ensley raised a few eyebrows by maintaining third position throughout in his indecently quick standard XK120 model. Stewart led the 75-mile race for five laps when he overtook Saunders on the second lap, before being overtaken by Russ Boss, who retained his lead unchallenged for the remainder of the

Jim Kimberly's Ferrari 340AM stands in the paddock at Turner AFB. (Courtesy Stacey Hopkins Collection)

race. Meanwhile, Saunders was losing ground by having to pit several times due to his Jaguar having overheating problems, allowing Stewart into second position. Stewart held his place despite a challenge from Ensley, and they finished the race in that order.

The fourth event, known as the Strategic Air Power Trophy race, was 252 miles for production and modified sports cars of all classes. A formidable array of cars made their way to the start grid. Among their number were the three Cunningham team cars, plus Charles Moran driving his own Cunninghan Coupé, ten Allards, six Ferraris, three of which belonged to Spear, and a Kurtis, as well as OSCAs, Porsches and Jaguars.

Forty-three cars lined up on the grid, which had been arranged by engine capacity – largest at the front – and set off on a paced lap before the pace car pulled off, allowing the cars to thunder over the start line. In the heat and confusion of a rolling start, George Huntoon experienced what was possibly the shortest race of his career as he made solid contact with a marker barrel within 400ft of the start line. It threw the front-end alignment out on his C-type Jaguar, and he could not continue. Meanwhile, Spear in his 340MM and Walters in the Cunningham C5R were fighting for the lead with Fitch, Scott, Cunningham, Kimberly, and Ensley – having abandoned his Jaguar in favour of a Kurtis – in hot pursuit. This represented the first showing of the Kurtis in the east, and it made a creditable debut, running eighth for many laps. The pace soon began to take its' toll, as first Scott, then Lloyd and Tilley retired by the end of the ninth lap. By lap 20 Walters had built his lead to 34 seconds over Spear, but more retirements came during the next ten laps. Ensley reluctantly retired the Kurtis with a faulty fuel pump, Samulson came into the pits with his Ferrari, never to return to the race, Duntov retired his Allard with a damaged oil sump, and Phil Hill's Ferrari 340 Mexico lost its oil. Minding his own business, Baron von Kreidner,

Briggs Cunningham's C4R and C5R models on the runway, in preparation for the Strategic Air Power Trophy race. Phil Waters, in the C5R, would finish 3rd while Briggs Cunningham, in the C4R, would finish in fifth place. (Courtesy Stacey Hopkins Collection)

driving a Crosley LM, had the biggest shock of the day as Ben Sands, driving Ensley's Jaguar XK120, passed him travelling backwards at some 90mph, having lost control of the car in a spin.

On the 33rd lap Walters pitted the C5R for new rear tyres and fuel, and to check a possible faulty fuel system. It was a delay that was to cost him dearly, as he could only sit and watch as Spear came past the pits and began building up a commanding lead. Fitch also gained from Walter's misfortune, as he established himself in second position. With time running out, Walters could not make up the necessary ground to catch the leading cars, so the race finished with Spear as the winner, nearly two minutes ahead of Fitch, gaining 1000 points towards the championship title. Fitch came second, Walters third, and Kimberly fourth. Unluckiest driver of the race was Erickson, who had managed to keep his Jaguar C-type in sixth place for most of the time, but on the final lap the car completely lost oil pressure. He had to abandon the car on the backstretch of the course with less than half a lap left, and dejectedly walk back to the pits.

It was fitting that the victory dinner was held in the new picnic pavilion, constructed at Turner AFB with some of the profits from the 1952 Sowega races, proving to some of the doubters of the SCCA/SAC alliance that something constructive had happened with the money. It later emerged that the profit from the second meeting at Turner AFB was substantially lower than the first event, with a figure of nearly $4000 being muted. Unfortunately the source of that figure is unclear, though it is assumed that it was produced from Turner AFB, as it was the one used by Senator Errett Scrivner in his report presented to Congress in 1954.

March AFB, Riverside, California, 8.11.1953

"The main event saw some of the finest machinery in the country on the starting grid." (Road & Track)

An Official Entry Blank for the event at March AFB. (Courtesy Bruce Perry Collection)

The final SCCA/SAC national race of 1953 was held at one of the air force's oldest military installations: March AFB, in the Moreno Valley, east of Los Angeles, near Riverside, California. The base was home to the 12th Air Division, which comprised the 22nd and 320th Bomb Wings, equipped with B-47 Stratojet bombers, together with the 807th Air Base Group. Both bomb wings had seen active service in World War II and the Korean conflict.

Sports car racing in southern California had, by now, become a regular occurrence, with the California Sports Car Club the predominant organiser, and the Four-Cylinder Car Club, to a lesser degree, holding regular meetings. The SCCA had been in negotiation to use Castle AFB, but it came to nothing, so it saw this event at March Field as a great opportunity for the Los Angeles region to expand its activities in this part of America, and, hopefully, enhance its reputation by doing so. The SCCA Los Angeles region, headed by Don Schoenert, had the responsibility for organising the event at March Field, known as the Orange Empire National Sports Car Races, with the proceeds going to the Airmen's Living Improvement Fund. Such was the importance to the SCCA to make this a success, they announced that it was a national event counting towards the championship – the first to be held in southern California. Civic groups in Riverside and Orange Counties

Track layout at March AFB. (Terry O'Neil Collection)

showed remarkable interest in the event, and pledged their co-operation in making it a success.

A 3.5-mile course was laid out on two tarmac runways and the connecting taxi strips of the base, encompassing two straightways of 5000ft, and nine bends, five of which were 90 degree or more turns. The pits were located on the inside of the track, and grandstands erected on the outside for the spectators, along three sides of the circuit.

Billed as an 'east versus west' competition, the event did not live up to its name. Debates had raged all season as to which part of America had the best drivers and the fiercest competition, and so far none of the mid-west venues had produced an answer to that question. It was hoped that this last major event on the 1953 calendar might give some clues, but strong entries from the east were unfortunately not matched by those from the west, especially for the over 1500cc categories. Strange, really, as this was the final chance for valuable points to be picked up towards the SCCA 1953 national championships. Instead, Phil Hill, Bill Stroppe, and Jack McAfee turned up in Mexico for the Carrera Panamericana. Bill Spear turned up at March AFB to defend his lead in the championship, though if he failed and either Makins or Kimberly put in a strong performance, the situation could change.

The first race of the day had at least 50 starters, novice drivers in all displacement classes of sports cars. It was won easily by Riddelle Gregory in the C-type Jaguar belonging to his brother, Masten, with Max Briney second in an Allard J2 Lincoln owned by C C Asimus, and Paul Miller third in an Allard J2 Cadillac. Not so fortunate was Jim Harrison from Colorado Springs in another C-type Jaguar, who had a close encounter with a hay bale and came off worse. MG models dominated the positions in class F, with Lewis finishing first, followed by Mack and Friedman.

The second race was for production sports cars in all classes. From the start Thornton High took the lead in an Allard LM, followed by Borden in a Jaguar XK120M, and MacKay Fraser in a similar model. The Allard proved too powerful for High to control, and he spun the car several times, losing considerable ground to the Jaguars. MacKay Fraser managed to pass Borden into first place and won by a comfortable margin. Jaguars took the first four places, followed by the Porsche 356 of Glen Hunter, first in class F. The first MG to cross the finish line was the MG TD owned and driven by John Benton in eighth position.

The main event for cars under 1500cc counted towards the national championship standings, and was to prove a closely fought affair. Ken Miles stood an outside chance of securing a top five place in the national championship, depending on how other drivers performed in the over 1500cc race. The level of excitement was maintained throughout the race as Miles took an immediate lead from the start, closely followed by James Simpson in his OSCA MT4, and Beavis in the Offenhauser-powered MG. On the tenth lap Simpson took over first place and began to draw away from Miles. Further down the field there was a three-way battle between Yedor, Van Dyke, and Drake before the pace became too much for Yedor, who retired his MG Special. At the front the lead was steadily cut back by Ken Miles, and possibly due to the pressure Miles was exerting, Simpson spun the OSCA on the penultimate lap, allowing Miles through to take victory. In doing so, Miles gained 1000 points to add to his championship total. Simpson recovered the OSCA to finish second, ahead of Von Neumann who finished the race in third, one lap down on the leaders.

As the result of a vote taken by the drivers, it was decided that the

Ken Miles (MG Special) and James Simpson (OSCA) side by side as they battle for first place in the third race. Miles eventually took the chequered flag ahead of Simpson. (Courtesy Ron Kellogg Collection)

main event for over 1500cc cars would not have a Le Mans-type start. Instead, lots were drawn for the grid positions. A powerful selection of cars took to the grid, including a team of Cunningham cars driven by Briggs Cunningham, Phil Walters, and John Fitch. The team was using its well-raced C4R models and the not-so-frequently-used lighter C5R model. Pitted against the Cunninghams were the Ferraris of Spear, Edwards, and Kimberly, the Siata V8 of Ernie McAfee, and the C-type Jaguar driven by Masten Gregory. There was also a Kurtis 500 owned by Bill Stroppe, but driven by Tony Ruttman in Stroppe's absence, together with a host of various powered Allards, Kurtis and potent Specials.

James Chapman's Allard, driven by Tom Bamford, led for the first lap, after which it was caught and passed by Walters in the Cunningham on lap two. Spear, Fitch and Kimberly followed him past Bamford, and the positions remained that way until the Cunningham C5R of Walters had to go into the pits suffering from low oil pressure. To save any further damage to the car, it was withdrawn from the race. Spear inherited the lead, but only for a short time, having to pit for new tyres. It was now Fitch out in front on lap 15, and although Spear got to within six seconds of catching him, his Ferrari had a puncture, resulting in another pit stop. This allowed Cunningham into second place, with Spear finishing third. Masten Gregory in his Jaguar C-type held on to finish in fourth place, ahead of Jim Kimberly who had to endure a four-

minute pit stop while mechanics checked for suspension defects and changed the tyres on his Ferrari.

By taking third place Spear ensured that he had done enough to win the SCCA drivers' national championship for 1953, after being runner-up to Sherwood Johnston by a substantial margin in 1952. The Spear/Momo partnership had proved formidable all season, and the title was richly deserved.

At the victory dinner held later that Sunday evening, the event at March AFB was heralded as a great success, and it was announced that over 70,000 spectators had turned up for the races. The author could find no accurate financial data published to say how much the Airmen's Living Improvement Fund benefited from the event, but an unsubstantiated source estimated that it was in the region of $23,500.

Jim Kimberly at speed in his Ferrari 340AM. He finished fifth in the 175-mile feature race. (Courtesy Ron Kellogg Collection)

William Pollack drove the Glasspar Mameco Special to a well-deserved sixth place in the 175-mile feature race. (Courtesy Ron Kellogg Collection)

4

1953 Statistical review

MacDill AFB 21.2.1953

Race 1	12 laps	Race distance 50 miles	Class Unrestricted Prod	Starters @29

Race winner's time 38mins 57.6secs		Average speed 77.0mph	

27	Jaguar XK120	Erickson E	1oa	1cl C	
47	Jaguar XK120	Edmison R	2oa	2cl C	
38	Jaguar XK120	Rosenberger A	3oa	3cl C	
	Jaguar XK120	Wilson D	4oa	4cl C	
34	Jaguar XK120	Hendricks F	5oa	5cl C	
55	MG TC	Fergus R	6oa	1cl F	
56	MG TD	Fleming W	7oa	2cl F	
68	MG TC	Gardner R	8oa	3cl F	
21	Jaguar XK120	Rainwater L	Dnf		
61	MG TD	Culler T			
16	Jaguar XK120				
115	Renault 106S	MacCabe J			
110	Austin A90	Sharpe V			
113	Jaguar XK120				
41	Jaguar XK120	Wallace C			

Programme cover for the MacDill AFB event.
(Courtesy Bruce Perry Collection)

36	Jaguar XK120		Ryberg R		
99	Jowett Jupiter		Pace A		
39	Nash-Healey		MacNaughton D		
65	MG TD		Harbour J		
63	Jowett Jupiter		King W		
60	MG TC		Lyon R		
24	Jaguar XK120		King B		
76	MG		Granby E		
81	MG		Koenig O		
54	MG		Kelly L		

102	Siata 300 BC Crosley		Samuelson R	Dnf	
114	Siata 300BC 750		Kousar B	Dnf	
71	Porsche 356		Clovis P		
87	VW-Porsche Special		Brundage H		
74	MG TD		Holbert R		
121	Siata 300 BC Crosley		Ludington R		
112	Crosley LM		Von Kreidner E	Dnf	
83	H R G		Morton J		
30	Jaguar XK120		Davis R		

Race 2 12 laps	Race distance 50 miles	Class Unrestricted Mod	Starters 36

6 Hr Collier Memorial 120 laps	Race distance 492 miles	Class Unrestricted	Starters 57

Race winner's time 37mins 7.7secs	Average speed 80.8mph

Race winner's time 6 hours	Average speed 82.2mph

31	Jaguar C-type	XKC 013	Blackwood R	1oa	1cl CM
40	Jaguar XK120 Special		Whitmore C	2oa	2cl CM
32	Jaguar XK120 Silverstone		Leighton C	3oa	3cl CM
45	Jaguar XK120M		Wyllie M	4oa	4cl CM
80	Porsche 356 Super		Haycraft C	5oa	1cl F
98	Porsche 356 America		Goldman M	6oa	2cl F
48	Jaguar XK120		Pace T	7oa	5cl CM
37	Jaguar XK120		Meagher R	8oa	6cl CM
62	Jaguar XK120		Carver C	9oa	7cl CM
25	Jaguar XK120 Special		Fageol L	10oa	1cl B
88	MG TC		Gary R	11oa	3cl F
93	OSCA MT4 1100	1112	Makins R	12oa	1cl GM
11	Cisitalia 202 MM Spyder		Ceresole P		2cl GM
101	Siata 300BC 1100 Spyder		Haskell I		3cl GM
106	Bandini Crosley		Riley J		1cl HM
9	Allard J2X Cadillac	J2192	Warner F	Dnf	
4	Cunningham C3 Coupe	5208	Stiles P	Dnf	
3	Allard J2 Lincoln		Brundage J	Dnf	
72	OSCA MT4 1350	1124	Cunningham B		
55	Jaguar XK120		Fergus R		
94	Glockler Porsche		Brocken K		
42	Allard K1 Mercury		Puleston R	Dnf	
26	Jaguar XK120		Wing R		

1	Cunningham C4R		Fitch J	1oa	1cl BM
10	Ferrari 340 Mexico	0228 AT	Spear W / Hill P	2oa	1cl CM
5	Ferrari 225 S	0220 ED	Kimberly J / Huntoon G	3oa	2cl CM
24	Jaguar C-type		Johnston S	4oa	3cl CM
311	Jaguar C-type	XKC 030	Gegen R/Hirsch D	5oa	4cl CM
28	Jaguar C-type	XKC 022	Wessells III H / Carson J	6oa	5cl CM
9	Allard J2X Cadillac	J2192	Warner F	7oa	2cl BM
72	OSCA MT4 1350	1124	Cunningham B	8oa	1cl FM
70	Ferrari 166 MM	0054 M	Lunken E / Hassan C	9oa	1cl EM
50	Ferrari 212 Ex	0100 E	Moran C / Benett J	10oa	1cl D
40	Jaguar XK120 Special		Whitmore C / Cheatham A	11oa	6cl CM
94	Glockler Porsche		Brocken K	12oa	2cl FM
75	Siata 208 CS	CS 060	Linton O	13oa	2cl E
45	Jaguar XK120		Wyllie M / Sabel J	14oa	7cl CM
35	Jaguar XK120		Ryberg R / Hugus E	15oa	1cl C
93	OSCA MT4 1100	1112	Makins R / Bott F	16oa	1cl GM

47	Jaguar XK120		Whitz D / Edmison R	17oa	2cl C
97	Porsche 356 1500		Proctor F / Koster A	18oa	3cl FM
26	Jaguar XK120 Special		Wing R / Spitler S	19oa	8cl CM
100	Siata 300BC 1100 Spyder	ST404BC	Keller R / Farago P	20oa	2cl GM
95	Lester-Offenhauser	8	Lloyd W / Thorpe L	21oa	4cl FM
11	Cisitalia 202MM Spyder		Ceresole P	22oa	3cl GM
98	Porsche 356 America		Goldman M	23oa	5cl FM
33	Jaguar XK120		Bridges D	24oa	3cl C
109	Nardi Crosley Spyder		Gougelman P	25oa	1cl HM
55	MG TC		Fergus R / Watts F	26oa	1cl F
62	Jaguar XK120		Carver C / Franklin J	27oa	4cl C
85	MG TD		Rainwater L / Richmond R	28oa	2cl F
88	MG TC		Gary R / Nelson R	29oa	3cl F
64	MG TD		Hildebrand K / Seaverns B	30oa	4cl F
69	MG TD		Allen F	31oa	5cl F
112	Crosley LM		Von Kreidner E	32oa	2cl HM
111	Palm Beach Crosley Spec.		Schrafft G	33oa	3cl HM
90	Siata 208CS		Flink L	34oa	6cl F
108	Crosley Hotshot		Sanderson G	35oa	4cl GM
2	Cunningham C4R		Walters P	Dnf	
74	MG TD		Holbert R	Dnf	
8	Allard J2X Cadillac	J1577	Wacker F	Dnf	
4	Cunningham C3 Coupe	5208	Stiles P	Dnf	
46	Jaguar XK120		Larson F	Dnf	
110	Austin A90		Haycraft C	Dnf	
43	Jaguar XK120		Victor W	Dnf	
67	Maserati A6GCS	2039	Koster F	Dnf	
39	Nash-Healey		Naughton D	Dnf	
7	Frazer Nash LM Rep	421/100/110	Boynton E	Dnf	
65	MG TD		Harbour J	Dnf	
19	Allard J2 Chrysler	J2020	Negley J	Dnf	
31	Jaguar C-type	XKC 013	Blackwood R	Dnf	
91	OSCA MT4 1350	1123	Simpson J	Dnf	
73	BMW 328		Tobin E	Dnf	
3	Allard J2 Lincoln		Brundage J	Dnf	
116	Siata 300BC Spyder	ST425BC	Ahr K	Dnf	
22	Allard J2X Cadillac		Ensley J	Dnf	
56	MG TD		Fleming W	Dnf	
14	Jaguar C-type	XKC 010	Feuerbacher A	Dnf	
37	Jaguar XK120		Meagher R	Dnf	
115	Renault 106S		MacCabe J	Dnf	
83	HRG Aerodynamic		Morton J	Dns	

* winner on handicap basis was Cunningham in the OSCA MT4.

Bergstrom AFB 12.4.1953

Race 1	12 laps	Race distance 53.76 miles	Class Unrestricted Prod	Starters

Race winner's time 40mins 5secs		Average speed 74.9mph	

33	Jaguar XK120		Newcomer T	1oa	1cl C
21	Jaguar XK120		Rainwater L	2oa	2cl C
23	Jaguar XK120		Fenner H	3oa	3cl C
27	Porsche 356 America		Brocken K	4oa	1cl F
15	Porsche 356 Super		Richter R	5oa	2cl F
77	MG TC		Banes W	6oa	3cl F
7	MG TD		Williams R	7oa	4cl F
39	Morgan Plus 4		Staley J	8oa	4cl C*
42	MG TD		Chaney-Brown S	9oa	5cl F
67	Crosley		Clifford H	10oa	6cl F**
61	MG TC		Wilkins F	11oa	7cl F
37	Jaguar XK120		Erickson E		
55	Jaguar XK120		Wallace C		
60	Jaguar XK120		Rose D		
43	Aston Martin DB2		Harrison E		
13	MG TD		Smith E		
19	MG TD		Galbraith G		
34	Porsche 356 Super		Cook F		

| 36 | MG TC | | Tomforde A | | |
| 53 | MG TC | | Beeler H | | |

* moved from Class D. ** moved from Class H

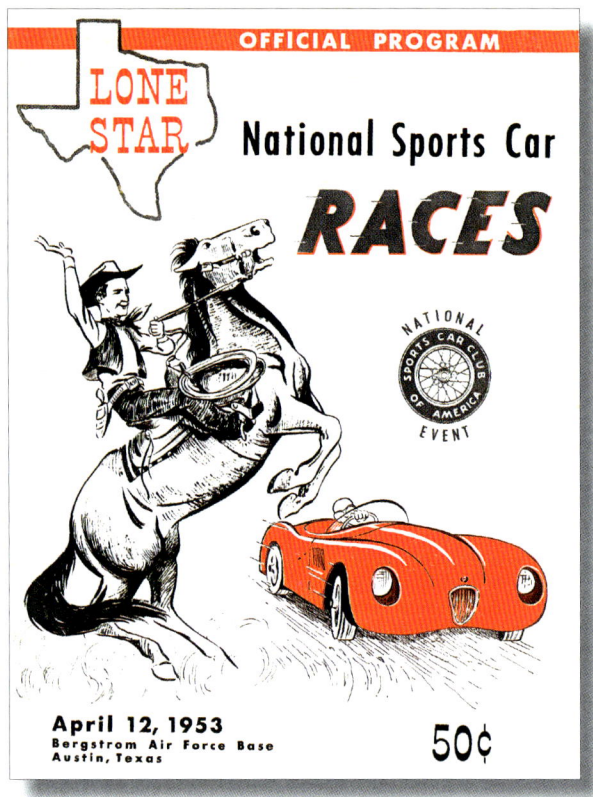

*Programme cover for the Bergstrom AFB event.
(Courtesy Bruce Perry Collection)*

| **Race 2** | 17 laps | Race distance 75 miles | Class Unrestricted Mod | Starters | |

Race winner's time 52mins 50secs	Average speed 85.7mph

10	Ferrari 340 Mexico	0228 AT	Spear W	1oa	1cl CM
8	Allard J2X Cadillac	J1577	Wacker F	2oa	1cl BM
5	Ferrari 340 AM	0204 A	Kimberly J	3oa	2cl CM
9	Allard J2X Cadillac		Ensley J	4oa	2cl BM
3	Jaguar C-type		Duncan D	5oa	3cl CM
55	Jaguar C-type		Wallace C	6oa	4cl CM
4	Allard J2 Oldsmobile	J1859	Gray W	7oa	5cl CM

16	Jaguar C-type	XKC 020	Larson F	8oa	6cl CM
41	Jaguar XK120 Silverstone		Leighton C	9oa	7cl CM
35	Jaguar XK120M		Schroeder R	10oa	8cl CM
25	Jaguar XK120M		Koehne G	11oa	9cl CM
32	Ford Special		Vanbeuren E	12oa	10cl CM
80	Jaguar C-type	XKC 024	Thomson A	13oa	11cl CM
29	Jaguar XK120M		Lavely R	14oa	12cl CM
58	OSCA MT4 1350	1127	Said B	15oa	1cl FM
91	OSCA MT4 1350	1123	Simpson J	16oa	2cl FM
51	OSCA MT4 1100	1112	Makins R	17oa	1cl GM
48	Nardi-Crosley Spyder		Gougleman P	18oa	1cl HM
24	MG TD		Fenner H	19oa	3cl FM
44	MG TC		Hill F Hann J	20oa	4cl FM
62	MG TC		Bartendale R	21oa	5cl FM
45	Fibresport		Mays J	22oa	2cl GM
18	Siata 300BC 750 Spyder		Samuelson R	23oa	2cl HM
12	MG TC		Shelby C	24oa	6cl FM
68	Crosley		Clifford H	25oa	3cl HM
11	Allard J2 Cadillac	J3146	Scott R	Dnf L4	
56	Allard J2X Cadillac		Skogmo D		
1	Jaguar C-type	XKC 010	Johnston S		
31	Jaguar C-type	XKC 013	Blackwood R		
46	Ferrari 340 AM	0118 A	Hill P	Dns?	
52	Invicta		Beeler H		
75	Ferrari 340 AM	0206 A	McAfee J		
28	Jowett Jupiter		Saunders J		
30	MG TD		Sallisbury J		
47	MG TD		Peebles K		
62	MG TC		Bartindale B		
98	MG TD		Linxwiller J		
100	MG TD		Flinton S		
54	Cisitalia 202MM Spyder		Ceresole P		

| **Race 3** | 23 laps | Race distance 103 miles | Class U 1500cc | Starters |

Race winner's time 1hr 25mins 33secs	Average speed 79.66mph

| 58 | OSCA MT4 1350 | 1127 | Said B | 1oa | 1cl FM |
| 49 | Glockler Porsche | 10447 | Von Neumann J | 2oa | 2cl FM |

51	OSCA MT4 1100	1112	Makins R	3oa	1cl GM
44	MG TC		Hill F	4oa	3cl FM
15	Porsche 356 Super		Richter R	5oa	1cl F
48	Nardi-Crosley Spyder		Gougleman P	6oa	1cl HM
18	Siata 300BC 750 Spyder		Samuelson R	7oa	2cl HM
28	MG TD		Harbour J	8oa	2cl F
38	Jowett Jupiter		Wright G	9oa	3cl F
68	Crosley		Clifford H	10oa	3cl HM
14	Porsche 356		Shelby C		
17	MG TD Mk II		Talley J		
47	MG TD		Peebles K		
61	MG TC		Wilkins E		
65	MG TC Special		Banes W		
91	OSCA MT4 1350	1123	Colby G		
99	MG TD Mk II		Keyes R		
100	MG TD		Flinton S		
27	Porsche 356 America		Brocken K		
34	Porsche 356 Super		Cook F		
42	MG TD		Chaney-Brown S		
54	Cisitalia 202MM Spyder		Ceresole P		
22	Crosley		Betts W		

Race 4	45 laps	Race distance 201.6 miles	Class O 1500cc	Starters	19

Race winner's time 2hr 31mins 48secs	Average speed 86.4 mph

5	Ferrari 340 AM	0204 A	Kimberly J	1oa	1cl CM
80	Jaguar C-type	XKC 024	Hill P	2oa	2cl CM
2	Jaguar C-type	XKC 015	Gregory M *	3oa	3cl CM
9	Allard J2X Cadillac		Ensley J	4oa	1cl BM
16	Jaguar C-type	XKC 020	Larson F	5oa	4cl CM
75	Ferrari 340 AM	0206 A	McAfee J	6oa	5cl CM
4	Allard J2 Oldsmobile	J1859	Gray W	7oa	2cl BM
21	Jaguar XK120		Rainwater L	8oa	1cl C
35	Jaguar XK120M		Schroeder R	9oa	6cl CM
33	Jaguar XK120		Newcomer T	10oa	2cl C
32	Ford Special		Vanbeuren E	11oa	7cl CM
41	Jaguar XK120 Silverstone		Leighton C	Dnf L23	

1	Jaguar C-type	XKC 010	Johnston S	Dnf L17	
8	Allard J2X Cadillac	J1577	Wacker F	Dnf L4	
20	Jaguar XK120M		Shelby C	Dnf	
3	Jaguar C Type		Duncan D		
56	Allard J2X Cadillac		Skogmo D		
20	Jaguar XK120		Linxwiler J		
31	Jaguar C-type	XKC 013	Blackwood R		
40	Jaguar XK120		Grose R		
52	Invicta		Beeler N		
55	Jaguar XK120		Gray T		
46	Ferrari 340 AM	0118 A	Brown C	dns	
11	Allard J2 Cadillac	J3146	Scott R	dns	
10	Ferrari 340 Mexico	0228 AT	Spear W	dns	

*Gregory originally entered and practised in Allard-Chrysler, #3202 but lost second gear.

Offutt AFB 5.7.1953

Race 1	17 laps	Race distance 51 miles	Class Unrestricted Prod	Starters	22

Race winner's time 43mins 50.4secs	Average speed 69.78mph

99	Jaguar XK120		Newcomer T	1oa	1cl C
76	Jaguar XK120		Wing R	2oa	2cl C
15	Jaguar XK120		Erickson E	3oa	3cl C
54	Porsche 356 Super		Moore P	4oa	1cl F
50	Jaguar XK120		Seibert J	5oa	4cl C
39	Jaguar XK120		Grove J	6oa	5cl C
65	MG TD		Fleming W		2cl F
64	MG TD		McGrade E		3cl F
2	MG TD		Katskee L		4cl F
46	MG TD Mk II		Stipe H		5cl F
68	MG TD		Spilman E		6cl F
98	Jaguar XK120		Rosenberger A	Dnf L15	
28	Jaguar XK120		Heath R	Dnf L3	
21	MG TD		Cosgrove M	Dnf L6	
3	MG TD		Chaney Brown S		
14	Porsche 356 Super		Richter R		
25	MG TC		McCleery J		

30	Jaguar XK120		Suebert J		
38	Jaguar XK120		Stahel K		
40	Jaguar XK120		Lyeth J		
42	MG		Rydjord J		
49	MG TD		Jones S		
60	MG TD Mod		Saltzgager R		
62	MG TD		Locarni R		
63	MG TC		Livingstone R		
66	Morris Minor		McCall R		

Race 2 25 laps	Race distance 75 miles	Class Unrestricted Mod	Starters 27

Race winner's time 59mins 26.7secs	Average speed 75.69mph

11	Allard J2X Cadillac	J3146	Shelby C	1oa	1cl BM
45	Allard J2X Chrysler		Hall J	2oa	2cl BM
13	Jaguar C-type	XKC 020	Larson F	3oa	1cl CM
17	Ferrari 225S	0166 ED	Lloyd W	4oa	1cl DM
9	Allard J2X Cadillac		Ensley J	5oa	3cl BM
57	Allard J2X Cadillac		Skogmo D	6oa	4cl BM
41	Jaguar C-type	XKC 033	McManus R	7oa	2cl CM
40	Jaguar XK120M		Lyeth J	8oa	3cl CM
4	MG TD Mod		Benett J	9oa	1cl FM
61	MG TD Mod		Salzgaber R	10oa	2cl FM
7	OSCA MT4 1100	1112	Makins R	11oa	3cl FM
31	Jaguar XK120		Lavely R	12oa	4cl CM
50	MG TC s/c		Larson R	13oa	2cl DM
43	MG TD s/c		Rowley E	14oa	3cl DM
47	HRG		Montgomery B	15oa	4cl FM
26	Siata 300BC 750 Spyder		Brown C		1cl HM
37	Fairy Special		Howell J		2cl HM
89	Sparrow Crosley		Mac Arthur S		3cl HM
75	Ferrari 340AM	0032 A	McAfee J	Dnf L19	
19	Allard J2X Cadillac	J2192	Warner F	Dnf L19	
51	Allard J2 Oldsmobile	J1859	Gray W	Dnf	
29	Allard J2 Cadillac		Koehne G	Dnf L3	
34	Jaguar XK 120		Crimm L	Dnf L3	
22	Siata 300BC 750 Spyder		Robb H		
48	MG TD Mk II		Bye D		
20	MG TC		O'Hare F		
6	Ferrari 225 S	0220 ED	Lewis M		

Race 3 33 laps	Race distance 100 miles	Class U 1500cc	Starters 19

Race winner's time 1hr 25mins 35.5secs	Average speed 70.08mph

91	OSCA MT4 1450	1133	Simpson J	1oa	1cl FM
4	MG TD Mod		Benett J	2oa	2cl FM
61	MG TD Mod		Salzgaber A	3oa	3cl FM
7	OSCA MT4 1100	1112	Makins R	4oa	4cl FM
48	MG TD Mk II		Bye D	5oa	5cl FM
47	HRG		Montgomery B	6oa	6cl FM
26	Siata 300BC 750 Spyder		Samuelson R	7oa	1cl HM
65	MG TD		Fleming W	8oa	1cl F
14	Porsche 356 Super		Richter R	9oa	2cl F

Programme cover for the Offutt AFB event. (Terry O'Neil Collection)

2	MG TD		Katskee L	10oa	3cl F
22	Siata 300BC 750 Spyder		Robb H		2cl HM
88	Bandini Crosley		Riley J		3cl HM
33	Uihlein Special		Brocken K	Dnf	
21	MG TD		Hackerot J	Dnf	
100	MG TC		Newcomer T		
20	MG TC		O'Hare F		
63	MG TC		Livingstone R		
64	MG TD		McGrade E		
23	Cisitalia 202MM Spyder		Ceresole P		
89	Sparrow Crosley		MacArthur S		
37	Fairy Special		Howell J		
3	MG TD		Chaney-Brown S	Dnf	

Race 4	67 laps	Race distance 200 miles	Class O 1500cc	Starters 33

Race winner's time 2hrs 36mins 32.1secs		Average speed 76.66mph	

58	Jaguar C-type	XKC 015	Gregory M	1oa	1cl CM
12	Ferrari 340 Mexico	0226 AT	Shelby C & McAfee J	2oa	2cl CM
13	Jaguar C-type	XKC 020	Urbas J Dr	3oa	3cl CM
41	Jaguar C-type	XKC 033	Hassan C	4oa	4cl CM
1	Allard JR Cadillac	3404	Wacker F	5oa	1cl BM
6	Ferrari 225S	0220 ED	Lewis M	6oa	1cl DM
11	Allard J2 Cadillac	J3146	Scott R	7oa	2cl BM
45	Allard J2X Chrysler	J1732	Duncan D	8oa	3cl BM
17	Ferrari 225S	0166 ED	Lloyd W	9oa	2cl DM
10	Ferrari 166 MM	0054 M	Lunken E	10oa	1cl EM
16	Excalibur J		Ullrich H	11oa	3cl DM
99	Jaguar XK120		Newcomer T	12oa	1cl C
19	Allard J2X Cadillac	J2192	Warner F	Dnf L46	
9	Allard J2X Cadillac		Ensley J	Dnf L3	
51	Allard J2 Oldsmobile	J1859	Gray W	Dnf L40	
29	Allard J2 Cadillac		Koehne G		
57	Allard J2X Cadillac		Skogmo D		

5	Ferrari 340 AM	0204 A	Kimberly J	Dnf L65	
18	Jaguar XK120		Edwards S		
90	Ferrari 166 MM	0010 M	Simpson J		2cl EM
34	Jaguar XK120		Crim L		
38	Jaguar XK120		Stahel K		
39	Jaguar XK120		Grove J		
31	Jaguar XK120M		Lavely R		
	Jaguar XK120M				
27	Ferrari 340 AM	0118 A	Brown C		
75	Ferrari 340 AM	0032 A	McAfee J	Dnf	
24	MG TD		Schleicher V		

Lockbourne AFB 8.8.1953

Race 1	14 laps	Race distance 50 miles	Class U 1500cc	Starters 46

Race winner's time 38mins 47secs		Average speed 77.7mph	

40	Porsche 356 Super		Kerner B	1oa	1cl F4
34	Porsche 356 Super		Moore P	2oa	2cl F4
72	Porsche 356 Super		Cornett D	3oa	3cl F4
42	Porsche 356 Super		Van Antwerpen P	4oa	4cl F4
44	Porsche 356 Super		Kerrigan W	5oa	5cl F4
41	Porsche 356 Super		Davis C	6oa	6cl F4
53	Porsche 356 America		Magenheimer R	7oa	1cl F3
38	Porsche 356 America		Short W	8oa	2cl F3
52	Porsche 356 America		Hanna H	9oa	3cl F3
36	Porsche 356 America		Klinger R	10oa	4cl F3
21	MG TC		Fergus R	11oa	1cl F1
24	MG TC		Marsh D	12oa	2cl F1
12	MG TD Mk II		Stoll C	13oa	3cl F1
4	MG TD		Andrews W	14oa	4cl F1
2	MG TD		Williams J	15oa	5cl F1
23	MG TD		Brooks J	16oa	6cl F1
46	Singer SM 1500		Cole R	17oa	1cl F5
43	Porsche 356 Super		Schaffer J		7cl F4
55	Porsche 356 Super		Fleming G		8cl F4
45	Porsche 356 Super		Dietrich C		9cl F4
33	Porsche 356 America		Hoff I		5cl F3

*Programme cover for the Lockbourne AFB event.
(Terry O'Neil Collection)*

27	MG TD		Moore W	20cl F1
57	MG TD		Gleason	21cl F1
54	MG TD		Kuhn J	22cl F1
58	MG TD		Locarni R	23cl F1
25	MG TD		Davenport F	24cl F1
29	MG TD		Shaw C	25cl F1
6	MG TD		Vollmer P	26cl F1
9	MG TD		Harbour J	27cl F1
1	MG TC		Wyllie M	Dnf L5
14	MG TD		Dickey H	Dnf L5
20	MG TD		Chakmakian C	Dnf L5

Race 2 21 laps	Race distance 75.2 miles	Class FM,GM,HM	Starters 37

Race winner's time 56mins 4secs		Average speed 80.4mph	

91	OSCA MT4 1450	1133	Simpson J	1oa	1cl FM
12	Glockler Porsche	10447	Proctor F	2oa	2cl FM
39	Porsche 356 Super		Goldman M	3oa	3cl FM
4	MG TD Special		Benett J	4oa	1cl F-MG
22	OSCA MT4 1100	1112	Makins R	5oa	1cl GM
77	Porsche 356 Super		Bentley J	6oa	4cl FM
45	MG TC S/C		Atkins G	7oa	5cl FM
35	Nardi Crosley Spyder		Gougleman P	8oa	1cl HM
6	MG TC Mod		Mangenheimer R	9oa	2cl F-MG
111	Palm Beach Crosley		Schrafft G	10oa	2cl HM
2	MG Mod		Kriplen D	11oa	3cl F-MG
21	Cisitalia 202		Gent R	12oa	2cl GM
17	MG TD		Krasberg R	13oa	4cl F-MG
55	Porsche 356 Super		Fleming G	14oa	6cl FM
25	MG TD		McPherson L	15oa	5cl F-MG
20	Cisitalia 202MM Spyder		Ceresole P	16oa	3cl GM
31	Siata 300BC 1100 Spyder		Haskell I	17oa	4cl GM
11	Crosley		Dodds W	18oa	3cl HM
28	Crosley		Brooks J	19oa	4cl HM
89	Sparrow Crosley		MacArthur S	20oa	5cl HM
22	MG TD		Staples W	21oa	6cl F-MG

49	Simca 8	Goldich R	1cl F7
7	MG TD	Bastrup L	7cl F1
8	MG TD	Cooper M	8cl F1
15	MG TD	Smith E	9cl F1
5	MG TD	Fergus J	10cl F1
50	MG TD	Katskee L	11cl F1
17	MG TD	Russell R	12cl F1
11	MG TD	Tinder R	13cl F1
3	MG TD	Kuhn R	14cl F1
51	MG TD	Harris B	15cl F1
19	MG TD	DePanaloza E	16cl F1
16	MG TD	Durbin R	17cl F1
10	MG TD	Ward M	18cl F1
28	MG TD	Davis L	19cl F1

57	MG TD		Lyle L	22oa	7cl F-MG
33	Siata 300BC 750 Spyder	ST 407 BC	Yares R	23oa	6cl HM
23	Fiat Ballila		Forsythe P	24oa	5cl GM
18	Cisitalia 202		Taylor W	Nraf L14	6cl GM
29	Bandini Crosley		Rudkin H	Nraf L14	7cl HM
5	MG Special		O'Hare F	Nraf L14	7cl FM
8	MG TD Special		Salzgaber R	Nraf L10	8cl FM
32	Siata 300BC 750 Spyder		Roberts G	Nraf L8	8cl HM
19	Fiberglass Special		Mays J	Nraf L7	7cl GM
16	Uihlein Special		Brocken K	Nraf L7	9cl FM
24	Siata 750 Spyder Special		Keller R	Nraf L4	9cl HM
36	Siata 208S		Adams W	Nraf L4	10cl FM
9	MG TD		Howell E	Nraf L2	8cl F-MG

Race 3 21 laps	Race distance 75.2 miles	Class C	Starters 30

Race winner's time		Average speed	

C2-18	Jaguar XK 120	Ryberg R	1oa	1cl CSM
15	Jaguar XK 120M	Wyllie M Dr	2oa	1cl C
C2-52	Jaguar XK120M	Gary R	3oa	1cl C2
76	Jaguar XK120	Wing R	4oa	1cl C1
4	Jaguar XK120	Manting J	5oa	2cl C1
12	Jaguar XK120M	Cooper W		2cl C
25	Jaguar XK120	Ensley J		3cl C1
C2-11	Jaguar XK120M	Noonan W		2cl C2
18	Jaguar XK120M	Kerr B		3cl C
C2-19	Jaguar XK120M	Heerman W		3cl C2
C2-15	Jaguar XK120M	Heldt W		4cl C2
19	Jaguar XK120M	Shaeffer J		4cl C
98	Jaguar XK120	Rosenberger A		4cl C1
7	Jaguar XK120	Palmer D		5cl C1
C2-17	Jaguar XK120M	Donnelly R		5cl C2
23	Jaguar XK120M	Moncur J		5cl C
2	Jaguar XK120	McComb D		6cl C1

C2-16	Jaguar XK120M		Skillman N		6cl C2
17	Jaguar XK120M		Karber L		6cl C
11	Jaguar XK120		Wilson C		7cl C1
C2-20	Jaguar XK120M		Klinger R		7cl C2
1	Jaguar XK120		Tjaarda J		8cl C1
	Jaguar XK120		Brown S		
	Jaguar XK120		Haskell I		
C1-3	Jaguar XK120		Crove J		
C1-5	Jaguar XK120		Gedney G		
C1-6	Jaguar XK120		Carver C		
C2-22	Jaguar XK120		Davis R		
C2-21	Jaguar XK120		Bott F		
C2-19	Jaguar XK120		Heerman W Dr		

Race 4 28 laps	Race distance 100.2 miles	Class BM,CM,DM,EM	Starters 38

Race winner's time 1hr 7mins 5secs	Average speed 89.9mph

11	Ferrari 340 Mexico Spyder	O228 AT	Spear W	1oa	1cl CM
58	Jaguar C-type	XKC 015	Gregory M	2oa	2cl CM
5	Ferrari 340 AM	O204 A	Kimberly J	3oa	3cl CM
30	Ferrari 225S	O218 ET	Johnston W	4oa	1cl DM
74	Jaguar C-type		Wallace C	5oa	4cl CM
8	Allard J2 Chrysler	J2020	Negley J	6oa	1cl BM
14	Jaguar C-type	XKC 010	Fergus R	7oa	5cl CM
38	Maserati A6 GCS	2039	Koster F	8oa	1cl EM
75	Jaguar XK120 Silverstone		Leighton C	9oa	6cl CM
6	Allard JX2 Cadillac	J2192	Warner F	10oa	2cl BM
7	Fraser-Nash Le Mans Rep	421/100/110	Boynton E	11oa	2cl EM
10	Whitmore-Jaguar XK120		Whitmore C	12oa	1cl U
27	Siata 208 CS	CS 060	Linton O	13oa	3cl EM
22	Jaguar XK120M		Davis D	14oa	2cl U
19	Excalibur J		Ulrich H	15oa	2cl DM
12	Jaguar C-type	XKC 022	Wessells III H	16oa	7cl CM
21	Healey Silverstone		Penn A	17oa	3cl DM
31	Siata 208 CS		Blackwood R	18oa	4cl EM
39	Allard J2X		Salzgaber R	19oa nraf	3cl BM

44	Allard J2 Le Mans	J3153	Patten N	20oa	4cl BM
51	Allard J2 Oldsmobile	J1859	Gray W	21oa	5cl BM
28	MG TC S/C		Larson R	22oa	5cl EM
25	MG TC S/C		Dietrich S	23oa	6cl EM
24	Ferrari 166 MM	0054 M	Lunken E	24oa	7cl EM
26	MG TD S/C		Schleicher V	25oa	8cl EM
2	Ford Special		Chamberlain R	Dnf L19	3cl U
9	Allard L4		Bosken H	Dnf L14	4cl U
22	Norris Special		McIntire C	Dnf L13	
66	Allard J2		Lee D	Dnf L8	
23	MG TD Special		Edmison R	Dnf L5	
4	Allard J2X Cadillac		Ensley J	Dnf L5	
1	Allard JR Cadillac	3403	Tilley R	Dnf L1	
29	MG TD S/C		Randle W	Dnf L1	
37	Kieft		Hassan C	Dnf	
57	Jaguar C-type		Duncan D	Dnf	
15	Jaguar XK120M		Wyllie M	Dnf	
16	Jaguar XK120		Skillman N	Dnf	
17	Jaguar XK120		Karber L	Dnf	

58	Jaguar C-type	XKC 015	Gregory M	18oa	6cl CM
16	MG TD		Durbin R	19oa	5cl F
52	Porsche 356 America		Hanna H	20oa	6cl F
11	MG TD		Tinder R	21oa	7cl F
38	Maserati A6 GCS	2039	Koster F	22oa	1cl EM
9	MG TD		Harbour J	23oa	8cl F
E3	Giaur			R*	
U3	Alfa Romeo 2C			R	
				R	
				R	
				R	
				R	
				R	
				R	
				R	
				R	
				R	
				R	
				R	

*R = running, though not enough completed laps to be classified.

Race 5 H'cap 21 laps	Race distance 75 miles	Class Unrestricted	Starters 30+

Race winner's time	Average speed

Stead AFB. 17.10.1953

Sagebrush Trophy 10 laps	Race distance 28 miles	Class Novice U 1500cc	Starters 30

Race winner's time 28mins 33.8secs	Average speed 58.84mph

6	Allard JX2 Cadillac	J2192	Warner F	1oa	1cl BM
10	Whitmore-Jaguar XK120		Whitmore C	2oa	1cl CM
21	MG TC		Fergus R	3oa	1cl F
45	MG TC s/c		Atkins G	4oa	2cl F
31	Siata 300BC 750 Spyder		Haskell I	5oa	1cl HM
20	Cisitalia 202MM Spyder		Ceresole P	6oa	1cl GM
111	Palm Beach Crosley		Schrafft G	7oa	2cl HM
25	Jaguar XK120		Ensley J	8oa	1cl C
5	Ferrari 340 AM	0204 A	Kimberly J	9oa	2cl CM
30	Ferrari 225 S	0218 ET	Johnston S	10oa	1cl D
74	Jaguar C-type		Leighton C	11oa	3cl CM
12	Jaguar C-type	XKC 022	Wessells III H	12oa	4cl CM
76	Jaguar XK120		Wing R	13oa	2cl C
53	Porsche 356 America		Magenheimer R	14oa	3cl F
11	Ferrari 340 Mexico	0228 AT	Spear W	15oa	5cl CM
22	OSCA MT4 1100	1112	Makins R	16oa	2cl GM
46	Singer SM 1500		Cole P	17oa	4cl F

66	MG Special		Qvale K	1oa	1cl F
117	Simca 8 Special		Taylor L	2oa	2cl F
49	Porsche 356		Helm C	3oa	3cl F
155	MG TD Mk II		Talbot P Dr	4oa	4cl F
12	MG TD		Mack E	5oa	5cl F
22	Giaur		Hicks R	6oa	1cl G
17	MG TD Mk II		Halverson A	7oa	6cl F
87	MG TD		Jolly G	8oa	7cl F
40	Singer SM 1500		Tschopp E	9oa	8cl F
118	Jowett Jupiter		Carbury J	10oa	9cl F
21	MG TD		Swain S	11oa	10cl F
47	MG TD		Thomas L	12oa	11cl F

121	MG TD	Vincent C	13oa	12cl F
110	MG TC	Cleghorn W	14oa	13cl F
42	MG TD Mk II	Bury R	15oa	14cl F
82	MG TD Mk II	Baxter S	16oa	15cl F
30	MG TD Mk II	Zimmerman D	17oa	16cl F
109	MG TD	Standers E	18oa	17cl F
59	MG TD Mk II	Heaney G	19oa	18cl F
71	MG TD	Hewitt W	20oa	19cl F
63	MG TD	Bremmer W	21oa	20cl F
123	MG TD	Hoyer L	22oa	21cl F
27	Singer SM 1500	Franges J	23oa	22cl F
89	MG TD	Smith R	24oa	23cl F
62	MG s/c Special	Chatfield T	Dnf L3	
39	MG TD	Inch M	Dnf	
51	MG TD Mk II	Warwick J		
	OSCA 1350	(Leson's mechanic)	Dnf	

Biggest Little Race 10 laps	Race distance 28 miles	Class Novice O 1500cc	Starters 14

Race winner's time 25mins 43.5secs	Average speed 65.3mph

101	Allard J2X Cadillac	Cochrane J	1oa	1cl B
711	Allard J2 LM Chrysler	Block C	2oa	2cl B
33	Jaguar XK120M	Henderson T	3oa	1cl C
96	Jaguar XK120M	Byrd R	4oa	2cl C
60	Jaguar XK120	Ramsey J	5oa	3cl C
65	Austin-Healey 100	McDonald W	6oa	1cl D
20	Ford Special	Balchowsky M	7oa nraf	3cl B
131	MG TC s/c	Duncan J	8oa	1cl E
126	Jaguar XK120M	Teran S	9oa	4cl C
106	Kurtis 500 S Cadillac	Sawyer G		
107	Kurtis 500 S Cadillac	Rhode F		
105	Allard J2X Cadillac	Barneson J	Dnf	
4	Ferrari		Dnf	
64	BMW 328	Cartwright D	Dnf	

*Programme cover for the Stead AFB event.
(Courtesy Bruce Perry Collection)*

Survival Race & Airman's Cup 10 laps	Race distance 28 miles	Class C, F (MG)	Starters

Race winner's time	Average speed

28	Jaguar XK120	Seher R	1oa	1cl C
55	Jaguar XK120M	Weiss S	2oa	2cl C
72	Jaguar XK120	Fraser	3oa	3cl C
200	Jaguar XK120M	Montonen H	4oa	4cl C
33	Jaguar XK120M	Henderson T	5oa	5cl C
60	Jaguar XK120	Ramsey J	6oa	6cl C
83	MG TD	Banta H	7oa	1cl F MG
42	MG TD Mk II	Byrd R	8oa	2cl F MG
47	MG TD	Thomas L	9oa	3cl F MG

30	MG TD		Zimmerman D	10oa	4cl F MG
83	MG TD		Scoville J	11oa	5cl F MG
82	MG TD		Fawcett E	12oa	6cl F MG
110	MG TC		Skivington J	13oa	7cl F MG
53	MG TD		Thomas D		

Comstock Race 10 laps	Race distance 17 miles	Class Novice & F3	Starters

Only 6 laps completed

Race winner's time		Average speed	

101	Allard J2X Cadillac		Cochrane J	1oa	1cl B
96	Jaguar XK120M		Byrd R	2oa	1cl C
60	Jaguar XK120		Ramsey J	3oa	2cl C
65	Austin-Healey 100		McDonald W	4oa	1cl D
155	MG TD Mk II		Talbot P Dr	5oa	1cl F
40	Singer SM 1500		Tschopp E	6oa	2cl F
12	MG TD		Mack E	7oa	3cl F
144	Cooper Mk VI F3		Trimble R	1oa F3	1cl F3
31	Cooper Norton F3		Swift G	2oa F3	2cl F3
97	Cooper Mk VI F3		Steiner R	3oa F3	3cl F3
711	Allard J2 LM Chrysler		Block C	Dnf L3	

Race 5	Race distance	Class Unrestricted Prod	Starters 33

Race winner's time 2hrs 30mins	Average speed	5.33-mile course used

26	Ferrari 340 AM	0350 AM	Edwards S	1oa	1cl C
2	Ferrari 250 MM	0260 MM	Hill P	2oa	1cl D
9	OSCA MT4 1350	1127	David W	3oa	1cl F
23	OSCA MT4 1100	1122	Coppel A	4oa	1cl G
711	Allard J2 LM Chrysler		Block C	5oa	1cl B
5	Ferrari 166 MM II	0342 M	McDougall E	6oa	1cl E
11	Porsche 356 America		Von Neumann J	7oa	2cl F
66	MG TC Special		Gillespie R	8oa	3cl F
38	Frazer-Nash LM Rep	421/200/183	Lowe J	9oa	2cl E
80	Mercury Special		Louis R Dr	10oa	2cl C
22	Giaur Crosley		Lovely P	11oa	2cl G
100	Austin-Healey 100		Snell W	12oa	2cl D
70	Jaguar XK120M		Rice R	13oa	3cl C

20	Ford Special		Balchowski M	14oa	2cl B
54	Crosley Special		Eyerly H	15oa	1cl H
116	Singer SM 1500		Gardner V	16oa	4cl F
88	MG TD		Banta H	17oa	5cl F
44	MG TD		Adams R	18oa	6cl F
36	Allard J2 Cadillac		Fox J	19oa	3cl B
113	MG TD		Grube L	20oa	7cl F
85	MG TC		Mahon D	21oa	8cl F
25	Crosley Special		Young J	22oa	3cl G
77	MG Special		Wright V	23oa	9cl F
121	MG TD		St Louis G	24oa	10cl F
	Ferrari 250MM	0312 MM	Devin W	dnf	
58	Jaguar C-type	XKC 015	Gregory M	Dnf L9	
106	Kurtis 500 S Cadillac		Sawyer G	dnf	
107	Kurtis 500 S Cadillac		Rhode F	dnf	
101	Allard J2X Cadillac		Cochrane J	dnf	
10	Allard J2		Dickey D	dnf	
46	Jaguar XK120		Pinkerton F	dnf	
74	Nash-Healey			dnf	
87	MG TC		Wallace R	dnf	

Turner AFB 25.10.1953

King George Cup 17 laps	Race distance 75 miles	Class unlimited Mod	Starters 47

Race winner's time 49mins 33.6secs	Average speed 90.80mph

59	Cunningham C4R		Fitch J	1oa	1cl BM
60	Cunningham C4R		Cunningham B	2oa	2cl BM
28	Allard J2X Cadillac		Scott R	3oa	3cl BM
27	Jaguar C-type	XKC 032	Erickson E	4oa	1cl CM
15	Jaguar C-type	XKC 034	Huntoon G	5oa	2cl CM
29	Hansgen Jaguar Special		Hansgen W	6oa	3cl CM
101	Ferrari 225S	0218 ET	Lloyd W	7oa	1cl DM
62	Fageol-Porsche Special		Fageol L	8oa	2cl DM
82	Allard J2		Hall J	9oa	4cl BM

58	Cunningham C5R	5319R	Walters P	10oa	5cl BM
57	OSCA MT4 1350	1124	Keller R	11oa	1cl FM
77	OSCA MT4 1350	1132	Makins R	12oa	2cl FM
12	OSCA MT4 1350	1127	Moffett G	13oa	3cl FM
7	Frazer-Nash LM Rep	421/100/110	Boynton E	14oa	1cl EM
36	Allard J2		Brundage J	15oa	6cl BM
31	Siata 208 CS		Blackwood R	16oa	2cl EM
48	Allard JR Cadillac	3403	Tilley R	17oa	7cl BM
20	Porsche 356 America		Brundage H	18oa	4cl FM
51	PBX Special		Poole C	19oa	1cl HM
111	Palm Beach Crosley		Schrafft G	20oa	2cl HM
70	Nardi Crosley Spyder		Gougelman P	21oa	3cl HM
26	Siata 300BC 750 Spyder		Robb H	22oa	4cl HM
87	Sparrow Crosley		MacArthur S	23oa	5cl HM
119	Siata 300BC 750 Spyder		Rose D	24oa	6cl HM
41	Ferrari 340 Mexico	0226 AT	Duncan D	Dnf	
110	Jaguar Special	ex XKC-015	Ceresole P	Dnf	

92	Porsche 550 Spyder	550-03	Kling K	Dnf	
93	Porsche 550 Spyder	550-04	Von Hanstein H	Dnf	
				L11	
140	Jaguar XK120		Leighton C		
54	Kieft MG		Derujinsky G	Dnf	
6	Kurtis 500 S		Ensley J	Dnf	
49	Allard JR Cadillac	3402	Schilling D		
109	Multiplex 186		Fanelli H		
46	Ferrari 166 MM	0054 M	Lunken E	Dnf	
66	Allard J2X Cadillac	J3146	Shelby C		
118	Ferrari 250 MM	0260 MM	Brown C		
141	Jaguar C-type		Wallace C		
80	Jaguar C-type	XKC 033	Gregory R		
134	Disbrow Special		Disbrow		
102	Lagonda Rapide		Vaughn M		
35	Siata 300BC 750 Spyder		Samuelson R		
127	Morris-MG		Luddington F	Dnf	
45	Maserati A6 GCS	2039	Koster F		
47	Kieft MG		Howell E		
39	Porsche 356 America		Crawford E		
112	Crosley LM		Von Kreidner E		
89	Siata 300BC 750 Spyder		Jones E		

Tift Pioneer Trophy 17 laps	Race distance 75 miles	Class U 1500cc	Starters 29

Race winner's time 1hr 0mins 45secs	Average speed 74.07mph

Programme cover for the Turner AFB event. (Terry O'Neil Collection)

18	Porsche 356 Super		Thompson R	1oa	1cl F
116	Porsche 356 Super		Goldman M	2oa	2cl F
121	Porsche 356 Super		Cornett D	3oa	3cl F
22	Porsche 356 Super		Jenkins E	4oa	4cl F
19	Porsche 356		Browne P	5oa	5cl F
23	Porsche 356		Hopkins R	6oa	6cl F
97	Porsche 356		Bentley J	7oa	7cl F
14	Porsche 356		Pace R	8oa	8cl F
105	Porsche 356		Brons J	9oa	9cl F
132	Porsche 356		Hanna H	10oa	10cl F
33	Porsche 356		Schillinger G	11oa	11cl F
55	HRG		Trager A	12oa	12cl F

79	MG TC		Fergus R	13oa	1cl MG
74	MG TD		Durbin R	14oa	J2cl MG
53	MG TD		Bailey P	15oa	J2cl MG
30	MG TD		Wells R	16oa	4cl MG
25	MG TD		Cooper M		
21	MG TD		O'Hare F		
65	MG TC		Banes W		
47	MG TD Mk II		Howell E		
52	MG TD		Compton G		
72	MG Mod		Allen F		
83	MG TD		Pettit M		
85	MG TD		Atkins G		
88	MG TD		Fleming W		
106	MG TD		McKinsey R		
120	MG TD		Kaperonis J		
122	MG TD		Shupe		
115	MG TD		Sheppard J		
145	MG TD		Harbour J		
69	Porsche 356 Super		Shuck W Dr		
44	Porsche 356		Richter R		
24	Simca		Noriega		
38	Jowett Jupiter		Hopkins R	Dns	

Keenan Sowega Trophy 17 laps	Race distance 75 miles	Class Jaguar	Starters @22

Race winner's time 58mins 34secs	Average speed 77.40mph

104	Jaguar XK120M		Boss R	1oa	1cl CM
43	Jaguar XK120M		Stewart P	2oa	2cl CM
3	Jaguar XK120		Ensley J/Sands B	3oa	1cl C
17	Jaguar XK120M		Gray H	4oa	3cl CM
16	Jaguar XK120M		Pace T	5oa	4cl CM
143	Jaguar XK120		Blackwood R	6oa	2cl C
56	Jaguar XK120		Hendricks J	7oa	3cl C
4	Jaguar XK120M		Frankland J	8oa	5cl CM
64	Jaguar XK120		Dukes D		4cl C
42	Jaguar XK120M		MacArthur A		6cl CM
129	Jaguar XK120M		Saunders W		7cl CM
96	Jaguar XK120M		Spracino P		8cl CM
113	Jaguar XK120M		Kaplan J		
137	Jaguar XK120M		Constantine G		

67	Jaguar XK120M		Crowder R		
32	Jaguar XK120M		Cooper W		
81	Jaguar XK120		Wilson D		
103	Jaguar XK120		Cheatham A		
149	Jaguar XK120		Habersin A		
139	Jaguar XK120		Wing R	Dnf	
144	Jaguar XK120		MacArthur J		

Strategic Air Power Tr 57 laps	Race distance 250 miles	Class Unrestricted	Starters 43

Race winner's time 2hrs 40mins 28.8secs	Average speed 93.47mph

90	Ferrari 340 MM	0324 AM	Spear W	1oa	1cl CM
59	Cunningham C4R		Fitch J	2oa	1cl BM
58	Cunningham C5R	5319R	Walters P	3oa	2cl BM
5	Ferrari 340 AM	0204 A	Kimberly J	4oa	2cl CM
60	Cunningham C4R		Cunningham B	5oa	3cl BM
61	Cunningham C4RK	5218R	Moran C	6oa	4cl BM
45	Maserati A6 CGS		Koster A & Benett J	7oa	1cl DM*
123	Excalibur J		Ullrich H	8oa	2cl DM
57	OSCA MT4 1350	1124	Johnston S	9oa	1cl FM
29	Hansgen Jaguar Special		Hansgen W	10oa	3cl CM
62	Fageol-Porsche Special		Fageol L	11oa	3cl DM
12	OSCA MT4 1350	1127	Moffett G	12oa	2cl FM
40	Glockler Porsche	10447	Urbas J	13oa	3cl FM
33	Porsche 356		Schillinger G		1cl F
132	Porsche 356		Hanna H		2cl F
74	MG TD		Durbin R		3cl F
81	Jaguar XK120		Wilson D		1cl C
111	Palm Beach Crosley		Schrafft G		1cl HM
26	Siata 300BC 750 Spyder		Connoly J		2cl HM
56	Jaguar XK120		Hendricks J		2cl C
51	PBX Special		Vilardi D		3cl HM
124	Excalibur J		Reidy H		4cl DM
101	Ferrari 225S	0218 ET	Lloyd W	Dnf L9	
15	Jaguar C-type	XKC 034	Huntoon G	Dnf L1	

#	Car	Chassis	Driver	Result	
50	Allard JR Cadillac	3404	Scott R	Dnf L8	
27	Jaguar C-type	XKC 032	Erickson E	Dnf L56	
6	Kurtis 500 S		Ensley J	Dnf L23	
100	Ferrari 340 Mexico Spyder	0228 AT	Hill P	Dnf L30	
49	Allard JR Cadillac	3402	Duntov Z	Dnf L26	
93	Porsche 550 Spyder	550-04	Von Hanstein H	Dnf	
92	Porsche 550 Spyder	550-03	Kling K	Dnf	
48	Allard JR Cadillac	3403	Tilley R	Dnf L9	
109	Multiplex 186		Fanelli H	Dnf L36	
54	Kieft MG		Derujinsky G		
118	Ferrari 340 AM	0118 A	Samuelson R	Dnf L29	
46	Ferrari 225	0220 ED	Lunken E	Dnf L42	
3	Jaguar XK120		Sands B		
112	Crosley LM		Von Kreidner E		
76	Ferrari 340 MM	0350 AM	Edwards S	Dns	
114	Jaguar C-type		Gregory M	Dns	

John Negley killed during practise. Allard J2LM#J2020   * moved up from class EM

March AFB 8.11.1953

Race 1 10 laps	Race distance 35 miles	Class Novices	Starters 51

Race winner's time 27mins 3secs	Average speed 77.62 mph

#	Car	Chassis	Driver	Pos	Class
58	Jaguar C-type	XKC 022	Gregory R	1oa	1cl CM
12	Allard J2X Lincoln		Briney M	2oa	1cl BM
138	Allard J2 Cadillac		Miller P	3oa	1cl AM
22	Jaguar XK120M		Turnstall W	4oa	1cl C
32	Jaguar XK120M		Masterson R	5oa	2cl C
85	Jaguar XK120M		MacGregor S	6oa	3cl C
63	Jaguar XK120M		Weller R	7oa	4cl C
38	Siata 208 S		Stables D	8oa	1cl EM
133	MG Special		Lewis S	9oa	1cl FM
24	Kurtis 500 S DeSoto		Wynn K	10oa	2cl BM
37	MG Special		Mack E	11oa	2cl FM
131	Jaguar Special		Sullivan S	12oa	2cl CM
7	MG TC		Friedman H	13oa	3cl FM
14	Kurtis 500 S Mercury		Buderin A	14oa	3cl CM
21	Ford Special		Murphy R	15oa	4cl CM
105	Simca V8-60		Salisbury R	16oa	1cl DM
80	Sunbeam Alpine		Stevens R	17oa	2cl DM
102	Nash-Healey		Gilbert W	18oa	5cl CM
86	Jowett Jupiter		Carberry J	19oa	1cl F
94	MG TD		Flintom S	20oa	4cl FM
97	Volkswagen		Smith RD	21oa	5cl FM
132	MG TC		White G	22oa	6cl FM
39	MG TD		Brigham R	23oa	1cl MG
69	Porsche 356		Porter J	24oa	7cl FM
83	MG TD		Youngberg J	25oa	2cl MG
65	MG TC		Harris R	26oa	8cl FM
8	Siata 300BC 750 Spyder		Cannon J	27oa	1cl HM
103	MG TD		Garlick W	28oa	3cl MG
114	MG TD		Speer M Jr	29oa	4cl MG
33	Jowett Jupiter		Weissman J	30oa	2cl F
82	MG TD		Wood H	31oa	5cl MG
117	MG TD		Parker F	32oa	6cl MG
122	Edwards R-62 Special		Edwards W	33oa	3cl BM
137	Allison Scorpion		Also I	34oa	2cl HM
40	MG TD		Driver K Jr	35oa	7cl MG
99	MG TD		Boyer C	36oa	8cl MG
59	MG TD		MacNeil A	37oa	9cl MG
118	MG TD		Horvath J	38oa	10cl MG
56	MG TC V8-60		McHenry T Dr	39oa	3cl DM
116	Porsche 356		Arnold H	40oa	3cl F
42	MG TD Mk II		Phillips R	41oa	9cl FM
134	Siata 208 S		Wilder W	42oa	4cl F
66	MG TD		Aldridge J	43oa	11cl MG
115	Singer SM 1500		McGuire C	44oa	5cl F
77	Simca Special		Campbell F	45oa	10cl FM
106	MG TC		Mahon E	46oa	11cl FM
113	MG TD		Hart P	47oa	12cl FM
112	Jaguar C-type	XKC 024	Harrison J	48oa dnf L4	6cl CM
28	MG TD		Panuse L	49oa dnf	13cl FM
120	Crosley		Holloway C	50oa dnf	3cl HM

Programme cover for the March AFB event. This iconic cover features Bill Stroppe's famous Kurtis-Mercury. Sitting inside is Miss Marge Ruvald talking with a B-47 bomber pilot, Earl Gordon. (Terry O'Neil Collection)

Race 2 10 laps	Race distance 35 miles	Class Unrestricted Prod	Starters

Race winner's time 28mins 4secs		Average speed 74.84mph	

72	Jaguar XK120M	MacKay Fraser H	1oa	1cl CM
11	Jaguar XK120M	Borden J Dr	2oa	2cl CM
84	Jaguar XK120M	Montonen H	3oa	3cl CM
85	Jaguar XK120	MacGregor S	4oa	1cl C
110	Porsche 356	Hunter G	5oa	1cl F
66	Jowett Jupiter	Aldridge J	6oa	2cl F
26	Singer SM 1500	McDonald R	7oa	3cl F
25	MG TD Mk II	Benton J	8oa	4cl F
108	MG TD	Critchlow L	9oa	1cl MG
114	MG TD	Speer M	10oa	2cl MG
83	MG TD	Youngberg M	11oa	3cl MG
127	Allard J2 LM	High T	12oa	1cl BM
31	Jaguar XK120M	Masterson R	13oa	4cl CM
124	Jaguar XK120	Seher R	14oa	2cl C
86	Jowett Jupiter	Carberry J	15oa	5cl F
142	Morgan	Thompson C Dr	16oa	1cl D
66	MG TD	Aldridge J	17oa	4cl MG
1	MG TD	Barrett C	18oa	5cl MG
81	BMW 328	Blumenfeld D	19oa	1cl EM

Race 3 30 laps	Race distance 105 miles	Class U 1500cc	Starters

Race winner's time 1hr 19mins 11secs	Average speed 79.55mph

50	MG TD R-1 Special		Miles K	1oa	1cl FM
9	OSCA MT4 1350	1133	Simpson J	2oa	2cl FM
111	Porsche 356 America		Von Neumann J	3oa	3cl FM
101	Simca 8 Comp		Van Dyke L	4oa	4cl FM
49	MG TD		Drake R	5oa	5cl FM
43	Nardi		Hilderbrand K	6oa	1cl GM
44	Singer SM 1500		Van Laanen R	7oa	6cl FM
86	Jowett Jupiter		Carberry J	8oa	1cl F
141	VW-Porsche		Wilder S	9oa	7cl FM
97	VW Special		Anderson R	10oa	8cl FM
48	Offenhauser Special		Beavis G	11oa dnf	9cl FM
27	MG TD		Hanford H	12oa	10cl FM
73	DB Panhard		Peron P	13oa	1cl G
119	Porsche 356 LM		Mullin S	14oa	11cl FM
1	MG TD		Barrett C	15oa	2cl F
133	MG Special		Behel W	16oa dnf	12cl FM
74	Porsche 356		Shillam D Dr	17oa	13cl FM
8	Siata 300BC 750 Spyder		Manney H III	18oa	1cl HM
95	MG TD		Barker E	19oa	14cl FM
13	MG TC		Anderson A	20oa	15cl FM
62	Jowett Jupiter		Marks C	21oa	3cl F
26	Singer SM 1500		McDonald R	22oa	4cl F
106	MG TC		Mahon D	23oa	16cl FM

6	MG TC Special		Yedor C	24oa dnf L9	17cl FM
45	Young Special s/c		Young J	25oa dnf	2cl HM
87	MG TC		Banta H	26oa dnf	18cl FM
128	Porsche 356		Whittington W	27oa dnf	5cl F

Race 4	Race distance 175 miles	Class O 1500cc	Starters 36

Race winner's time 1hr 59mins 50secs	Average speed 87.62mph

15	Cunningham C4R		Fitch J	1oa	1cl BM
3	Cunningham C4R		Cunningham B	2oa	2cl BM
30	Ferrari 340 MM	0324 AM	Spear W	3oa	1cl CM
58	Jaguar C-type	XKC 022	Gregory M	4oa	2cl CM
5	Ferrari 340 AM	0204 A	Kimberly J	5oa	3cl CM
20	Glasspar Nameco Spl		Pollack W	6oa	4cl CM
104	Ferrari 212 Ex	0078 E	Wheeler H	7oa	1cl DM
17	Ferrari 250 MM	0312 MM	Devin W	8oa	2cl DM
64	Frazer-Nash LM	421/200/183	Lowe J	9oa	1cl EM
38	Siata 208 CS	BS 537	McAfee E	10oa	2cl EM
24	Kurtis 500 S De Soto		Trennert R	11oa	3cl BM
126	Allard J2 Cadillac		Kuchenbecker C	12oa	4cl BM
23	Veritas		Biehl J	13oa	3cl EM
143	Jaguar XK120		Jackson C	14oa	5cl CM
109	Kurtis 500 S Mercury		Ruttman T	15oa dnf L30	6cl CM
129	La Salle Ford		Bachowsky M	16oa	1cl AM
60	MG-Willys		Lowe M	17oa	3cl DM
96	Allard J2 Cadillac		Bamford T	18oa	5cl BM
4	Cunningham C5R	5319R	Walters P	19oa dnf L12	6cl BM
85	Jaguar XK120		MacGregor S	20oa	1cl C
71	Allard J2 Oldsmobile		Swartley S	21oa	7cl BM
121	Bristol Special		Scott E	22oa	4cl EM
53	Ferrari 340 MM	0350 AM	Edwards S	23oa	7cl CM
55	Jaguar Special		Pickford W	24oa	8cl CM
54	Kurtis 500 S De Soto		Murphy W	25oa	9cl CM
34	Jaguar XK120		Wilder E	26oa	8cl BM
138	Allard J2 Cadillac		Cochran J	27oa	2cl AM
				28oa	
47	Kurtis 500 S Cadillac		Sawyer G	29oa	3cl AM
29	Allard J2X	J3208	Barneson J	30oa dnf	9cl BM
19	Jaguar XK120 Special		Mendelson M	31oa dnf	10cl CM
88	MG TC Special		Stubbs A	32oa dnf	5cl EM
91	MG TC s/c Special		Erb H	33oa dnf	6cl EM
12	Allard J2X Lincoln		Briney M	34oa dnf	10cl BM
	Mercury Special		Bird T	35oa dnf	11cl CM
78	Ferrari 340 AM	0032 A	McAfee J	36oa dnf	12cl CM

5

SCCA national & regional races at other military bases 1953

Chanute AFB, Rantoul, Illinois

14.6.1953 (Regional/AFB)

"How the ex-Wilbur Shaw Maserati qualified as a sports car is somewhat of a mystery, but it was allowed to run, and finished in fifth position in the feature race." (Road & Track)

Chanute AFB was situated on a 2125-acre site, located on the southern edge of Rantoul, and was the headquarters for 3496 Air Training Command. The primary mission of the AFB was to provide military and technical training to Air Force officers and airmen, as well as civilians working for the military.

For a regional event, the races at Rantoul took on a magnitude unsurpassed by anything that had preceded it, as the number of entrants exceeded 150. In late autumn of 1952, having noted the successful event held at Turner AFB, Ben Harris III of the Chicago Region had started making arrangements with the Air Force Base Commander at Chanute, Major General Byron E Gates, for use of the Base. What they failed to see immediately was the need to use the Base over a four-day period to cope with the number of entrants for the races. Major General Gates

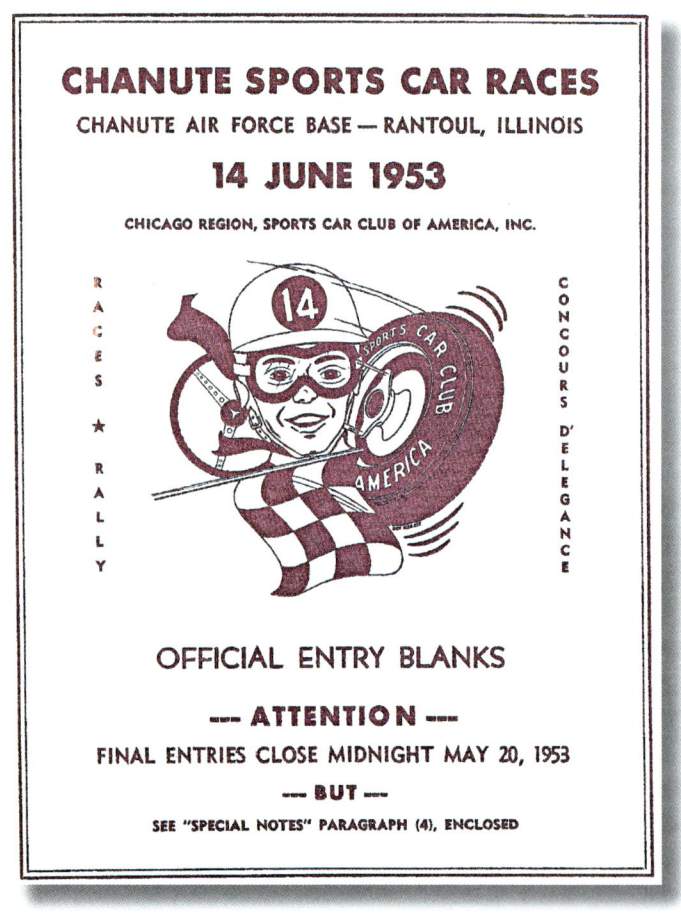

An Official Entry Blank for the event at Chanute AFB. (Courtesy Bruce Perry Collection)

granted the extra days of access to the Base, and luckily SCCA Chicago chairman Ben Harris III had a good organisational team in place to administer the event. Plenty of practical help was given by numerous members of the Air Force Technical Training Command to make this a memorable occasion. Two aircraft hangars were vacated and used as garages, so that the drivers could prepare their cars prior to the races, and up to 1200 airmen were made available to help with the running of the event. As with the National SCCA events held at airbases, it was agreed that all proceeds of the event would go to the Airmen's Living Improvement Fund.

The planned course was 3.3 miles in length, including one straightway of 6000ft. The start/finish line was located opposite a grandstand area that had been erected, as was the pit area, located on the inside of the track. The first part of the course was quite torturous, consisting of a left-hand curve, followed by a 90-degree bend to the right, swiftly followed by a right-hand curve that led directly onto another 90-degree bend. After that, there was a short respite for the drivers as a 1900ft straight led to a curve, then onto another short straight, before the cars had to take two more 90-degree right turns that led onto the main 6000ft straightway. From the end of the straightway, a hairpin bend led back to the pit area and the start/finish line.

The lead-up to the races was well documented in the local papers, and it was noticeable that there was a certain fascination with what was described as "... one of the most colourful entrants," namely Jim Kimberly. There was no crusade, either for or against him, the fascination was simply a result of the amount of money spent in creating a team that was capable of winning most events by an 'amateur' driver. It had led an astute journalist to look in detail at the entourage of red vehicles and people in red uniforms following Kimberly to each venue, and comparing the situation to the drivers that turned up in their MGs, having driven home from work in them the day before.

Considering that it was classified as a regional event, the races were extremely well supported, with estimates of a 75,000 crowd in attendance for the five-race programme, a tribute to the work and advertising that Chanute personnel had done on behalf of the SCCA. However, it was stated that only 60,000 of them paid to get in, as the people selling tickets were overwhelmed by the size of the crowd.

The first race, 'The Gates 50,' was for production sports cars under 1500cc. The field consisted mainly of Porsche or MG models, and attracted 38 entries. The Porsche contingent, led by Max Goldman, was too strong for the MGs, and finished in the first four positions. It was the MG TC of Robert Fergus that came fifth overall, and first in Class, maintaining his magnificent record of Class placing in the MG TC.

The second race, 'The Harper 50,' was for production sports cars over 1500cc, and, in effect, was a Jaguar race between ordinary production models and factory modified production models. It was anticipated that the XK120M models would have everything in their favour, but much to everyone's surprise, Tom Newcomer crossed the line in a standard production model to take first place. In a close finish, John Kilborn was classified second, and Riddelle Gregory third, both in modified cars.

The large crowd witnessed the welcome return of a Ladies' Race, as this was the first time since the abandonment of this event at Elkhart Lake in 1951 that a Ladies' Race had been run in this part of America. Eleven starters took to the grid, driving a variety of cars, and it was no surprise to see Sally Chapin (possibly recognised more for her skill in piloting aircraft than cars), driving Kimberly's Ferrari, pull out a substantial lead over the remainder of the field. Margaret Wyllie in a Jaguar was the only competitor to stay on the same lap, and in third place came Suzy Dietrich in her husband's MG TC s/c. Sally Chapin nearly came to grief when she

Track layout at Chanute AFB.
(Terry O'Neil Collection)

*Competitor's plaque for the event at Chanute AFB.
(Courtesy Bruce Perry Collection)*

was about to overtake Mary Stipe on the right. Upon hearing the Ferrari engine, Miss Stipe swung her MG to the right. Sally Chapin was forced to brake violently and cut back to the left quickly to avoid hitting the MG. After the race, she stated, " I must have been doing around 100 … maybe a little better. My heart was going bang-bang-bang!" (*The News-Gazette*, Champaign) More than likely, Kimberly's heart was also pounding!

Race four was the first of the two main feature races – this one, The Eubank Cup was for modified cars under 1500cc and attracted thirty-nine starters to the grid for the 102-mile race. Unlike the production car race, this one was not a fight between the Porsche marque alone, as there was a genuine challenge from OSCA and MG.

John Urbas driving Ed Trego's Glockler Porsche won the race, but was closely followed over the finish line by the OSCA driven by James Simpson, and the MG Special driven by Bob Salzgaber. Talking about Urbas after the race, Ed Trego said, "It was the first time he had ever driven a Porsche, and he did a wonderful job didn't he?" (*The News-Gazette*, Champaign)

The final race of the day was the 102-mile Technical Training Trophy Race for modified cars over 1500cc, with a special class for production Jaguars. Forty-seven cars came to the grid for the start of the race, and, as the flag fell, it was Jack Ensley in an Allard who took an instant lead ahead of Kimberly and Lewis both in Ferraris, Duncan in an Allard, and Urbas and Wallace, both driving Jaguars. Urbas had started in 26th position, but soon carved his way through the field. Ensley was unable to maintain his lead over Kimberly, due to spinning off the track twice in the opening laps, leaving Kimberly to stretch his lead over the chasing pack. By the end of the race, Kimberly had lapped everyone with the exception of Urbas, who had steadily made his way up to second place. Wallace, in the other C-type Jaguar, finished third ahead of Lewis in fourth position. It turned out to be a good day for Ferrari, as Lewis was first in Class D and Lunken's Ferrari won Class E. Bob McManus entered the Maserati 8CTF monoposto that Wilber Shaw had driven at Indianapolis, and Chuck Hassan was nominated to drive it. The car, which had won the Indianapolis 500 in 1939 and 1940, was still competitive enough to finish in fifth place. Strictly, the car was not eligible for this race, and as such would not be eligible for a prize, though none of the other competitors made any complaints, such was the sporting nature of the drivers.

At the Victory dinner, General Gates summed up the reaction of the spectators, and Chanute personnel when he said, "A month ago, not many of us in this area were sure what a sports car race was like. Now we know, and we like it. If you'll bring your cars back next year, every person who was here today will be back with all his friends." Just to add to the plaudits, Lieutenant Colonel Harry W Douglas, project officer for the races, declared that the undertaking had been a "… fine demonstration of how a community and the air force can work together." (*The News-Gazette*, Champaign.)

As it was a SCCA regional event, news coverage was purely on a local basis, and nothing was mentioned as to the extent the Base benefited from the races. Based on the parameters used by the General Accounting Office, it is doubtful if it was possible in pure financial terms to call the event profitable, though in terms of public relations, it did no harm at all.

Paine AFB, Everett, Washington

8.8.1953 (national/AFB)

"Lou Fageol, world famous speedboat driver, was on hand with his twin engine Porsche. Not particularly concerned about carrying luggage Lou has added a second Porsche engine in front, giving four wheel drive." (Bill Brent, Road & Track)

Originally called Snohomish County Airport, Paine Field, the civil airport, was constructed in 1936 with two runways. During WWII, the Army Air Corps manned Paine Field and stayed there until 1946. During that time, significant expansion and improvements took place, including the construction of two more

An Official Entry Blank for the event at Paine AFB. (Courtesy Bruce Perry Collection)

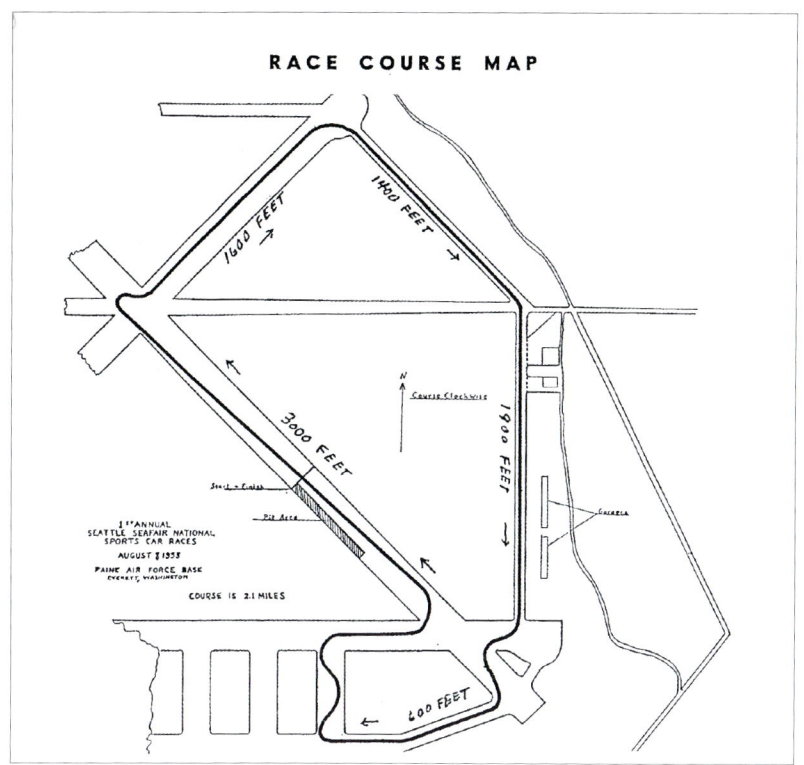

Track layout at Paine AFB. (Terry O'Neil Collection)

runways. In 1948, the airbase went back under the control of Snohomish County, but with the commencement of the Korean War, Paine Field was once again occupied by the military. In 1951, the 4753rd Air Force Aerospace Defence command unit was stationed there, and the name was changed from Paine Field to Paine Air Force Base. Due to the small numbers of military personnel involved, total control of Paine Field was not turned over to the Air Force. Instead, it set in place a shared-usage agreement, whereby commercial flights could continue to use the four active runways.

Paine Air Force Base played host to the first event organised by the Pacific Northwest region of the SCCA. During the summer of 1952, a small group of sports car enthusiasts from all over western Washington State formed an organisation to promote sports car racing in the Puget Sound area. Within weeks, the group, known as the Puget Sound Sports Car Club, boosted its membership to around 150, and became affiliated to the SCCA. Greater Seattle Inc, sponsors of the Seafair, heard about the Club's efforts to promote racing and came forward with an offer to include sports car races in the Seafair Celebration gala. The invitation was accepted, and arrangements put into place for the races to commence on August 8 1953. In conjunction with the SCCA and the Seattle Seafair Celebration, the Air Force was the co-sponsors of the event, with all proceeds going to benefit the Air Force Chaplain's Fund. So as to play its part fully, the SCCA decided to make this a National event, and, in doing so, hoped that the lure of points towards the National Championship would attract SCCA drivers from further afield than Washington State. Up to this point in time, races in the area had mainly been organised by the Sports Car Club of British Columbia, and as a consequence, a fair few Canadians from the Vancouver area would enter to compete against the local racers. There was another National event being run this weekend, but that was at Lockbourne AFB in Columbus Ohio, and because of the distance between them, would not detract from either entry list.

A 2.1-mile racecourse was mapped out along the runways and taxi strips, with the addition of an interesting loop that almost circled one of the hangars. The pits were located on the outside of the track on the main 3000ft straight, just before the start/finish line. So as to prepare local drivers and ensure the safety of the course, a practice session was held on June 7. Despite the rainy conditions, those SCCA members who tried the course deemed it safe and satisfactory for a major race to take place.

Race day started as wet and misty, conditions certainly not conducive to standing around, unless appropriately clothed. Consequently, the public didn't make an early entrance to the Air Base to watch the racing, but waited for conditions to improve. The event had certainly caught the imagination of the comparatively sparsely populated area, and, as weather conditions improved, the crowds took to the Washington State highways. So intense was the traffic that it backed up along old Highway 99, then the only major north-south highway connection in the State, much to the concern of the local police, who had not witnessed anything like this before. The event organisers decided to delay the start of the first race by an hour, to allow spectators to park their cars and find a viewing spot.

Newspaper reports claimed that 20,000 people were in attendance, but apparently many of them got in without paying, when the ticket sellers were overwhelmed by the unexpected amount of people and ran out of admission tickets. The organisers quickly came to the realisation that they had misjudged the magnitude of the crowd. They had to find extra parking spaces and allow spectators beyond the fenced areas of the track surround so they could view the races – shades of road racing in Northeast America at Bridgehampton and Watkins Glen. Luckily, though, there were no problems resulting from this action.

Three races were planned, a smaller than usual amount, especially for a National event, but the vast expanse of sparsely populated territory in this corner of Northwest America meant that entries would be much lower than in other parts of the country.

The first race of the day was for novice drivers. Twelve drivers entered the race, run over twelve laps of the track, and in addition, Charles Fifield (married to Temple Buell's daughter) entered his Allard for an observation run to check it out. The field consisted of two modified Jaguars, a Porsche 1500, and nine MGs. The start flag dropped, and the two Jaguars positioned on the front row of the grid jumped into an immediate lead, followed by the Porsche. These three cars lapped the remainder of the field before the end of the first lap. The Allard didn't fair so well, losing the gear linkage, and as a result, coasted to a standstill. The two Jaguars traded the lead several times before Tom Henderson took the chequered flag ahead of Bob Byrd's Jaguar, with the Porsche trailing in 3rd place, well ahead of the MGs.

Twenty-four under-1500cc cars entered the Colonel's Cup race, which was originally intended to be a 48-lap, 100-mile race, but was shortened to 30 laps due to the late start to the race programme. Nine of the cars belonged to the Canadian contingent of drivers, who had come to support the races. John Hudson in his Porsche 356 Super took the lead, and soon built up a 50-second cushion ahead of the second place car, the Morgan driven by Gary McDonald. Hudson remained unchallenged throughout the race, finishing an easy winner. Making its debut in this corner of America was the Crosley Special built by Harry Eyerly, but unfortunately it would be no fairytale finish, as the car lost

Lou Faegol's twin-engine Porsche special is prepared for the Seafair Trophy race. (Courtesy S Rutherford)

the left rear wheel on the first lap, sliding to a stop on the course. The Crosley was one of six cars that failed to complete the race.

The Seafair Trophy was the main feature event of the day, and had attracted some top drivers in a small field of eleven cars. Bill Stroppe had turned up with his Kurtis 500 and Bill Pollack was given a drive in a C-type Jaguar, belonging to the Henderson family, due to Tom Carstens' Allard not being available for him to drive. Frank Hern also had the use of Tom Henderson's Jaguar XK120M, winner of the first race. Lou Fageol had brought his unique twin-engine Porsche to the event, and there were three Specials entered by local lads Ray Hansen, Kolar, and Thompson.

By the time the grid lined up, the weather had taken a turn for the better, and the track was drying out quickly. Stroppe and Pollack were on the first row of the grid, and it was Bill Stroppe in his Kurtis who took the lead as the flag dropped, followed closely by the Ford Special of Ray Hansen, much to the delight of the crowd. Hansen maintained that position ahead of Pollack for 18 laps, before the oil pressure disappeared from his car and he was forced to retire. Lou Fageol had been running well in fourth place, but had to drop out with clutch problems on the 10th lap. Stroppe took the chequered flag well in the lead with a conservatively driven C-type Jaguar, with Pollack at the wheel coming in second. Frank Hern crossed the line in 3rd place, driving a Jaguar XK120M minus a left rear tyre. His tyre blew 1200ft from the chequered flag and he crossed the finish line on the wheel rim. Unfortunately, this was the most action seen by the crowd, as no exciting battles had taken place in the race, in which only seven cars completed the 100-mile grind.

Despite the small size of the fields for each race, the organisers of the event were delighted with their achievement of successfully putting on the races, even though they realised that certain areas of their planning would need improvement, should the event be held again.

Moffett NAS, Sunnyvale, California

16.8.1953 (National/NAS)

"The slings and arrows of outrageous fortune: A broken axle put Phil Hill's Ferrari hors de combat after travelling exactly three feet." (Road & Track)

The first Naval Air Station circuit race in the country was held at Moffett Field on a 3.5-mile long track laid out on the asphalt runways and taxiways of the Base. Moffett Field was home to Air

An Official Entry Blank for the event at Moffett Field NAS. (Courtesy Bruce Perry Collection)

Transport Squadron Three, and Five, Composite Squadron Three, Air Development Squadron Five and Carrier Air Group Nineteen. Located on a 1,000-acre site in Santa Clara County near the southern tip of San Francisco Bay, the base was originally commissioned as NAS Sunnyvale in 1933 to serve as a base for the West Coast dirigibles of the Navy's lighter-than-air programme. Hangar 1 was built to house the USS Macon (785ft long), intended to provide long range reconnaissance for the Pacific Fleet. The Macon only flew eight missions, before it crashed in 1935. In 1942, the base was re-named NAS Moffett Field.

The event at Moffett Field was organised on behalf of the SCCA by the San Francisco Region, and sponsored by the Naval Air Station and the Fleet Air Detachment based at Moffett Field for the Combined Moffett Field Charity Fund, established in 1950. Initial arrangements were conducted by Edward Gasper on behalf of the SCCA and the Base Commanding Officer Captain BB Nichol, whilst invaluable assistance came from the Guardsmen of San Francisco in the planning of the races. The event was the tenth race meeting on the SCCA National calendar for 1953, with all proceeds from this race event donated to the Charity Fund, Navy Relief, and the American Red Cross, as well as other local charities.

The most striking feature of the circuit layout was the 8000ft straightway, helping to make this the fastest track in western America. The track had seven turns, and the pits were located halfway along the inside of the straightway, and not, as indicated on the track plan, on the outside of the track. To help the competitors and their pit crews stay out of the blazing sun, tarpaulins had been supplied along the length of the pit area, generating much-needed shade. The downside to the track layout was the distance between the paying spectators and the competitors. Safety was never going to be an issue on the wide open spaces of the Base, but the criticism from the spectators was that they were too far removed from the action to be able to appreciate what was going on. Six blocks of bleachers were erected by naval personnel at various points around the outside of the track for the spectators, but proved inadequate for the estimated 50,000 people who turned out to watch the races. In fairness to the organisers, they had attempted to help keep the spectators better informed as to what was going on. The SCCA had the use of an electronic timer called the DSG Interval Computer, accurate to measuring time to the nearest one ten thousandth of a second. With the use of this device, the announcer could relay speeds, lap times, and even the intervals between two cars.

Three races were on the programme for the event, the first being the Captain's Cup Race, a 77-mile grind for cars under 1500cc, with Championship points at stake.

A strong field of 25 cars had entered for the race, though only about 20 took to the start line. Leson and Pringle turned out in their competitive Simcas, while Jack McAfee drove Von Neuman's Porsche 356 America. Strong opposition was expected to materialise in the form of Coppel's OSCA (ex MacDougall) and the very quick MG TD Special, driven by Ken Miles. As predicted, it turned out to be a fiercely contested race, with the lead being exchanged from Miles to Coppel and McAfee, until Miles went out of the race with no clutch, and Coppel retired with no oil pressure. For Miles in particular, this was an unusual 'did not finish,' as the MG had proved exceptionally reliable throughout the season. This left McAfee with a comfortable lead, which he maintained unchallenged to the finish line. Leson finished in second position, and Gillespie, driving an MG TC Special, in third place. John Young with his 'Young Special' was the only Class G car in the field, and finished in eleventh position, while the Class H cars had been transferred to the second race.

The second race was, by comparison, a sprint, covering just 21 miles, having being shortened from the original 35 miles. Named the Navcad Trophy, the race was open to novice drivers. It brought a varied mix of cars to the grid – everything from six-litre Allards to 726cc Crosley

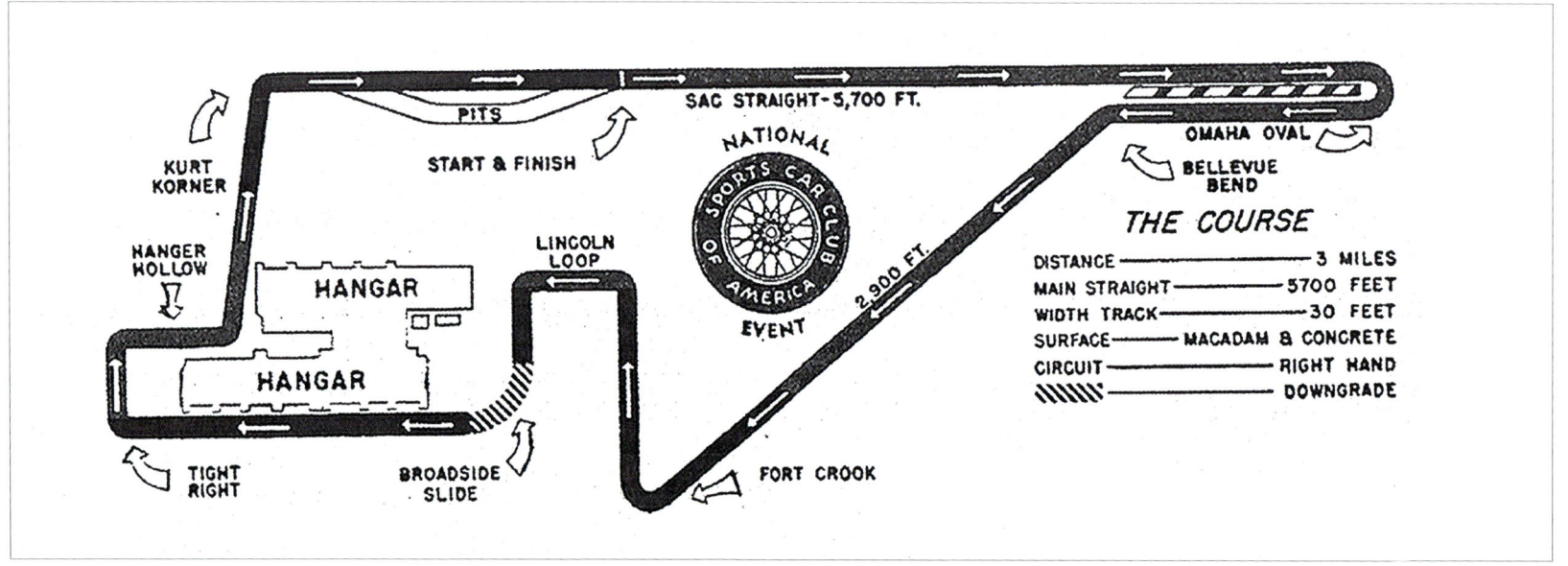

Track layout at Moffett Field NAS. (Terry O'Neil Collection)

Al Coppel had to retire his OSCA in the Captain's Cup race. (Courtesy Ron Kellogg Collection)

models. At least 43 cars started the race, with the inevitable conclusion being a victory for an Allard, as they were far more formidable than the smaller Class F cars, of which there were many. At the finish of the shortened race, three Allards were in the top four positions, the only interloper being the Class EM Frazer-Nash, owned by Jim Lowe but driven by Chuck Daigh to third place overall. Donald James driving a 'Special' won Class C, while the large Class F was won by Larry Taylor driving Chuck Leson's Simca 8 Special. Way down the field in 24th place, was a car better known for its rally qualities in Europe than racing capability – a Sunbeam Alpine. Nevertheless, it won Class D, but to put

Jack McAfee leads Ken Miles around the Moffett Field track. McAfee went on to win the Captain's Cup, while Miles had to retire his MG Special. (Courtesy Ron Kellogg Collection)

Chuck Daigh drove Jim Lowe's Frazer-Nash to third place in the Navcad Trophy Race. (Terry O'Neil Collection)

its performance into context, finished behind the Class HM winner, William Harper, driving Al Coppel's Nardi-Danese.

The feature race of the day was the Moffett Field Handicap Race, with a duration of 150 minutes. Unfortunately for the spectators, there was no explanation given in the programme as to how the Handicap was derived or how it worked, so they felt bemused, and were left to wonder what was going on as the cars circulated.

Fortunately, the drivers were aware of the handicap system, and the race attracted a lot of the top drivers from the West Coast of America.

Phil Hill brought his Ferrari 250MM along, while Bill Stroppe, on a roll following victories in seven of his eight starts, was in the Clay Smith-owned Kurtis 500. John Von Neumann was in the Ed Trego-owned Glockler Porsche, Ken Miles in his MG TD Special, the clutch now repaired, and Doug Trotter in the Aston-Martin GMC ex-Phil Hill road car. Allards, Jaguars, MGs, and Specials, including the ex-Parkinson Jaguar now owned by Jay Beezemeyer, and Pickord's Jaguar Special, made up the competitive field.

The race commenced with a Le Mans type start, the Kurtis of Stroppe and the Allard of Swartley getting away well. The start was not without its problems though, as Phil Hill broke the rear axle on his Ferrari before he had travelled 3ft, leaving him disconsolately watching the rest of the field disappear into the distance. Bill Stroppe covered 192.5 miles in the 150 minutes, for an overall win on distance classification, followed by Doug Trotter in the Aston-Martin GMC in second place, and Ken Miles in third. The James Chapman-owned Allard J2 Cadillac was plagued with pit stops every few laps, but, nevertheless, it finished fourth in the hands of Jack Armstrong. As the race ended, the Allard stalled 1000ft from the finish line, so Jack Armstrong jumped out, and, showing equal amounts of both strength and determination, pushed the heavy car over the finish line. Ken Miles was declared the winner of the race, based on the handicap time/distance formula, with Stroppe in second place, and Dr F Hodges, driving a Jaguar XK120M, in third position. The heat took its toll on drivers and cars with fifteen of the starters failing to finish the race.

Stout Field NGB, Indianapolis, Indiana

"Drivers said the Stout Field course was the shortest they had ever run on and tyre wear was extreme."
(National Speed Sport News)

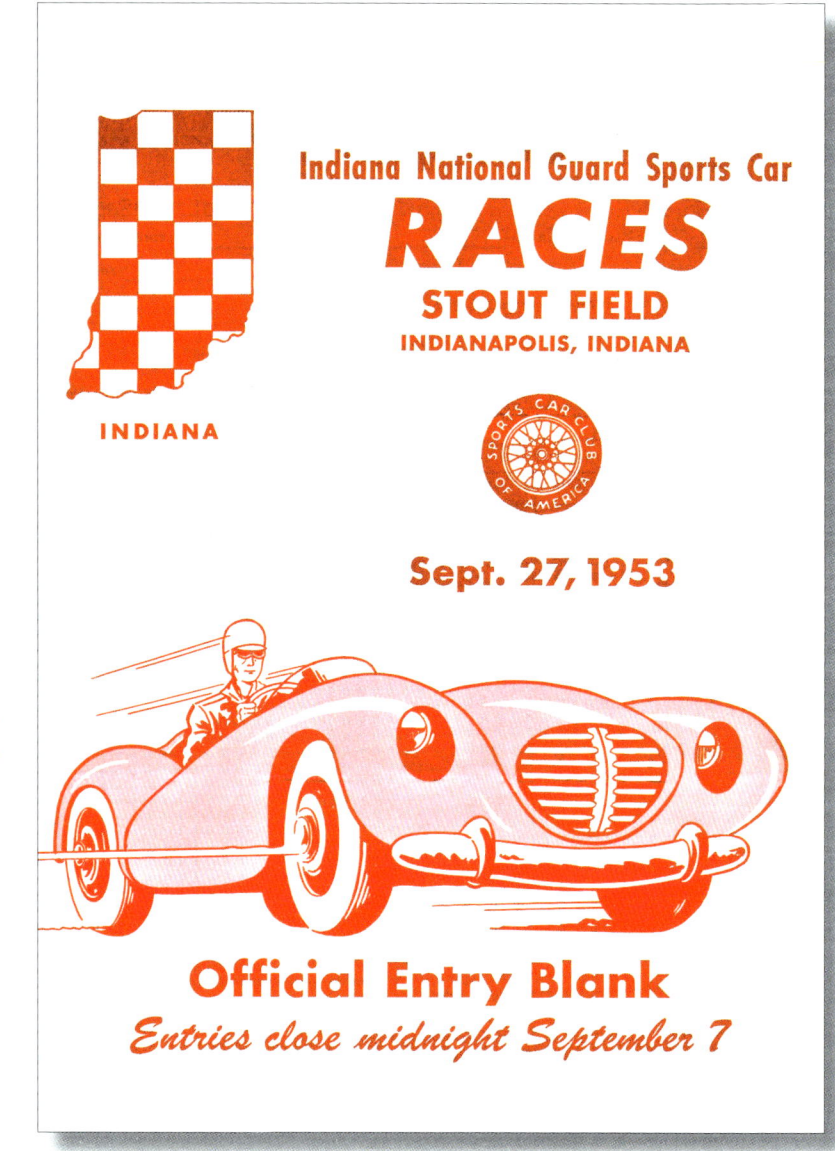

An Official Entry Blank for the event at Stout Field NGB. (Courtesy Bruce Perry Collection)

The first race event staged by the Indianapolis Region of the SCCA took place at Stout Field, a 357-acre site located five miles south-west of Indianapolis and was sponsored by the Indiana National Guard. The staging of the event was due largely to the efforts of Sandy McArthur, Robert Magenheimer, and Harry Reid of the Indianapolis Region, and Brig Gen Dougherty of the Indiana National Guards based at Stout Field, together with State Governor George N Craig.

Stout Field came into being in 1927, and was used as a local airport before being leased by the US Government during WWII, for the purpose of using it as the headquarters of the newly formed Troop Carrier Command. In 1947, the site was returned to the State of Indiana, and became home to the Indiana National Guard. The SCCA became attracted to the site, as runway improvements had been made during the period when in Government hands, and after inspection was deemed suitable for sports car races by the SCCA. After protracted negotiations with Governor Craig and the Base Commander, a deal was set up, whereby all proceeds of the event would go to the Indiana National Guard Armoury Fund.

A course was planned, utilising parts of all three main runways plus the main taxiway, roughly triangular in shape and 1.6 miles in length, one of the shorter circuits used for racing by the SCCA. The longest straightway was a mere 2400ft in length. It did bring adverse comments from the drivers of the heavier cars, as tyre wear was excessive, due to gear changes and constant braking on the tight circuit.

Six races had been planned for the event on what turned out to be a bright and sunny day. The first race was for cars under 1500cc, excluding the Porsche models, and was dominated by MG cars. Durbin took the lead and held onto it for several laps, before being overtaken first by Bob Fergus, then by Andrews, and finally by Brooks. Fergus,

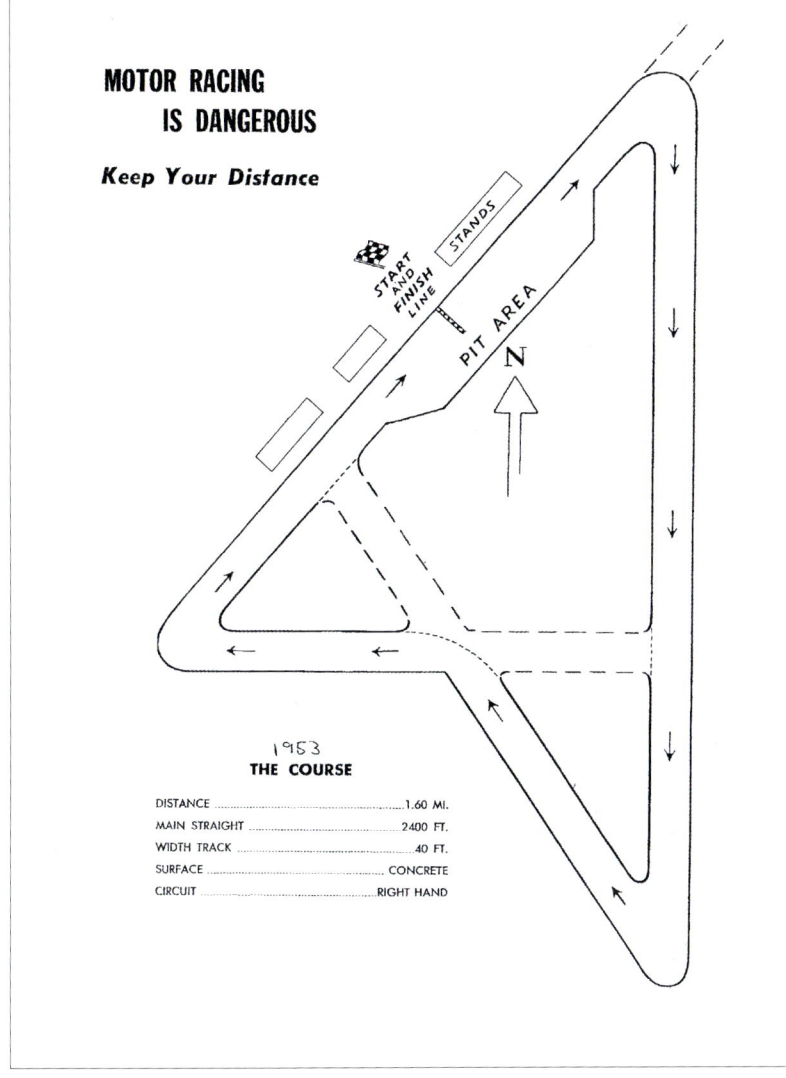

Track layout at Stout Field NGB. (Terry O'Neil Collection)

driving his very quick and successful MG TC, held onto the lead and finished in first place, followed by Andrews and Brooks.

The second race of the day brought out the standard production Jaguars, together with the Porsche models. Sandy McArthur, race chairman, had made pre-race predictions forecasting the Porsche models to run high up the field, because they were well suited to the twisty small tracks – more so than the Jaguars. However, with the exception of Cornett's Porsche Super that worked its way up to third place, the predictions were misplaced, as Jaguars dominated the proceedings. Even on this small track, their pace outstripped the agility of the smaller cars. Kilborn's Jaguar took the lead from the start and maintained the position throughout the race, followed by Ensley in his Jaguar. Two laps from the end, Ensley's car blew the right rear tyre, but carried on with a flailing shredded tyre to finish second, ahead of Cornett's Porsche Super. It was also a traumatic race for Roger Wing, as his Jaguar caught fire while on the back straight of the track, when the engine blew. Luckily, the fire was soon put out, but damage to the engine was extensive and would keep the car out of the remainder of the races.

In the third race for the under 1500cc cars, John Urbas, driving Ed Trego's Glockler Porsche (the same one Von Neumann drove at Moffett a month previously), gave a somewhat erratic display by spinning off the track three times, but still managed to finish first. Each time he left the track, he lost the lead to Rees Makins in his OSCA, but managed to claw it back again prior to his next spin. Urbas reported that the cause of his erratic driving was that the throttle was sticking open, causing him to take the corners too quickly. It must have been a very bewildered Makins that finished second ahead of the Porsche America of Ed Crawford, and the highly modified MG driven by Bob Salzgaber. In the production MG class, Don Marsh, a salesman working for Bob Fergus, drove the MG TC belonging to Bob Fergus to another victory, Andrews again finishing second, with Durbin in third place.

The fourth race brought together some of the quickest cars in the mid-west of America. Jim Kimberly and Jack Ensley were the pre-race favourites, while Lunken had his Ferrari (ex-Kimberly) competing against Lou Fageol's four-wheel drive, twin-engine Porsche, making its first appearance in the mid-west. Kimberly won the race by driving smoothly, as all around him were spinning off the track. He was ahead of Charles Wallace driving the Feuerbacher Jaguar Silverstone, and Jack Ensley, who was third in his Allard. Lunken won his battle against Fageol's Porsche, winning class D, while Hassan won class E in Lunken's old Ferrari. Katskee was first home of the Jaguar XK120M drivers, and John Kilborn first with the standard production Jaguar XK120.

The penultimate race was for modified under 1500cc cars, though a few of the owners opted to miss this event having used their cars in race three, while the Glockler Porsche was invited to join race six. Ed Crawford drove a smooth race in his Porsche America, and took first place with little opposition from the depleted field. Salzgaber moved into second place in his MG, with Magenheimer gaining ground steadily, until he threw a con-rod on the last lap of the race. This left John Whitlack to take third place driving an MG TD. In class H, Eddie Jones won his second class victory of the day, driving a Siata Spyder.

Such was the concern of the drivers of the larger cars that the final race of the day was curtailed to 67.2 miles. So much rubber had been expended that the drivers were worried about safety, and they correctly requested that the 100-mile race be reduced. Several drivers, including

*Competitor's plaque for the event at Stout Field.
(Courtesy Bruce Perry Collection)*

Bob Fergus, opted not to run at all, having used all of their tyres, though in the main, the drivers from race four turned out again. There were also one or two new faces, with the appearance of Rosenberger in the Nash-Healey Le Mans, and Fuerbacher in his C-type Jaguar.

It was Kimberly who took the early lead, followed by Lunken's Ferrari 225S, and it remained that way until the twelfth lap when Kimberly spun and retired with transmission problems. In the meantime, Rosenberger had already retired on the third lap, the Nash-Healey reportedly overheating. Lunken pitted on lap seventeen to allow Hassan to take over the driving of his Ferrari, and Ensley's Allard J2X took the lead. Ensley retained the lead until the 32nd lap when the transmission on the Allard locked, allowing Hassan to take the lead. Hassan was to experience brief success as the car had transmission trouble, and he went out together with Feuerbacher's Jaguar and Goldich's Excalibur on the next lap. With all this carnage around him, Wallace in the Jaguar Silverstone continued to circulate and keep out of trouble. His consistency paid off, as he took the lead, and unexpectedly finished the race in first place, ahead of the Excalibur-Willys of Lowrey and the Du Pont Ford Special of Chamberlain.

The Victory dinner was held that same evening, where it was stated that the excellent food served to the guests atoned for Indiana's no alcohol-on-Sunday law.

At the prize awards ceremony, The Governor Craig Award was presented to Chuck Wallace for winning the main race, the Shell Sportsmanship Award went to Phil Reddig, who had worked all night to get his car ready for the races, and the 'Hard Luck Trophy' to Andy Rosenberger.

6

1953 Statistical Review

Chanute AFB 14.6.1953

The Gates 50 16 laps	Classes Under 1500cc	Entrants 38	Starters
Race winner's time 45min 54.6sec	Average speed 69mph	Race distance 52.8 miles	

12	Porsche 356 Super	Goldman M	1oa	1cl F-P
	Porsche 356	Kerner B	2oa	2cl F-P
149	Porsche 356	Chamberlain R	3oa	3cl F-P
144	Porsche 356 Super	Cornett D	4oa	4cl F-P
111	MG TC	Fergus R	5oa	1cl F-MG
100	Porsche 356	Brocken K		5cl F-P
108	Porsche 356	Short W		6cl F-P
36	Porsche 356	Carroll G		
67	Porsche 356	Howell J		
56	Porsche 356	Klinger H		
61	Porsche 356 Super	Van Antwerpen P		
19	Porsche 356	Warren D		
60	Porsche 356	Williams F		
104	MG TD	Fleming W		2cl F-MG
63	MG TD	Kuhn R		3cl F-MG
72	MG TD	Dorn H		4cl F-MG
102	MG TC	Smith W		5cl F-MG

Programme cover for the Chanute AFB event. (Courtesy Bruce Perry Collection)

25	MG TD		Harbour J		6cl F-MG
15	MG TD Mk II		Davis D		1cl
48	MG TD Mk II		Bye D		2cl
140	MG TD Mk II		Stipe H		3cl
38	MG TC		Chaney Brown S		
99	MG TD		Cummings L		
125	MG TD		Cooper M		
30	MG TD		Erffmeyer R		
70	MG TD		Gleason C		
121	MG TD		Hackeroot J		
14	MG TD		Harris B		
85	MG TC		Jarvis N		
78	MG TD		Koenig O		
133	MG TD		Laflin L		
85	MG TC		Newcomer T		
128	MG TD		Peavey S	Dnf	
139	MG TD		De Penaloza E		
46	MG TD		Schroeder J		
16	MG TD		Williams J		
11	Simca		Goldich R	Dnf	
103	MG TD		Burgess D	Dns	

The Harper 50 16 laps	Classes Over 1500cc	Entrants 29	Starters

Race winner's time 42min 55.5sec	Average speed 73.8mph	Race distance 52.8 miles.

94	Jaguar XK120		Newcomer T	1oa	1cl C
134	Jaguar XK120M		Kilborn J	2oa	1cl CM
53	Jaguar XK120M		Gregory R	3oa	2cl CM
40	Jaguar XK120		Porter J	4oa	2cl C
98	Jaguar XK120		Rosenberger A	5oa	3cl C
126	Jaguar XK120		Manting J	6oa	4cl C
138	Jaguar XK120		Stahel K	7oa	5cl C
83	Jaguar XK120		Carlson N	8oa	6cl C
	Jaguar XK120		Warren D	9oa	7cl C
69	Jaguar XK120M		McRae D	10oa	3cl CM
101	Jaguar XK120M		Victor W	11oa	4cl CM
58	Jaguar XK120M		Lyeth J	12oa	5cl CM
116	Jaguar XK120M		Noonan W	13oa	6cl CM
21	Jaguar XK120M		Lamberson G	14oa	7cl CM
20	Jaguar XK120		Dormeyer K		
76	Jaguar XK120		Feuerbacher A	Disq	
32	Jaguar XK120		Friedmann T		

147	Jaguar XK120		Grove J		
34	Jaguar XK120		Hamill C		
146	Jaguar XK120		Kennedy V		
57	Jaguar XK120M		Klingler R		
80	Jaguar XK120		Kopplin K		
45	Jaguar XK120		Montgomery B		
96	Jaguar XK120		Scherer F		
97	Jaguar XK120		Selzer W		
	Jaguar XK120		Short D		
117	Jaguar XK120		Snowden J		
145	Jaguar XK120		Tjaarda J		
153	Jaguar XK120		Welge L		
143	Jaguar XK120		Parker D		
33	Jaguar XK120M		Van Arsdale M	Dns	

Chanute Classic 8 laps	Classes Ladies	Entrants 11	Starters 11

Race winner's time 20min 39sec	Average speed 76.7mph	Race distance 26.4 miles

6	Ferrari 225 S	O220 ED	Chapin S	1oa	1cl D
17	Jaguar XK 120M		Wyllie M	2oa	1cl C
34	Jaguar XK 120		Hamill J	3oa	2cl C
112	MG TC s/c		Dietrich S	4oa	1cl E
71	MG TD mod		Schleicher V	5oa	2cl E
	Jaguar XK 120		Dormeyer E	6oa	3cl C
45	Jaguar XK 120		Coan M		4cl C
93	MG TC		Seaverns N		1cl F
38	MG TD		Chaney Brown S		2cl F
152	MG TD		Arnolt G		3cl F
140	MG TD MkII		Stipe M	11oa	4cl F

Eubank Cup 31 laps	Classes Under 1500cc	Entrants 39	Starters 39

Race winner's time 1hr 25min 14.2sec	Average speed 71.8mph	Race distance 102 miles

154	Glockler Porsche	10447	Urbas J	1oa	Icl F
91	OSCA MT4 1100		Simpson J	2oa	2cl F*
115	MG TD mod		Salzgaber R	3oa	3cl F
18	Porsche 356		Finkl C	4oa	4cl F

12	Porsche 356 Super		Goldman M	5oa	5cl F		54	Allard J2X Chrysler	J1732	Duncan D	1cl BM
77	MG TC mod		Magenheimer R	6oa	6cl F		124	Kurtis 500 S		Walsh E	2cl BM
120	MG TD MkII		Garland G		7cl F		113	Jaguar C-type		Fergus R	4cl CM
68	Crosley		Howell J		1cl H		51	Allard J2X Oldsmobile	J1859	Gray W	5cl CM
122	Crosley		Dodds W		2cl H		75	Jaguar XK120 Silverstone		Leighton C	6cl CM
63	MG TD		Kuhn R		1cl MG		81	Excalibur J		Knudsen R	2cl DM
25	MG TD		Harbour J		2cl MG		3	Ferrari 166 MM	0054 M	Lunken E	1cl EM
104	MG TD		Fleming W		3cl MG		7	Frazer-Nash LM	421/100/110	Boynton T	2cl EM
121	MG TD		Cosgrove J		4cl MG		62	MG TC s/c		Larson R	3cl EM
73	MG TD		Andrews W				76	Jaguar XK120		Wing R	1cl C
123	Uihlein Special		Brocken K	Dnf			69	Jaguar XK120M		McRae D	2cl C
31	MG TD		Brooks J				17	Jaguar XK120M		Wyllie M Dr	3cl C
36	Porsche 356		Carroll G				98	Jaguar XK120		Rosenberger A	4cl C
4	MG TD mod		Dickens R				138	Jaguar XK120		Stahel K	5cl C
112	MG TC s/c		Dietrich C				134	Jaguar XK120M		Kilborn J	6cl C
84	MG TD mod		Eichrodt F				83	Jaguar XK120		Carlson N	
14	MG TD MkII		Harris BIII					Jaguar Special		Colby J	
118	Porsche 356		Kerner B				13	Jaguar XK120M		Cooper W	Dnf L8
56	Porsche 356		Klingler R				112	MG TC s/c		Dietrich C	
78	MG TD MkII		Koenig O				9	Allard J2X Cadillac		Ensley J	Disq L9
50	Fibersport Special		Mays J				32	Jaguar XK120		Friedmann T	
89	Sparrow Crosley		MacArthur S				86	Jaguar XK120M		Gary R	
42	MG TC mod		Meiners F				52	Jaguar C-type	XKC 015	Gregory M	
79	HRG		Montgomery B				53	Jaguar XK120M		Gregory R	
87	MG TD mod		Nelson W				147	Jaguar XK120		Grove J	
94	MG TD		Newcomer T				131	Jaguar XK120M		Heldt W	
92	MG TD mod		Reddick D					Jaguar XK120		Jones E	
88	Bandini Crosley		Riley J				47	Jaguar XK120M		Joseph O	
140	MG TD MkII		Stipe H				126	Jaguar XK120		Manting J	
19	Porsche 356		Warren D				29	Jaguar XK120		Mueller J	
142	Nardi-Crosley		Arnolt W	Dnf			22	Jaguar XK120M		Murphy R	
							94	Jaguar XK120		Newcomer T	

• moved from class G

Technical Training Tr 31 laps	Classes Unlimited	Entrants 39	Starters 47

Race winner's time 1hr 14min 43.5sec	Average speed 81.9mph	Race distance 102 miles

5	Ferrari 340 AM	O204A	Kimberly J	1oa	1cl CM
154	Jaguar C-type		Urbas J Dr	2oa	2cl CM
74	Jaguar C-type		Wallace C	3oa	3cl CM
6	Ferrari 225 S	O220 ED	Lewis M	4oa	1cl DM
43	Maserati 8C TF	3032	Hassan C	5oa	Unrestricted

143	Jaguar XK120		Parker D	
44	Allard LM	J3153	Patton N	
96	Jaguar XK120M		Scherer F	
71	MG TD s/c		Schleicher V	
97	Jaguar XK120		Selzer W	
137	Allard J2 Cadillac		Skogmo D	
101	Jaguar XK120M		Victor W	

84	MG TD mod		Eichrodt F		
82	Excalibur J		Ullrich H		
59	Allard J2X Cadillac	J2192	Warner J		
66	Clovis Special		Clovis P		
49	Comet-Mercury Special		Ballenger R		

Paine AFB 8.8.1953

Puget Sound H'cap 12 laps	Classes Novice	Entrants 15	Starters 12

Race winner's time	Average speed	Race distance 25.2 miles

10	Jaguar XK120M	Henderson T	1oa	1cl C
96	Jaguar XK120M	Byrd R	2oa	2cl C
6	Porsche 356 Super	Hudson J	3oa	1cl FP
58	MG TD	Grube L	4oa	1cl F Sp
47	MG TD	Thomas L	5oa	2cl FP
43	MG TC	Dickson W	6oa	2cl F Sp
82	MG TD Mk II	Ferguson S	7oa	3cl FP
34	MG TC	Kemper W	8oa	4cl FP
92	MG TD	Thomas D	9oa	5cl FP
53	MG TD MkII	Frey E	10oa	6cl FP
42	MG TD	Ormsbee R	Dnf	
57	MG TD MkII	Jossy E	Dnf	
17	Allard J2	Fifield C	N/C L1	

Colonel's Cup 30 laps	Classes Under 1500cc	Entrants 26	Starters 24

Race winner's time	Average speed	Race distance 63 miles

6	Porsche 356 Super	Hudson J	1oa	1cl F P
15	Morgan 4/4	McDonald G	2oa	1cl F Sp
46	MG TD	Wilson C Dr	3oa	2cl F Sp
39	MG TD	Pigott P	4oa	2cl F P
90	MG TD	Meredith C	5oa	3cl F P
20	Singer SM 1500	Denby R	6oa	4cl F P
4	MG TC	Toews R	7oa	5cl F P
83	MG TD	Scoville J	8oa	6cl F P
11	MG TD	Brouillard W	9oa	7cl F P
8	MG TD	Hardisty W	10oa	8cl F P
19	Porsche 356 America	Lovely P	11oa	9cl F P
89	MG J2 Special	A'Court E	12oa	3cl F Sp
7	MG TC	Balfe M	13oa	10cl F P
32	MG TC	Brown D	14oa	11cl F P
35	MG TD MkII	Hill G	15oa	12cl F P
95	MG TD MkII	Lee J	16oa	13cl F P
12	MG TD MkII	Walkem J	17oa	14cl F P
62	MG TD	Schultze M	18oa	15cl F P
54	Crosley Special	Eyerly H	Dnf L1	

Programme cover for the Paine AFB event.
(Courtesy Bruce Perry Collection)

22	Giaur-Crosley		Hicks R	Dnf	
40	MG TC		Braley R	Dnf	
41	Siata BC300 750 Spyder		Keck G	Dnf	
52	Austin Special		Kong W	Dnf	
88	Crosley		Rattenbury D	Dnf	

Seafair Trophy 48 laps	Classes Over 1500cc	Entrants 11	Starters 11

Race winner's time 1hr 33min 42sec	Average speed 64.42mph	Race distance 100 miles

30	Kurtis 500 S Mercury		Stroppe W	1oa	1cl CM
44	Jaguar C-type	XKC 023	Pollack W	2oa	2cl CM
10	Jaguar XK120M		Hern F	3oa	1cl C
21	Porsche 356 Super		Lovely P	4oa	1cl E
18	Jaguar XK120M		Tiedemann E	5oa	2cl C
91	MG TC s/c		Talkins F	6oa	2cl E
25	Dodge Special		Thompson A	7oa	3cl C
60	Fageol-Porsche Special		Fageol L	8oa dnf L10	1cl D
48	Ford Special		Hansen R	Dnf L18	
81	Mercury Special		Kolar G	Dnf	
28	Jaguar XK120M		Wiseman R	Dnf	

Moffett NAS 16.8.1953

Captain's Cup 22 laps	Classes Under 1500cc	Entrants	Starters

Race winner's time 1hr 4min 56sec	Average speed 71.1mph	Race distance 77 miles

75	Porsche 356 America		McAfee J	1oa	1cl F
117	Simca 8 Comp Sport		Leson C	2oa	2cl F
66	MG TC Special		Gillespie R	3oa	3cl F
112	Porsche 356		Armstrong J	4oa	4cl F
61	Simca 8 Comp Sport		Pringle W	5oa	5cl F
70	MG TD		Brumby J	6oa	6cl F
37	MG TD		Pendergraft P	7oa	7cl F
28	MG TC		Lyons D	8oa	8cl F
85	MG TD		Preston G Dr	9oa	9cl F
110	MG TC		Skivington J Dr	10oa	10cl F
35	Young Special s/c		Young J	11oa	1cl G

12	MG TD		Barrett C	Dnf	
23	OSCA MT4 1100	1122	Coppel A	Dnf	
32	Porsche 356		Hildebrand K	Dnf	
44	MG TD		Adams R	Dnf	
50	MG TD MkII R-1 Special		Miles K	Dnf	
87	MG TC		Banta H	Dnf	
90	MG TD		St Louis G	Dnf	
100	Singer SM 1500		Snell W	Dnf	
111	Porsche 356		Kieckhefer W	Dnf	
9	OSCA MT4 1350	1127	David W	Dnf	
11	Glockler Porsche	10447	Von Neumann J	Dnf	
18	MG TC		Hayes J		
41	MG TD		Grube L		
78	VW Special		Muller A		
95	Porsche 356 LM		Robbins I		

NavCad Trophy 10 laps	Classes Novices	Entrants	Starters

Race winner's time 16min 22sec	Average speed 77.0mph	Race distance 21 miles

20	Allard J2X Chrysler		Cardwell R	1oa	1cl BM
59	Allard J2X Cadillac	J3208	Barneson J	2oa	2cl BM
34	Frazer-Nash LM MkII Rep	421/200/183	Daigh C	3oa	1cl EM
6	Allard J2 LM		Sawyer G	4oa	3cl BM
114	James Special		James D	5oa	1cl CM
10	Jaguar XK120M		Nix R	6oa	2cl CM
42	Allard J2 LM Chrysler		Block C	7oa	4cl BM
48	Jaguar XK120M		O'Brian J	8oa	3cl CM
91	Jaguar XK120M		Hodges E	9oa	4cl CM
135	Jaguar XK120		Lainas T	10oa	5cl C
117	Simca Comp		Taylor L	11oa	1cl F
66	MG TD Special		Qvale K	12oa	2cl F
36	Allard J2 Cadillac		Gunderson R	13oa	5cl BM
121	Jaguar XK120		Gagen D	14oa	cl C
76	Jaguar XK120		Lozano I	15oa	cl C
68	Jaguar XK120		Miranda M	16oa	cl C
58	Porsche 356		Losey G	17oa	3cl F
75	Porsche 356 America		McAfee J	18oa	4cl F
84	Jowett Jupiter		Connelly D	19oa	5cl F
56	MG TD MkII		Knutson A	20oa	6cl F
103	MG TD		Dalton J	21oa	7cl F

Programme cover for the Moffett Field NAS event. (Terry O'Neil Collection)

116	Singer SM 1500		Gardner V	22oa	8cl F
5	Nardi Danese 750		Harper C	23oa	1cl H
43	Sunbeam Alpine		Ganschow C	24oa	1cl D
17	MG TD MkII		Halverson A	25oa	9cl F
81	MG TD		Kinsley W	26oa	10cl F
27	MG TD		Tuttle M	27oa	11cl F
89	MG TD MkII		Fox B	28oa	12cl F
99	MG TD		Valens J	29oa	13cl F
47	MG TD		Jewell M	30oa	14cl F
54	MG TD MkII		Watson J	31oa	15cl F
128	MG TD		Healy J	32oa	16cl F
49	MG TD		Powell S	33oa	17cl F
19	MG TD		Smith E	34oa	18cl F
110	MG TC		Cleghorn W	35oa	19cl F
123	MG TD MkII		Carillon W	36oa	20cl F
71	MG TD		Dickenson C	37oa	21cl F
94	MG TD		Vann G	38oa	22cl F
77	MG Special		Wright V	39oa	23cl F
67	MG TC Special		Odom B	Dnf	
79	Porsche 356		Cardwell J	Dnf	
53	Siata 300BC 1100 Spyder		Loughridge J	Dnf	
72	Crosley		Dyer J	Dnf	

Moffett Field H'cap	Classes Unlimited	Entrants	Starters

Race winner's time 2hr 30min	Average speed 77mph	Distance covered 192.5 miles	

301	Kurtis 500 S Mercury		Stroppe W	1oa	1cl BM
24	Aston Martin DB2-GMC		Trotter D	2oa	1cl CM
50	MG TD Mk II R-1 Special		Miles K	3oa	1cl FM
130	Allard J2 Cadillac		Armstrong J	4oa	2cl CM
91	Jaguar XK120M		Hodges F Dr	5oa	3cl CM
112	Porsche 356 LM		Mullen S	6oa	2cl FM
67	MG TC Special		Gillespie R	7oa	3cl FM
60	Morgan Plus 4		Caton L	8oa	1cl DM
113	Jaguar Special		Pickford B	9oa	4cl CM
44	MG TD		Adams R	10oa	4cl FM
117	Simca 8 Comp		Leson C	11oa	5cl FM
43	Sunbeam Alpine		Ganschow C	12oa	2cl DM
37	MG TD		Pendergraft P	13oa	6cl FM
85	MG TD		Preston G Dr	14oa	7cl FM
12	MG TD		Barrett C	15oa	8cl FM
110	MG TC		Skivington J Dr	16oa	9cl FM
8	Siata 300BC 750 Spyder		Manney H III	17oa	1cl HM
237	Allard J2X Oldsmobile		Swartley J	Dnf	
9	OSCA MT4 1350	1127	David W	Dnf	
11	Glockler Porsche	10447	Von Neumann J	Dnf	

29	Baldwin Special		Von Neumann Jo	Dnf
32	Nardi Spyder		High T	Dnf
34	Frazer-Nash LM MkII Rep	421/200/183	Hildebrand K	Dnf
36	Allard J2 Cadillac		Lowe J	Dnf
45	Jaguar XK120		Fox J	Dnf
46	Jaguar XK120M		Pinkerton F	Dnf
52	MG TC V8-60		Pedigo P	Dnf
53	Siata 300BC 1100 Spyder		Loughridge J	Dnf
66	MG TD Special		Graham M	Dnf
61	Simca 8 Comp Special		Van Dyke L	Dnf
80	Mercury Special		Louis R Dr	Dnf
131	MG TC s/c		Erb H	Dnf
15	Jaguar Special		Beezemyer J	Dnf
2	Ferrari 250 MM	0260 MM	Hill P	Dnf

Stout Field NGB 27.9.1953

Race 1	20 laps	Classes F, G, H	Entrants 26	Starters

Race winner's time 31min 6.07sec	Average speed 61.73mph	Race distance 32 miles

96	MG TC	Fergus R	1oa	1cl F
32	MG TD	Andrews R	2oa	2cl F
41	MG TD	Brooks J	3oa	3cl F
38	MG TD	Durbin R	4oa	4cl F
51	Singer SM 1500	Cole P		
55	Volkswagen	Webb R		
43	Lancia	McWhirter F		
37	MG TD	Vollmer P		
92	MG TD	McPherson L		
35	MG TD	Whitlock J		
76	MG TD	Cooper M		
75	MG TD	Cooper W		
34	MG TD	Phillips G		
85	MG TD	Moore W		
86	MG TD	Short W		
14	MG TD	McCann J		
33	MG TD	Wilson C		
62	MG TD	Bunker A		

23	MG TD	Lange A	
71	MG TD	Snowden J	
78	MG TD	Brewer J	
39	MG TD	Marlett C	
40	MG TD	Earl J	
42	MG TD	De Penaloza E	
54	MG TD	Davenport F	

Race 2	20 laps	Class Porsche, Jaguar	Entrants 18	Starters

Race winner's time 28min 6.62sec	Average speed 68.32mph	Race distance 32 miles

19	Jaguar XK120	Kilborn J	1oa	1cl C
99	Jaguar XK120	Ensley J	2oa	2cl C
72	Porsche 356 Super	Cornett D	3oa	1cl F
15	Jaguar XK120	Grove J	4oa	3cl C
18	Jaguar XK120	Kopplin K	5oa	4cl C
	Jaguar XK120	Wing R	dnf	
28	Aston Martin DB2	Sugarman B Dr		
50	Porsche 356 Super	Kerrigan W		2cl F
48	Porsche 356 Super	Shuck W Dr		3cl F
77	Porsche 356 America	Magenheimer R		4cl F
49	Porsche 356 Super	Van Antwerpen P		
83	Porsche 356 Super	Lyeth J		
13	Jaguar XK120	Reid H		
20	Jaguar XK120	Pierson R		
52	Jaguar XK120	Gary R		
12	Jaguar XK120	Blackman S		
30	Jaguar XK120	Wilson C		

Race 3	45 laps	Class F, G, H, GM, HM	Entrants 44	Starters

Race winner's time 1hr 3min 5.33sec	Average speed 68.04mph	Race distance 72 miles

64	Glockler Porsche	10447	Urbas J Dr	1oa	1cl FM
84	OSCA MT4 1350	1132	Makin R	2oa	2cl FM
97	Porsche 356 America		Crawford E	3oa	3cl FM
46	MG TD Special		Salzgaber R	4oa	4cl FM
96	MG TC		Marsh D		1cl F
32	MG TD		Andrews W		2cl F

Programme cover for the Stout NGB event.
(Courtesy Bruce Perry Collection)

38	MG TD		Durbin R		3cl F
37	MG TD		Vollmer P		4cl F
51	Singer SM 1500		Cole P	Dnf	
9	Siata 300BC 750 Spyder		Jones E		1cl HM
92	Crosley		McNamara J		2cl HM
89	Swallow Crosley		MacArthur S	Dnf	
31	Bandini		Kuhn R	Dnf	
88	Siata 300BC 750 Spyder		Keller R	Dnf	
47	MG TD MkII		Howell E		
22	MG TD mod		Eichrodt F		
45	MG TD mod		Reddig P		
36	MG TD mod		Whitlack J		

90	Siata Amica		Deremiah R		
58	Siata 208 GS		Blackman S		
53	OSCA MT4		Moffett G		
56	Cisitalia		Gent R		
43	Lancia		McWhirter F		
55	Volkswagen		Webb R		
54	MG TD		Davenport F		
41	MG TD		Brooks J		
92	MG TD		McPherson L		
71	MG TD		Snowden J		
76	MG TD		Cooper M		
34	MG TD		Phillips G		

Race 4 45 laps	Classes B-F, BM-EM	Entrants 44	Starters

Race winner's time 1hr 2min 56.4sec	Average speed 69.05sec	Race distance 72 miles

5	Ferrari 340 AM	0204A	Kimberly J	1oa	1cl C
	Jaguar XK120 Silverstone		Wallace C	2oa	2cl C
4	Allard J2X Cadillac		Ensley J	3oa	1cl B
7	Ferrari 225 S	0220 ED	Lunken E		1cl D
21	Jaguar XK120M		Katskee L		1cl CM
81	Jaguar XK120M		Klingler R		2cl CM
66	Jaguar XK120M		Stewart P		3cl CM
25	Jaguar XK120M		Heldt W		4cl CM
6	Ferrari 166 MM	0054 M	Hassan C		1cl E
19	Jaguar XK120		Kilborn J		
18	Jaguar XK120		Kopplin K		
20	Jaguar XK120		Pierson R		
15	Jaguar XK120		Grove J		
17	MG TC s/c		Dietrich C		2cl E
29	MG TD s/c		Randle W		3cl E
72	Porsche 356 Super		Cornett D		1cl F
	Porsche 356 America		Magenheimer R		2cl F
82	Jaguar XK120M		Lyeth J		
93	Jaguar XK120M		Kerr B		
60	Fageol-Porsche Special		Fageol L	Dnf	
44	Porsche 356 America		Tappan R	Dnf	
50	Porsche 356 Super		Kerrigan W	Dnf	
49	Porsche 356 Super		Van Antwerpen P	Dnf	
83	Porsche 356 Super		Lyeth J	Dnf	
28	Aston-Martin DB2		Sugarman B		

94	Jaguar XK120M		Donnelly R		
95	MG TD s/c		Schleicher V		
98	Nash-Healey LM		Rosenberger N		
73	DuPont		Chamberlain M		
12	Jaguar XK120		Blackman S		
16	Jaguar XK120		Hugus E		
52	Jaguar XK120		Gary R		
30	Jaguar XK120		Wilson C		
26	MG V8-60		Salzgaber R		

Race 5 28 laps	Classes FM, GM, HM	Entrants 18	Starters

Race winner's time 37min 1.57sec	Average speed 72.33mph	Race distance 44.8 miles

97	Porsche 356 America		Crawford E	1oa	1cl FM
46	MG TD V8-60		Salzgaber R	2oa	2cl FM
36	MG TD mod		Whitlack J	3oa	3cl FM
77	MG TC mod		Magenheimer R	Dnf L27	
9	Siata 300BC 750 Spyder LM		Jones E		1cl HM
92	Crosley		McNamara J		2cl HM
45	MG TD mod		Reddig P		
87	MG TD V8-60		Whitz D		
29	MG TD s/c		Randle W		
17	MG TC s/c		Dietrich C		
47	MG TD MkII		Howell E		
58	Siata 208 GS		Blackman S		
84	OSCA MT4		Makins R		
89	Swallow		MacArthur S		
31	Bandini		Kuhn R		

Race 6 42 laps run*	Class O-1500cc	Entrants 24	Starters

*(race scheduled for 65 laps, 104 miles)

Race winner's time 1hr 13min 48.64sec	Average speed 54.87mph	Race distance 67.2 miles

	Jaguar XK120 Silverstone		Wallace C	1oa	1cl CM 68
73	Du Pont Ford Special		Chamberlain R	3oa	1cl U
81	Jaguar XK120M		Klingler R	4oa	1cl C
98	Nash-Healey LM		Rosenberger A	Dnf L3	
21	Jaguar XK120M		Katskee L		
69	Excalibur J		Goldich R	Dnf L32	
	Jaguar C-type	XKC 010	Fuerbacher A	Dnf L32	
25	Jaguar XK120M		Brown S	dnf	
64	Glockler Porsche	10447	Urbas J Dr		
7	Ferrari 225 S	0220 ED	Hassan C & Lunken E	Dnf L32	
4	Allard J2X Cadillac		Ensley J	Dnf L31	
5	Ferrari 340 AM	0204 A	Kimberly J	Dnf L12	
	Jaguar C-type		Fergus R	Dns	

7

Other motor clubs using military bases

Luke AFB, Glendale, Arizona

3.5.1953

"A nasty, rubber-eating dog-leg proved too dangerous for the drivers at the Luke AFB auxiliary strip, and they balked at driving the course." (Arizona Republican)

The Phoenix National Road Race was instigated by the Arizona Region of the Four Cylinder Club of America and the Commander of Luke AFB, General Charles F Borne, and was the first race event of its kind in this part of Arizona. Part of their overall agreement to hold the races was that there would be no cash prizes, only glittering trophies, and all proceeds of the race would be shared between the Airmen's Fund for Luke AFB and the Girl Scouts. The race trophies were donated by local business leaders, as was the usual practice – benefits usually accrued from them doing this, so to them it was another way of advertising.

Luke AFB was located twenty miles north west of Phoenix, on the outskirts of the city of Glendale, Arizona. Established in 1941, the Arizona base began as Litchfield Park Air Base, but was de-activated in 1946. The Base was re-named as Luke Air Force Base and came under the control of the Air Training Command when it was reactivated in 1951, though it is noted that Litchfield Park is still referred to in the literature for the race event. Pilots were trained to fly P-51 Mustangs and F84 fighter planes, and the Thunderbirds were formed at Luke AFB in 1953, when the US Air Force took its best pilots to establish a demonstration team. The base covered a large site, and apart from the main base area, there were auxiliary landing strips. It was on one of these strips, Auxiliary 3, that the races took place, albeit that Auxiliary 4 is erroneously mentioned in one of the newspaper articles leading up to the races.

Auxiliary 3 was located five miles north of the main base, and it soon became apparent to the drivers as they went out for practice, that the layout of the 2.5-mile course had a very bumpy and abrasive surface. The drivers were particularly unhappy about one section of the layout and appointed a spokesman to approach the organising committee. After discussions between the drivers' representative and the officials of the Four-Cylinder Club, the decision was taken on the morning before the races to delete a section of tight double bends from the original course, the section in question being the one deemed too dangerous by the drivers. The revised course measured 2 miles in length, and was roughly triangular in shape, though had 15 turns within the layout over the airstrip. Revising the line of the course meant that qualifying for grid position for the different races had to be abandoned on Saturday, so the drivers and officials agreed that lots would be drawn instead for the Sunday race start positions.

Estimates of the crowd size varied widely depending on which source one believes. *The Phoenix Gazette* suggested 4500, the *Arizona*

Republican 8000, and the *National Speed Sport News* put the figure at 15,000. Luckily, their reports on six of the seven races were more harmonious. There were five 16-mile sprint races for different Classes, the first of these starting at 10.30am, a 40-mile race for novices and the main event, an 80-mile race for the Governor's Cup, which started at 1.30pm.

The winner of the first sprint race, for production cars under 1500cc, was Speedway bike rider Wilbur Lamoreaux in his Singer 1500 SM. Lamoreaux had bought two cars to the event and after practising in his MG, decided to race his Singer. He fought off the attentions of two Jowett Javelins that far out-paced the rest of the field made up of MGs, a couple of Porsches, and Dyna-Panhards to win by a comfortable margin. Jackson in a modified Jaguar XK120 took the second race, for production cars over 1500cc, in which there was a tie for second place between Bellesiles and McPherson, also in Jaguars. The three drivers kept the crowd on their toes as they fought for position throughout the race.

Ken Miles in his well-raced and much feared MG TD-RI easily took the third race for modified cars under 1500cc, ahead of the modified MGs of Bob Menefee and Tracy Bird. The next race brought out the larger capacity cars, and Jack McAfee driving a Ferrari 340AM took the honours ahead of Morgensen in his Fiberglas Special, powered by a Cadillac engine, Yates in an Allard J2 Cadillac, and Wheeler in his Ferrari 212 Export. Myra Zeller (Mendelson) in a Jaguar XK120M came first in the Ladies Race, ahead of Helen Cavin also driving a Jaguar and Ruby Conway in a Porsche 356.

There appears to be some confusion as to who won the 40-mile novice race. According to the *Phoenix Gazette* and the *Arizona Republic*, Lou Yates in an Allard-Cadillac narrowly won the race after Bill Murphy spun his Kurtis-De Soto on the fifteenth lap, but another source, *National Speed Sport News*, indicated Murphy as the winner. If the newspapers are correct, then Murphy in the Kurtis-De Soto was second and Dick Morgensen in his Special-Cadillac was third.

The main race for the Governor's Cup attracted a field of at least 27 cars, and pre-race predictions were that it would be a three-way fight between McAfee in a Ferrari, Stroppe in his red Kurtis 500, and Hill in his Ferrari. Phil Hill had practised on Saturday afternoon, but a flying rock had pierced the radiator on his Ferrari and he decided not to run, complaining that the track was unsuitable. He was not the only driver to complain about the state of the track – John Von Neumann was also in attendance, and he decided that the track was too rough, so, like Phil Hill, decided to sit the race out.

The grid line up draw was kind to McAfee, as he was on the first row, though not as kind for Stroppe, as he found himself way back on the ninth row of three-a-breast sports cars. The disadvantage was quickly wiped out as the flag fell, Stroppe carving his way through the field to second place within a distance of 250 yards. By the end of the first of forty twisting two-mile laps, Stroppe had taken a narrow lead over McAfee, a lead he would maintain for the remainder of the race. Stroppe savoured his victory that put an end to the road racing domination of Jack McAfee and the Ferraris in this part of America, as two months previously, McAfee had beaten him at Palm Springs. McAfee had been the only real challenger, until he had a puncture, and had to pit on lap 32. In the meantime, Morgensen's car broke a fan belt, and dropped out of contention, finishing in 14th place. McAfee eventually finished in second place after making up ground on the leader, and Ken Miles drove his reliable MG Special into third place, ahead of Crean's Porsche 356.

After the races, a victory banquet was held at the Westward-Ho Hotel, where prizes were awarded to the leading drivers in each race.

In view of the vast discrepancies in the reporting of the event, final results are sketchy and with regard to the wide variance in the attendance figures, no comment can be made on the financial success of this event. It is doubtful if the information was ever published, though it was mentioned in the *Phoenix Gazette* that a representative from the Bank of Douglas was going to count the receipts the afternoon after the races had taken place.

Fort Worth NGB, Newark Tx

23.8.1953 (FASCA)

"Jones performed a notable feat by winning the third race in his modified Jaguar, before returning to take second place in the big event."
(Fort Worth Star-Telegram)

This event, planned by the Foreign Auto and Sports Car Association to take place at the Eagle Mountain National Guard Base, was the first ever sports car race event to be held in the Fort Worth area of Texas. It was sponsored by Combat Command 'A' 49th Armoured Division of the Texas National Guard, and, according to commanding officer Col Burton Lyons, all proceeds of the event would be going to the Guard units for use in equipping day rooms, buying athletic equipment, and defraying recreational expenses.

For a small motor club, this was an ambitious project, but as the majority of the Foreign Auto Sports Car Association members were also members of the SCCA, the race chairman, Eddie Becker, decided to run the races under SCCA rules, in order that the competitors were familiar with them. It also goes a long way to explaining how the Club acquired

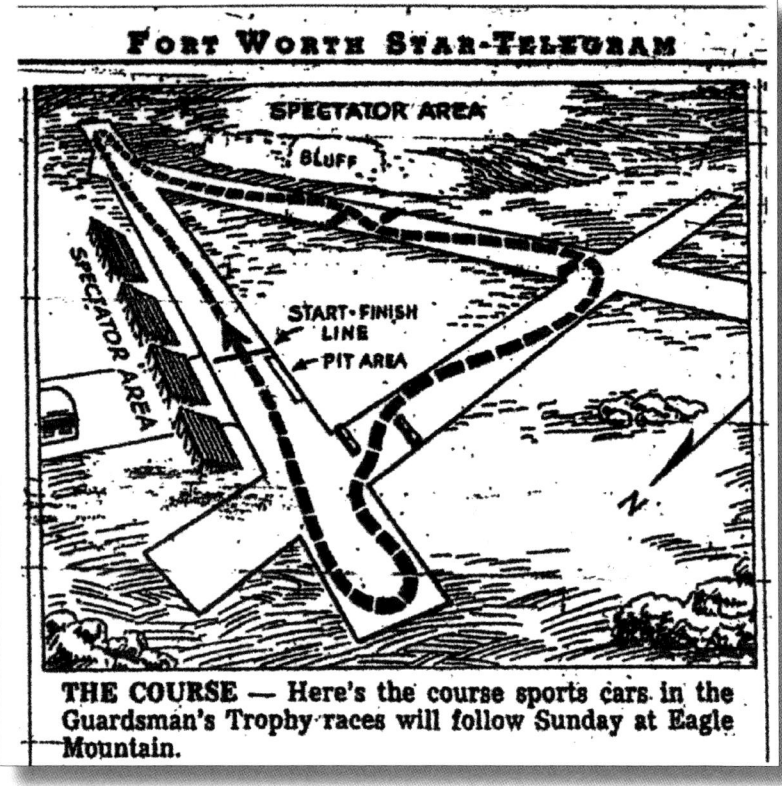

Track layout at Fort Worth NGB, together with aerial photo of runway layout. (Terry O'Neil Collection)

the 'know how' to fulfil their ambitious plans in putting the event on, successfully attracting drivers from Texas and the surrounding States of Louisiana, Oklahoma, Kansas, and Missouri.

To give the venue its full title, it was known as the Eagle Mountain Lake Marine Air Corps Air Station originally. Built during WWII, the Base was used to provide information on the viability of building amphibious gliders. The Base had three runways, each 6000ft long, and towards the end of 1945, the location was used for night fighter training. In the early 1950s, Eagle Mountain was handed over to the National Guard.

The Eagle Mountain was a hard surface triangular course of approximately 3.5 miles laid out over the main runways, which drivers termed as 'excellent.' It contained a straightway of 5000ft, together with turns of 70, 80, and 150 degrees, and two of 180 degrees, and the hilly terrain surrounding the Base provided safer and better vantage points for the spectators than was usual at airport locations. Col Lyons, Commanding Officer of the Base, gave a commitment of co-operation, and said that guardsmen would control the traffic onto the Base, look after ticket sales, provide and set up bleachers for the spectators and set up a loudspeaker system for the event.

A total of five races were scheduled, including the twenty-lap feature, The Guardsman's Trophy Race. Technical inspection and practise sessions for the competitors were held on the day, prior to the races, and, being a completely new course, practise was not without its problems for some of the cars and drivers. The race programme commenced at 1pm on Sunday with a ten-lap race for standard production MGs, and featured a 'Le Mans' start, with the drivers running twenty-five yards across the tarmac, before jumping in their cars to start them. Bill Steiner managed to edge out James Gilchrist and Jim Roberts after thirty miles of hard motoring to take first place.

The second race was for cars of up to two litres and included mainly modified MGs. They would have been joined by two Porsche 356 models, however, both succumbed to mechanical ailments during the morning practice session and failed to make it to the start grid. Fred Hill eventually won the race in his modified MG after following the Continental-MG Special of Norman Scott for most of the race, but the unfortunate Scott was robbed of victory when the car blew a piston on the last lap of the race. Bill Clifford finished the race in second place behind Hill driving in his very quick 746cc Crosley. Clifford's Crosley gave a creditable performance that surprised a number of other competitors. Racing with the modified machinery were some standard production sports cars, Dale Duncan taking the honours in this division in an MG TC. Duncan was more than pleased with his performance in the little MG, as he was more used to driving an Allard.

Over-two-litre cars took to the track for the third race, segregated into two divisions and run concurrently over fifteen laps; the first for modified cars and the other for standard production cars. Springer Jones won the modified section in a Jaguar XK120M, ahead of Bob Schroeder and Bill McPherson driving similar cars, while the standard production section went to Dr Harold Fenner, also in a Jaguar XK120.

Before the final event, a five-lap ladies' race took place, run on a handicap basis. The MGs were given a good start ahead of the Allard. Mrs G Galbraith driving an MG TD finished first, ahead of Mrs George Koehne, who failed narrowly to make up the handicap in her husband's Allard J2 Cadillac. Betty Stafford was third, Jo McKinney fourth. and Rita Joerns fifth in another MG.

The main event was a 72-mile race for sports cars of over 3000cc, eagerly anticipated by the 11,000 spectators. While the field was made up predominantly of Jaguars, there were three Allards, one belonging to Roy Cherryhomes, and a Ferrari entered by AV Dayton, present. Had it not been for mechanical ailments during the practice session, there would also have been the C-type Jaguar of Joe Mabee, who ran an oil drilling company for a living. Carroll Shelby, driving Cherryhome's Allard J2X Cadillac, and Dale Duncan, back in his Allard, were on the first row of the grid, Warren Turner in another Allard on the second row,

Grid line-up for the feature race, with Shelby and Duncan on the front row, both driving Allards. (Courtesy Michael T Lynch)

while Dayton's Ferrari was placed on the third row. As the starter, Brian Bartindale, dropped the green flag, Shelby jumped ahead of Duncan at the start, beat the pack to the first turn, and stayed ahead for the remainder of the twenty-lap race. For two laps, Shelby was pursued closely by Dale Duncan in his Allard J2 Chrysler, and George Koehne driving Dayton's Ferrari 340 Mexico. Duncan pulled out of the race on the third lap, due to failing oil pressure, which gave Koehne second place. He held that position for fourteen laps on a track that was becoming increasingly treacherous because of heavy rain showers, despite not being used to the left-hand gear change in the car, then was severely handicapped when he blew a tyre. Springer Jones, in his Jaguar XK120M, overtook Koehne to inherit second place, with Schroeder moving up into third. Riddelle Gregory moved into fourth spot, but the C-type didn't have the legs to catch the XK120M models. Koehne's Ferrari managed to limp halfway round the course to the pit area to have the wheel changed with enough time to rejoin the race, eventually finishing back in eighth place. Such was Shelby's dominance of the race, he had the opportunity to ease up over the closing stages, and still finished over one lap ahead of Springer Jones.

Floyd Bennett Field NAS, New York

29.8.1953 (AAA)

"The official temperature stood at 120°F during the running of the sports car races." (New York Times)

On an extremely hot day in August, sports car racing came as near to the centre of New York City as it was going to get. Floyd Bennett Field NAS was located on the southwest edge of Long Island, within easy commuting distance to the city centre. It was the first time that a sports car race had been held in metropolitan New York, since the race held at the New York World's Fair in 1940.

The event, consisting of three races, was organised by Base Commander Harold C Jipson and JS Donaldson, promoter of the Freeport stock car events and president of Grand Prix of Endurance Inc, with input from Alec Ullman, representing the American Automobile Association, who helped in the running of the event. The races were

*An Official Entry Blank for the event at Floyd Bennett Field.
(Courtesy Bruce Perry Collection)*

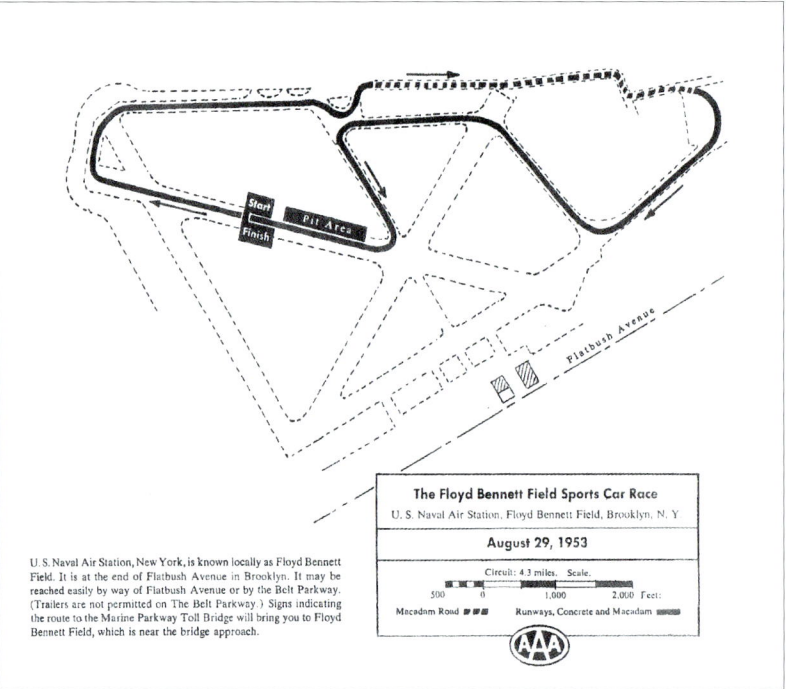

*Original track layout at Floyd Bennett Field.
(Courtesy Michael Eaton Collection)*

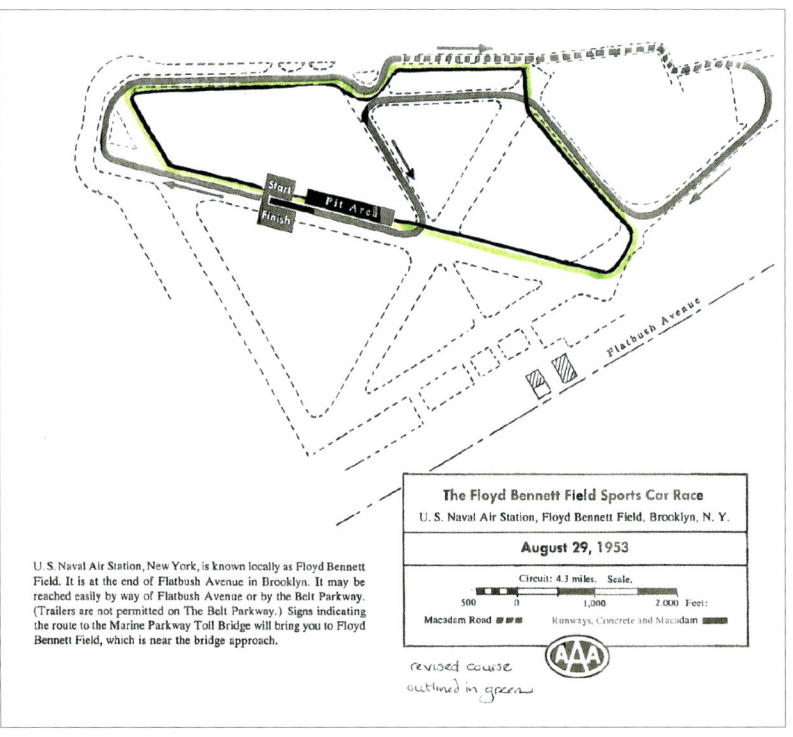

Revised track layout at Floyd Bennett Field. (Terry O'Neil Collection)

sponsored by Grand Prix of Endurance Inc and run under the sanction of the Contest Board of the American Automobile Association, and were subject to the rules of the FIA. All proceeds of the races went to the Service Personnel Welfare Fund. While the majority of events in the Northeast of America had SCCA involvement, this event had no input from the SCCA, as was quite evident by both the structure of the meeting and the planning leading up to the event. Fortunately though, one prominent feature of other AAA races held in the past was

William Wonder and friends contemplate the forthcoming race. (Courtesy Michael Eaton Collection)

missing. In 1950, the AAA had instituted a new method of scoring road races, whereby only the top three finishers per class would be scored and listed in the results. This meant that overall finishing positions were rarely published. Anyone outside of the top three per class would be flagged off and not listed as finishers. This approach was not popular with the drivers, and for this particular event, the system was scrapped.

Floyd Bennett Field was used as a reserve training base for both Naval and Marine air reserve training. It was the proximity to New York City and the facilities that it offered that attracted the race organisers to the site. Having reached agreement with the Base Commander, Harold Jipson, Ulmann, and Donaldson set about designing a racecourse that stretched 4.3 miles in length (according to the programme), utilising the principal runway of the base, together with several taxiways, and a station street. The proposed course consisted of eleven turns and had a straightway of 7200ft. It ended up as an interesting, but unusual shape – it almost looked as if two separate courses had been joined together by a narrow apron of black asphalt. There was no doubt that the organisers fully intended using the course as mapped out in the race application details, as the races were described as being run over 10 laps (43 miles) and 50 laps (215 miles). In view of the statistical information available about each race, grave doubts exist as to how much of the originally planned course was actually used. It is most likely that a course of 2.15 miles in length was used, exactly half that as stated on the map in the programme. The theory is supported by a track sketch secured from the David Ash Collection, that indicates that the course used followed only portions of the original planned course and extended onto other runways as well. Why this last minute change of route and length of the course was made at such short notice is not clear and not explained in any of the race reports available. However, by the time the official programme had gone to print, an amended course had obviously been decided on, as indicated by the number of laps published against each race distance.

Totally unaware of the changes made to the route of the course, an estimated crowd of 50,000 spectators came out in the blistering heat to watch the races. The strict Class structure for cars adopted by the SCCA was not used by the race organisers of this event, instead, an arbitrary lumping together of small engine capacity cars or large capacity cars was as sophisticated as it was going to get. The first race, entitled the

Wonder's MG ready to move to the grid for the start of the Floyd Bennett Cup race. (Courtesy Michael Eaton Collection)

Part of the grid line-up for the start of the Floyd Bennett Cup Race. (Ozzie Lyons, courtesy Pete Lyons Collection)

Sheephead Bay Trophy, was for cars under 1500cc, and attracted a field of 28 cars lined up on the grid four across, made up mainly of MG models. However, it was Lamoreaux, driving a twin caburettor Singer that jumped into the lead, upon receiving the green flag and continued pulling away from the rest of the field. At middle race distance, he was a good thirty car lengths ahead of Bill Lloyd's Jowett Jupiter, followed by a hoard of MGs. Disaster struck Lamoreaux on lap seventeen, as the oil pressure dropped dramatically in the Singer and he was forced to retire. This presented Bill Lloyd in his Jowett Jupiter with the lead and he covered the remaining three laps to win the 43-mile race. Gus Ehrman and Mark Rodney, both driving MG TD models, finished the race in second and third places. Despite having to retire, Lamoreaux was classified as finishing in sixth place on distance covered.

The second race was also run over 43 miles, and was for production cars exceeding 1500cc. Twenty-two cars, predominantly Jaguar and Porsche models, lined up for the start of the race on the wide runway in the hot sun. Miller in his Porsche and Goldschmidt in his Kieft-MG made the best start, but at the end of the first lap, it was Goldschmidt who had taken the lead. He led the race for the first three laps, then spun, allowing Russell Boss, in a modified Jaguar, to overtake him. Boss hung on to his lead, despite a determined effort by Goldschmidt to re-take the lead. Boss crossed the finish line just one second ahead of Goldschmidt, with Hassan in a modified Jaguar a distant third, ahead of the Jaguar driven by 'John Marshall.' It turns out that 'John Marshall' was an alias used by Miles Collier – he raced under that name due to family pressure after the death of his brother

At the 'business' end of the grid, the Cunninghams and Perry Fina's Cadillac-engine Special receive last minute attention. (Ozzie Lyons, courtesy Pete Lyons Collection)

Sam, in 1950. Charles Wallace won Class CP in a standard Jaguar, finishing the race in fifth position overall, while Brett Hannaway won Class F in his Porsche.

The main race was the Floyd Bennett Cup, set to run for 100 laps, a distance of 215 miles. According to sketchy reports published in the *New York Times*, around forty cars lined up for the Le Mans-type start of the race, including the official Cunningham Team, the Ferraris of Spear and Lloyd, Goldschmidt's Allard, and the Jaguars of Hansgen, Schott, and Hirsch. An eventful practice session earlier that morning had seen Masten Gregory split the petrol tank on his C-type Jaguar after sliding off the track and landing in a ditch. Gregory escaped injury, but had to stand and watch as the car caught fire because of the escaping fuel and was rapidly engulfed by flames. Eager to participate in the race, Gregory managed to persuade another competitor, Henry Wessells III, to sell his brand new C-type to him in time to drive it in the race. Luckily for Gregory, Wessells had his eye on purchasing an OSCA, so he was not particularly disinclined to do a deal with Gregory.

The temperature was still rising in the early afternoon as the starter, Myke Collins, dropped the flag for the start of the race. Gregory sprinted ahead of the other drivers across the tarmac to be first away, followed by Walters and Cunningham in their Cunninghams. On the second lap, Spear, driving a Ferrari 340 Mexico, came through the pack to displace Cunningham in third place, then on the next lap overtake Walters, and on the fourth lap take the lead from Gregory.

*A chase through the hangar complex, as Jim Pauley's Special is hunted down by Dominianni's Giaur and Grier's Siata 208CS.
(Ozzie Lyons, courtesy Pete Lyons Collection)*

*Hansgen and Eager finished fifth in the Floyd Bennett Cup Race in the Hansgen Jaguar Special.
(Ozzie Lyons, courtesy Pete Lyons Collection)*

*Hansgen was a busy man, as he also co-drove the Aston-Martin DB2 with Pearsall, finishing in tenth place.
(Ozzie Lyons, courtesy Pete Lyons Collection)*

Fanelli's Multiplex Special failed to complete the 215-mile race. (Ozzie Lyons, courtesy Pete Lyons Collection)

Spear's Ferrari 340 Mexico and one of the Cunninghams battle for position. Spear and Benett were to finish second overall in the Floyd Bennett Cup race. (Ozzie Lyons, courtesy Pete Lyons Collection)

Line-up for the start of the Brighton Beach Trophy race showing #21 Porsche 356 Speedster of Tex Hopkins and the Kieft-MG #99 driven by Erwin Goldschmidt. (Courtesy Stacey Hopkins Collection)

Gregory was forced to retire, his newly acquired Jaguar suffering rear end trouble, and on lap 63, the heat claimed its first victim, as Harry Gray pitted the C-type Jaguar and retired with heat exhaustion, allowing Hassan to jump in the car and continue the race in his place. Two laps later, Spear also pitted in his Ferrari, on the point of collapse – another victim of the sun. John Benett took over the car and began the chase after Walters, who had inherited the lead. Although his car was suffering from brake-judder, and he had to pit twenty laps from the end of the race, Walters had enough time in hand to win by the distance of one lap over the Spear/Benett Ferrari in second place, and Briggs' Cunningham in third place. Fourth place in the race went to Lloyd in his Ferrari 225S, ahead of the Hansgen Jaguar Special, and Gray's Jaguar C-type. James Simpson ended up a creditable seventh place in the small OSCA MT4.

Class awards went to Walters in Class BM, Spear and Benett in Class CM, Lloyd in Class DM, Bonadies in Class E, Simpson in Class FM, Roth in Class F, and Poole and Vilardi in Class HM.

Although the event suffered from a stuttering start, it turned out to be vastly successful, attracting a large crowd that was kept well under control by the officials. To illustrate the latter point, some spectators had managed to penetrate the inner field and park their cars in an unauthorised area. That problem was solved by the introduction of a mobile crane which, literally, hoisted the cars away. Only the Navy could get away with that!

Long Beach (NAVSTA)/ Reeves Field, California

3/4.10.1953 (LBMGCC)

"As the race came into the final laps, the big question was, can Stroppe lap the field?" **(Car Craft)**

Reeves Field was located on Terminal Island, a man-made sand-filled island adjacent to the port of Los Angeles. Expanding between the harbours of San Pedro and Long Beach, it came within the corporate city limits of Los Angeles. The changes in name of this airstrip are as convoluted as the history of the Base. Initially, the site was Allen Field, a small 410-acre civilian airport built in 1927. Allen Field consisted of three paved runways, the largest of which was 4200ft in length, a seaplane ramp, and several hangars. In 1935, the Navy took control over Allen Field and designated it as a Naval Air Base (NAB San Pedro), then promptly renamed it Reeves Field. In 1942, it

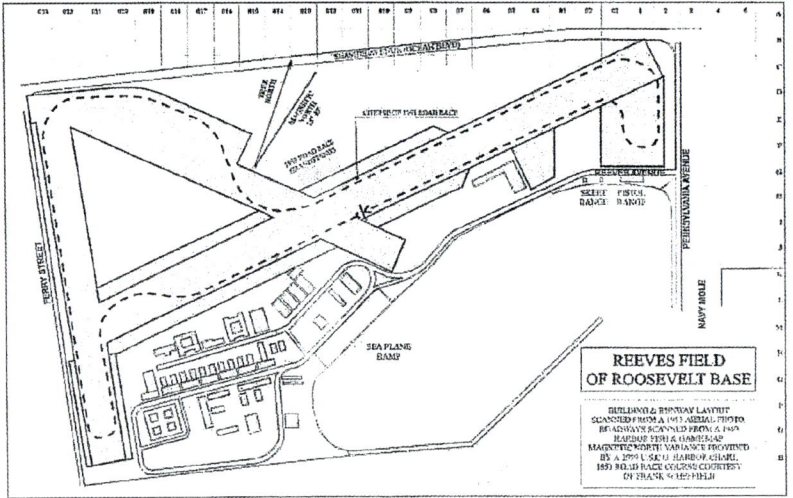

Track layout at Reeve Field NAVSTA. (Terry O'Neil Collection)

was re-designated as a Naval Air Station (NAS Terminal Island), but was disestablished in 1947. Long Beach Naval Station (NAVSTA Long Beach) was established in 1941, and located adjacent to Reeves Field, so continued to use Reeves Field as an auxiliary airfield subsequent to 1947.

Both the location of Reeves Field and the occasion proved to be unique in so far as it was the first race to be held within the corporate city limits of Los Angeles, and the first race to benefit a charitable organisation, The Navy-Marine Corp Relief Society. The location was only used once for sports car racing, and was also the only race meeting solely organised and sponsored by the Long Beach MG Club. A point that was not unique was that the Long Beach MG Club, as an organising body, reportedly lost a great deal of money in this ambitious venture, proving that motor racing was not only expensive for the racers, but for the organisers as well. In theory, any profits accrued would have been donated to The Navy Relief Society. The Long Beach MG Club's previous involvement with the organisation of a race event had been at Palm Springs, where they and the Sports Car Racing Association had jointly organised the fifth Annual Road Race event.

Having negotiated a deal with the Navy for the use of the site, Long Beach MG Club set about planning a course that measured 2.3 miles across asphalt, concrete runways, and taxi aprons. The longest straight measured 3750ft, with the pits to the outside of the circuit along the straight, and a grandstand built opposite the start/finish line.

The planned itinerary was to have ten events for sports cars, plus two races for motorcycles, held over the weekend, and it was anticipated that attention would centre on the races that included the modified cars, as they were the ones that could take advantage of the track layout.

Action from the eighth race as a horde of MGs chase a Jowett Javelin into a corner. (Courtesy Ron Kellogg Collection)

However, despite the build-up in advertising for the two days of racing, it was estimated that only 10,000 people paid to watch the events over the Saturday and Sunday, proving a big disappointment and financial disaster to the organisers. On reflection though, without some of the better known named drivers in attendance, the incentive to stand in the scorching sun was diminished somewhat.

Saturday's races commenced with a ladies' race over six laps of the track, which was won by Janet Anderson in a Volkswagen Special, ahead of Wilder in a Jaguar XK120, and Mary Davis driving an MG TD Special. The Anderson/Volkswagen combination was proving to be the team to beat, having also won at Santa Barbara. The remaining five races on the Saturday afternoon brought wins for Hayward in the well supported MG novice drivers' race, ahead of Johnson and Wright. Around 38 MGs, the majority of them TD models, started the six-lap race. Hayward started half way down the grid, but soon forced his car to the front, being challenged all the way by Johnson. Bob Norton's Porsche proved to be too quick for the Jowett Jupiter and the Singer, bringing a well deserved victory to Norton in the under 2-litre production car race. Norton won easily, ahead of Earl in the Singer 1500 and Carberry in a Jowett Jupiter.

The winner of the feature race, Bill Stroppe, is about to overtake the Jowett Jupiter driven by Marks. (Courtesy Ron Kellogg Collection)

Robert Menefee won the over 2-litre production car race, finishing just ahead of James Lowe in his quick Frazer-Nash, and then went on to win the Jaguar race in his XK120, ahead of Jenkins and Marks in similar cars. The up-and-coming Charles Daigh won the ten-lap over 2-litre modified car race, driving the successful ex-Parkinson Jaguar Special. This car was now owned by Jay Beesemyer, Vice-President of General Petroleum based in California, and had been subject to some serious internal improvements since his ownership. To the disappointment of the crowd, both Ken Miles and Bill Stroppe opted not to join in the ten-lap race, but to save their cars for the 30-lap feature race on Sunday. The Asimus-owned Allard J2 Lincoln, driven by Max Briney, took Class BM honours, while James Lowe was back to win his Class in the Frazer-Nash.

Sunday's event started with a six-lap MG race, having a field of around 23 entries, and was won by Trennent, ahead of Bowering and Wright, all driving TD models. Next up was another six-lap race, this one for the under 1500cc cars, in which Dave Shillam drove away from the rest of the field in his Porsche 356 to win comfortably ahead of MacDannold's Singer, and the Jowett Jupiter's of Marks and Carberry.

The first of the two feature races was for Class F, FM, and GM, which attracted a diverse array of cars to the grid for the ten-lap race. Pre-race favourites for the trophy were Ken Miles, in his potent and extremely successful MG Special, George Beavis, in his Beavis-Offenhauser Special, together with the reliable modified MGs of Drake and Bird. Lots were drawn for start positions, and found Miles well down the grid among what were to become 'also rans,' whereas Beavis was near the front of the grid. However, when the flag dropped, the Offy was left at the start line due to a lock-up in the starter motor. Miles set off in his familiar style, weaving through the pack to take the lead by the time they had rounded the first turn. From that point on, the race for first place was over for everyone else. Even though he slowed down for the last five laps, his lead was such that nobody was going to catch him, and his domination of Class FM racing in California was maintained. Second-placed man was Tracy Bird, driving the modified MG TD that used to be successfully driven by John von Neumann, while Bob Drake took third place in another modified MG TD.

No sooner had the race finished, the top drivers from that race were

Pickford's Jaguar Special leads Stroppe's Kurtis at the start of the feature race. (Courtesy Ron Kellogg Collection)

on the grid for the 30-lap race amongst the larger capacity cars. It was reported that about 40 cars lined up for the start of the race, though I have been unable to confirm the accuracy of that number. Among the entries to take to the grid were at least four Allards, four Kurtis 500s, and a number of production Jaguars, two Jaguar Specials, and, of course, Ken Miles in his MG TD R-1 Special.

When that colourful character Al Torres dropped the green flag, Stroppe's Kurtis sliced through the pack with ease, followed closely by Daigh and Miles in that order. Stroppe quickly pulled away from Daigh, and, by the end of the third lap, was about a mile ahead of the battle being waged between Daigh and Miles for second position. After several laps, Daigh was forced to make a pit stop for what sounded like a stuck exhaust valve. Since nothing could be done by the mechanics, he was waved out of the pits. It took him several laps to catch up with Miles, but with the car sounding and becoming rougher, he fell back and was passed by Max Briney in the Asimus-owned Allard J2 Lincoln.

At the front, Stroppe and Miles were lapping the slower cars, though Stroppe was progressing through the field at a faster rate. As the race came towards its conclusion, the question was ... Could Stroppe lap Miles? He almost made it – as Stroppe's car started the last lap, he was four seconds behind Miles and as they progressed around the circuit, Stroppe began closing him down. As they approached the finish line, Stroppe was literally one car-length behind Miles, but just failed to pass him. Briney finished a distant third in the Allard, and Daigh struggled round the circuit to the sound of expensive metallic noises to finish in fourth place, in Beesemyer's Jaguar Special.

The start/finish official, Al Torres, keeps a careful watch as the cars speed towards the finish line. (Courtesy Ron Kellogg Collection)

Fort Worth NGB, Newark Tx

6.12.1953 (FASCA)

"Riddelle Gregory, University of Texas law student, broke Carroll Shelby's domination of Texas sports car racing at Eagle Mountain, with a victory in the 75-mile feature event." **(Fort Worth Star-Telegram)**

The second running of the Guardsman's Trophy Races took place within an unusually short period of time, after the first meeting in August. A small club it might have been, but the Foreign Auto and Sports Car Association obviously considered the first event successful, and didn't want to waste any time when it came to building its reputation. It was intent on attracting top calibre drivers to this 'out of season' event, referred to by some as the 'frost bite' races. The National Guard Base Commander, Col Burton Lyons, was happy to accommodate the FASCA again, and was instrumental in making improvements based on experience of the previous event, such as ticketing procedures, so as to avoid congestion at the entrance, and traffic management to and from the base. As with the previous event, proceeds were donated to the National Guard Base, in order to improve facilities and recreational amenities.

From the details available in the *Fort Worth Star-Telegram*, it would appear that the organisers were pleased with the response to this event, as well known drivers and owners such as Masten and Riddelle Gregory, Tom Davis, Springer Jones, Jo Mabee, and Bill Jarnigan, had sent back entry forms. At a pre-race meeting held on the Wednesday prior to the races, the race committee made up of members of the FASCA and the Fort Worth Sports Car Club agreed that the line of the course would be changed from that of the previous event. They proposed shortening the circuit to three miles in length and having only one uninterrupted straightway, but still using the main runways of the Base. A crowd in excess of the 11,000 at the previous races was expected, and bleachers were placed on the outside of the entire start/finish straight for their convenience by the Base personnel. They served two purposes: one, to keep spectators within a safe confined area, and two, to give the spectators a degree of comfort.

Practice was scheduled for Saturday afternoon, and unfortunately witnessed the elimination of some prominent entrants to the feature event. The cars of Masten Gregory, Sherwood Johnston, and Joe Mabee all developed mechanical ailments, and weren't able to take part in the five-race programme that began on Sunday afternoon at 1pm. A particular disappointment was the elimination of Joe Mabee's Chrysler-powered Special, which had recently upped the world sports car speed record to 203.105mph at the Bonneville Salt Flats.

The first event of the programme was a ten-lap race for production MGs, and the 8000 spectators were thrilled by the close racing, as eleven cars set off from the start. At the finish of ten laps, James Gilchrist just beat off the constant challenge of Walter Gladson to take first place, while Robert Rodier followed both of them to finish a close third in his MG TC.

The second race, affectionately called the 'powder puff derby,' was a five-lap handicap race for ladies and attracted nine entrants. Given a substantial start, the winning car was the unlikely choice of many, the Hillman Minx driven by Wanda Moody, followed by the Jaguar XK120 of Barbara Bayer and the Allard J2 Cadillac driven by Mrs George Koehne.

The largest field of the day, for cars of less than 2000cc, saw a diverse array of cars line up for the third race, run over forty-five miles. Both modified and production cars lined up together, with Class wins more realistic for the majority of the entrants than an over all win. As expected by many following his performance in the August event, it was Scott's Continental-MG Special that led the rest of the field over the finish line. Charles Bowen finished in second place in his modified MG, ahead of the Porsche 356 driven by Fred Cook. Competition was fierce in Class H, where Bob Samuelson, driving his Siata, just staved off the challenge of Hank Robb in a similar car, and the Crosley driven by Betts, to win the Class. The Class F winner was James Sanders in a Jowett Jupiter, finishing ahead of Dick Jones in an MG.

The fourth race featured cars of over 2000cc divided into modified and standard production sections. Judging by the initial entry list, the field was made up entirely of Jaguars with the exception of a lone Aston Martin, driven by Lorin McMullen. It was no surprise to see the modified Jaguar of Springer Jones take the chequered flag, ahead of Dr Sherrod and Charlton Jones in similar cars. The Aston Martin managed to finish in third position in the production class, behind the two standard Jaguars driven by Harold Fenner and Bob Masterson.

A slightly depleted field took to the grid for the 25-lap feature race, the Guardsman's Trophy, though, even without Mabee, Johnston, and Masten Gregory, there was still enough talent in the diverse field to make it competitive. Roy Scott was to drive Tom Davis' bored out Allard J2 in Class A, Carroll Shelby had Roy Cherryhomes' Allard J2X in Class B, Bill Jarnigan was to drive the Ferrari 340AM belonging to Charles Brown, and Riddelle Gregory had his C-type Jaguar on the grid.

From the start, it was Shelby who led into the first corner, followed closely by Scott and Riddelle Gregory. Shelby maintained his lead for nine laps, and then his Allard J2X began having ignition problems. Roy Scott took over the lead in Tom Davis' Allard J2 Cadillac on the tenth lap, and held it until the start of lap twenty. Riddelle Gregory, however, had been creeping up steadily in his Jaguar C-type, and had cut Scott's lead to three seconds when Scott's Allard lost its transmission, putting him out of the race. Having inherited the lead five laps from the finish, Gregory made sure he stayed out in front, and eventually took the chequered flag 1000 yards ahead of Shelby, who had nursed his Allard round with persistent ignition trouble. Another Allard J2, driven by Warren Turner, finished in third place, followed by the two standard specification Jaguars of Charles Jones and Bob Masterson. Riddelle Gregory's victory broke the domination of Carroll Shelby in Texas sports car races during 1953.

Reports on the races in general are sketchy, and the published results for the final race in the local newspaper tend to conflict with the Classes eligible to compete in this race. Whilst it is advertised as being for cars of 3000cc or above, the results show a Class for F or FM cars. In view of the small number of entrants to this race, the organisers may have extended invites to other competitors. However, as no comparative data is to hand, it is inconclusive as to whether or not the Class F and FM cars ran in this race.

8

1953 Statistical Review

Luke AFB 3.5.1953

Race 1 8 laps	Race distance 16 miles	Class U 1500cc	Starters

Race winner's time 15min 58sec		Average speed 60mph	

1A	Singer SM 1500	Lamoreaux W	1oa	1cl F
7A	Jowett Jupiter	Marks C	2oa	2cl F
69A	Jowett Jupiter	Hackney H	3oa	3cl F
2A	MG TD	Webb C		
3A	Porsche 356	Conway G		
6A	Porsche 356	McGregor S		
8A	MG	Blaisdell J		
9A	MG TD	Barrett C		
12A	MG	Yourdon R		
14A	MG	Potts J		
28A	MG	Chamberlain J		
50A	MG	Cleveland N		
4A	Panhard Dyna	Datig F		
5A	Panhard Dyna	Ryan F		

Programme cover for the Luke AFB event. (Terry O'Neil Collection)

Race 2	8 laps	Race distance 16 miles	Class O 1500cc Prod	Starters

Race winner's time 13min 57.2sec	Average speed 68.57mph

71D	Jaguar XK120M	Jackson J	1oa	1cl C
14B	Jaguar XK120	Bellesiles J	J2oa	J2cl C
5B	Jaguar XK120	McPherson W	J2oa	J2cl C
2B	Jaguar XK120	Painter C	4oa	4cl C
4B	Jaguar XK120	Dobson W		
3B	Jaguar XK120	Yoder T		
15B	Jaguar XK120	O'Brien T		
1B	Jaguar XK120	Hackney H		

Race 3	8 laps	Race distance 16 miles	Class FM	Starters

Race winner's time 17min 4sec	Average speed 56.4mph

1C	MG TD Special R-1	Miles K	1oa	1cl FM
6C	MG TD Special	Menefee B	2oa	2cl FM
9C	MG TD Special	Bird T	3oa	3cl FM
42C	Porsche 356	Crean J	4oa	4cl FM
2C	MG TD mod	Kingsley M		
3C	Volkswagen mod	Lee J		
4C	MG mod	Burkhard J		
5C	MG mod	Dolden H		
10C	MG mod Special	Bell W		
15C	MG mod	James G		
22C	Singer 1500 SM mod	Van Laanen R		
14D	Simca 8 Special	Pringle W		

Race 4	8 laps	Race distance 16 miles	Class BM, CM, DM	Starters

Race winner's time 13min 51.3sec	Average speed 69.3mph

98D	Ferrari 340 AM	0032 A	McAfee J	1oa	1cl CM
7D	Morgensen Special-Cadillac		Morgenson R	2oa	1cl BM
2D	Allard J2 Cadillac		Yates L	3oa	2cl BM
8D	Ferrari 212 Ex	0078 E	Wheeler H	4oa	1cl DM
3D	MG TD-Ford Special		Lee G		
77D	Allard J2 Oldsmobile		Swartley S		
32D	Allard J2 Lincoln		Stubbs A		
9D	Jaguar XK120M		Montrose G		
10D	MG-V8 Special		Mahon D		
11D	Allard J2 Lincoln		Sanderson D		
13D	Kurtis-DeSoto		Murphy W		
19D	Jaguar XK120M		Mendelson M		
71D	Jaguar XK120M		Jackson J		

Race 5	20 laps	Race distance 40 miles	Class Novice	Starters

Race winner's time 34min 38sec	Average speed

2D	Allard J2 Cadillac	Yates L	1oa
13D	Kurtis 500 De Soto	Murphy W	2oa
7D	Morgenson Special-Cadillac	Morgenson R	3oa
11D	Allard J2 Lincoln	Sanderson D	4oa

Race 6	8 laps	Race distance 16 miles	Class Ladies	Starters

Race winner's time 16min 38sec	Average speed 58mph

	Jaguar XK120M	Zeller M	1oa
	Jaguar XK120	Cavin H	2oa
3A	Porsche 356	Conway R	3oa
50A	MG	Cleveland A	4oa
71D	Jaguar XK120M	Jackson J	
4C	MG mod	Burkhard J	

Race 7 Govenor's Cup 40 laps	Race distance 80 miles	Class Unrestricted	Starters 27

Fort Worth NGB 23.8.1953

Race winner's time 1hr 5min 33sec	Average speed 73.28mph

13D	Kurtis 500 S Mercury		Stroppe W	1oa	1cl B
98D	Ferrari 340 AM	0032 A	McAfee J	2oa	1cl CM
1C	MG TD Special R-1		Miles K	3oa	1cl FM
42C	Porsche 356		Crean J	4oa	2cl FM
6C	MG TD Special		Menefee R	5oa	3cl FM
8D	Ferrari 212Ex	0078 E	Wheeler H	6oa	1cl DM
	Siefried-Mercury Special		Wilder S	7oa	
3B	Jaguar XK120		Dobson W	8oa	
3C	Volkswagen mod		Lee J	9oa	
1D	Glaspar Cadillac		Fickas W	10oa	
69A	Jowett Jupiter		Hackney H		1cl F
7A	Jowett Jupiter		Marks C		2cl F
7D	Morgensen Special-Cadillac		Morgensen R	14oa	
2C	MG TD mod		Kingsley M	15oa	
19D	Jaguar XK120M		Mendelson M		
11D	Allard J2 Lincoln		Sanderson D		
2D	Allard J2 Cadillac		Yates L		
9C	MG TD Special mod		Bird T		
10C	MG Special mod		Bell B		
3D	MG-Ford		Lee G		
13D	Ferrari		Hill P	Dns	
7C	Porsche 356 America		Von Neumann J	Dns	

Race 1	10 laps	Race distance 36 miles	Class MG	Starters

Race winner's time	Average speed

	MG	Steiner W	1oa	1cl G
	MG	Gilchrist J	2oa	2cl G
	MG	Roberts J	3oa	3cl G
	MG			
	MG			

Race 2	15 laps	Race distance 54 miles	Class U 2 litres	Starters

Race winner's time	Average speed

	MG TC mod	Hill F	1oa	
	Crosley	Clifford W	2oa	1cl HM
17	MG mod	Symmonds J	3oa	
43	MG TC	Duncan D		1cl G
21	MG TD	Peterson G		
	MG TC	Spelman E		
44	MG TC mod	Banes W		
	Continental-MG Special	Scott N	Dnf	

Race 3	15 laps	Race distance 54 miles	Class O 2 litres	Starters

Race winner's time	Average speed

Jaguar XK120M	Jones S	1oa	1cl CM
Jaguar XK120M	Schroeder R	2oa	2cl CM
Jaguar XK120M	McPherson W	3oa	3cl CM
Jaguar XK120	Fenner H		1cl C
Jaguar XK120	Jarnigan W		

Race 4	Race distance	Class Ladies H'cap	Starters

Race winner's time		Average speed	

	MG TD	Galbraith G	1oa	
	Allard J2 Cadillac	Koehne J	2oa	
		Stafford E	3oa	
		McKinney J	4oa	
	MG	Joerns R	5oa	

Race 5 Guardsman's Trophy 20 laps	Race distance 72 miles	Class Unrestricted	Starters

Race winner's time 54 min 45 sec		Average speed 78.9mph	

11	Allard J2X Cadillac	J3146	Shelby C	1oa	1cl B
	Jaguar XK120M		Jones S	2oa	1cl C
	Jaguar XK120M		Schroeder R	3oa	2cl C
	Jaguar C-type	XKC 033	Gregory R	4oa	3cl C
	Jaguar XK120		Jarnigan W	5oa	4cl C
55	Allard J2 Chrysler		Turner W	6oa	2cl B
	Jaguar XK120M		McPherson W	7oa	5cl C
	Ferrari 340 Mexico	0226 AT	Koehne G	8oa	6cl C
54	Allard J2X Chrysler	J1732	Duncan D	Dnf	
20	Jaguar XK120M		Greenberg H		
56	Special			Dnf	

Floyd Bennett Field NAS 29.8.1953

Sheepshead Bay Trophy 20 laps	Race distance 43 miles	Class u 1500cc	Starters 28

Race winner's time 44min 37.17sec		Average speed 57.9mph	

84	Jowett Jupiter Mk 1A		Lloyd W	1oa	1cl F

27	MG TD		Ehrman G	2oa	2cl F
73	MG TD		Rodney M	3oa	3cl F
74	MG TD		Rabe G	4oa	4cl F
46	MG TD		Hunt G	5oa	5cl F
50	Singer 1250		Lamoreaux W	6oa nraf	6cl F
81	MG TD		Decker W	7oa	7cl F
67	MG TD		Meyer R	8oa	8cl F
64	MG TD		Rathke R	9oa	9cl F
63	MG TD		Gedeon R	10oa	10cl F
35	MG TD		Cornman R	11oa	11cl F
4	MG TD		Patterson A	12oa	12cl F
29	MG TD		Beer E	13oa	13cl F
77	MG TD MkII		Witalis E	14oa	14cl F
108	MG		Mooney J	15oa	15cl F
104	MG		Maronie	16oa	16cl F
78	MG TD		Comito L	17oa	17cl F
94	MG TD		Black D	18oa	18cl F
93	MG TD		Feldman A	Dnf	
16	MG TC		Janis C	Dnf	
26	MG TC		Miller J	Dnf	
103	MG		Abry C	Dnf	
34	MG TD		Alderman G	Dnf	
79	MG TC		McCleery J	Dnf	
95	MG TD		Iacono J	Dnf	
61	MG TD		Bastrup L	Dnf	
47	MG TC		Ranzenhofer H	Dnf	
72	MG TD		Sheldrale C	Dnf	

Brighton Beach Trophy 20 laps	Race distance 43 miles	Class O 1500cc	Starters 24

Race winner's time 37min 55.27sec		Average speed 67.98mph	

12	Jaguar XK120M		Boss R	1oa	1cl CM
99	Kieft-MG		Goldschmidt E	2oa	1cl FM
65	Jaguar XK120M		Hassan C	3oa	2cl CM
31	Jaguar XK120M		Marshall J	4oa	3cl CM
60	Jaguar XK120		Wallace C	5oa	1cl C
71	Jaguar XK120		Grossman R	6oa	2cl C
109	Jaguar XK120M		Kaback S	7oa	4cl CM
882	Jaguar XK120M		Derujinsky G	8oa	5cl CM
57	Jaguar XK120M		Woodbury W	9oa	6cl CM

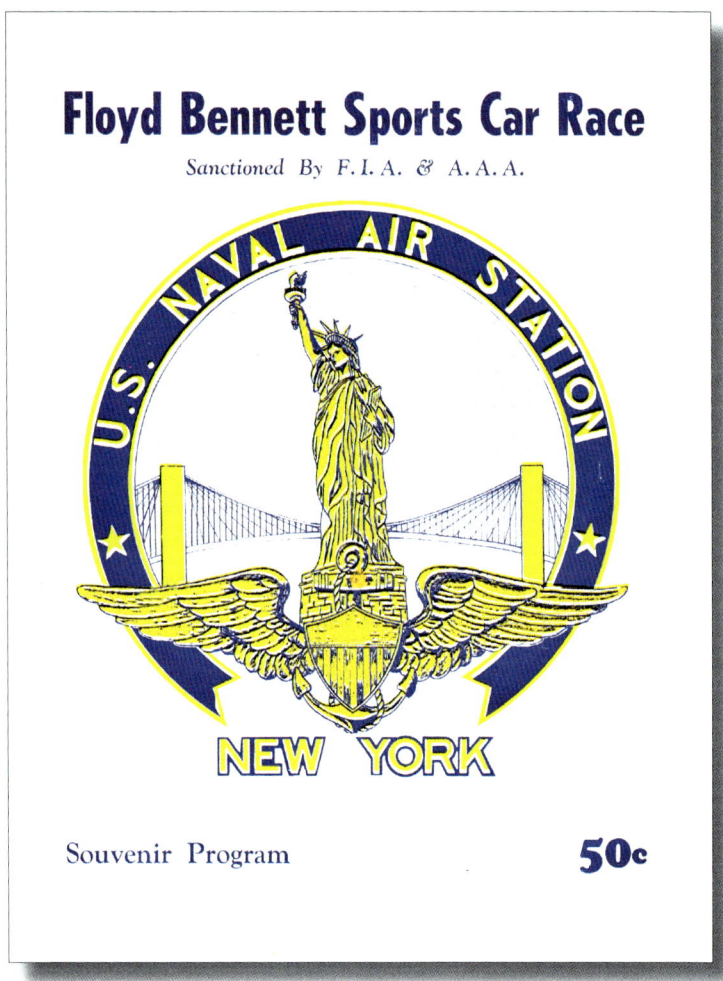

Programme cover for the Floyd Bennett Field NAS event.
(Terry O'Neil Collection)

Race 3 Floyd Bennett Cup 100 laps	Race distance 215 miles	Class Unrestricted	Starters 41

Race winner's time 2hr 54min 9.36sec	Average speed 74.07mph

2	Cunningham C4R		Walters P	1oa	1cl BM
10	Ferrari 340 Mexico	0228 AT	Spear W / Benett J	2oa	1cl CM
1	Cunningham C4R		Cunningham B	3oa	2cl BM
85	Ferrari 225S	0166 ED	Lloyd W	4oa	1cl DM
37	Hansgen Jaguar Special		Eager W / Hansgen W	5oa	2cl CM
311	Jaguar C-type	XKC 030	Gray H / Hassan C	6oa	3cl CM
91	OSCA MT4 1450	1133	Simpson J	7oa	1cl FM
9	Frazer-Nash LM MkII	100/174	Bonadies A	8oa	1cl E
30	OSCA MT4 1350	1127	Moffett G	9oa	2cl FM
17	Aston Martin DB2		Hansgen W / Pearsall R	10oa	2cl DM
53	JP Special		Pauley J	11oa	3cl FM
22	Frazer-Nash		Smyth P	12oa	2cl E
19	Jaguar XK120M		McKenna T	13oa	4cl CM
117	Porsche 356 America		Weinmann M	14oa	4cl FM
18	MG TD		Wonder W	15oa	5cl FM
92	Siata 208 CS	CS 056	Brewster W	16oa	3cl E
43	MG TD Special		Roth I	17oa	1cl F
44	MG Special		Allen F	18oa	2cl F
7	Siata 208 CS	CS 071	Grier R	19oa	4cl E
41	PBX Crosley Special		Poole C / Vilardi A	20oa	1cl HM
24	Deutsch Bonnet Panhard		Cook B	21oa	2cl HM
100	Giaur		Dominianni F	22oa	3cl HM
74	MG TD		Rabe G	23oa	3cl F
86	Crosley		Ingleheart J	24oa	4cl HM
20	Cisitalia 202MM Spyder		Ceresole P	25oa	1cl GM
6	Jaguar C-type	XKC 015	Gregory M	Dnf	
71	Jaguar XK120		Grossman R	Dnf	
109	Jaguar XK120M		Kyback S	Dnf L8	
3	OSCA MT4 1350		Johnston S	Dnf	
90	Nardi-Cadillac Special		Fina P	Dnf	
23	Jaguar Special		Schott C	Dnf	
56	Bandini 750 Spyder		Scatchard T	Dnf	
82	Multiplex Special		Fanelli H	Dnf	

15	Jaguar XK120	Conley A	10oa	3cl C
55	Morgan Plus 4	Rothschild M	11oa	1cl D
105	Porsche 356	Hannaway H	12oa	1cl F
89	Allard Palm Beach	Dexter H	14oa	1cl E
75	MG TD MkII	Dressel J	15oa	2cl FM
16	Jaguar XK120	Laird R	16oa	4cl C
59	Porsche 356	Miller P	17oa	2cl F
54	Jaguar XK120	Dagavar F	18oa	5cl C
28	Jaguar XK120M	Kaplan J	19oa	7cl CM
21	Porsche 356	Hopkins T	20oa	3cl F
107	Jaguar XK120	Hugus E	Dnf	
62	Porsche 356	Killgore J	Dnf	
52	Singer 1500 SM mod	Vaughan W	Dnf	3cl FM
106	BMW	Meinhardt V	Dnf	

96	MG TD		Sinon F	Dnf	
111	Frazer-Nash		Donaldson J	Dnf	
48	Siata 300BC 1100 Spyder		Keller R	Dnf	
116	Singer 1500 SM		Vaughan W	Dnf	
98	Allard J2 Cadillac		Goldschmidt E	Dnf	
97	MG TD		Keeley J	Dnf	
101	Frazer-Nash		Rogers	Dnf	
36	Bandini		Rudkin H	Dnf	

138	MG TD		Wilder J		
68	MG TD		Snow R		
96	MG TD		Datig F		
119	MG TC		Dolden H		
69	MG TD		Davis M		
53	MG TD		Peel D		
27	MG TD		Sinclair S		
97	MG TD		Scott W		

Long Beach NAVSTA/Reeves Field 3.10.1953

Race 1	6 laps	Race distance 13.8 miles	Class Ladies & F3	Starters

Race winner's time		Average speed	

42	Volkswagen Special		Anderson J	1oa	
34	Jaguar XK120M		Wilder L	2oa	
69	MG TD		Davis M	3oa	
79	MG TC		Mahon E		
38	Willys-MG		Lowe M		
49	MG TD		Hayward E		
85	MG TD		Parker M		
120	MG TD		DeOlivera H		
111	F3 500 Special		Bracken R		
134	Morrow Special		Morrow H		
153	Cooper 500 F3		Trimble R		

Race 2	6 laps	Race distance 13.8 miles	Class MG Novice	Starters 38

Race winner's time		Average speed	

49	MG TD		Hayward D	1oa	1cl G
91	MG TD		Johnson H	2oa	2cl G
135	MG TD		Wright A	3oa	3cl G
129	MG TD		Anderson F		
29	MG TD		Stone W		

Programme cover for the Reeve Field NAVSTA event. (Terry O'Neil Collection)

41	MG TD		Spear D		
127	MG TD		Boyer C		
73	MG TD		Peron P		
89	MG TD		Jeffries H		
5	MG TD		Swarthout J		
93	MG TD		Huff J		
51	MG TD		Miles M		
63	MG TD		Valdez F		
136	MG TD		Brisbin S		
	MG TC				
	MG TD				
	MG TD				
	MG TD				
	MG TD				
	MG TD				
	MG TD				
	MG TD				
	MG TD				
	MG TD				
	MG TD				
	MG TD				
	MG TD				
	MG TD				
	MG TD				

Race 3 8 laps	Race distance 18.4 miles	Class B, C, D, E	Starters

Race winner's time	Average speed

23	Jaguar XK120		Menefee B	1oa	1cl C
39	Fraser-Nash LM MkII	421/200/183	Lowe J	2oa	1cl E
66	Jaguar XK120		Bloxham R	3oa	2cl C
107	Willys Studebaker		Green P		
30	Morgan Plus 4		Thompson C		
38	Willys-MG		Lowe M		
100	Austin-Healey 100		Mayer H		

Race 4 6 laps	Race distance 13.8 miles	Class F & G	Starters

Race winner's time 16min 4sec	Average speed 51.58mph

60	Porsche 356		Norton B	1oa	1cl F
118	Singer SM 1500		Earl M	2oa	2cl F
86	Jowett Jupiter		Carberry J	3oa	3cl F
73	Dyna-Panhard		Peron P		
82	Dyna-Panhard		Crouzet F		
4	MG TD		Barker E		
161	MG TD				
94	MG T		Byrom R		
88	Singer SM 1500		Lamoreaux W		

Race 5 8 laps	Race distance 18.5 miles	Class Jaguar	Starters

Race winner's time	Average speed

23	Jaguar XK120		Menefee R	1oa	1cl C
	Jaguar XK120		Jenkins B	2oa	2cl C
	Jaguar XK120		Marks C	3oa	3cl C
	Jaguar XK120				
	Jaguar XK120				
	Jaguar XK120				
	Jaguar XK120				
	Jaguar XK120				

Race 6 10 laps	Race distance 23 miles	Class O 1500cc	Starters

Race winner's time	Average speed

55	Jaguar Special		Daigh C	1oa	1cl CM
116	Jaguar XK120M		Evans H	2oa	2cl CM
12	Allard J2X Lincoln		Briney M	3oa	1cl BM
39	Frazer-Nash LM MkII	421/200/183	Lowe J		1cl DM
66	Jaguar XK120		Bloxham R		
23	Jaguar XK120		Menefee R		

	Jaguar XK120		Jenkins B		
	Jaguar XK120		Marks C		
35	Jaguar XK120M		Playan M		
11	Jaguar XK120M		Borden J		

Race 7 6 laps	Race distance 13.8 miles	Class MG	Starters 23

Race winner's time 15min 28.8sec	Average speed 53.42mph

74	MG TD		Trennert D	1oa	1cl G
131	MG TD		Bowering B	2oa	2cl G
135	MG TD		Wright A	3oa	3cl G
150	MG TD		Anakin B		
58	MG TD		Parker F		
61	MG TD		Thomas W		
37	MG TD		Reynolds R		
83	MG TD		Anderson R		
80	MG TD		Marshall C		
126	MG TD		Brigham R		
148	MG TD		Pichette J		
159	MG TD			dnf	
	MG TC				
123	MG TD		Collins J		
98	MG TD		Bradley J		
	MG				
	MG				
	MG				
	MG				
	MG				
	MG				
	MG				
	MG				

Race 8 8 laps	Race distance 18.5 miles	Class U 1500cc	Starters 28

Race winner's time	Average speed

25	Porsche 356		Shillam D	1oa	1cl F
104	Singer 1500 SM		McDannold R	2oa	2cl F
169	Jowett Jupiter		Marks C	3oa	3cl F
86	Jowett Jupiter		Carberry J		
60	Porsche 356		Norton R		
79	MG TC		Mahon E		
4	MG TD		Barker E		
31	MG TC		Smith M		
143	MG TC		Yedor C		
	MG TD				
	MG TD				
	MG TD				
	MG TD				
	MG TD				
	MG				
	MG				
	MG				
130	Crosley		Anderson M		
18	Crosley		Gardner C		

Race 9 10 laps	Race distance 23 miles	Class FM, GM, F, G	Starters

Race winner's time 23min 17.4sec	Average speed 59.2mph

50	MG TD R-1 Special		Miles K	1oa	1cl FM
9	MG TD Special		Bird T	2oa	2cl FM
69	MG TD mod		Drake R	3oa	3cl FM
39	Frazer-Nash LM MkII	421/200/183	Lowe J		
	MG TC mod		Andersen V		
10	Beavis Offenhauser Special		Beavis G	Dnf L1	

Fort Worth NGB 6.12.1953

Race 10 30 laps	Race distance 69 miles	Class Unrestricted	Starters 40

Race winner's time 1hr 2min 5.8sec	Average speed 66.67mph

110	Kurtis 500 S Mercury		Stroppe W	1oa	1cl BM
50	MG TD R-1 Special		Miles K	2oa	1cl FM
12	Allard J2X Lincoln		Briney M	3oa	2cl BM
55	Jaguar Special		Daigh C	4oa	1cl CM
24	Kurtis 500 S Cadillac		McGurk F		
64	Allard J2 Cadillac		Kuchenbecker C		
84	Kurtis 500 S De Soto		Murphy W		
124	Allard J2 Cadillac		Bythiner K		
71	Jaguar XK120M		Jackson J		
35	Jaguar XK120M		Playan M		
116	Jaguar XK120M		Evans H		
81	Jaguar XK120		McGregor J		
100	Austin-Healey 100		Mayer H		
107	Willys Studebaker		Green P	Dnf	
69	MG TD		Drake R		
9	MG TD Special		Bird T		
39	Frazer-Nash LM MkII	421/200/183	Lowe J		
141	Siata Dinna GS		Wilder W		
156	Siata 208S		Stables D		
	Singer SM 1500		Snell W		
52	MG TC V8-60		Pedigo P		
114	Jaguar XK120		Garlick W		
20	Allard J2X				
86	Jowett Jupiter		Carberry J		
	Siata 300 BC				
118	Singer SM 1500		Earl M		
36	Kurtis 500				
113	Jaguar Special		Pickford W		
14	Jaguar XK120		Royle J		
165	Jaguar XK120				
66	Jaguar XK120		Bloxhan R		
30	Morgan		Thompson C		
28	MG TC V8-60		Conway V		
11	Jaguar XK120M		Borden J		
169	Jowett Jupiter		Marks C		

Race 1 10 laps	Race distance 30 miles	Class MG	Starters

Race winner's time	Average speed

46	MG		Gilchrist J	1oa	1cl F
4	MG		Gladson W	2oa	2cl F
28	MG TC		Rodier R	3oa	3cl F
14	MG		Crim L		
19	MG		Matthews B		
24	MG		Barnett F		
33	MG TD		Galbraith G		
39	MG		Ross W		
42	MG		Steiner W		
69	MG		Fillmore C		
90	MG		Blum S		

Race 2 5 laps	Race distance 15 miles	Class Ladies H'cap	Starters

Race winner's time	Average speed

25	Hillman Minx		Mooney W	1oa	
	Jaguar XK120		Bayer B	2oa	
7	Allard J2 Cadillac		Koehne J	3oa	
4	MG		Gladson M		
9	Jaguar XK120		Bymmonda M		
13	Nardi-Danese		Crim N		
33	MG TD		Galbraith C		
34	MG		Joerns R		
41	MG		Jelley W		
77	Jaguar XK120		Leaf D		

Race 3	15 laps	Race distance 45 miles	Class U 2000cc	Starters
Race winner's time			Average speed	

16	Continental-MG Special		Scott N	1oa	1cl FM
27	MG mod		Bowen C	2oa	2cl FM
	Porsche 356		Cook F	3oa	3cl FM
22	Jowett Jupiter		Saunders J		1cl F
42	MG		Jones R		2cl F
40	Singer 1500 SM		Allen G		3cl F
35	Siata 300BC 750 Spyder		Samuelson R		1cl HM
1	Siata 300BC 750 Spyder		Robb H		2cl HM
29	Crosley Special		Betts W		3cl HM
5	MG mod		Wolski A		
8	MG mod		Hubbs C		
10	Jowett Jupiter		Wright G		
17	Morris Minor		Spencer M		
18	MG mod		Ong J		
25	MG mod		Wilson W		
28	MG TC		Rodier R		
30	Crosley mod		Place A		
33	MG		Galbraith G		
43	MG		Jones R		
44	Porsche 356		Richter R		
48	Hillman Minx		Webb G		
90	MG		Blum S		

Race 4	15 laps	Race distance 45 miles	Class U 3500cc	Starters
Race winner's time			Average speed	

31	Jaguar XK120M		Jones S	1oa	1cl CM
23	Jaguar XK120M		Sherrod V Dr	2oa	2cl CM
	Jaguar XK120M		Jones C		3cl CM
3	Jaguar XK120		Fenner H		1cl C
32	Jaguar XK120		Masterson R		2cl C
21	Aston Martin DB2		McMullen L		1cl D
4	Jaguar XK120M		Mabee L		
6	Jaguar XK120		Martin H		
9	Jaguar XK120		Symmonds J		
12	Jaguar XK120M		Crim L		
26	Jaguar XK120M		Hoppener G		
36	Jaguar XK120M		Woodward V		
59	Jaguar XK120		Gregory M		
66	Aston-Martin s/c		Harrison E		

Race 5	25 laps	Race distance 75 miles	Class Unrestricted	Starters
Race winner's time			Average speed	

80	Jaguar C-type	XKC 033	Gregory R	1oa	1cl CM
11	Allard J2X Cadillac	J3146	Shelby C	2oa	1cl B
47	Allard J2 Chysler		Turner W	3oa	2cl B
	Jaguar XK120M		Jones C	4oa	2cl CM
32	Jaguar XK120		Masterson R	5oa	3cl CM
85	Allard J2 Cadillac		Scott R	nraf	3cl B
22	Jowett Jupiter		Saunders J		1cl F
44	Porsche 356		Richter R		2cl F
25	MG mod		Wilson W		3cl F
71	Ferrari 340 AM	0118 A	Jarnigan W		
20	Healey-Chrysler		Larson D		
27	Allard J2 Chrysler		Hall J		
58	Jaguar C-type	XKC 015	Gregory M	Dns	
65	Mabee Chrysler Special		Mabee J	Dns	
	Ferrari 225S	0218 ET	Johnston S	Dns	

9

SCCA National/SAC base races 1954

For the SCCA, the year began full of optimism. The Contest Board of the SCCA had effected a new contract with Strategic Air Command for eight Air Force Base races for 1954, thereby making racing under safe conditions available to a greater number of members, and, at the same time, providing a patriotic service. The SCCA would return to MacDill AFB, Bergstrom AFB, Offutt AFB, Lockbourne AFB and March AFB, with other races being introduced at Hunter AFB, Andrews AFB, and Chanute AFB. The latter named AFB had been used as a regional venue in 1953, and the event had been successful in attracting a large number of entrants and spectators. Well over $250,000 in proceeds from the seven 1953 national events was used to improve living conditions of Air Force Base personnel, and the hope was that this figure would be even greater this time round.

It was not only the SAC that had benefited from the 1953 events. By the end of the 1953 season, SCCA membership had increased by 37 per cent, and, for the first time in its history, the SCCA was on a solid financial footing.

Within the SCCA, an important change was made to the competition points scoring method at the beginning of 1954. Instead of having one National Champion, there was now a National Champion for each of the car Classes, some 15 in all, thus encouraging more entrants to participate in the races in the hope of winning something. Four main divisions took shape based on engine capacity, each encompassing several Classes that distinguished between standard and modified cars. It was along these lines that the races were organised.

Other changes with a long lasting affect for the Club were also taking place, as several privately owned road courses were being developed at an accelerating pace in different parts of America. Thompson, Willow Springs, and Wilmot Hills were operational in 1954, and a new track at Elkhart Lake, to be called Road America, was scheduled to be open in mid-1955. Further track development was planned at Paramount Ranch, Bridgehampton, Lime Rock, Marlboro, Vineland, and Riverside beyond 1955, but in the meantime, the SAC bases were by far the best venues on offer.

Unfortunately, the optimism at the beginning of the year soon turned to genuine concern for the future of the SCCA, and for sports car racing in general. A decision taken by Congress halfway through the year to stop the use of SAC and active Air Force bases for racing, potentially had major implications for the SCCA. This decision, following on from the ban of road racing on public roads in many states across America, was a bitter blow, not only for the SCCA, but for other sports car clubs as well. For future event programme planning within the SCCA, alternative sites would need to be found at both national and regional levels. As a result, in the latter half of 1954, Club officials found themselves hastily conducting initial enquiries with all possible site authorities, such as the Municipal Airport Commission and City Councils, in order to resolve their dilemma.

MacDill AFB, Tampa, Florida

31.1.1954

"Kimberly's new car was an exciting thing to watch and according to Kimberly, was an exciting thing to drive." (Road & Track)

The 1954 programme of national events started with this meeting at MacDill AFB, and like last year, was planned to take place prior to the race at Sebring, though with a gap of over four weeks between the two events, disruption to the rival meeting was minimal. It was at last being acknowledged by the SCCA, albeit begrudgingly, that the Sebring race was there to stay.

Significant changes to the track layout at MacDill accounted for the fact that the circuit now measured only 3.44 miles, but with one long straight measuring 1.1 miles and fourteen corners of varying difficulty, the challenge to the drivers was every bit as much as in 1953. Although still under the banner of the Florida National Sports Car Races, the format of the race programme had also changed from the 1953 programme. The six-hour Sam Collier Trophy race was dropped, and in its place, a 200-mile event, the Governor Dan McCarty Memorial Trophy race, was introduced.

One thing had remained unchanged though; the co-operation between the SAC and the SCCA in putting the race organisation into practice. The SAC personnel played their part in preparing the track layout, putting up safety barriers, arranging car parking, and selling tickets. In return, proceeds from the races went to the MacDill Airmen's Living Improvement Fund.

Interestingly, on the day prior to the races, an article appeared in the *Tampa Morning Tribune*, submitted by Millard C Cleveland, for the Committee of Tampa Ministers Association: "Tampa ministers yesterday told off the Air Force for conducting all-day Sunday sports car races at MacDill AFB, in a sizzling letter addressed to US Senator Smathers." Briefly, the points raised in the minister's letter were:

Being host to 100,000 civilians is not 'recreation' for MacDill airmen.

Deployment of Air Force personnel in uniform to peddle tickets for Sundays' race is uneconomical.

Making ticket salesmen of ranking officers 'is beneath the dignity of the Air Force.'

In a curt reply, Senator Smathers stated that, "… the sports car races are classed as a recreational event and recreation is most important to our servicemen."

It appears strange that in writing a letter on behalf of church ministers, not one issue relating directly to religion was raised in the letter, and one wonders if it was part of an ongoing campaign contrived to cause embarrassment to Curtis LeMay. Three things were for sure; firstly Millard C Cleveland was no economist; secondly he was not a sociologist, and, thirdly, the correspondence did nothing to detract from the enjoyment that the 40,000 spectators experienced from watching the four races.

Saturday was devoted to a driver's school, and to practise sessions for all Classes of cars, all of which went off without incident. Sunday morning dawned and at 9.45am, the first event, the Imperial Polk County Trophy Race for modified cars under 1500cc, commenced. Thirteen cars sped away from the grid on their 50-mile journey, with Rees Makins' OSCA 1100cc first away, though he was soon caught and passed by Sherwood Johnston, driving in James Simpson's OSCA. Briggs Cunningham, also in an OSCA, joined in the tussle for the lead, until he spun his car and stalled the engine, putting him back down the field. This put Brewster in a fourth OSCA, in contention ahead of Crawford in a Porsche America. At the front, Johnston maintained his substantial lead, and even received

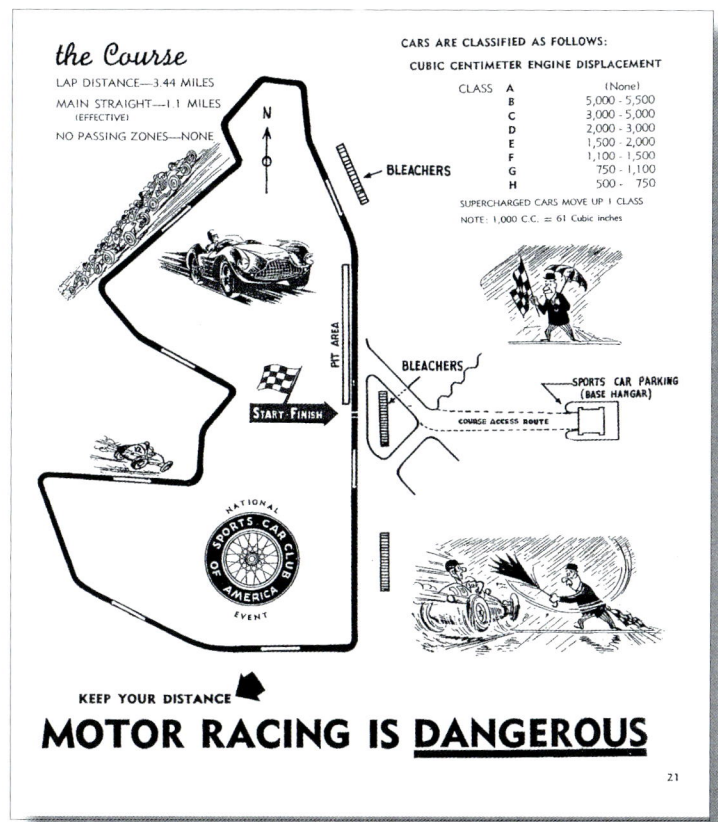

Track layout at MacDill AFB. (Terry O'Neil Collection)

*Isabelle Haskell sits in her Siata at MacDill AFB.
(Terry O'Neil Collection)*

*The Strategic Air Command team of Allard JRs line up prior to the feature race in which they finished in 6th, 7th, and 8th places.
(Courtesy Dean Butler)*

the 'slow down' signal from his pits, before taking the chequered flag 12 seconds ahead of Brewster, with Cunningham managing to claw his way back to take third place. Makins finished 6th overall, first in Class GM, ahead of Richard Gent's Cisitalia and Bob Keller's Siata, while George Schrafft finished a creditable ninth overall, and first in Class HM in the Palm Beach Crosley.

The second race brought the over-1500cc modified cars to the start line. 17 cars lined up, including Curtis LeMay's Allard JR, but in the hands of Texan driver, Roy Scott. Bill Spear opted not to run, saving his tyres on the Ferrari for the feature race later in the day, but Kimberly obviously felt more bullish and decided to try out his new Ferrari, a powerful 4.5-litre 375MM, the first to be delivered to the USA.

It took only half a lap for Kimberly to dominate the proceedings by taking the lead. Kimberly was followed by Scott, who was driving LeMay's Allard, and Phil Walters driving a Cunningham-entered Ferrari 250 MM. Their positions remained unchanged, until the fifth lap when Curtis LeMay was on hand to watch Scott slide the Allard into the only drainage ditch anywhere in the vicinity of the course, and out of the race.

Kimberly's Ferrari went on to win the race with a huge distance to spare ahead of Walters' Ferrari, while Ron Tilley saved face for the SAC entries by coming third in an Allard JR. On the seventh lap, Erickson had moved his Jaguar C-type into fourth place, ahead of George Huntoon driving Sheppard's Jaguar C-type; positions they held until the end of the race. Also making its debut on American soil was the Kieft-Bristol, impressively driven by Paul Ceresole. The 2-litre car won its class comfortably and finished ninth overall.

Thirty-three production cars lined up for the start of the third event, the Gasparilla Trophy Race. The entry list was predominantly made up of MG, Jaguar, and Porsche models. As expected, the race ended up as two races in one, the Jaguars having their own contest, while the remainder of the field fought it out for Class honours. Ten of the first eleven places went to Jaguars, the lone intruder being the Austin-Healey driven by George Huntoon, who finished in sixth position. First across the line was the experienced Russ Boss, but he was challenged all the way by a driver making his first appearance, Major Warren Smith. In Class F, Porsche dominated the proceedings, Haycraft winning the class ahead of Proctor and Schmidt. First MG home was that of Bob Fergus in his well-raced and successful MG TC, ahead of Ralph Durbin in a MG TD. It appears that the drainage ditch visited by Scott in the previous race was an unattractive, but necessary, proposition for Paul Bailey, as he left the course trying to avoid a spinning car. The damage to the car was considerable, though the driver escaped serious injury.

The feature race was the 200-mile Governor Dan McCarty Memorial Race, introduced as a replacement for the six-hour event as held in 1953. Forty-four production and modified cars lined up on the

Roy Scott was the nominated driver to take charge of Curtis LeMay's Allard and finished in 6th place. (Courtesy Dean Butler)

grid, and as race starter Terry Field gave them the green flag, Walters in the Chrysler-powered Cunningham C4R was first away, but before he had reached the first corner he had been passed by Kimberly's new Ferrari. At the end of the first lap, Kimberly held a ten-second lead over Walters, followed by Spear, Scott and Fitch. There were duels between the cars in each Class as they jostled for early dominance in the long race, and it was not long before a few cars began to drop out, due to the ferocious pace. Schrafft went out on the 9th lap and Spear went out on lap 17, after a couple of visits to the pits, which meant he went home without any Championship points. Fitch moved into third place in Cunningham's Ferrari 250 MM, but was in no position to be able to mount a challenge to the top two placed cars. As the race progressed, Walters began closing the gap on Kimberly and they began swapping places, much to the delight of the estimated 40,000 excited spectators. Walters inched ahead on lap 45, and retained the slender advantage for three laps, before Kimberly took his opportunity to pass Walters for the final time. With a single lap to go, Kimberly took a sizeable lead to cross the finish line ahead of Walters, as the Cunningham dropped back due to clutch trouble. Fitch retained his third position from early on in the race ahead of Lloyd in another Ferrari, and Huntoon in a C-type Jaguar. The three SAC-entered Allard JRs, including Scott's car that had been recovered from the drainage ditch, finished in the next three positions. After the race, a happy Jim Kimberly said, "I still have much to learn about the new 4.5." That must have sounded quite ominous to the other competitors.

A Victory dinner was served at the MacDill Officer's Club in the evening, where major trophies and Class awards were presented to the winners, with due praise being given to the many people who had helped to organise this successful event.

There were no official financial figures published immediately after the event, so it is impossible to judge what benefits accrued for the Airmen's Living Improvement Fund. However, a figure of $23,393 net profit was later forthcoming from the offices of the General Accounting Office when it carried out its investigations into the races.

Rumblings of discontent continued to emanate from the Florida base weeks after the event had finished. This time, it was more than a passing remark that hit the newspaper headlines. It appeared that a concerted effort had been made to disrupt further races from taking place at MacDill AFB. Under the banner headline of "Did MacDill Races Cost Taxpayers $100,000?" the *Tampa Tribune* printed a lengthy anonymous letter sent by two disenchanted airmen. Basically, the letter was full of criticism of every aspect of the event, implying that the whole thing was set up to satisfy the whims of one man, General Curtis LeMay.

Needless to say, the article hit the desk of the Chairman of the House Subcommittee on Air Force Appropriations, Congressman Errett P Scrivner, giving him the opportunity to start an enquiry into the way the races were conducted.

Errett Power Scrivner was the Republican Representative from Kansas, born in 1898, and represented Kansas from 1943 to 1959. He

Dave Schilling drove his Allard JR to eighth place in the feature race. (Courtesy Dean Butler)

was an ambitious man and took every opportunity to score points against anyone who stood in his way, including Curtis LeMay. To say that their relationship was cold was an understatement, and the competition for publicity points was ongoing between them.

Hunter AFB, Savannah, Georgia

13/14.3.1954

"We thought we had seen a real battle at MacDill between Phil Walters and Jim Kimberly – then we saw the duel between 'Gentleman Jim' and Bill Spear at Hunter. Better just say it was the greatest thing since the wheel, and let it go at that." (Sports Car)

The second National event of 1954 was organised by one of the newly formed regions of the SCCA, the Savannah Region, and took place for the first time at Hunter AFB. Hunter was an established military facility dating back to the days of WWII. In 1946, it was de-activated and returned to the City of Savannah for use as a civilian airport, then re-activated in September 1950, when the City of Savannah swapped the airfield for a smaller site, 8 miles north of Savannah. Hunter AFB became home to the 2nd Bomb Wing, equipped with B-47 bombers, as depicted on the cover of the event programme.

The close co-operation between race chairman John Rueter of the Savannah Region and Colonel George Newton the Project Officer at Hunter was evident down to the finest details that required attention to make this meeting a success. They even laid out two circuits for the event, one of 3.5 miles that was used for the first three races, and a 5-mile circuit for the main race, part of which had been surfaced with an experimental 'tar-rubber' (which was developed as a less expensive alternative to concrete runways). The switch between the two was made by using the full length of a runway (2 miles) for the long circuit, and by turning off on a taxi way about halfway up the runway for the shorter circuit. Bleachers were erected along the turns, as well as the straightways, these being filled by an estimated 50,000 paying spectators.

It was an early start to the day for the participants of the day's first race, the Shamrock Cup, 52.5 miles for production and modified sports cars under 1500cc. Nineteen cars faced the green flag, which fell at precisely 8.30am. The field was predominantly made up of Porsches and MGs, but it was the OSCA driven by George Moffett and Lloyd Barton in the Glockler Porsche that sped away from the remainder of the pack. At the end of the

An Official Entry Blank for the event at Hunter AFB. (Courtesy Bruce Perry Collection)

first lap, Pace driving a Porsche came through in third place followed by the other Porsches and the HRG, before the first of the MGs appeared, led by Joe Sheppard in a new MG TF model. The top positions did not change throughout the race, Moffett winning by a margin of nearly two minutes ahead of Barton and Pace. The first MG across the finish line was that of R Jones, who finished in eighth place, while Lt Terpening driving a Crosley won Class H. One competitor was less fortunate; Donald Clark driving a Buckler Special flipped his car on the sharp turn coming onto the pit straight. Luckily, damage to both driver and machine was slight, but having come all the way from Canada to complete just two laps made them firm contenders for the 'hard luck trophy.'

The Azalea Cup race covering 77 miles was for production cars over 1500cc, but only ten cars started the race; two Austin-Healeys and eight Jaguars. For the majority of the race, it was a continuation of the battle that took place at MacDill AFB between Boss and Smith for top spot. The two raced within a car's length of each other, swapping the lead for fifteen laps until ill fortune struck Smith as the throttle linkage came adrift. Although Smith made the repairs quickly, Boss had built up a substantial lead. He won comfortably from Hodgeman and Tom Pace, both driving Jaguars, with Kincheloe finishing fourth in an Austin-Healey to win Class D.

Fourteen cars took to the grid for the start of the third race of the day, the Coastal Empire Cup. They were production cars under 1500cc, and modified cars under 1100cc. First away was Thompson in a Porsche 356, followed by two other Porsches, then accelerating from the last row of the grid into fourth position, the Palm Beach Crosley driven by New York cafeteria chain owner George Schrafft. Halfway through the race, Pace took the lead and Schrafft had moved into second place, due to Thompson's Porsche slowing down with plug trouble. At that point, Schrafft was some 30 seconds behind Pace, but a concerted effort over the next six laps saw him close the gap to 14 seconds. The gap continued to close, though Pace had the race under control, and he took the chequered flag six seconds ahead of Schrafft. Thompson in his ailing Porsche managed to secure third spot ahead of Morgan in another Porsche. Joe Sheppard finished in seventh place and was the first MG driver across the finish line.

The Savannah Grand Prix was the 150-mile feature race of the day, open to production cars over 1500cc and modified cars over 1100cc. Class winners were eligible for National Championship points, so it was not surprising that the top drivers were in attendance to try and boost their early season totals. Pre-race favourites for overall honours were the Ferrari 375MMs of Spear and Kimberly, but strong opposition in the form of the Allard JRs entered by SAC, the Cunningham team, a Jaguar C-type, and other Ferraris was also present. In the F Mod Class, it looked like a straight fight between the OSCAs, following a stunning performance at Sebring a week earlier, but with five entered, it was difficult to forecast which one would come out on top.

At the drop of the green flag, Kimberly was first away, followed by Spear in his new 375 MM and Johnston in a Cunningham. As they crossed the line at the end of the first lap, it was Spear in the lead followed by Kimberly, Johnston, Wyllie in a C-type Jaguar and the Ferraris of Lloyd and Lyeth. The order remained the same until the fourth lap when Wyllie's Jaguar sheared an axle shaft and he dropped out of the running. On the same lap, Lyeth and Dave Schilling in an Allard JR collided, resulting in Lyeth having to retire his Ferrari. In Class F Modified, George Moffett was making a break ahead of the other OSCAs and established a commanding lead that was never challenged throughout the race.

Lap seven saw the beginning of an exciting duel between Spear and Kimberly, the result of Kimberly spinning and allowing Spear a 35-second lead. Kimberly clawed his way back, lap by lap, cutting into Spear's lead, and by lap twenty he was only eight seconds behind. The decisive move was made on the 28th lap, when Kimberly covered a lap

Blackwood's Siata 208CS finished the feature race in third place, in Class EM. (Courtesy Michael Eaton Collection)

Charles Moran lines up on the grid for the start of the feature race in the Cunningham C4RK. (Courtesy Michael Eaton Collection)

at over 100mph and broke away from Spear. The final lap saw Kimberly take the chequered flag by a slight margin from Spear with Johnston third, Lloyd fourth and Moffett fifth, in his OSCA. Kimberly won Class CM, Lloyd Class DM, and Moffett took Class FM honours. In an attempt to salvage something from the race, Wyllie decided to take his three-wheel Jaguar out for the final lap, so that he could claim to be running at the end of the race. His audacious ploy gained him third place in Class C Modified.

The Victory banquet for the Savannah National Sports Car Races was provided at the General Oglethorpe Hotel where, after the speeches, the trophies were awarded to the winning drivers. One special award, the Dunlop Gold Cup for outstanding sportsmanship went to Russell Boss for withdrawing from the Savannah Grand Prix, so that he could donate his tyres to a friend with a faster car in the feature race, while the 'hard luck trophy' was awarded to Donald Clark.

No figures were available to indicate what level of money went to the Airmen's Living Improvement Fund.

Bergstrom AFB, Austin, Texas

27/28-3-1954

"... then there's 111-year old Colonel Walt Williams, America's oldest surviving Civil War veteran from Franklin, Texas, who, when requesting tickets to the races last week, was made 'honorary base commander' for Sunday." (Austin American)

Bergstrom AFB was established in 1941 on a 3000-acre site in Del Valley near to the City of Austin. The city's bonds bought the site and it was loaned to the US Government for an indefinite period, with the agreement that ownership would eventually revert back to the City of Austin. At the end of WWII, it was placed in the hands of Tactical Air Command, then transferred to Continental Air Command in 1948, and finally taken over by Strategic Air Command in 1949. Escort F-84E Mustangs were based there to protect the bomber force of B47 and B52 planes in the skies above America. (In reality, the propeller driven F84Es could hardly keep up with the jet engine powered B47 and B52s)

There was no shortage of publicity for this, the second race to be held at the Bergstrom Air Force Base outside Austin, Texas. The *Austin American* newspaper gave its full backing to the races and did a series of

An Official Entry Blank for the event at Bergstrom AFB. (Courtesy Bruce Perry Collection)

articles for the week leading up to race day, including one on a special guest to the event. The guest, Walter Williams, was 111 years old, had fought for the Confederate Army in the American Civil War, and had requested tickets for the races, as he had not attended one before. He was made 'honorary base commander' for the day, and even had the Confederate flag flown on the official's stand in honour of his presence.

Following on just two weeks after the previous National event, there was little time for the competitors to contemplate the rumblings coming

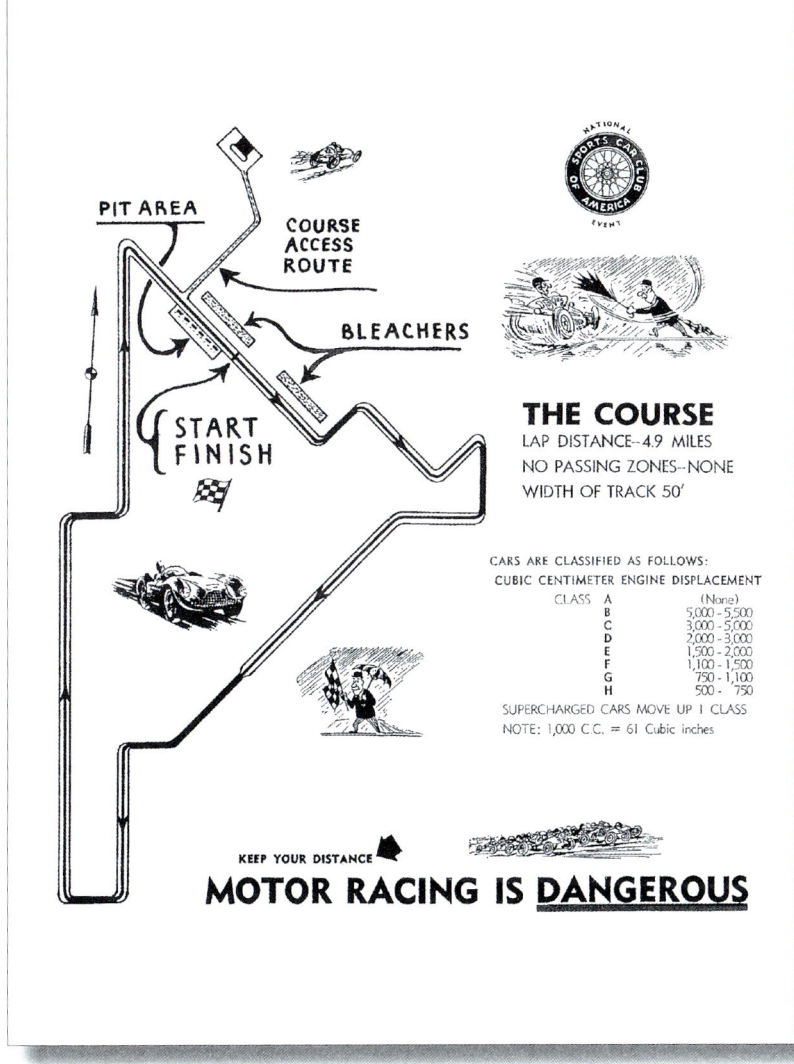

Track layout at Bergstrom AFB. (Terry O'Neil Collection)

from Congress regarding the future of the SAC/SCCA races. However, the SAC consciously cut its expenditure down by half for the Bergstrom event from that of last year, so as to create the right impression to Congress, and, at the same time, potentially make more money to go into the Airmens' Living Improvement Fund. To support the efforts of the Bergstrom AFB, a delegation from SAC headquarters came to add their support to the event. General LeMay was accompanied by Major General John Montgomery, commander of the Eighth Air Force, and Brigadier General Charles Schott, deputy commander. Their appearance was less than coincidental; they wanted to make a point to Congress that their commitment to the races was 100 per cent.

A significant number of changes had been made to the layout of the course from that of 1953. At a meeting between the Base commander, Col Ben W Lichty and officials of the SCCA race committee, two more corners were included to last year's straightway that went past the pits, and one more to the end of the following straightaway. The result of these changes was to increase the length of the course from 4.48 miles to 4.9 miles, and included thirteen turns, making it one of the longest used by the SCCA for National races.

A programme of two 50-mile events and two 100-mile races were planned, the second 100-mile race being a change from the original plan, as the fourth race was going to be 150-miles long. The change came about as a result of the tar on parts of the runway beginning to melt due to the high temperature. Surprisingly, some of the contenders for Championship honours were not in attendance for this meeting. Bill Spear and Russ Boss gave it a miss, as did all of the OSCA drivers, but at least it did give other drivers the opportunity to gain some valuable points.

The first race was for all production sports cars and modified cars up to 1100cc, the honours going to a group of Jaguar drivers who outpaced the other contenders in the race. Riddelle Gregory came home in first place with his Jaguar XK120M, followed by Springer Jones and Ted McGrade in similar cars. Banes driving an Austin-Healey won Class D, Staley in a Porsche 356 won Class F and Crouzet, who worked for Panhard in Los Angeles, won Class HM in a new DB Panhard that he drove from New Orleans to be at the event.

The second race was a warm-up for the main event, but the race was given surprisingly little press coverage, and as such, no great amount of detail of entrants or comprehensive results are available. Kimberly drove to an easy victory, ahead of Riddelle Gregory, this time driving a C-type Jaguar, while Dale Duncan finished in third place driving Dayton's Ferrari 340 Mexico, updated with a 4.5-litre engine. The fourth position was awarded to Bill Jarnigan in the Class D Ferrari 250 MM, as he out-paced the Allard J2s of Gray and Wickham, both of whom were in Class B.

The first of the 100-mile races involved Class F production cars and under 1100cc modified cars and counted towards the SCCA National Championship. With the OSCAs absent from the race, the Porsche drivers were expected to do well. They did not disappoint, as Staley and Bunker fought for the lead between them for eleven laps, before Staley spun out. Staley recovered, but couldn't quite reach Bunker when the chequered flag was shown. In third place came the DB Panhard driven by Crouzet. Despite the car being new (it had landed at New Orleans docks on the Thursday before the races), it proved to be very quick and its performance surprised many of the other drivers. Betts 750cc Giaur stopped 100 yards from the finish line sans oil and a clutch, but the determined Betts got out and pushed the car over the finish line to claim sixth place overall, not a bad effort considering that he had injured an ankle in a crash during practice. For this effort, he was awarded the Sportsmanship Trophy at the Victory dinner.

The second 100-mile race featured the over 1500cc cars, and brought a selection of Ferraris, Jaguars, and Allards to the line, all in contention for championship points.

Kimberly took an instant lead, and although challenged briefly by Carlos Braniff from Mexico in another Ferrari 375MM, the race result was never really in doubt as Braniff's brakes began to fade. Braniff's Ferrari was the one used by Ascari and Farina to win the Nürburgring 1000km in 1953, and, prior to the main race, had been subject to repairs, a new pinion being required. The Jaguar C-type cars of Shelby (owned by Guy and Joe Mabee) and Riddelle Gregory were incapable of the power output of the Ferraris, Shelby finishing in a commendable third place about 300 yards behind Braniff, but Riddelle Gregory retiring after twelve laps. Such was the margin of difference between the top three cars and the rest of the field, it took only twelve laps for Kimberly to overtake the fourth placed car, the Ferrari 250MM driven by Jarnigan was the car originally raced by Phil Hill, then sold to Charles Brown. The best performance of a smaller capacity car was that of John von Neumann's Porsche 550 Spyder, which only had a pushrod engine. It circulated consistently to finish in fifth position, ahead of a group of Jaguar XK120s. Second place in Class FM went to Norman Scott's Continental-MG Special, this being the car that had proved so successful in the Fort Worth races of 1953.

Special awards were handed out at the victory dinner, Jim Saunders taking the 'Hard Luck Trophy' when his MG Special failed after pushing Von Neumann's Porsche in the final race. The Airmen's Living Improvement Fund benefited to the tune of $8315, somewhat below the $24,337 raised in 1953, but followed the trend of lower income at AFBs holding the races the second time around.

Andrews AFB, Maryland, 1/2.5.1954

"Spear was last of 40 entrants to leave the start line when his 4.5 Ferrari stalled at the drop of the green flag." (Road & Track)

Established first as Camp Springs Army Airfield in 1941, the name was changed in 1945 to Andrews Airfield, in honour of Lt General Frank M Andrews, Commander of European operations for all Army Air Forces, who died in 1943. Andrews AFB was home to the 89 Airlift Wing and headquarters to the Military Air Transport Service. The 4320-acre site is located adjacent to Camp Springs, in Prince George County, Maryland, 10 miles southeast of Washington DC.

Considering it was towards the end of 1952 that the SCCA signed up with the SAC to use military bases for sports car races, it was maybe surprising it took the parties such a long time to hold a race event in the vicinity of America's capital city.

It couldn't have come at a better time though, as the very future of the SCCA/SAC races was under threat. If this meeting, held under the noses of the Senators and Congressmen, was to prove an outstanding success, it could sway any future decisions in favour of the races. The event at Andrews AFB, just outside Washington DC (advertised on the cover of the official programme as Washington DC, but actually in the State of Maryland) was the fifth SCCA national event of 1954, and followed on two weeks after the national races held at Pebble Beach. This was the first time that Andrews AFB had been used as a venue for motor racing, and was part of the programme of events organised between the SCCA and Strategic Air Command. Both Bill Spear and Jim Kimberly had missed the Pebble Beach race, and in their absence, Stirling Edwards had picked up valuable championship points. However, none of the established Californian drivers made the trip across from the West Coast to be at Andrews AFB, but representation from the East Coast was strong. Bill Spear, keen to retain his hard-won national title from 1953, was there to challenge Kimberly, who, so far, had got the upper hand with a string of race wins in the early part of 1954.

The paddock and pits were set up on the infield at Andrews AFB. Kimberly came prepared with his red transporter that doubled as a viewing platform. (Courtesy Michael Eaton Collection)

Track layout at Andrews AFB. (Terry O'Neil Collection)

The National Capital Sports Car Races received acclaim, even before a wheel was turned in anger. An article in the *Charleston Daily Mail* stated that Ted Fields, racing director of the SCCA indicated that 146 entries had been received for the 6 races, making this the largest field ever for a sports car event. While the report was in fact inaccurate in its detail at the time, it turned out that a record number of cars did eventually participate in the races.

A circuit of 4.3 miles had been mapped out on the runways of Andrews Air Force Base, containing nine tricky bends and three straightways, the longest of which was 5700ft. The pits were situated on the infield along the straightway where the start/finish line was located, opposite to which a bank of bleachers had been erected by Air Force volunteers. The event was sanctioned by the SCCA and endorsed by the Washington Board of Trade and the Junior Chamber of Commerce, with all proceeds of the event being divided between the Andrews AFB Airmen's Living Improvement Fund, the Washington Boy's Club and the Air Force Aid Society.

The SAC staff volunteered (or were volunteered) to carry out duties to aid with the preparation of the event, an event which held an additional significance to those involved, as President Eisenhower personally planned to present the winner of the 200-mile feature race with a cup. Bleachers had been set up along the start/finish straight, as well as on the far side of the track along the 5700ft straight, to help accommodate an estimated crowd of 60,000. It was rumoured that an Air Force sergeant complained to his Congressman about orders to work on details connected with preparing runways for the races, and, as a result, a few angry Congressmen demanded an investigation into the practice of using SAC bases for sports car races. If this rumour had any truth to it, it would have come on top of similar complaints following the races at MacDill Air Force base at the end of January.

The complaints had landed on the desk of Congressman Errett P Scrivner, who was the chairman of the House Subcommittee on Air Force Appropriations. It was through his position in government that he had to determine whether or not the agreement between the SAC and the SCCA should continue long term. Scrivner had been an adversary of Curtis LeMay, who was Commanding General of the SAC, for a long time, and saw the opportunity to take advantage of LeMay. Although it was denied, Scrivner allegedly expressed his views on the matter from the point of view of an accountant, and did not take into account the human and social aspects of the agreement. Consequently, he was on the warpath and it was a time when the Air Force could have done without the complaints coming from its personnel.

The first of the six races, the George Washington Trophy, provided an early start to the day for the competitors, and was a ten-lap run for production sports cars under 3000cc. Kincheloe and Thompson battled for the lead throughout the entire race, but Kincheloe's black Austin-Healey finally nosed out Thompson's Porsche to take the chequered flag. Roland McConkey came third driving his Triumph TR2, while Fred Allen finished in fourth place.

No sooner had Thompson finished the first race, he was back in action with his Porsche for the Congressional Trophy Race, for modified and production cars under 1500cc. The race attracted a large entry of cars, up to 50, and this time, Thompson was up against the OSCA of Rees Makins, the PBX of Candy Poole and several more Porsche models. Again, it was a closely fought affair between Makins and Thompson, but the PBX, with its smaller engine capacity, wasn't quite able to get on level terms with either of them.

Norwood's Siata passes McNamara's MG during the Congressional Trophy Race. Norwood finished third in Class GM. (Courtesy Michael Eaton Collection)

Henry Wessells III approaches the pits after a practice run in his OSCA. (Courtesy Michael Eaton Collection)

Henry Wessells' OSCA finished nineteenth in the Abraham Lincoln Trophy Race. (Courtesy Michael Eaton Collection)

Kimberly's Ferrari 375MM sits in the paddock. Kimberly won the Abraham Lincoln Trophy, but had the misfortune to retire one lap from the end of the feature race when he was well placed to win the event. (Courtesy Michael Eaton Collection)

The White House Trophy was a race for the MG marque and had a Le Mans-type start. Howard Hanna discusses tactics with his pit crew. (Courtesy Michael Eaton Collection)

Start time approaches for Howard Hanna. (Courtesy Michael Eaton Collection)

In a tight finish, Makins' lighter car just managed to beat Thompson to the chequered flag, with the little PBX finishing in third place ahead of a hoard of larger-engine Porsche and Siata models.

The third race of the morning, the Abraham Lincoln Trophy, was extended to seventeen laps, and was for modified and production cars over 1100cc. This brought out some of the contenders for the President's Cup, to be run in the afternoon, along with others who were hoping to put in a performance good enough to be able to qualify for that race. Some drivers declined to join the race, so saving their cars, assured of their places for the feature event. Among their number were Sherwood Johnston, Bill Spear, Jack Ensley and Fred Wacker. It turned out to be an easy victory for Jim Kimberly in his Ferrari 375MM. He was quickly into the first corner, ahead of the remainder of the field, and stayed there unchallenged for the seventeen laps, and in doing so, lapped most of the other cars. The C-type Jaguar of Erickson came in a distant second, just holding off the challenge of Lloyd and Lyeth, both driving Ferraris, while Hansgen finished in fifth place in George Tilp's Aston-Martin DB2 Offenhauser.

The Thomas Jefferson Trophy was a ten-lap race for production Jaguar and Porsche marques, but such was the difference in performance between the two marques, the overall outcome was never in doubt. It turned out to be two races in one, with the Jaguars taking the first overall ten places. The winner was the experienced Jaguar driver Charles Wallace, gaining additional valuable points towards the Class C National Championship, which he was already leading. The first Porsche across

Hanna gets away smoothly ahead of Nash, but Holbert's MG TD is about to overtake him. (Courtesy Michael Eaton Collection)

A foot race across the concrete, then Hanna and Nash jump into the cars and start their engines. (Courtesy Michael Eaton Collection)

Dust and smoke is all that remains as the field gets away for its ten-lap race. (Courtesy Michael Eaton Collection)

Richardson comes under pressure from Oliver's MG TD. Oliver finished in fifth place in the White House Trophy Race. (Courtesy Michael Eaton Collection)

Howard Hanna in his MG TF during the White House Trophy Race, in which he finished sixth. (Courtesy Michael Eaton Collection)

Dager and Holbert were nigh inseparable during the White House Trophy Race, Dager finishing just ahead of Holbert in seventh place. (Courtesy Michael Eaton Collection)

the finish line in eleventh place was that of Thompson in his third race of the day. He also gained much needed points in his battle with Art Bunker to gain the Class F Production National Championship.

The day's fifth race was another 10-lap affair, this time for production MGs. Grouped in with the production Porsche for Class Championship purposes, the MG drivers had little chance of gaining enough points to make an impact on the Class F Championship. This was due to the more even level of competition within the MG marque, though Bob Fergus and Ralph Durbin were near to the top of the MG rankings at the meetings they attended. This race would prove to be no different

Further down the field, Kahmer and Twist battle for position. (Courtesy Michael Eaton Collection)

Dick Thompson had a good race and finished in third place driving his MG TD. (Courtesy Michael Eaton Collection)

Howard Hanna appears to have the track to himself, as the field stretches out over the final laps of the race. (Courtesy Michael Eaton Collection)

Robert Fergus drives his quick MG TC to second place in the White House Trophy race. Ahead of him is an unidentified MG TD. (Courtesy Michael Eaton Collection)

for them, as Durbin finished first, and Fergus second, a rare defeat for Fergus' quick TC model. The durable Dr Thompson finished in third place, in an MG TD, marginally behind Fergus, with Len Bastrup in fourth place.

Anticipation amongst the spectators had been growing all day for the feature race, The President's Cup, a 203-mile event for modified sports cars from all Classes. Of the forty-one starters, the pre-race favourite was Jim Kimberly, based on his race record so far in 1954, where he had proved nigh unbeatable in his Ferrari 375MM. His closest adversary, Bill Spear, was there to do battle with Kimberly in an identical Ferrari, though, so far, he had come off second best to Kimberly at previous events. Also in the strong field were the Ferraris of Lloyd and Lyeth, together with Wyllie in a C-type Jaguar, Cunningham, Johnston, and Wessells in OSCAs, Hansgen in an Aston-Martin Offenhauser, and nightclub owner Jack Ensley in the Kurtis 500 which he drove in the Carrera Panamericana. Also in the line-up was Fred Wacker, despite blowing the Cadillac engine in his Allard during practice. Not to be put off by this minor inconvenience, Wacker decided to replace the engine with the only one available, that being the one from his truck. His crew worked furiously to remove the engine from the Ford truck that had hauled the car to Maryland. They added high compression heads, and placed the motor in the Allard, giving the car a new lease of life.

The start to the race saw Kimberly pull away into the lead, but as the tyre smoke dispersed, it could be seen that Spear was still in his grid slot, desperately trying to restart the Ferrari which had stalled. The rest of the field was round the first bend before Spear finally fired the car up. Despite his terrible start, Spear was in thirteenth position at the end of the first lap, and was second to Kimberly at the end of lap two. It took another twenty-two laps before Spear finally caught and passed Kimberly, and much to the crowd's delight, the two drivers swapped the lead with each other for the next twenty laps, neither driver being able to gain a significant advantage over the other. Finally, on lap forty-five the deadlock was broken, and Kimberly managed to draw away from Spear. The majority of the spectators anticipated that Kimberly would retain the lead and go on to win the race, but then disaster struck for Kimberly on the penultimate lap. Clouds of smoke poured from the Ferrari as it crossed the line for the last lap, the car slowed, then stopped two miles from the finish line. The Ferrari had thrown a rod, and the engine had seized. With victory in his hand, a quirk of mechanical fate had suddenly

Kimberly and Spear, both in Ferrari 375MM models, continued their season long battle for supremacy in Class CM. While Kimberly won the Abraham Lincoln Trophy Race, Spear went on to win the feature race, the President's Cup. (Ozzie Lyons, courtesy Pete Lyons Collection)

snatched it away from him. Spear couldn't believe his luck as he passed the stricken car and went on to take the chequered flag.

William Lloyd finished the race in second place, the only driver on the same lap as Spear, with Cunningham taking a commendable third place in the OSCA, ahead of Wyllie in the Jaguar C-type, and Lyeth in his Ferrari. Jack Ensley took Class BM honours in his Kurtis, Kincheloe was winner of Class D, and McNought the victor in Class EM in his Maserati. Wacker finished the race in his rebuilt Allard, though was not placed. After the race, the mechanics set to work on removing the engine, and replaced it in the truck, so that the car could be hauled away. Devastated by his bad luck, Kimberly could not bear to hang around after the race, and left the venue as soon as he could, an action quite out of character of this sportsman.

Spear was invited to the White House to receive the President's Cup from President Dwight Eisenhower. (Courtesy Abbie Rowe)

On the next day, Bill Spear and Alfred Momo, Spear's chief mechanic, went to the White House, where President Dwight D Eisenhower presented Bill Spear with the President's Cup.

As for the National Championship standings, Spear made gains over Kimberly in the Class C Modified section, though it might have proved to be too little too late to make any difference to the ultimate result. Meanwhile, Cunningham took a useful lead in the Class F Modified section with his third overall position in the race.

Chanute AFB, Rantoul, Illinois

6.6.1954

"Poor man races, too – but doesn't win ... How about the guy, who, instead of wearing red gloves, wears an oil-soaked red baseball cap, canvas sneakers, wrinkled slacks, and Walgeen sun glasses? What's he doing out there, rubbing elbows with the got-rocks? Bert Bertine (Champaign – Urbana Courier) interviewing race entrant Norm Patton

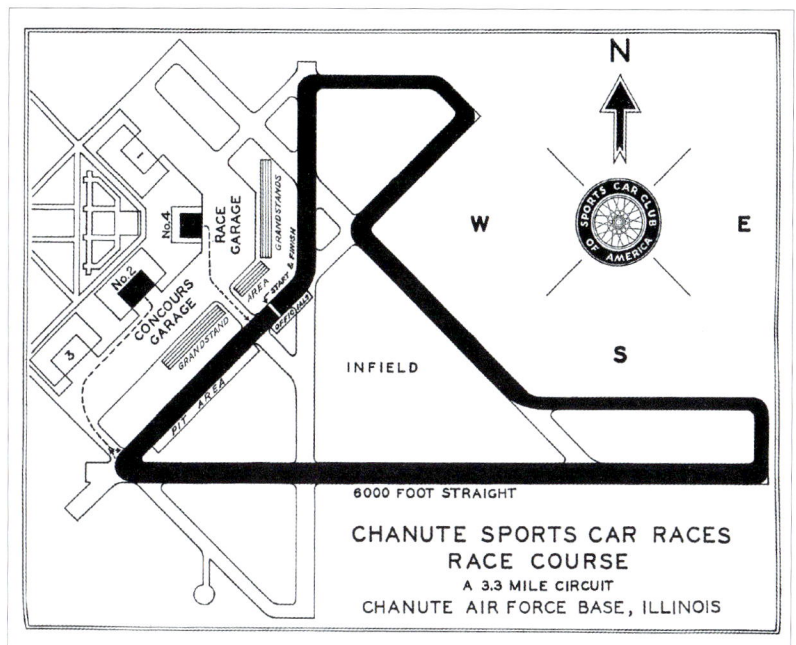

Track layout at Chanute AFB. (Terry O'Neil Collection)

The success of last year's Regional event at Chanute helped elevate the venue to National event status for 1954, and was the seventh National event of the year. After the excitement of the Andrews AFB races the next National race was held at Golden Gate, San Francisco, and was another opportunity for the West Coast drivers to earn Championship points in the absence of such people as Spear, Cunningham and Kimberly. McAfee, Edwards, David, Coppell and Stroppe were the beneficiaries.

Although a National event, it was once more down to Ben Harris III and the Chicago Region to liase with Major General Byron Gates, Commander of Chanute AFB, to ensure that this event was as good, if not better than the 1953 meeting. Early signs indicated that it would be, with a staggering 292 entries received by the organisers. To accommodate all of these entries, technical inspection of the cars started on Thursday prior to the races on Sunday. Hundreds of military personnel were assigned duties on a shift roster, and were allowed to watch the races, and those airmen who worked in the concession stands received a percentage commission on their sales.

The importance of the Chanute race was emphasised when it was announced that three media teams would be present; *NBC television*, *Fox Movietone News*, and *Time Magazine*, and that the races would be featured on the *Dave Garraway Show*.

The same 3.3-mile track layout of 1953 was used, described in the *Waukesha Daily Freeman* as "… one of the most difficult airport road racing tracks in America. Two hairpin bends and three right-angle turns are interspersed around the curvy track. The main feature of the course is a 1-mile straightway, which ends with one of the hairpin bends." The *Champaign-Urbana Courier* said, "Sports car drivers all feel that pushing one of the sleek little jobs around the Chanute layout is tougher than driving in the '500' at Indianapolis, because of the turns – all of them flat."

The large number of entries did, in theory, create a problem for the race committee, as they needed to limit the number of cars in any one race to a certain number, so as to conform to safety standards. Taking into consideration the length of the track, together with the width of the runways, it was decided by the race committee that a maximum limit of 70 cars per race would be acceptable. Any entries beyond that number would only be permitted to enter if the equivalent number of the top 70 dropped out before the start of a race. Fortunately for the organisers, their fears were allayed because a number of entrants pulled out due to technical problems following practice sessions.

The first race started at 9.30am when the crowd was still building up, and involved production cars of unlimited capacity together with modified cars up to 1100cc. According to the scant race reports available, around 76 cars entered the race, with 10 cars withdrawing after practise. Chuck Wallace drew a good grid position and pulled away in his Jaguar at the start of the race. If the report in the Champaign-Urbana Courier is to be believed, then the expected challenge from the other Jaguars failed to materialise - instead the challenge came from a Moretti and a MG TD. At the end of sixteen laps, Wallace was first over the finish line, and depending on which source is taken as being correct, either Robb in the Moretti or Allin in the MG TD was second, and the other car third. Len Franke, driving his new Austin-Healey 100, finished in fourth place.

The second race, for modified cars over 1100cc, saw the greatest number of entries withdraw, either because of mechanical ailments following practice, or the feeling of a need to conserve the car for the feature race when Championship points were at stake. 35 cars arrived at the start line and as the flag dropped, pre-race favourite Jim Kimberly, with a rebuilt engine in his Ferrari, sped away from the rest of the field. Main interest focused on further down the field, where there was a tussle between Fred Wacker's Arnolt-Bristol and Ted Boynton's Frazer-Nash, for the Class EM accolades. Wacker was originally scheduled to race his Allard J2X Cadillac, but a crash at Elkhart Lake the previous week put his car out of action. He adapted well to the Arnolt-Bristol, but not well enough to stop Boynton from taking first place in class EM. In the overall results, Katskee's C-type Jaguar was second to Kimberly, with Lunken third in his newly acquired Ferrari 340AM. He had bought the car on the Friday prior to the race from Jim Kimberly. Lyeth finished fifth overall and first in Class DM, while Jack Ensley won Class BM in his Kurtis, and Frank Bott was victorious in Class FM driving an OSCA.

The Central Illinois Cup was the third race of the day, and was for production cars under 1500 cc and modified under 1100cc. It turned out to be a straight fight between the OSCA of Rees Makins and three Porsche 356 models, with Makins managing to hold them off over the 16 laps to finish first. Max Goldman, who was last year's winner, finished second with Ballenger's Porsche Super in third place.

The feature race of the day started promptly at 2.30pm, and, by now, an estimated crowd of over 45,000 spectators had gathered. 43 of the original entry of 61 lined up on the grid for the race start, one notable absentee being Bill Spear. Kimberly in his Ferrari sped into the lead from his starting position in the second row, shortly after the second turn, and was never headed. Kimberly's nearest competitor, Ernie Erickson, was a full lap behind at the finish. Erickson fought hard to get on terms with Kimberly, but the Ferrari had too much power for the Jaguar C-type. Katskee's C-type finished in third place. The expected duel between Kimberly and Dale Duncan in a similar car never materialised, when Duncan's Ferrari, owned by Dayton, broke down in the second race and couldn't be repaired in time for the feature race. Duncan drove an Allard J2X instead, and finished in fifth place. Lunken, in the ex-Kimberly Ferrari 340AM, had to drop out of the race while running in second position, when first he had fuel pump problems, then the clutch burned out.

Kimberly averaged just over 79mph for the race to chalk up his ninth victory in ten major sports car races during 1954. Kimberly's average speed was slower than the previous year, despite having a more powerful car, but, this time round, he was never challenged for the lead.

Class wins went to Ensley in Class BM, Kimberly in Class CM, Hassan in Class DM, Wacker in Class EM and Stewart in Class FM, though not in his new OSCA. It seemingly had trouble and he borrowed the Uilhein Special from Karl Brocken for the race. Overall, thirty-two of the forty-three starters finished the race.

The day ended with a big Victory banquet for drivers and owners, at which Class prizes were announced and distributed. While financial details of the event were still being calculated, it was apparent that the Chanute event had provided substantial evidence to support hopes of the SCCA that it would be allowed to continue its races at the Air Force bases in future years.

At the Victory dinner, Major General Gates gave an enlightening speech in which he frankly conceded that the hundreds of Chanute men whose work made the races possible were 'not volunteers.' He stated: "You can't get something for nothing," referring to the funds for the Airmen's Living Improvement Fund.

He pointed out: "In the military, no one volunteers. But they will pitch in when they are told, and particularly when it is explained to them what is being accomplished. In this case, they were ordered to help themselves at the same time that they were receiving valuable training." He readily conceded that an investigating congressman could easily find men "… who didn't like it," but again, he pointed out, "… there are a lot of things about military training that men don't like, but which they must do if we are to have an effective military force." He declared that the men were receiving "… wonderful training in logistics." He added, "… no one has yet devised a method of getting things like this for nothing. As long as I am in command, we will not sit back and wait for Congress or anyone else to give us something for nothing. We'll work to earn these things for ourselves." (Quotes extracted from *The News-Gazette* newspaper.) Major General Gates finished by arguing that the policing of such events represented a useful exercise of manpower. The Air Force (and the SCCA) position was stated eloquently when he said: "You don't offer your kid a dime to shine your shoes, then, when he's done the job, withhold the dime because he's used up shoe polish, electric light and a polishing cloth."

Following on from the newspaper coverage given to Jim Kimberly in 1953 by the *Champaign-Urbana Courier*, the newspaper carried an article that personified the SCCA in the eyes of many outsiders. The gist of the article was concerning the opportunities available to the amateur drivers with low budgets to win prizes. It didn't take them long to figure out that the chances were pretty slim, and that an elite band of drivers were the recipients of many of the prizes. So was it fair competition, or was it just a rich man's game? Despite this notion being denied by the SCCA publicity director, Dave Allen, the conclusion drawn was that poorer men might dare to own a sports car – but they wouldn't win any races unless it was among themselves.

While the article provided food for thought, it didn't influence the people that mattered – the race drivers. For many a driver, the idea was to participate and enjoy the spectacle, a notion that the newspaper interviewer had obviously not got to grips with.

Offutt AFB, Omaha, Nebraska

4.7.1954

"Ruth Hampton, who appears in the Universal-International sports car motion picture Johnny Dark awarded McAfee a big kiss in the victory lane after the feature event. The conversation between McAfee and Miss Hampton went like this: 'Well, what are you going to do, give me a kiss or the roses?' He received both." **(Sports Car)**

The 9th national event was back at the headquarters of the SAC - what better place to be on the 4th of July? The race programme itself was no problem, however, the backdrop to the meeting was clouded by the issues raised by Congress, regarding the costs involved in running such events. In late April, according to the *Kansas City Times* (29 April edition), Republican Congressman Errett P Scrivner was reported as saying: "They (the races) cost Uncle Sam far more than is contributed to the recreational funds of sponsoring bases. It would be far better and cheaper if Congress, upon need shown, appropriated more money, $3 or $4 or $5 per airman, for added comforts, rather than have these races disrupt base operations."

Scrivner cited Offutt as a case in point in 1953, where, according to him, more money was spent than netted. Col AJ Beck, Commander of Offutt, refuted these claims. "Simply not so. Our records are open for inspection by Congressman Scivener or anyone else, any time. I cordially invite the citizens of Omaha and the State of Nebraska and Iowa to come to the races on 4 July and see for themselves the manner in which it is conducted, and to inspect the many benefits provided by last year's race." The war of words had commenced, and it was against this backdrop of claim and counter-claim that preparation for the races took place.

An Official Entry Blank for the event at Offutt AFB. (Courtesy Bruce Perry Collection)

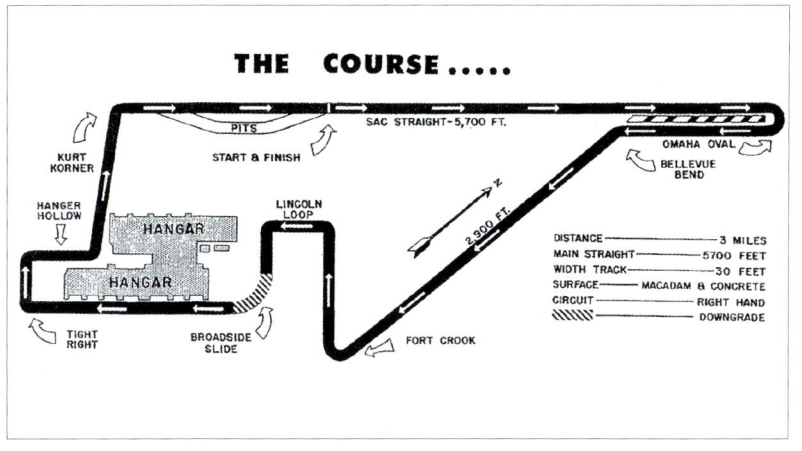

Track layout at Offutt AFB. (Terry O'Neil Collection)

One week after the Chanute event, a national event had been held at Westover AFB, where Kimberly re-asserted his dominance of Class C Modified cars, with Wallace, Bentley, and Makins picking up maximum Championship points in their Classes.

A gap of three weeks made a welcome break, which allowed for repairs to various cars, and, as a result, there was a full entry list for the Offutt meeting. Well, nearly a full entry list, as on the evening before race day, a distraught Jim Kimberly had to pick up the telephone and tell the organisers he would not be able to compete in the event, due to transmission problems on his Ferrari 375MM.

Advertised as another 'East meets West' race event, it was down to the Project Officer, Col W Gray, to ensure that he secured promises from the West Coast drivers to compete at Offutt. His success was limited to a few commitments, though, importantly, he managed to secure an entry from Parravano for Jack McAfee to drive his Ferrari 375MM.

Once again, despite the rumblings emanating from Congress, General LeMay fully committed the SAC airmen to the tasks involved in making this a memorable event for a gathering of more than 25,000 spectators. He even went to the extent of personally taking Congressman Roman Hruska for a ride around the track in a Cunningham. The course was the same three-mile circuit as used at the 1953 event, with the pits situated on the inside of the track, along the 5700ft straightway. 23,000 bleacher seats were set out along the outside of the track in anticipation of the large crowd turning out to watch the races. Not wishing to ruffle even more feathers back in Washington, LeMay also made sure that he didn't fall foul of the Nebraska Liquor Commission, following some adverse publicity about the illegal sale of alcohol that had filtered through to Congressman Scrivner from other events. Although technically, the AFB didn't come under the jurisdiction of the State of Nebraska, LeMay conceded that the sale of liquor on the base would have an adverse impact upon the sales of civilian licensees in the vicinity of the base.

As was now customary, all proceeds of the event went towards the Airmen's Living Improvement Fund at the base holding the event, in this instance, Offutt AFB.

For the first time in SCCA history, grid positions for each race were determined by the times obtained during the mandatory practice runs on Saturday.

The four-race programme started on Monday with the Strategic Air Command Trophy Race, a fifty-mile event for production sports cars. Jaguars dominated the proceedings, the OSCA driven by Rees Makins being the only other marque to come within the top ten overall finishers. Loyal Katskee took over the lead on the fourth lap, and steadily increased the gap between his car and the rest of the field, finishing the race one lap ahead of the other competing cars. Art Bunker was first in

Ralph Dubin was a serious contender for the Class F Driver's Championship and scored valuable points in the Ak-Sar-Ben Trophy Race at Offutt AFB. (Courtesy Michael Eaton Collection)

Despite his winning performance at Andrews AFB, Spear was losing ground to Kimberly in the Class CM Driver's Championship. With Kimberly not in attendance at Offutt, Spear picked up valuable points by finishing second in the Omaha Grand Prix event. (Ozzie Lyons, courtesy Pete Lyons Collection)

Class F and Makins first in Class GM, while the Siata Spyder driven by AG Place won Class HM.

Thirty minutes later, Katskee was back on the start line, this time in his C-type Jaguar for the seventeen-lap Cornhusker Cup Race. Despite there being a competitive field of Ferraris and another Jaguar C-type, Katskee took the lead on the first lap, and was unchallenged for the duration of the race, finishing 48 seconds ahead of the second-place car, the Jaguar C-type driven by Ernie Erickson. Finishing in third, fourth, and fifth places were the Ferraris of Lloyd, Irish, and Lyeth. Walter Gray was sixth overall and first in Class BM, while Boynton took Class EM honours in his Frazer-Nash, and Marvin Weinman won Class FM in an OSCA MT4.

Race three was for championship points, the thirty-three laps, 100-mile Ak-Sar-Ben Trophy, for production cars under 1500cc and modified cars under 1100cc. The race was completely dominated by the OSCA driven by Rees Makins. Makins had managed to lap the complete field by the end of the twenty-first lap, and went on to win the race easily. His closest competitor was Art Bunker in his Class F Production Porsche, who finished in second place, followed by Paul Van Antwerpen in a similar car. In Class HM, Roy Cherryhomes drove his Moretti to a Class victory and surprised a lot of people by finishing the race in sixth position. The points earned by Makins made him the second highest point scorer in the Championship to date.

The final race of the day was the Omaha Centennial Grand Prix, a two hundred-mile event for production cars over 1500cc and modified cars over 1100cc. With Kimberly missing from the field, it was a great opportunity for the other drivers to make up lost ground in Class C Modified of the Championship, something that didn't escape the notice of defending champion Bill Spear in particular. From the time the flag dropped, it was a race that would be determined between the Ferraris of McAfee and Spear – a case of 'East meeting West' on equal terms.

The temperature was reaching near to 100°F as the race started. McAfee made the better start and led at the end of the first lap, but, second time around, it was Spear in front. It only took four laps into the race before the leading pair were overtaking the back markers in the field, with Spear maintaining his fragile lead. Never more than a few seconds separated the two cars, until the 57th lap, when McAfee edged in front. By now, Spear was without meaningful brakes and had to downshift to make his way round the ninety degree bends, and, to add to his discomfort, the tailpipe of his Ferrari was dragging on the tarmac. Meanwhile, McAfee was gradually pulling away in the lead, and there he stayed for the next ten laps to cross the finish line twenty seconds ahead of Spear, thus denting his hopes of retaining his title.

Katskee, driving his C-type Jaguar for the second time that day, moved up to third place on the twenty-second lap and remained there to finish in that position ahead of the OSCA driven by Phil Stewart, who finished six laps behind first place McAfee. There were Class wins for Charles Moran driving a Cunningham C4RK (Class B), Lyeth and Schaeffer in Class DM, Ted Boynton in a Frazer-Nash in Class EM, and Phil Stewart driving an OSCA in Class FM.

Jack McAfee was well rewarded for his efforts at the end of the race, as not only had he accumulated 1000 points, but he was also presented with a kiss and a bunch of roses from film actress Ruth Hampton. Not a bad days work.

Lockbourne AFB, Columbus, Ohio

8.8.1954

"Marshall kept me posted from the pits on just how the race was progressing. All I had to do was follow his instructions" – Jim Kimberly (Columbus Dispatch)

By now, it had been recognised that the whole future of the SCCA/SAC races was in the balance. Not that the drivers could do anything about it - they still turned up in their droves to support the Second National Sports Car Races at Lockbourne AFB. Despite other claims, this truly was the largest entry to a sports car race to date, with a total of 188 entrants, including the Cunningham team, just back from their trip to Europe.

Curtis LeMay was keen for the SAC to continue playing an active part in promoting the events, as was chronicled by the *Charleston Daily Mail* on 28th July. "A B-47 jet bomber will appear over Charleston on Wednesday 4 August, in connection with the promotion of ticket sales for sports car races at Lockbourne AFB." Project Officer Lt Col Donald McCash was equally aware of his responsibility of ensuring that everything was geared to catering for an estimated crowd of over 60,000 turning up to watch the races. Everything from traffic management, car parking, ticket sales, and the placement of bleachers fell to him and his vast army of volunteers.

The layout of the track had been modified slightly for this meeting from the one of the previous year. Two hairpin bends had been replaced by gentler curves at the northern end of the circuit and one straightway reduced by 50ft, which caused a slight reduction in the length of the track to 3.53 miles. The pits were located to the inside of the 4600ft straightway, while the back straight measured 6800ft, allowing high speed runs for the larger cars.

After the cars were checked in for inspection, they were housed in

An Official Entry Blank for the event at Lockbourne AFB. (Courtesy Bruce Perry Collection)

Admission ticket to the event at Lockbourne AFB. (Courtesy Wolery Collection IMRRC)

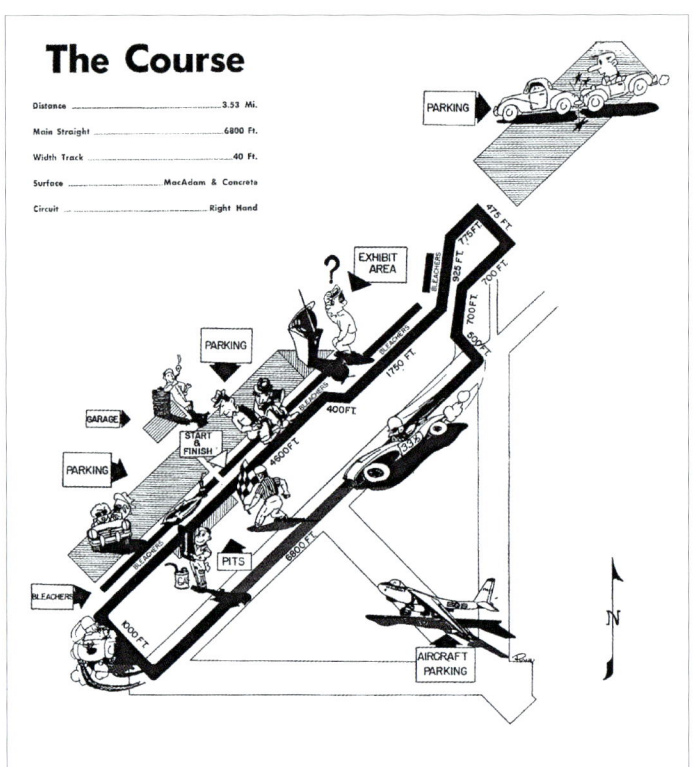

Track layout at Lockbourne AFB. (Terry O'Neil Collection)

one of Lockbourne's large hangars. There they would stay, to be tuned and worked on between races. Meanwhile, in the pit area, an increasing number of teams were parking large tractor-trailer units fitted out as repair shops. In stark contrast, one competitor with a Formula 3 car, Harry Whitney, turned up with his car on a trailer pulled by a 1937 LaSalle hearse. "My wife and I sleep in the hearse when we go to the races," he said. (*Columbus Dispatch*)

Practice on Saturday afternoon gave way to frantic work on the cars housed in the hangars on Saturday evening, and long into the night. One car in particular was a centre of attraction, that being the Siata belonging to John Bentley. The Siata had sustained a good deal of bodywork damage after being run into, and the mechanics were determined to have it repaired and ready for the first race in the morning. Their determination paid off, as the car was on the grid for the 'Skyhawker 50' event, albeit in less than pristine condition.

Sunday dawned bright, earlier for some than others, as the first race was scheduled to start at 9am. The 'Skyhawker 50' was a 14-lap event for production sports cars of less than 1500cc, and modified sports cars of less than 1100cc. 56 cars appeared on the grid, and, at the drop of the green flag, shattered the early morning silence. They departed with much noise and confusion as they sorted themselves out. Bunker and

A view of the open pit area at Lockbourne, with the Cunningham team truck dominating the scene. (Courtesy Wolery Collection IMRRC)

A British-made Triumph TR2 was provided as the official pace car for the races. (Courtesy Wolery Collection IMRRC)

One of the giant hangars at Lockbourne was made available to competitors to store and prepare their cars. Fred Wacker's Arnolt-Bristol receives some attention. (Courtesy Wolery Collection IMRRC)

*An unidentified MG TD corners hard during the Skyhawker 50 Race.
(Courtesy Wolery Collection IMRRC)*

*Hannig's Siata finished 5th in Class GM in the Skyhawker 50 Race.
(Courtesy Wolery Collection IMRRC)*

*Alfred Momo standing behind the OSCA driven by Rees Makins.
(Courtesy Wolery Collection IMRRC)*

*Dr Robert Quinn and friends discuss their chances of success in the Lockbourne Trophy Race.
(Courtesy Wolery Collection IMRRC)*

*In the Skyhawker 50 Race, John Norwood's Siata is being challenged for position by Charles Stoll's MG TD.
(Courtesy Wolery Collection IMRRC)*

Jim Brookes drove the Triumph TR2 to 6th place in the Ohio Valley Cup Race. (Courtesy Wolery Collection IMRRC)

Kerr's Jaguar XK120 looks to be about to overtake Glowacke's Austin-Healey 100 in the Ohio Valley Cup Race. (Courtesy Wolery Collection IMRRC)

Thompson, both driving Porsches, occupied the first two positions with Makins' OSCA in third place at the end of the first lap. By the third lap, Makins had caught and passed both Porsches, and it was very soon after that Thompson dropped out of the race with failing oil pressure.

Steele, driving a Porsche, moved up into third place, followed by Bentley in a Siata Spyder, and Van Antwerpen's Porsche. Towards the close of the race, Bentley moved ahead of Steele, but other than that, the top positions remained the same. As the chequered flag dropped, it was Makins first, followed by Bunker and Bentley. Candy Poole put in a remarkable performance in his HM Class PBX to finish sixth overall, well ahead of the first MG home, that of Norm Patton in ninth place.

The Ohio Valley Cup Race was for production cars over 1500cc, and brought together Jaguars, Austin-Healeys and TR2s. Like so many of these races held previously, it would end up as two separate events in one – in this case, it was Jaguar versus the rest. Excitement was not the order of the day, as Wallace, to his credit, took an immediate lead as the flag dropped, and remained unchallenged throughout the race in his Jaguar XK120M, gaining more championship points. Katskee led Manting briefly, then the roles reversed for the remainder of the race, while further down the field, Bob Fergus was trying to get his Austin-Healey among the Jaguars. He, in turn, was followed by the Triumph TR2 driven by Jim Brookes, taking advantage of the gaps being opened up by Fergus. While neither of them was in contention for top overall placing, they managed to finish fifth and sixth, each taking a Class victory.

The third race of the day, the Scioto 50, brought the modified under-2-litre cars to the start grid. The OSCAs had dominated this class of racing for the whole of the season, and a strong presence of OSCAs was evident here. There were five entered in Class FM and one in Class GM, that of Rees Makins who had already built up an unassailable lead in the Class GM championship race. It also marked a rare appearance of Jim Kimberly driving something other than his usual Ferrari 375MM that had been so dominant during the season. He had purchased an OSCA from James Simpson, who, in turn, had just acquired a new one. Pitted against the OSCAs was an assortment of Siatas, Arnolt-Bristols, Porsches, and various other marques, many of which entered the race more in hope than belief of a good Class result.

From the start of the race, Simpson took an immediate lead, followed by Schrafft in a new 2-litre Siata, and Kimberly in his OSCA, Briggs Cunningham in another OSCA, and Paul Ceresole with a Kieft-Bristol. On the next lap, Shrafft had dropped down to fifth with Linton's OSCA coming through to take fourth place. The picture was beginning to look familiar, as OSCAs quickly filled the top spots. It wasn't until

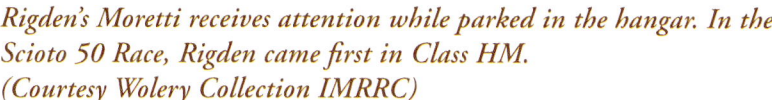

Rigden's Moretti receives attention while parked in the hangar. In the Scioto 50 Race, Rigden came first in Class HM. (Courtesy Wolery Collection IMRRC)

the ninth lap that their domination was dented, as Karl Brocken took over fourth place in his Uihlein Special. As the end came into view, it was Simpson who took the chequered flag. Briggs Cunningham took the second spot together with valuable Championship points, and Jim Kimberly was third ahead of Brocken and Kuhn, who had made a late dash to take fifth place. Rees Makins took the honours in Class GM with his OSCA, while Class HM went to Jerry Rigden driving a Moretti.

Finishing in 20th place was John Bentley in his Siata 1100cc Spyder. By doing so, he finished 2nd in Class GM, maintaining a wonderful record for the season of not finishing outside of the top two places in his Class, for the numerous races he entered. It also left him in an unassailable second position in Class GM of the National Championship.

Forty-seven production Porsches and MGs lined up for the fourth race, and in addition, there was one Formula 3 car, determined to start, despite there being no Class for the car. Brig General Hewitt Wheless, Lockbourne AFB commander, started the race, and it was the experienced Porsche driver Dick Thompson who took an early lead, gradually pulling away from second-place Warren Steele, as the race progressed. Harry Whitney delighted the crowd by making his way up to third place in his Cooper F3 car, but disappointment was to follow as the little car stopped on the circuit, having lost the engine. "I think I could have beaten the Porsches if the engine had held up," said Whitney after the race. Meanwhile, Thompson continued his way unhindered to the finish, followed by Steele, Bunker, and Van Antwerpen, all driving Porsches. The first MG to finish was that driven by Bob Fergus, narrowly beating Durbin to fifth place.

The Buckeye Cup produced what was probably the most competitive field for the season so far. Although most of the Championship Class awards were settled, there was still personal pride at stake for the drivers,

The Uihlein Special was driven by Karl Brocken to 4th place in the Scioto 50 Race. (Courtesy Wolery Collection IMRRC)

Karl Brocken in the Uihlein Special during the Scioto 50 Race. (Courtesy Wolery Collection IMRRC)

The two Porsche 356 America models were entered by Bob Steele from Michigan, and ran in the Skyhawker 50 Race. (Courtesy Wolery Collection IMRRC)

Van Antwerpen drove the Porsche 356 Super to 5th place in the Skyhawker 50 Race. (Courtesy Wolery Collection IMRRC)

The grid line-up for the start of the Skyhawker 50 Race. (Courtesy Wolery Collection IMRRC)

Dr Robert Quinn's MG TC. (Courtesy Wolery Collection IMRRC)

The Cunningham Team cars were parked together in one corner of the garage. Briggs Cunningham drove the OSCA to second place in the Scioto 50 Race. (Courtesy Wolery Collection IMRRC)

and, in some cases, a few points to be made. Five Ferraris, five Allards, four Jaguar C-types – two each of Excalibur – Cunningham, and Kurtis were on the grid alongside the smaller OSCA, Arnolt-Bristol, Austin-Healey, and TR2 models. Pre-race favourites had to be the Ferraris, based on what had happened so far in the season, though circumstances emanating from the start, and the first lap of the race, could well have changed people's minds. First of all, and not for the first time this year, Bill Spear stalled his Ferrari when the starting flag dropped. He hastily tried to start it again and kangarooed his car about thirty yards, and after making terribly expensive noises from the rear end, it finally died. Exit one Ferrari from the fray. Meanwhile, the other cars had made off in a crescendo of sound as far as the first corner, where there was a mix-up involving about six cars, among them Kimberly and Walters, both driving Ferraris. Kimberly lost some spokes from the front left wheel, and Walters stopped to pull away his right wing from the wheel, and, in so doing, found himself two laps down on the rest of the field. Away from the carnage, Lunken had taken the lead ahead of Katskee's C-type Jaguar, and they held these positions until the seventh lap. Having been given re-assurance from his pit board on the state of his damaged wheel, Kimberly set about catching the leaders; on lap seven, he caught and passed Katskee. Walters, too, had been climbing his way back into contention, despite having to pit so that officials could inspect the damage to his car, though it was doubtful he could catch up with Kimberly. The two Cunninghams were also in contention together with Jack Ensley's Kurtis, which had lost fourth gear.

Walters was having the drive of his life. Leaving his pit area, he

William Spear sits in his Ferrari as Alfred Momo and other mechanics tune the car in preparation for the feature race. (Courtesy Wolery Collection IMRRC)

Spear alights from the Ferrari 375MM in the paddock next to Makins' OSCA. (Courtesy Wolery Collection IMRRC)

The Cunningham Team had a mobile workshop that was even larger than Kimberly's truck, though Cunningham did have four cars to look after. (Courtesy Wolery Collection IMRRC)

Something has caught Briggs Cunningham's attention as he stands with Alfred Momo, next to the Cunningham C4R that he would drive to 6th place in the Buckeye Cup Race. (Courtesy Wolery Collection IMRRC)

was two laps down on Kimberly, but with controlled aggression and superb driving skill through the corners, he un-lapped himself once, and, going through the speed traps at over 160mph, began to catch Kimberly for the second time. Unfortunately for him, he ran out of laps and finished under half a lap behind Kimberly, but well ahead of a third-placed man, Eb Lunken in another Ferrari. Sherwood Johnston drove a steady race to finish fourth in his Cunningham, ahead of Katskee and Briggs' Cunningham. Lloyd's Ferrari won Class DM, his Class Championship already assured, Salzgaber won Class E, extending his lead in that Class, and Frank Bott took Class FM in his OSCA. As Fred Wacker's Arnolt-Bristol was the only entry in Class EM, the car was moved up into Class DM, where it placed second in Class behind Lloyd's Ferrari.

By winning the Buckeye Trophy, Kimberly secured beyond challenge his claim to the 1954 sports car driving championship. After the race, Kimberly was full of praise for his mechanic, Marshall Lewis. "Give all the credit to this

A couple of army volunteers oversee the work being done on Briggs Cunningham's car. (Courtesy Wolery Collection IMRRC)

fellow here: Marshall kept me posted from the pit on just how the race was progressing. All I had to do was follow his instructions. Several spokes were knocked out of the left front wheel, but Marshall checked it from the pits and told me it was still running true, so I kept on going." (*Columbus Dispatch*)

The next SCCA/SAC race should have been held at Stead AFB, scheduled for the 26 September. In view of the alleged complaints being

Cunningham's mobile workshop was also used as a timing stand to plot the progress of team drivers. In front of it stand two C4R models. (Courtesy Wolery Collection IMRRC)

Competitor's plaque for the event at Lockbourne AFB. (Courtesy Bruce Perry Collection)

directed at Congress, and the nature of unhelpful signals emanating back from Congress, Curtis LeMay had no choice but to put all SAC races that had not been signed off by the Air Force and the SCCA on hold. According to a report in the Nevada State Journal, the Reno Chamber of Commerce, which had been assisting with the arrangements for the races at Stead AFB, asked General LeMay whether the event could be held at the Base if it was sponsored by the Chamber, rather than the Base. General LeMay reluctantly denied the request, so the Chamber then enquired of Major General Charles E Born, whose Crew Training Air Force would soon supplant the SAC as the agency in charge of the Stead AFB programme, whether he would assent to the races. Again, the answer was no, and, as a result, the Chamber of Commerce cancelled their plans to help with the races.

March AFB, Riverside, California

7.11.1954

"The crowd was treated to what was probably the greatest array of top drivers and machines ever assembled at an SCCA event." (Sports Car)

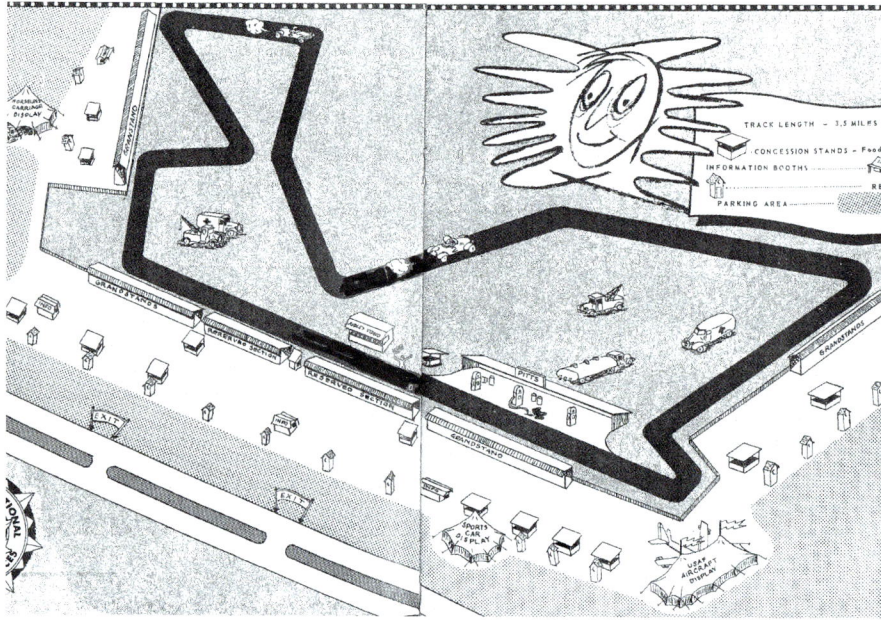

Track layout at March AFB. (Terry O'Neil Collection)

The final national meeting of the 1954 season went ahead at March AFB Riverside as originally planned, and followed on from three other national events; one on the northwest coast at Seattle, and the other two on the eastern side of America, at Thompson Raceway and Watkins Glen. The event at Seattle attracted drivers from the West Coast of America, but, apart from a handful of drivers including Leson, David, Kieckhefer, Eyerly, and Edwards, the results in terms of championship points gained would leave little impression on the final outcome in each of the championship Classes. Edwards, David and Kieckhefer turned out to be the beneficiaries from this event.

With Class C Modified already won, Kimberly sat out the Thompson meeting, and Spear, although at the event, also sat out the race that counted towards the championship, therefore not adding to his points total in that Class. Rees Makins won his race in the OSCA, and secured the Class G Modified title, while in Class F Modified, Cunningham drove his OSCA to victory and took the title.

Watkins Glen attracted many of the big names on the eastern coast of America, with Frank Bott winning the Queen Catherine Cup in his Class F Modified OSCA, while Phil Walters won the Grand Prix in a Cunningham C4R, with Kimberly in second place. Jack Ensley finished 9th overall and 3rd in Class B Modified, but it was enough to secure the Class B Modified title. Lloyd continued to dominate Class D Modified, having secured that Class championship a few races previously.

Agreements had already been signed by the SCCA and SAC to hold the Riverside event, prior to the order from Congress to stop the races coming into force. It would prove to be the very last race held jointly between the two parties, signalling the end of an era, and a successful working partnership. With the majority of the Class championship sorted out, it was perhaps surprising that a few of the leading drivers from the East Coast made their way to California for this, the final National race of the season. It could be that the occasion was not to be overlooked as the SAC/SCCA races had been rewarding for them, and there was no chance of anymore to follow. If Lockbourne had been good, then this was going to be its equal. The SCCA were leaving the SAC bases with a bang, not a whimper!

This, the Second Annual Orange Empire National Sports Car Races, was run under the auspices of the Los Angeles Region of the SCCA, and sponsored by the March AFB Airmen's Living Improvement Fund, with all proceeds going to that cause. There were high hopes that the revenue would exceed that of 1953, when more than $24,000 was netted.

The circuit had been changed beyond recognition from the previous meeting, only the main straightway remaining the same. The other previous straightway had disappeared, and there were now eleven turns instead of nine. Looks were obviously deceptive though, as according to the official information, the track still measured 3.5 miles in length.

There were seven races on the programme this year, the day's programme opening with a seven-lap race over the 3.5-mile course for junior drivers in cars under 1500cc. An assorted group of twenty-four cars lined up on the grid, and, as the flag dropped, it was Frank Monise in an MG Special owned by Ed Freutel (formerly the Barlow Simca) that took the lead. Monise was followed closely by Eschrick driving a Simca, Chapman in an OSCA, and Stevens in a Jupiter Special. Eschrick dropped out on the second lap, and, with one lap to go to the finish, Monise had to retire with a blown piston, elevating Chapman into the lead. Meanwhile, Mauser in another MG Special, owned by Joe Playan, had been moving steadily through the pack, and gained second place from Stevens on the last lap. In fourth place overall and first in Class F Production was James Orr in a Porsche, followed by Class HM winner Ray Howard driving Ray Biehl's Moretti.

The second race brought out the junior drivers with over 1500cc cars, with at least thirty-nine cars on the grid. Bob Smith in a Kurtis 500 took the lead ahead of Eric Hauser in a Special, and Howard Hively in his Ferrari 250MM. Hively took the lead on the second lap, building up a considerable lead over Hauser who had also gone past Smith. Worse was to come for Smith, as Morgensen and McGraw also passed him, but he fought back to regain fourth place from McGraw before the end of the race. Hively finished first, well ahead of Morgensen and Hauser. Fifth overall and first in Class C Production was Bill Miller in a Jaguar. Other Class winners were Knowle in a Triumph TR2 Class EM, and George Rosenthal in a TR2, Class EP.

Standard production MGs took to the grid for the start of the third race. What should have turned out to be an uneventful seven-lap race turned into one of controversy: three of the top four finishing cars were subject to protests, which were upheld by the technical inspectors, and which led to the disqualification of the cars driven by Trennert, Parkinson and Kaplan. The official order of finish thus became Meyers (elevated from second place), Choisser (elevated from fifth), and Curland (elevated from sixth place.) As to how, or why, the cars passed their original technical inspection was open to debate.

It was back to normality for the next race involving production cars in all classes. The field consisted mainly of Jaguars and MGs interspersed with Porsches, Corvettes, Panhards and HRG cars. It was more a case of racing for Class honours, as the Jaguars were expected to sweep the field. They didn't disappoint, taking the first eight places overall, with Jim Peterson leading them home. Second place went to Bill Miller, and third place to Loyal Katskee, while the best of the rest was the Corvette driven by Peterson, followed by Kunstle in his Porsche. First MG home was that of Robert Brigham in fifteenth place.

Race five was unique in that it marked the first time that a Ladies' race had been included in a National event. Just as significant was that out of the twenty-nine original entries, the nineteen starters represented the largest field for a Ladies' race ever to take the start grid for the five-lap race. Their cars were divided into two categories, under 1500cc and over 1500cc, with awards given to the winners of both groups.

When the flag dropped, Ina Balchowsky, driving her husband's Bu-Ford Special, took the lead, followed by Mary Davis in a Triumph TR2, and Jane McBratney in a Morgan Plus 4. On the third lap, Dr H Hoppe, at the wheel of a Corvette, took over third place, and on the last lap moved into second, making the finishing order Balchowsky, Hoppe, Davis, and McBratney. In the under 1500cc class, Pat Sawyer in a Singer led from start to finish, followed by Cosette Lawrence in an MG and Jan Stevens in a Jowett Jupiter Special.

The sixth race, which was for under 1500cc cars, should have witnessed the appearance of John von Neumann, with his new Porsche 550 Spyder sporting a 4-overhead cam engine. Unfortunately however, the car was badly damaged by fire during practice after an encounter at high speed with an MG, and was withdrawn from the race. It would have been interesting to see it in action against the all-conquering OSCAs, of which there were five entered for this race where Championship points were at stake. Thirty-seven cars were on the start grid, and it was Pete Lovely in his VW-Porsche Special that took the lead on the first lap. He was quickly caught and then passed by Simpson and Stewart, both driving OSCAs, and was closely followed by a third one, that driven by Bill David, and Marion Playan in his MG Special. The two OSCAs at the head of the field battled for superiority, until on the tenth lap, Stewart dropped out with engine trouble. Just as intense was the struggle between Lovely and David. David had taken second place and successfully staved off the challenge of Lovely, until the final corner of the last lap, when Lovely managed to get ahead of David and beat him to the chequered flag.

By the time the final race was due, weather conditions had changed, and a strong wind whipped up the dust and sand, making visibility less than ideal for drivers and the estimated 40,000 paying spectators. At least forty-one cars lined up for the start of the race, among them a Mercedes 300SL making its race debut on the West Coast of America. There should also have been Jim Kimberly's latest Ferrari purchase, a Ferrari 410S, but after practising in the car, Jim declared that it was not yet prepared to his liking, and preferred to race his trusty Ferrari 375MM. After achieving seventeen victories out of nineteen starts in it, who could blame him? The rumour down the pit lane was that the new Ferrari 375 Plus was putting out a bit too much power for Jim's liking, and this was not the occasion to try it out. Also on the start line, making a welcome return after illness, was Phil Hill. Hill had had a bad year following his accident in Mexico at the end of 1953, and had suffered from stomach ulcers. Just before the March AFB race, Hill had received a note attached to a photograph of a newly bodied Ferrari from Allen Guiberson which read: "Guaranteed not to cause ulcers." Hill responded positively and accepted the drive in the Ferrari 375MM used by Braniff at Bergstrom AFB earlier in the year.

Kimberly and Hill were joined on the grid by seven other Ferraris, two Jaguar C-types, three Kurtis, two Allards, a host of Specials, and various other marques. It was a disappointment, though, not to have the Cunningham team in attendance, as last year, the team had taken the first two places of the main event. Possibly, Briggs Cunningham already knew what lay in store for him in 1955, realising that his own cars were rapidly becoming less competitive, and he decided to end on a high note with the win at Watkins Glen.

As the flag dropped, the decibels increased, and, as a cloud of smoke cleared, the crowd could see that Michael Wysong, driving Guy Mabee's Mabee Special, had out-dragged his rivals to take the lead. Wysong was overtaken by Kimberly before the first corner, and had to give way to Johnston and Spear in very quick time. Kimberly was not renowned for making serious mistakes, but this was one occasion when he paid the penalty of spinning on the approach to the main straight. He went off track, hit a hay bale and had to wait for the entire field to go by before he was able to restart. A pit stop to change a bent wheel left him more than a lap behind the leaders.

Spear had taken the lead after Kimberly's mishap, followed by the Ferraris of Hill, Johnston, and Edwards. The top four positions remained that way – only the fifth position was contested. In the end, that position went to Lou Brero in his Jaguar C-type, a lap down on the leader, with Kimberly closing him down in sixth, having worked his way back through the field. In the gathering darkness, Spear reached the chequered flag, followed by Hill and Johnston. If OSCAs had proved dominant in their Class throughout the season, Ferraris had matched in this race, with six of them finishing in the top seven places.

Michael Wysong finished in a creditable ninth position, taking Class BM, Howard Hively in a Ferrari winning Class DM, and Walter Kieckhefer in a Triumph TR2 winning Class EP, and securing joint second place in Class EP National Championships.

Racing at SAC bases had an obvious advantage that would be lost to competitors in future – the use of expansive covered hangars, so that drivers could work on their cars in comparative comfort and safety. (Courtesy Michael Eaton Collection)

1954 Statistical Review

MacDill AFB 31.1.1954

Imperial Polk County Tr 15 laps	Race distance 50 miles	Class FM, GM, HM	Starters 13

Race winner's time 42min 51.4sec	Average speed 69.99mph

91	OSCA MT4 1450	1133	Johnston S	1oa	1cl FM
2	OSCA MT4 1450	1138	Brewster W	2oa	2cl FM
1	OSCA MT4 1450	1137	Cunningham B	3oa	3cl FM
46	Porsche 356 America		Crawford E	4oa	4cl FM
14	Porsche 356 America		Lipe G	5oa	5cl FM
77	OSCA MT4 1100	1112	Makins R	6oa	1cl GM
42	Cisitalia 202 MM Corsa		Gent R	7oa	2cl GM
34	Porsche 356 America		Brundage H	8oa	6cl FM
111	Palm Beach Crosley		Schrafft G	9oa	1cl HM
28	Siata 300BC 1100 Spyder		Keller R	10oa	3cl GM
20	Bandini Crosley		Goldman M	11oa	2cl HM
81	Renault Special		Gauding H	12oa	3cl HM
43	Siata 300BC 1100 Spyder		Haskell I	13oa	4cl GM

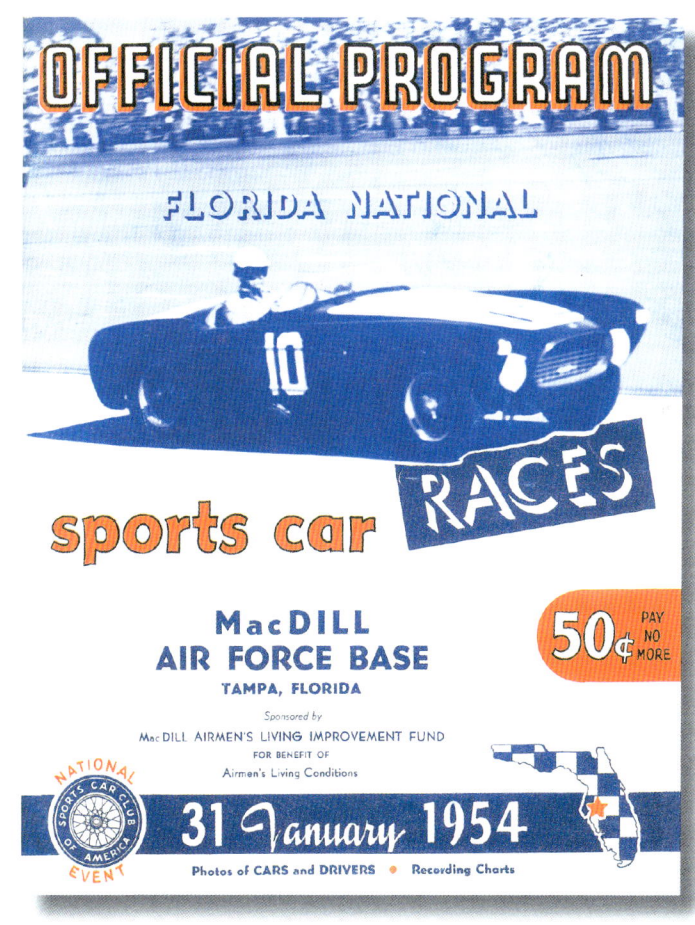

Programme cover for the MacDill AFB event.
(Terry O'Neil Collection)

Festival of States Tr

Festival of States Tr 15 laps	Race distance 50 miles	Class BM, CM, DM, EM	Starters 17

Race winner's time 38min 54.6sec	Average speed 77.04mph

5	Ferrari 375 MM	0364 AM	Kimberly J	1oa	1cl CM
6	Ferrari 250 MM	0348 MM	Walters P	2oa	1cl DM
38	Allard JR Cadillac	3403	Tilley R	3oa	1cl BM
27	Jaguar C-type	XKC 032	Erickson E	4oa	2cl CM
15	Jaguar C-type	XKC 034	Huntoon G	5oa	3cl CM
10	Ferrari 225 S	0166 ED	Lloyd W	6oa	2cl DM
7	Kurtis 500 S Cadillac		Johnston S	7oa	2cl BM
23	Ferrari 225 S	0220 ED	Lunken E	8oa	3cl DM
53	Kieft-Bristol		Ceresole P	9oa	1cl EM
49	Allard JR Cadillac	3402	Schilling D	10oa	3cl BM
31	Siata 208 CS	CS 069	Blackwood R	11oa	2cl EM
40	Jaguar XK120M		Stiles P	12oa	4cl CM
33	Fageol-Porsche Special		Fageol L	13oa	3cl EM
26	Allard J2X		Carveth R	14oa	4cl BM
37	Allard JR Cadillac	3404	Scott R	Dnf L5	
54	Jaguar C-type	XKC 030	Katskee L		
45	Allard J2		Grey W		

Gasparilla Trophy

Gasparilla Trophy 15 laps	Race distance 50 miles	Class C, D, F	Starters 33

Race winner's time 44min 12.9sec	Average speed 67.85mph

19	Jaguar XK120M	Boss R	1oa	1cl CM
65	Jaguar XK120M	Smith W	2oa	2cl CM
101	Jaguar XK120M	Victor W	3oa	3cl CM
71	Jaguar XK120M	Bentley J	4oa	4cl CM
62	Jaguar XK120M	Pace T	5oa	5cl CM
35	Austin-Healey 100	Huntoon G	6oa	1cl D
4	Jaguar XK120M	Frankland J	7oa	6cl CM
41	Jaguar XK120M	Kaplan J	8oa	7cl CM
11	Jaguar XK120M	Sparacino P	9oa	8cl CM
73	Jaguar XK120M	Ludington F	10oa	9cl CM
12	Jaguar XK120	Young A	11oa	1cl C
80	Porsche 356	Haycraft C	12oa	1cl F
29	Porsche 356 Super	Proctor F	13oa	2cl F
79	Porsche 356	Schmidt J	14oa	3cl F
75	Porsche 356	Pace R	15oa	4cl F
51	MG TC	Fergus R	16oa	5cl F
18	MG TD	Durbin R	17oa	6cl F
56	MG TD	Compton G	18oa	7cl F
47	MG TC	Fowler T	19oa	8cl F
57	MG TD	Roemer R	20oa	9cl F
50	Jaguar XK120	Puleston R		2cl C
21	Austin-Healey 100	Bailey P	dnf	
16	Jaguar XK120M	Lavac H		
30	MG TC	Lyle L		
32	MG TC	Lindenmeier H		
39	MG TD	Boyles T		
55	MG TD	Dupree J		
58	Jowett Jupiter	Welles R		
60	Jaguar XK120 M	Gary R		
61	Jaguar XK120	Hendricks J		
64	MG TD	Pesslano L		
69	MG TD	Lyon R		
72	MG TD	Daly J		
76	MG TD	Kelley L		

Gov D McCarty Memorial

Gov D McCarty Memorial 60 laps	Race distance 200 miles	Class Unrestricted	Starters 44

Race winner's time 2hrs 38mins 8.64secs	Average speed 75.88mph

5	Ferrari 375 MM	0364 AM	Kimberly J	1oa	1cl CM
3	Cunningham C4R		Walters P	2oa	1cl BM
6	Ferrari 250 MM	0348 MM	Fitch J	3oa	1cl DM
10	Ferrari 225 S	0166 ED	Lloyd W	4oa	2cl DM
15	Jaguar C-type	XKC 034	Huntoon G	5oa	2cl CM
37	Allard JR Cadillac	3404	Scott R	6oa	2cl BM
38	Allard JR Cadillac	3403	Tilley R	7oa	3cl BM
49	Allard JR Cadillac	3402	Schilling D & Hassan C	8oa	4cl BM
27	Jaguar C-type	XKC 032	Erickson E	9oa	3cl CM
19	Jaguar XK120M		Boss R		1cl C
120	Jaguar XK120M		Habersin A		2cl C
68	Jaguar XK120M		Wilson D		3cl C
12	Jaguar XK120		Young A & Morton J		1cl CP
23	Ferrari 225 S	0220 ED	Lunken E	Dnf L41	3cl DM
31	Siata 208 CS	CS 069	Blackwood R		1cl EM
53	Kieft-Bristol		Ceresole P		2cl EM
1	OSCA MT4 1450	1137	Cunningham B		1cl FM
46	Porsche 356 America		Crawford E		2cl FM
14	Porsche 356 America		Lipe G & Irish R		3cl FM

29	Porsche 356 Super		Proctor F		1cl F-P
70	Porsche 356		Bentley J		2cl F-P
18	MG TD		Durbin R		1cl F-MG
51	MG TC		Fergus R		2cl F-MG
30	MG TC		Lyle L		3cl F-MG
77	OSCA MT4 1100	1112	Makins R & Bott F		1cl GM
28	Siata 300BC 1100 Spyder		Keller R		2cl GM
81	Renault Special		Gauding H		1cl HM
20	Bandini Crosley		Goldman M		2cl HM
9	Ferrari 340 MM	0324 AM	Spear W	Dnf L17	
42	Cisitalia 202MM Corsa		Gent R		
111	Palm Beach Crosley		Schrafft G	Dnf L9	
	Cunningham C3		Stiles P	Dnf	
54	Jaguar C-type	XKC 030	Katskee L		
62	Jaguar XK120M		Pace T		
2	OSCA MT4 1450	1138	Brewster W		
91	OSCA MT4 1450	1133	Johnston S		
4	Jaguar XK120M		Frankland J		
33	Fageol-Porsche Special		Fageol L	Dnf	
11	Jaguar XK120M		Sparacino P		
22	Glockler Porsche	10447	Cooper W		
26	Allard J2X		Carveth R	Dnf	
45	Allard J2 Oldsmobile	J1859	Gray W	Dnf	

26	MG TD		Whitaker J	10oa	6cl F
59	MG TD		Boyles W	11oa	7cl F
65	MG TD		Richardson R	12oa	8cl F
50	Crosley		Terpening P	13oa	1cl H
46	MG TD		Shields J	14oa	9cl F
25	MG TC		Lyle L	Dnf L3	
55	Buckler Special		Clark D	Dnf L2	
92	MG TD		Rahal E	Dnf	
23	MG		Quinn R	Dnf	
56	Porsche 356		McLaughlin D	Dnf	
77	Siata 300BC 1100 Spyder	ST 435 BC	Bentley J	Dnf	

Azalae Cup 22 laps	Race distance 77 miles	Class O 1500cc	Starters 10

Race winner's time 59min 9.3sec	Average speed 78.1mph

3	Jaguar XK120M		Boss R	1oa	1cl C
28	Jaguar XK120M		Hodgman H	2oa	2cl C

Hunter AFB 14.3.1954

Shamrock Cup 15 laps	Race distance 52.5 miles	Class U 1500cc	Starters 19

Race winner's time 41min 30.12sec	Average speed 75.9mph

2	OSCA MT4 1450	1139	Moffett G	1oa	1cl FM
40	Glockler Porsche	10447	Barton L	2oa	2cl FM
33	Porsche 356		Pace R	3oa	1cl F
21	HRG		Flickinger P	4oa	2cl F
35	Porsche 356		Waring T Dr	5oa	3cl F
73	Porsche 356		Morgan J	6oa	4cl F
60	Allard Palm Beach		Wilson C	7oa	3cl FM
37	MG TD		Jones R	8oa	4cl FM
115	MG TF		Sheppard J	9oa	5cl F

Programme cover for the Hunter AFB event.
(Courtesy Bruce Perry Collection)

29	Jaguar XK120M		Pace T	3oa	3cl C
48	Austin-Healey 100		Kinchloe W	4oa	1cl D
49	Jaguar XK120		Young A	5oa	4cl C
66	Jaguar XK120M		Woodbury W	6oa	5cl C
39	Jaguar XK120M		Smith W	7oa	6cl C
31	Jaguar XK120M		Blackmar A	8oa	7cl C
11	Jaguar XK120M		Sparacino P	Dnf	
64	Austin-Healey 100		Dantone W	Dnf	

Coastal Empire Cup 22 laps	Race distance 77 miles	Class F, GM, HM	Starters 14

Race winner's time 1hr 6min 28.4sec	Average speed 69.5mph

33	Porsche 356 Coupe		Pace R	1oa	1cl F
111	Palm Beach Crosley		Schrafft G	2oa	1cl GM*
1	Porsche 356		Thompson R Dr	3oa	2cl F
73	Porsche 356		Moran J	4oa	3cl F
77	Siata 300BC 1100 Spyder	ST435BC	Bentley J	5oa	2cl GM
70	Porsche 356		Hawthorne D	6oa	4cl F
115	MG TF		Sheppard J	7oa	5cl F
25	MG TC		Lyle L	8oa	6cl F
65	MG TD		Richardson R	9oa	7cl F
46	MG TD		Shields J	10oa	8cl F
42	Siata 300BC 750 Spyder		Haskell I	Dnf L7	
20	Crosley		Stetson H	Dnf	
61	Porsche 356 Super		Antwerpen P	Dnf	
34	Siata 300BC 750 Spyder		Jones E	Dnf	

* moved from Class HM

Savannah GP 30 laps, 5 miles	Race distance 150 miles	Class C, BM, CM, EM, FM	Starters 31

Race winner's time 1hr 32min 55.8sec	Average speed 97.2mph (5-mile circuit used)

5	Ferrari 375 MM	0364 AM	Kimberly J	1oa	1cl CM
9	Ferrari 375 MM	0382 AM	Spear W	2oa	2cl CM
51	Cunningham C4R		Johnston S	3oa	1cl BM
44	Ferrari 225 S	0166 ED	Lloyd W	4oa	1cl DM
2	OSCA MT4 1450	1139	Moffett G	5oa	1cl FM
52	OSCA MT4 1450	1137	Cunningham B	6oa	2cl FM
63	OSCA MT4 1450	1138	Brewster W	7oa	3cl FM
43	Cunningham C4RK	5218R	Moran C	8oa	2cl BM
91	OSCA MT4 1450	1133	Simpson J	9oa	4cl FM
22	Ferrari 225 S	0218 ET	Melville A	10oa	2cl DM
32	OSCA MT4 1350	1114	Linton O	11oa	5cl FM
97	Kieft Bristol		Carpenter W	12oa	1cl EM
39	Jaguar XK120M		Smith W	13oa	1cl C
11	Jaguar XK120M		Sparacino P	14oa	2cl C
54	Jaguar XK120M		Schmidt J	15oa	3cl C
14	MG Special		Allen F	16oa	6cl FM
40	Glockler Porsche	10447	Cooper W	17oa	7cl FM
30	Kieft Bristol		Ceresole P	18oa	2cl EM
19	Kieft MG		Howell E	19oa	8cl FM
64	Austin-Healey 100		Dantone B	20oa	3cl DM
24	Allard JR Cadillac	3402	Schilling D	21oa	3cl BM
45	Siata 208 CS	CS 069	Blackwood R	22oa	3cl EM
16	Jaguar C-type	XKC 009	Wyllie M Dr	23oa	3cl CM
67	Allard JR Cadillac	3403	Tilley R	Dnf	
57	Ferrari 250 MM	0348 MM	Lyeth J	Dnf L4	
1	Porsche 356		Thompson R	Dnf L3	
3	Jaguar XK120M		Boss R	Dns	
7	MG mod		Franklin W	Dnf	
28	Jaguar XK120M		Hodgman H	Dnf	
39	Jaguar XK120M		Smith W	Dnf	
4	Lester-MG		Black D	Dnf	

Bergstrom AFB 28.3.1954

Race 1 10 laps	Race distance 50 miles	Class Prod & HM	Starters

Race winner's time 42min 1.2sec	Average speed 71.39mph

81	Jaguar XK120M		Gregory R	1oa	1cl C
31	Jaguar XK120M		Jones S	2oa	2cl C
54	Jaguar XK120M		McGrade E	3oa	3cl C
3	Jaguar XK120M		Fenner H	4oa	4cl C
16	Austin-Healey 100		Banes J	5oa	1cl D
60	Austin-Healey 100		Roberts J	6oa	2cl D
81	Alfa Romeo		Velasquez J	7oa	3cl D
39	Porsche 356		Staley J	8oa	1cl F
66	DB Panhard		Crouzet F	9oa	1cl HM
49	Porsche 356 Super		Bunker A	10oa	2cl F
18	Porsche 356		Richter R	11oa	3cl F
23	Nardi		Whitehead B		2cl HM
58	Siata 300BC 750 Spyder		Place A		3cl HM
15	Jaguar XK120				

21	Siata 300BC 750 Spyder		Rose D		4cl HM
82	Jaguar XK120		Talley C		
85	Porsche 356		Rich J		
45	MG TD		Chaney-Brown S		
6	Jaguar XK120		Koehne G Mrs		
88	Porsche 356 Special		Rodier R		
46	MG		Joerns J		

Race 2 10 laps	Race distance 50 miles	Class BM, CM, DM, FM	Starters

Race winner's time 37mins 7.2secs	Average speed 80.82mph

5	Ferrari 375 MM	0364 AM	Kimberly J	1oa	1cl CM
80	Jaguar C-type	XKC 033	Gregory R	2oa	2cl CM
1	Ferrari 340 Mexico	0226 AT	Duncan D	3oa	3cl CM
52	Ferrari 250 MM	0260 MM	Jarnigan W	4oa	1cl DM
20	Allard J2 Oldsmobile	J1859	Gray W	5oa	1cl BM
43	Allard J2		Wickman R	6oa	2cl BM
9	Porsche 550 Spyder	550-003	Von Neumann J	7oa	1cl FM
22	MG Special		Saunders J	8oa	2cl FM
24	Aston Martin DB2		McMullen L	9oa	2cl DM
32	Continental-MG Special		Scott N	10oa	3cl FM
10	Ferrari 166 MM	0024 M	Lozano I	11oa	3cl DM

Programme cover for the Bergstrom AFB event. (Courtesy Bruce Perry Collection)

44	Ferrari 375 MM	0286 AM	Braniff C	Dnf
77	OSCA MT4 1100	1112	Makins R	Dnf
26	Ford Special		Van Buren F	Dnf
36	Maserati A6GCS		Braden	
42	MG Special		Wickman R	
43	Allard J2X		Fenner H	
99			Vakovenko P	
30	Chysler Special		Peebles K	dns

Race 3 20 laps	Race distance 98 miles	Class U 1500cc	Starters

Race winner's time 1hr 26min 45.6sec	Average speed 69.16mph

49	Porsche 356 Super		Bunker A	1oa	1cl F
39	Porsche 356		Staley J	2oa	2cl F
66	DB Panhard		Crouzet F	3oa	1cl HM
50	Porsche 356		Rydford J	4oa	3cl F
85	Porsche 356		Rich J	5oa	4cl F
59	Giaur Crosley		Betts W	6oa	2cl HM
58	Siata 300BC 750 Spyder		Place A		3cl HM
64	MG TC				
45	MG TD		Chaney-Brown S		
88	Porsche 356 Special		Rodier R		
46	MG		Joerns J		
51	MG		Reinberg D		
2	Siata 300BC 750 Spyder		Robb H		
18	Porsche 356		Richter R		
19	MG 1250		Heath R		
21	Siata 300BC 750 Spyder		Rose D		
23	Nardi		Crimm L		
25	MG		Spillman E		
27	MG		Barnett F		
34	MG		Gilbert R		
35	MG		Peterson H		
55	Porsche 356		Cook F		

Race 4 20 laps*	Race distance 98 miles	Class O 1500cc	Starters

Race winner's time 1hr 7min 51sec	Average speed 88.43mph

*(30-lap race re-scheduled to 20 laps.)

5	Ferrari 375 MM	0364 AM	Kimberly J	1oa	1cl CM
44	Ferrari 375 MM	0286 AM	Braniff C	2oa	2cl CM
48	Jaguar C-type	XKC 022	Shelby C	3oa	3cl CM
52	Ferrari 250 MM	0260 MM	Jarnigan W	4oa	1cl DM

9	Porsche 550 Spyder	550-003	Von Neumann J	5oa	1cl FM
53	Jaguar XK120M		Attaway C	6oa	1cl C
54	Jaguar XK120M		McGrade T	7oa	2cl C
32	Continental-MG Special		Scott N	8oa	2cl FM
3	Jaguar XK120M		Fenner F	9oa	3cl C
20	Allard J2 Oldsmobile	J1859	Gray W	10oa	1cl BM
7	Allard J2 Cadillac		Joerns J / Koehne G Mrs	11oa	2cl BM
16	Austin-Healey 100		Banes W	12oa	2cl DM
15	Jaguar XK120				
49	Porsche 356 Super		Bunker A		
39	Porsche 356		Staley J		
80	Jaguar C-type	XKC 033	Gregory R	Dnf L12	
77	OSCA MT4 1100	1112	Makins R	Dnf	
	Alfa Romeo Disco Volante		Velasquez J		
26	Ford-Mercury Special		Van Beuren F		
22	MG Special		Saunders J	Dnf	
24	Aston Martin DB2		McMullin L		
30	Chrysler Special		Peebles K	dns	

Also in the entry list

27	MG		Barnett F	F
4	MG 1250		Gladston W	F
56	Jowett Jupiter		Wright G	FM
55	Porsche 356		Cook F	F
2	Siata 300BC 750 Spyder		Robb H Jr	HM
14	Jaguar XK120		Mudge J	C
			Petrie W	
51	MG		Reinberg D	
33	MG1250		Clifford H	F
37	Jaguar XK120		Smith E	
			Smith T	
88	Porsche 356 Special		Rodier R	F
34	MG 1250		Gilbert R	F
35	MG1250		Petersen H	F
29	Jaguar XK120		Masterson R	C
36	Maserati A6 GCS		Burns R	E
			Grasscock L	
19	MG1250		Heath R	F
21	Siata 300BC 750 Spyder		Rose D	HM
99			Yakovenko P	
25	Ford Special		Spilman E	CM
17	Kurtis 500 S Cadillac		Ensley J	BM

Andrews AFB 2.5.1954

George Washington Tr 10 laps	Race distance 43 miles	Class U 3 litres	Starters

Race winner's time 37min 53.8sec		Average speed 68.08mph	

85	Austin-Healey 100		Kincheloe W	1oa	1cl D
65	Porsche 356		Thompson R Dr	2oa	1cl F
149	Triumph TR2		McConkey R	3oa	1cl E
45	Austin-Healey 100		Allen F	4oa	2cl D
152	Austin-Healey 100		Bulck E	5oa	3cl D
89	Austin-Healey 100		Holley J	6oa	4cl D
93	Austin-Healey 100		Dantone W	7oa	5cl D
25	Porsche 356 Super		Lilley W	8oa	2cl F
100	Austin-Healey 100		Fusca J	9oa	6cl D
71	Porsche 356 Super		Fleming W	10oa	3cl F
66	MG TF		Durbin R	11oa	4cl F
163	MG TF		Hanna H	12oa	5cl F
174	MG TD		Long W	13oa	6cl F
170	Porsche 356		Flynn J	14oa	7cl F
177	MG TD		Pessolano L	15oa	8cl F
146	Triumph TR2		Robinson J	16oa	2cl E
73	Morgan		McKinsey R	17oa	7cl D
90	Austin-Healey 100		Zuver G		SGP 1
7	Porsche 356		Jenkins E		SGP 28
19	Porsche 356 Super		Bunker A		SGP 16
48	Porsche 356 Super		Graham J		SGP 19
113	MG TC		Black D		SGP 14
127	Austin-Healey 100		Livingstone K		SGP 2
134	Porsche 356		Mahoy C		SGP 24
150	MG TD		Perry H		SGP 27
168	Austin-Healey 100		Campbell Schmidt A		SGP 6
172	MG TD		Kahmer R		SGP 25
130	MG TD		Twist T		SGP 18

Congressional Trophy 10 laps	Race distance 43 miles	Class F, GM, HM	Starters @50

Race winner's time 38min 8.88sec		Average speed 67.63mph	

107	OSCA MT4 1100	1112	Makins R	1oa	1cl GM
65	Porsche 356		Thompson R Dr	2oa	1cl F
74	PBX Crosley		Poole C	3oa	1cl HM

#	Car	Chassis	Driver	Pos	Class
71	Porsche 356 Super		Fleming W	4oa	2cl F
118	Porsche 356 Super		Koster A	5oa	3cl F
60	Porsche 356 Super		Cooper J	6oa	4cl F
77	Siata 300BC 1100 Spyder	ST435BC	Bentley J	7oa	2cl GM
159	Porsche 356		Baker R	8oa	5cl F
59	Bandini Crosley		Rudkin H	9oa	2cl HM
119	Siata 300BC 1100 Spyder		Norwood J	10oa	3cl GM
68	MG TD		Bastrup L	11oa	6cl F
62	MG TD		Richardson R	12oa	7cl F
153	Porsche 356		Link H	13oa	8cl F
163	MG TF		Hanna H	14oa	9cl F
172	MG TD		Richardson T	15oa	10cl F
30	Siata 300BC 1100 Spyder		Pompeo T	16oa	4cl GM
128	MG TC		Baptista F	17oa	11cl F
38	Siata 300BC 750 Spyder	ST 407 BC	Yares R	18oa	3cl HM
112	MG TD		Kegeles S	19oa	12cl F
177	MG TD		Pessolano L	20oa	13cl F
66	MG TF		Durbin R	21oa	14cl F
32	MG TD		Ryan J	22oa	15cl F
24	MG TD		McNamara J	23oa	16cl F
150	MG TD		Perry H	24oa	17cl F
171	MG TD		Richardson T	25oa	18cl F
56	MG TC		Wyllie M	26oa	19cl F
144	Nardi		Vitale D	27oa	4cl HM
7	Porsche 356		Jenkins E	Dnf	
19	Porsche 356 Super		Bunker A		SGP 7
21	Siata 300BC 750 Spyder		Keller R		SGP 36
25	Porsche 356 Super		Lilley W		SGP 3
31	Crosley		Stetson H		SGP 49
39	MG TD		Holbert R		SGP 29
41	MG TD		Ward M		SGP 28
48	Porsche 356 Super		Graham J		SGP 4
70	Siata 300BC 750 Spyder	ST 425 BC	Ahr K		SGP 47
72	Cisitalia 202MM Corsa		Gent R		SGP 38
81	Giaur		Dominianni F	Dnf	SGP 48
108	Siata 300BC Spyder		Flink L		SGP 44
111	Palm Beach Crosley		Schrafft G	Dnf	
113	MG TC		Black D		SGP 24
123	MG TC		Fergus R		SGP 33
131	MG TD		Kraus E		SGP 25
134	Porsche 356		Mahoy C		SGP 8
147	MG TD		Chaney Brown S		SGP 34
154	MG TD		Miller C		SGP 19
170	Porsche 356		Thorpe R		SGP 9
174	MG TD		Long W		SGP 31
75	MG TD		Dager H		SGP 22
130	MG TD		Twist T		SGP 13

Abraham Lincoln Tr 17 laps	Race distance 73 miles	Class O 1500cc mod	Starters 62

Race winner's time 56min 0.4sec	Average speed 78.11mph

5	Ferrari 375 MM	0364 AM	Kimberly J	1oa	1cl CM
137	Jaguar C-type	XKC 032	Erickson E	2oa	2cl CM
2	Ferrari 225 S	0166 ED	Lloyd W	3oa	1cl DM
94	Ferrari 250 MM	0348 MM	Lyeth J	4oa	2cl DM
8D	Aston-Martin DB2 Offy		Hansgen W	5oa	3cl DM
46	Maserati A6 GCS	2053	McNought D	6oa	1cl EM
40	Jaguar Special		Schott C	7oa	3cl CM

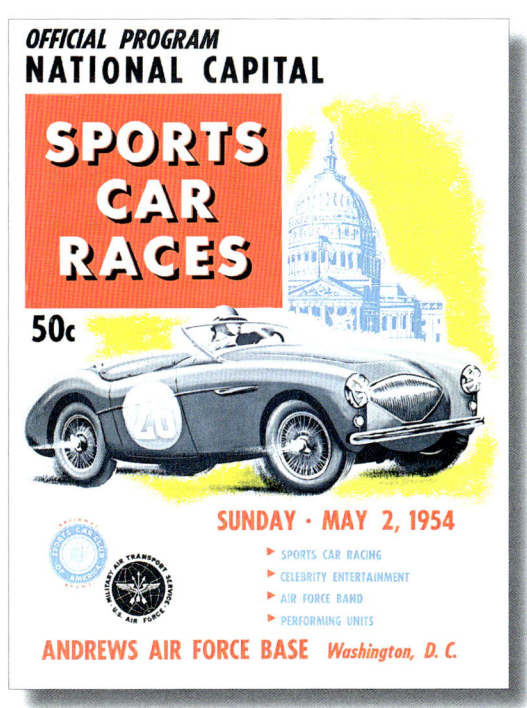

Programme cover for the Andrews AFB event. (Terry O'Neil Collection)

#	Car	Chassis	Driver	OA	Class
49	Allard JR Cadillac	3402	Schilling D	8oa	1cl BM
55	Jaguar C-type	XKC 009	Wyllie M Dr	9oa	4cl CM
117	Maserati A6 GCS	2039	Koster F	10oa	2cl EM
63	OSCA MT4 1450	1138	Brewster W	11oa	1cl FM
26	Maserati A6 GCS		Proctor F	12oa	3cl EM
47	OSCA MT4 1450	1139	Moffett G	13oa	2cl FM
42	OSCA MT4 1450	1137	Cunningham B	14oa	3cl FM
61	OSCA MT4 1350	1114	Linton O	15oa	4cl FM
91	OSCA MT4 1450	1133	Simpson J	16oa	5cl FM
10	Jaguar XK120M		Wallace C	17oa	1cl C
15	Ferrari 340 AM	0204 A	Lunken E	18oa	5cl CM
121	OSCA MT4 1350	1124	Wessells III H	19oa	6cl FM
145	Kurtis 500 S		Roberts G	20oa	2cl BM
4	Lester MG		Black D	21oa	4cl EM
104	Jaguar XK120		McGrade E	22oa	2cl C
122	Arnolt Bristol Bolide		Fergus R	23oa	5cl EM
84	Allard J2		Losse F	24oa	3cl BM
136	Jaguar XK120		Sarle C	25oa	3cl C
35	Siata 208 S Spyder	BS 530	Kuhn R	26oa	6cl EM
44	MG Special		Ehrman G	27oa	7cl FM
85	Austin-Healey 100		Kincheloe W	28oa	1cl D
95	Porsche 356 America		McLaughlin D	29oa	1cl F
178	Jaguar XK120		Smidt C	30oa	4cl C
64	Jaguar XK120		White D	31oa	5cl C
52	Siata 208 S	BS 501	Circurel R	32oa	7cl EM
45	Austin-Healey 100		Allen F	33oa	2cl D
89	Austin-Healey 100		Holley J	34oa	3cl D
152	Austin-Healey 100		Bulck E	35oa	4cl D
96	Jaguar XK120		Coldwell M	36oa	6cl C
127	Austin-Healey 100		Livingstone K	37oa	5cl D
29	MG Special		Atkins G	38oa	8cl FM
90	Austin-Healey 100		Zuver G	39oa	6cl D
93	Austin-Healey 100		Dantone W	40oa	7cl D
146	Triumph TR2		Robinson J	41oa	8cl EM
142	MG TD		Trenholm J	42oa	2cl F
126	MG TC Special		Bradford D	43oa	9cl FM
1	Ferrari 375 MM	0382 AM	Spear W		SGP 11
6	Ferrari 225 S	0220 ED	Lunken E	dns	SGP 27
11	Jaguar XK120M		Sparcino P		SGP 22
12	OSCA MT4		Weinman M		SGP 59
17	Kurtis 500 S Cadillac		Ensley J		SGP 5
36	Allard J2X		Rutherford S		SGP 6
37	Jaguar XK120		McKenna T		SGP 12
53	Bandini Siluro-Siata 1500		Pauley J		SGP 57
80	Jaguar XK120M		Mull J		SGP 16
92	Jaguar XK120		Reiland R		SGP 24
8	Allard J2X Cadillac	J2086	Wacker F	Dnf	SGP 2
100	Austin-Healey 100		Fusca J		SGP 38
110	Ferrari 166 MM	0054 M	Heldt W		SGP 43
138	Jaguar XK120		Waddleton T		SGP 17
139	Jaguar XK120M		Constantine G		SGP 23
148	Jaguar XK120		Dunham W		SGP 25
149	Triumph TR2		McConkey R		SGP 47
168	Austin-Healey 100		Campbell Smidt H		SGP 31
175	MG TD		Donoghue W		SGP 62

Thomas Jefferson Tr 10 laps	Race distance 43 miles	Class Porsche, Jaguar	Starters

Race winner's time 35min 57.6sec	Average speed 71.74mph

#	Car	Driver	OA	Class
10	Jaguar XK120M	Wallace C	1oa	1cl C
87	Jaguar XK120	Crusoe J	2oa	2cl C
54	Jaguar XK120	Bird J	3oa	3cl C
3	Jaguar XK120M	Boss R	4oa	4cl C
64	Jaguar XK120M	White D	5oa	5lc C
109	Jaguar XK120	Forno V	6oa	6cl C
34	Jaguar XK120	Woodbury W	7oa	7cl C
27	Jaguar XK120M	Manting J	8oa	8cl C
139	Jaguar XK120M	Constantine G	9oa	9cl C
129	Jaguar XK120M	Perrin R	10oa	10cl C
138	Jaguar XK120	Waddleton T	11oa	11cl C
65	Porsche 356 Super	Thompson R Dr	12oa	1cl F
160	Jaguar XK120M	Norair P	13oa	12cl C
71	Porsche 356 Super	Fleming W	14oa	2cl F
25	Porsche 356 Super	Lilley W	15oa	3cl F
7	Porsche 356	Jenkins E	16oa	4cl F
159	Porsche 356	Baker R	17oa	5cl F
143	Jaguar XK120	MacKenzie	18oa	13cl C
148	Jaguar XK120	Dunham W	19oa	14cl C
48	Porsche 356 Super	Graham J	20oa	6cl F
178	Jaguar XK120M	Gilmartin R	21oa	15cl C
96	Jaguar XK120	Coldwell M		SGP 6
11	Jaguar XK120M	Sparcino P		SGP 9
16	Jaguar XK120	Vilardi D		SGP 18
18	Jaguar XK120M	Ensley J		SGP 4
19	Porsche 356 Super	Bunker A		SGP 27

162

33	Jaguar XK120		Valdez-Depena A		SGP 10
80	Jaguar XK120M		Mull E		SGP 21
92	Jaguar XK120		Reiland R		SGP 20
134	Porsche 356		Mahoy C		SGP 30
153	Porsche 356		Link H		SGP 26
167	Jaguar XK120M		Bucher J		SGP 5
170	Porsche 356		Thorpe R		SGP 29

150	MG TD		Perry H		Dnf
131	MG TD		Kraus E		SGP 32
154	MG TD		Miller C		SGP 23
155	MG TD		Werner D		SGP 25
171	MG TD		Richardson D		SGP 10
174	MG TD		Long W		SGP 36
113	MG		Lewis F		SGP 6
98	MG TD				

President's Cup 47 laps | Race distance 203 miles | Class Unrestricted | Starters 40

White House Trophy 10 laps | Race distance 43 miles | Class MG | Starters

Race winner's time 41min 20.4sec | Average speed 62.41 mph

66	MG TF		Durbin R	1oa	1cl F
123	MG TC		Fergus R	2oa	2cl F
99	MG TD		Thompson R Dr	3oa	3cl F
68	MG TD		Bastrup L	4oa	4cl F
166	MG TC		Oliver R	5oa	5cl F
163	MG TF		Hanna H	6oa	6cl F
75	MG TD		Dager J	7oa	7cl F
39	MG TD		Holbert R	8oa	8cl F
140	MG TF		Davidson M	9oa	9cl F
50	MG TD		Schields J	10oa	10cl F
124	MG TC		Rodier R	11oa	11cl F
147	MG TD		Robinson J	12oa	12cl F
41	MG TD		Ward M	13oa	13cl F
169	MG TD		Fair J	14oa	14cl F
172	MG TD		Kahmer R	15oa	15cl F
158	MG TD		Berckemeyer J	16oa	16cl F
161	MG TF		Nash R	17oa	17cl F
62	MG TF		Richardson R	18oa	18cl F
97	MG TD		Skitarelic B Dr	19oa	19cl F
130	MG TD		Twist T	20oa	20cl F
32	MG TD		Ryan J	21oa	21cl F
24	MG TD		McNamara J	22oa	22cl F
177	MG TD		Pessolano L	23oa	23cl F
56	MG TC		Wyllie M	24oa	24cl F
156	MG TD		Rocca L	25oa	25cl F
115	MG TD		Edwards W	26oa	26cl F
165	MG TD		Hall O	27oa	27cl F
128	MG TC		Baptista F	28oa	28cl F
112	MG TC		Kegeles S	Dnf	
83	MG TC		Sterner G	Dnf	

Race winner's time 2hr 28min 48.6sec | Average speed 81.85mph

1	Ferrari 375 MM	0382 AM	Spear W	1oa	1cl CM
2	Ferrari 225 S	0166 ED	Lloyd W	2oa	1cl DM
42	OSCA MT4 1450	1137	Cunningham B	3oa	1cl FM
55	Jaguar C-type	XKC 009	Wyllie M Dr	4oa	2cl CM
94	Ferrari 250 MM	0348 MM	Lyeth M & Hassan C	5oa	2cl DM
91	OSCA MT4 1450	1133	Johnston S	6oa	2cl FM
8D	Aston-Martin DB2 Offy		Hansgen W	7oa	3cl DM
46	Maserati A6 GCS	2053	McNought D	8oa	1cl EM
114	Kieft-Bristol		Carpenter W	9oa	2cl EM
17	Kurtis 500 Cadillac		Ensley J	10oa	1cl BM
121	OSCA MT4 1350	1124	Wessells III H	11oa	3cl FM
63	OSCA MT4 1450	1138	Brewster W	12oa	4cl FM
47	OSCA MT4 1450	1139	Moffett G	13oa	5cl FM
26	Maserati A6 GCS		Proctor F & Koster F	14oa	6cl FM
61	OSCA MT4 1350	1114	Linton O	15oa	7cl FM
8	Allard J2X (Ford)	J2086	Wacker F	16oa	2cl BM
35	Siata 208S Spyder	BS 530	Kuhn R	17oa	3cl EM
178	Jaguar XK120		Spitler S	18oa	1cl C
44	MG Special		Ehrman G	19oa	8cl FM
146	Triumph TR2		Wing R	20oa	1cl E
85	Austin-Healey 100		Kincheloe W	21oa	1cl D
10	Jaguar XK120		Wallace C	22oa	2cl C
136	Jaguar XK120		Sarle C	23oa	3cl C
71	Porsche 356 Super		Fleming W & Thorpe	24oa	2cl E*
152	Austin-Healey 100		Buick E	25oa	2cl D
7	Porsche 356		Daly J	26oa	3cl E*
93	Austin-Healey 100		Dantone W	27oa	3cl D
54	Jaguar XK120		Quackenbush J	28oa	4cl C

146	Triumph TR2		Robinson J		
78	Cunningham C4RK	5218R	Moran C		
5	Ferrari 375 MM	0364 AM	Kimberly J	Dnf L46	
15	Ferrari 340 AM	0204 A	Lunken E		
105	Ferrari 225 S	0218 ET	Melville A		
110	Ferrari 166 MM	0054 M	Heldt W		
27	Jaguar XK120M		Manting J		
14	Frazer-Nash		Grey H		
40	Jaguar XK120 Special		Schott C		
45	Austin-Healey 100		Allen F		
49	Allard JR Cadillac	3402	Schilling D / Hassan C		
52	Siata 208 S	BS 501	Cicurel R		
79	Jaguar-Cadillac Special		Whitmore C		

* cars moved to Class E from Class F

Programme cover for the Chanute AFB event. (Courtesy Bruce Perry Collection)

Chanute AFB 6.6.1954

Gates 50 16 laps	Race distance 52.8 miles	Class Unrestricted	Starters approx. 66

Race winner's time			Average speed		
121	Jaguar XK120		Wallace C	1oa	1cl C
1	Moretti		Robb H	2oa	1cl HM
134	MG TD		Allin A	3oa	1clF-MG
69	Austin-Healey 100		Franke L	4oa	1cl D
115	Jaguar XK120M		Schroeder J	5oa	2cl C
140	Jaguar XK120		Karlstrom J	6oa	3cl C
117	Jaguar XK120		Grove J	7oa	4cl C
124	Jaguar XK120M		Attaway C	8oa	5cl C
55	Jaguar XK120		Weber J		6cl C
122	Triumph TR2		Salzgaber R		2cl D
25	Austin-Healey 100		Davis D		3cl D
12	Porsche 356 Super		Goldman M		1cl F
77	Porsche 356 Super		Carlson N		2cl F
29	Porsche 356 Super		Bunker A		3cl F
126	MG TF		Durbin R		1cl F-MG
13	MG TD MkII		Garland G		2cl F-MG

47	OSCA MT4 1100	1112	Makins R		1cl GM
111	Siata 300BC 1100 Spyder	ST 435 BC	Bentley J		2cl GM
103	Nardi-Lancia Spyder		Gougleman P		2cl HM
88	Bandini Mercury		MacArthur S		3cl HM
38	Siata 300BC 750 Spyder	ST 407 BC	Yares R		
33	Jaguar XK120M		Kilborn J		
71	Jaguar XK120		Manting J		
19	Jaguar XK120M		Heerman W		
94	Jaguar XK120		Coffin T		
56	Jaguar XK120M		Coan B		
9	Lotus Mk VI-MG		Rubini G	Dnf L4	
92	Clovis Special		Lamberson G		
95	Porsche 356		Burgess D		
54	Porsche 356		Floria J		
58	Fibersport		Howell J		
45	Fibersport		Mays J		
49	Fibersport TXP		Townsend B		
16	MG TD		Blume B		
23	MG TC		Quinn R		
24	MG TC		Cummings L		

37	MGTD		Boardman M		
41	MG TD		Ward M		
81	Siata 300BC 750 Spyder	ST 425 BC	Ahr K		
31	Porsche 356 Super		Shuck W		
59	Porsche 356		Tappan R		
61	Porsche 356 Super		Van Antwerpen P		
66	Porsche 356 America		Steele W		
102	Porsche 356		Magenheimer R		
3	Jaguar XK120M		Boss R		
64	Triumph TR2		Dodds W		
118	Austin-Healey 100		Graham C		
33	Jaguar XK120M		Kilborn J		
44	MG TF		Patton N	Dnf	

Chicago Cup 16 laps	Race distance 52.8 miles	Class BM, CM, DM, FM	Starters 35

Race winner's time 38min 37.8sec	Average speed 82mph

5	Ferrari 375 MM	0364 AM	Kimberly J	1oa	1cl CM
21	Jaguar C-type	XKC 030	Katskee L	2oa	2cl CM
15	Ferrari 340 AM	0204 A	Lunken E	3oa	3cl CM
27	Jaguar C-type	XKC 032	Erickson E	4oa	4cl CM
17	Kurtis 500 S Cadillac		Ensley J	5oa	1cl BM
136	Ferrari 250 MM	0348 MM	Lyeth R		1cl DM
30	Austin-Healey 100M		Carkhuff S		2cl DM
90	Allard J2X Oldsmobile	J1859	Gray W S		2cl BM
7	Frazer Nash LM Rep	421/100/110	Boynton E		1cl EM
8	Arnolt-Bristol Bolide		Wacker F		2cl EM
161	Arnolt-Bristol Bolide		Fergus R		3cl EM
48	OSCA MT4 1350	1132	Bott F		1cl FM
157	Uihlein Special		Brocken K		2cl FM
76	OSCA MT4 1350		Stewart P		3cl FM
153	Ferrari 375 MM		Duncan D	dnf	
40	Glockler Porsche	10447	Cooper W		
2	Jaguar C-type	XKC 009	Wyllie M		
10	Siata 208S		Kuhn R		
112	MG TC s/c		Dietrich S		
51	MG TD		Schleicher V		
26	Jaguar XK 120M		Kerr B		
46	Porsche 550 Spyder		Crawford E		
65	Kurtis Kraft		Rigden J		
50	Alfa Romeo 2.9		Field J		

68	Arnolt Bristol		Boynton E		
70	Chrysler Special		Clovis P		
73	Fageol-Porsche Special		Fageol L		
79	Allard Palm-Beach		Wilson C		
129	Arnolt-Bristol		Arnolt S		
84	Jaguar XK120 Special		Skillman N		

Central Illinois Cup 16 laps	Race distance 52.8 miles	Class U 1500cc	Starters approx. 40

Race winner's time 43min 23.82sec	Average speed 73mph

47	OSCA MT4 1100	1112	Makins R	1oa	1cl GM
12	Porsche 356 Super		Goldman M	2oa	1cl F
39	Porsche 356 Super		Ballenger R	3oa	2cl F
139	Porsche 356 Super		Warren D	4oa	3cl F
111	Siata 300BC1100 Spyder	ST 435 BC	Bentley J	5oa	2cl GM
126	MG TF		Durbin R		1cl F-MG
105	MG TF		McGrade E		2cl F-MG
134	MG TD		Allin A		3cl F-MG
44	MG TF		Patton N		4cl F-MG
9	Lotus Mk VI-MG	26	Rubini G		3cl GM
38	Siata 300BC 750 Spyder	ST 407 BC	Yares R		
1	Moretti		Robb H		
54	Porsche 356		Floria J		
103	Nardi-Lancia		Gougelman P		1cl HM
85	Porsche 356		Van de Sande G		
106	Porsche 356		Hawthorne D		
58	Fibersport		Howell J		
45	Fibersport		Mays J		
49	Fibersport TXP		Townsend B		
81	Siata 300BC 750 Spyder	ST 425 BC	Ahr K		
92	Clovis Special		Lamberson G		
4	MG TD		Shaw C		
13	MG TD MkII		Garland G		
11	Porsche 356		Dormeyer K		
32	Porsche 356 Super		Steele M		
31	MG TD		Shuck W		
37	MG TD		Boardman M		
36	Porsche 356		Crane L		
66	Porsche 356 America		Steele W		
43	Siata 300BC Spyder		Rose D		

Offutt AFB 4.7.1954

Chanute Trophy 46 laps	Race distance 151.8 miles	Class Unrestricted	Starters 43

Race winner's time 1hr 55min 17.4sec			Average speed 79.15mph		
5	Ferrari 375 MM	0364 AM	Kimberly J	1oa	1cl CM
27	Jaguar C-type	XKC 032	Erickson E	2oa	2cl CM
21	Jaguar C-type	XKC 030	Katskee L	3oa	3cl CM
17	Kurtis 500 S Cadillac		Ensley J	4oa	1cl BM
90	Allard J2X Oldsmobile	J1859	Duncan D	5oa	2cl BM
152	Ferrari 340AM	0322 AM	Irish R	6oa	4cl CM
2	Jaguar C-type	XKC 009	Wyllie M Dr	7oa	5cl CM
136	Ferrari 250MM	0348 MM	Hassan C		1cl DM
98	Nash-Healey		Rosenberger A		3cl BM
121	Jaguar XK120M		Wallace C		1cl C
169	Jaguar XK120		Lawrence E		2cl C
117	Jaguar XK120		Grove J		3cl C
30	Austin-Healey 100		Carkhuff S		2cl DM
69	Austin-Healey 100		Franke L		1cl D
150	Austin-Healey 100		Vollmer P		2cl D
122	Triumph TR2		Salzgaber R		3cl D
8	Arnolt-Bristol Bolide		Wacker F		1cl EM
10	Siata 208S Spyder	BS 530	Kuhn R		2cl EM
112	MG TC s/c		Dietrich C		3cl EM
157	Uihlein Special		Stewart P		1cl FM
155	MG TD		Krasberg R		2cl FM
146	MG TD		Holland J		3cl FM
6	Excalibur J		Gary R	Dnf	
15	Ferrari 340 AM	0204 A	Lunken E	Dnf	
159	Allard J2X		Skogmo D	Dnf	
33	Jaguar XK120M		Kilborn J	Dnf	
7	Frazer-Nash LM Rep	421/100/110	Boynton E	Dnf	
	Excalibur J		Ullrich H		
65	Kurtis 500 S		Ridgen J		
141	Singer 1500		Goodman B		1cl F
40	Glockler Porsche	10447	Cooper W		
48	OSCA MT4 1350	1132	Bott F		
161	Arnolt-Bristol Bolide		Fergus R		
51	MG TD		Schleicher V		
148	Austin-Healey 100		Austin F		
135	Bandini		Whitlock J		
103	Nardi-Lancia Spyder		Gougleman P		
88	Bandini-Mercury		McArthur S		

(11 dnf)

SAC Trophy 17 laps	Race distance 50 miles	Class C, GM, HM	Starters

Race winner's time 43min 24sec			Average speed 70.50mph		
11	Jaguar XK120M		Katskee L	1oa	1cl C
3	Jaguar XK120M		Fenner H	2oa	2cl C
83	Jaguar XK120M		Lawrence E	3oa	3cl C
99	Jaguar XK120		Newcomer T	4oa	4cl C
43	Jaguar XK120M		Attaway C	5oa	5cl C
13	Jaguar XK120 M		Coan B	6oa	6cl C
77	OSCA MT4 1100	1112	Makins R	7oa	1cl GM
75	Jaguar XK120		Kopplin K	8oa	7cl C
103	Jaguar XK120M		Mason G	9oa	8cl C
102	Jaguar XK120		Mann D	10oa	9cl C
90	Porsche 356 Super		Bunker A		1cl F
81	Porsche 356 Super		Van Antwerpen P		2cl F
97	MG TF		Durbin R		3cl F
48	Lotus Mk VI-MG	26	Rubini G		2cl GM
59	Fibersport		Howell J		3cl GM
94	Siata 300BC 750 Spyder		Place A		1cl HM
93	Giaur Spyder		Betts W		2cl HM
54	Fibersport		Townsend B		3cl HM
33	Moretti		Cherryhomes R		
46	E.R.M. Special		Smith R		

Cornhusker Cup 17 laps	Race distance 50 miles	Class C, BM, CM, DM, EM, FM	Starters

Race winner's time 40min 02sec			Average speed 74.91mph		
12	Jaguar C-type	XKC 030	Katskee L	1oa	1cl CM
27	Jaguar C-type	XKC 032	Erickson E	2oa	2cl CM
25	Ferrari 225 S	0166 ED	Lloyd W	3oa	1cl DM
61	Ferrari 340 MM	0322 AM	Irish R	4oa	3cl CM
20	Ferrari 250 MM	0348 MM	Lyeth J	5oa	2cl DM
28	Allard J2X Oldsmobile	J1859	Gray W S	6oa	1cl BM
60	Cunningham C4RK	5218R	Moran C	7oa	2cl BM
85	Ferrari 250 MM	0260 MM	Brown C	8oa	3cl DM
96	Jaguar XK120M		Wallace C	9oa	1cl C
3	Jaguar XK120M		Fenner H	10oa	2cl C
13	Jaguar XK120M		Coan B		3cl C
43	Jaguar XK120M		Attaway C		4cl C

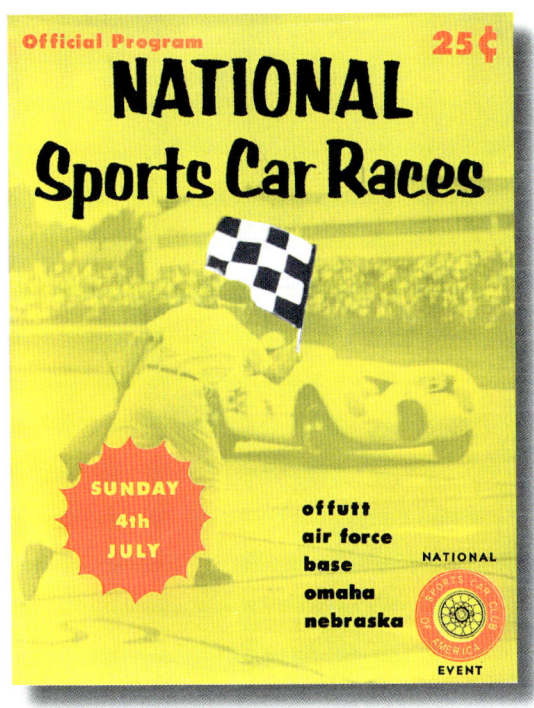

Programme cover for the Offutt AFB event. (Terry O'Neil Collection)

109	Allard J2		Rose D		3cl BM
7	Frazer-Nash Le Mans Rep	421/100/110	Boynton E		1cl EM
8	Arnolt-Bristol Bolide		Wacker F		2cl EM
4	Arnolt-Bristol Bolide		Arnolt S		3cl EM
63	MG TC s/c		Larson B		4cl EM
35	OSCA MT4		Weinman M		1cl FM
40	Glockler Porsche	10447	Barton L		2cl FM
29	Porsche 356 America		Crawford E		3cl FM
34	MG Special		Wilson W		4cl FM
62	Jaguar XK120		Larson R		
56	Jaguar XK120		Witt P		
82	Jaguar XK120		Leichter R		4cl CM
	Ferrari 225 S		Cooper W		4cl DM

AK-SAR-BEN Trophy 33 laps	Race distance 100 miles	Class F, GM, HM	Starters

Race winner's time 1hr 29min 30sec		Average speed 67.0mph	

77	OSCA MT4 1100	1112	Makins R	1oa	1cl GM
90	Porsche 356 Super		Bunker A	2oa	1cl F
81	Porsche 356 Super		Van Antwerpen P	3oa	2cl F
97	MG TF		Durbin R	4oa	3cl F
15	MG TF		McGrade E	5oa	4cl F
33	Moretti		Cherryhomes R	6oa	1cl HM
84	Nardi Spyder		Samuelson R	7oa	2cl HM
80	Porsche 356		Plue G	8oa	5cl F
19	MG TD MkII		Heath R	9oa	6cl F
64	MG TF		Elliott J	10oa	7cl F
48	Lotus Mk VI-MG	26	Rubini G		2cl GM
53	Fibersport		Mays J		3cl GM
54	Fibersport		Townsend B		3cl HM
59	Fibersport		Howell J		4cl GM
94	Siata 300BC 750 Spyder		Place A		4cl HM
46	ERM Special		Smith R		

Omaha GP 66 laps	Race distance 200 miles	Class BM, CM, DM, EM, FM, C	Starters

Race winner's time 2hr 32min 29sec	Average speed 79.09mph

55	Ferrari 375 MM	0374 AM	McAfee J	1oa	1cl CM
1	Ferrari 375 MM	0382 AM	Spear W	2oa	2cl CM
12	Jaguar C-type	XKC 030	Katskee L	3oa	3cl CM
66	OSCA MT4 1350		Stewart P	4oa	1cl FM
91	OSCA MT4 1350	1123	Simpson J	5oa	2cl FM
7	Frazer-Nash Le Mans Rep	421/100/110	Boynton E	6oa	1cl EM
20	Ferrari 250 MM	0348 MM	Lyeth J/Schaeffer	7oa	1cl DM
60	Cunningham C4RK	5218R	Moran C	8oa	1cl BM
29	Porsche 356 America		Crawford E	9oa	3cl FM
17	Kurtis 500 S Cadillac		Ensley J	10oa	2cl BM
92	Allard J2		Gray W		3cl BM
28	Allard J2X Oldsmobile	J1859	Gray W S		4cl BM
43	Jaguar XK120M		Attaway C		1cl C
14	Jaguar XK120M		McGrade E		2cl C
106	Jaguar XK120M		Masterson R		3cl C
36	Ferrari 225 S		Biggs D		2cl DM
26	Austin-Healey 100		Carkhuff S		3cl DM
25	Ferrari 225 S	0166 ED	Lloyd W		4cl DM
63	MG TC s/c		Larson R		2cl EM
4	Arnolt Bristol Bolide		Arnolt S		3cl EM
50	Allard JR Cadillac	3404	Warner F	Dnf L4	
58	MG TD MkII		Young J		
16	Austin-Healey 100		Richter R		

61	Ferrari 340 MM	0322 AM	Irish R		4cl CM
40	Glockler Porsche	10447	Barton L		4cl FM

Lockbourne AFB 8.8.1954

Skyhawker 50 14 laps	Race distance 50 miles	Class F, GM, HM	Starters

Race winner's time 38min 12.96sec	Average speed 78.5mph

4	OSCA MT4 1100	1112	Makins R	1oa	1cl GM
90	Porsche 356 Super		Bunker A	2oa	1cl F
77	Siata 300BC 1100 Spyder	ST 435 BC	Bentley J	3oa	2cl GM
61	Porsche 356 America		Steele W	4oa	2cl F
81	Porsche 356 Super		Van Antwerpen P	5oa	3cl F
174	PBX Special		Poole C	6oa	1cl HM
63	Siata 300BC 1100 Spyder		Haskell I	7oa	3cl GM
57	Porsche 356		Burgess D	8oa	4cl F
45	MG TF		Patton N	9oa	5cl F
41	Porsche 356 America		Kramer P	10oa	6cl F
123	Porsche 356		Shuck W	11oa	7cl F
131	Moretti		Rigden J	12oa	2cl HM
169	MG TF		Nash R	13oa	8cl F
94	MG TF		Wyllie P	14oa	9cl F
88	Bandini Mercury		Mac Arthur S	15oa	3cl HM
83	Clovis Special		Lamberson G	16oa	4cl HM
103	MG TF		Davidson M	17oa	10cl F
149	Siata 300BC 1100 Spyder		Norwood J	18oa	4cl GM
120	MG TD		McConnell R	19oa	11cl F
22	MG TC		Quinn Dr	20oa	12cl F
95	Siata 300BC 1100 Spyder		Hannig F		5cl GM
161	TXP Crosley		Townsend B		5cl HM
170	Crosley		Hill H		6cl HM
2	Porsche 356 Super		Thompson R	Dnf L3	
10	MG TD		Williamson H		
11	Porsche 356 Super		Goldman M		
29	MG TD		Williams		
30	Porsche 356 America		Johnson J		
38	Porsche 356 America		Ernst W		
47	MG TD		Ward M		
51	MG TD		Ward O		
58	MG TD		Gilbert R		
60	MG TD		McNamara J		

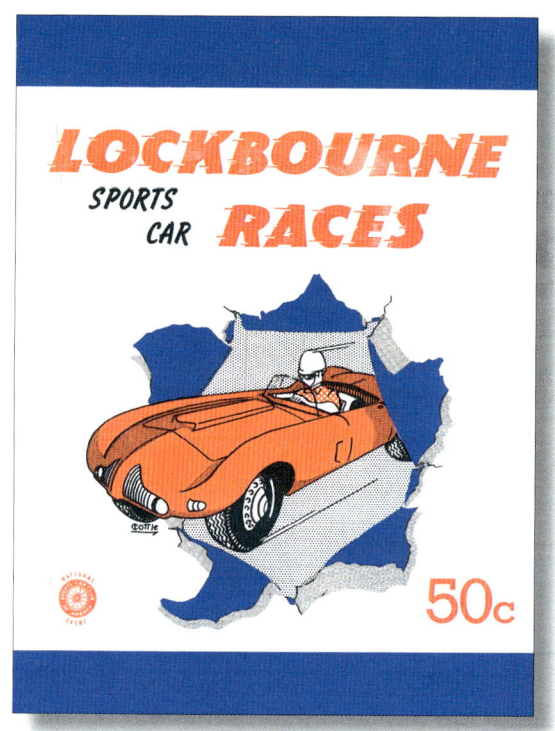

Programme cover for the Lockbourne AFB event. (Terry O'Neil Collection)

65	MG TD		Knoll R	Dnf
75	MG TD		Mills D	
76	Porsche 356		Ross B	
80	MG TD		Ryan J	
86	MG TD		Stoll C	
93	MG TC		Martin B	
96	MG TD		Boardman M	
101	MG TD		Cooper H	
107	MG TF		Durbin R	
108	MG TD		Durbin G	
109	MG TD		Cooper W	
114	MG TD		Skitarelic R	
116	MG MkII		Shaw C	
117	MG TD		Davis D	
121	MG TD		Lovell R	
124	Porsche 356 1300		Geoghegan R	
125	MG TD		Venhald J	
129	MG TC		Randle W	
141	MG TD		Davinport F	
148	Porsche 356		Earl J	
156	MG TD		Jayne E	

158	MG TC		Ferguson R		
160	MG TD		Steele M		
162	MG TD		Constant H		
165	MG TF		Richardson R		
172	MG TD		Rower A		
175	Singer SM 1500		Goodman B		
181	MG TC		Snowdon J		
183	Porsche 356		Lamb E		
186	MG TC		Bakker C		
37	Lotus Mk VI-MG	26	Rubini G		
102	Fiber Sport		Mays J		
159	Cisitalia 202MM Corsa		Gent R		
174	Fiat Balilla		Forsyth P		
182	Siata		Harris H		
16	Bandini Crosley		Brooks J		
34	Siata 300BC 750 Spyder		Mitchell W		
35	Bandini Crosley		Rudkin H		
43	Siata 300BC 750 Spyder		Dickens R		
46	Siata 300BC 750 Spyder	ST 425 BC	Ahr K		
78	Arnolt Bristol		Arnolt S		
126	Siata 300BC 750 Spyder	ST 407 BC	Yares R		
132	Siata 300BC 750 Spyder		Murphy R		
133	Siata 300BC 750 Spyder		Marsh D		
137	Renault Special		Pickrel W		

Ohio Valley Cup 21 laps | Race distance 75 miles | Class C, D, E | Starters 44

Race winner's time 52min 19.7sec | Average speed 86.0mph

79	Jaguar XK 120M		Wallace C	1oa	1cl C
74	Jaguar XK 120		Manting J	2oa	2cl C
14	Jaguar XK 120M		Katskee L	3oa	3cl C
134	Jaguar XK 120		Palmer D	4oa	4cl C
157	Austin-Healey 100		Fergus R	5oa	1cl D
71	Triumph TR2		Brooks J	6oa	1cl E
140	Austin-Healey 100		King J	7oa	2cl D
99	Austin-Healey 100		Stiles P	8oa	3cl D
171	Jaguar XK 120		Mason R	9oa	5cl C
84	Jaguar XK 120		Kerr T	10oa	6cl C
25	Austin-Healey 100		Glowacke E	11oa	4cl D
62	Austin-Healey 100		Dantone W	12oa	5cl D
111	Austin-Healey 100		Goldich R	13oa	6cl D
113	Triumph TR2		Wilson C	14oa	2cl E
122	Austin-Healey 100		McCann J	15oa	7cl D
20	Austin-Healey 100		Dukes D	16oa	8cl D
42	Austin-Healey 100		MacArthur A	17oa	9cl D
146	Austin-Healey 100		Kraft K	18oa	10cl D
139	Triumph TR2		Cathey G	19oa	3cl E
143	Jaguar XK 120		Kent G	20oa	7cl C
173	Triumph TR2		Davis A		4cl E
168	Triumph TR2		Salzgaber R		5cl E
54	Jaguar XK 120		Bird J		
15	Jaguar XK 120		Solavi F		
128	Jaguar XK 120M		Randle W		
127	Jaguar XK 120M		Lawrence E		
19	Jaguar XK 120M		McKenna T	R	
21	Jaguar XK 120M		Heerman W Dr	R	
82	Jaguar XK 120M		Ryan J		
70	Jaguar XK 120		Friedmann T		
85	Jaguar XK 120M		Woodnorth H		
144	Jaguar XK 120		Boeno J		
150	Jaguar XK 120M		Mull E		
164	Jaguar XK 120M		Livingston R		
185	Jaguar XK 120M		Dunham W		
188	Jaguar XK 120M		Hendricks J		
	Jaguar XK 120				
33	Austin-Healey 100		Advent C		
59	Austin-Healey 100		Tardif D		
64	Austin-Healey 100		Kunz H		
118	Austin-Healey 100		Allen F		
138	Austin-Healey 100		McCernise J		
166	Austin-Healey 100		Bulck E		
167	Austin-Healey 100		Ross R		
104	Austin-Healey 100		Schleicher V		

Scioto 50 14 laps | Race distance 50 miles | Class EM, FM, GM, HM | Starters

Race winner's time 34min 32.4sec | Average speed 86.85mph

91	OSCA MT4 1450	1133	Simpson J	1oa	1cl FM
73	OSCA MT4 1450	1137	Cunningham B	2oa	2cl FM
155	OSCA MT4 1450		Kimberly J	3oa	3cl FM
87	Uihlein Special		Brocken K	4oa	4cl FM
26	Siata 208 S Spyder	BS 530	Kuhn R	5oa	1cl EM
110	Siata 208CS	BS 501	Schrafft G	6oa	2cl EM
8	Arnolt Bristol Bolide		Wacker F	7oa	3cl EM
23	OSCA MT4 1350	1114	Linton O	8oa	5cl FM
152	Ferrari 166 MM	0054	Heldt W	9oa	4cl EM
4	OSCA MT4 1100	1112	Makins R	10oa	1cl GM
180	Arnolt Bristol Bolide		Cornett D	11oa	5cl EM

40	Glockler Porsche	10447	Cooper W	12oa	6cl FM
135	OSCA MT4 1450		Weinman M	13oa	7cl FM
36	Kieft Bristol		Ceresole P	14oa	6cl EM
9	Arnolt Bristol Bolide		Arnolt W	15oa	7cl EM
136	Kieft MG		Howell E	16oa	8cl EM
112	Porsche 356 America		Barton L	17oa	7cl FM
100	Porsche 356 America		Bunker A	18oa	8cl FM
39	Porsche 356 America		Crawford E	19oa	9cl FM
77	Siata 300BC 1100Spyder	ST435 BC	Bentley J	20oa	2cl GM
149	Siata 300BC 1100 Spyder		Norwood J		3cl GM
63	Siata 300BC 1100 Spyder		Haskell I		4cl GM
131	Moretti Coupe		Rigden J		1cl HM
88	Bandini Mercury		MacArthur S		2cl HM
43	Siata 300BC 750 Spyder		Seaverns B		3cl HM
161	TXP Crosley		Townsend B		4cl HM
137	Renault Special		Pickrel W		5cl HM
170	Crosley		Hill H		6cl HM
24	MG TC S/C		Dietrich C		
119	Siata 208S		Ball W		
142	Lea-Francis		McLarty A		
7	OSCA MT4 1350	1132	Bott F		
28	MG TD		Essex A		
44	Lester MG		Black D	Dnf	
48	Porsche 356 America		Johnston S		
52	MG Mk II		Queen J		
53	Bandini Siluro Offy		Pauley J		
72	MG TC		Quackenbush J		
106	Allard Palm Beach 21C		Kite H		
145	MG TD		Richredt F		
163	OSCA MT4 1350	1124	Wessells III H		
184	MG Special		Franklin B		
37	Lotus Mk VI-MG	26	Rubini G		
95	Siata 300BC Spyder		Hannig F		
102	Fiber Sport		Mays J		
159	Cisitalia 202MM Corsa		Gent R		
178	Fiat Balilla		Forsyth P		
182	Siata 300BC Spyder		Harris H		
16	Bandini Crosley		Brooks J		
34	Siata 300BC 750 Spyder		Mitchell W		
36	Bandini Crosley		Rudkin M		
46	Siata 300BC 750 Spyder	ST 425 BC	Ahr K		
78	Nardi Spyder		Arnolt S		

83	Fiat-Crosley		Lamberson G		
126	Siata 300 BC Spyder	ST 407 BC	Yares R		
132	Siata 300BC 750 Spyder		Murphy R		
133	Siata 300BC 750 Spyder		Marsh D		
174	PBX Crosley		Poole C		

Lockbourne Trophy 14 laps | Race distance 50 miles | Class F & F3 | Starters 52

Race winner's time 39min 20.4sec | Average speed 76.26mph

2	Porsche 356 Super		Thompson R	1oa	1cl F
61	Porsche 356 America		Steele W	2oa	2cl F
90	Porsche 356 Super		Bunker A	3oa	3cl F
81	Porsche 356 Super		Van Antwerpen P	4oa	4cl F
158	MG TC mod		Fergus R	5oa	1cl F-MG
107	MG TF		Durbin R	6oa	2cl F-MG
123	Porsche 356		Shuck W	7oa	5cl F
41	Porsche 356 America		Kramer P	8oa	6cl F
169	MG TF		Nash R	9oa	3cl F-MG
57	Porsche 356		Burgess D	10oa	7cl F
38	Porsche 356 America		Ernst W	11oa	8cl F
103	MG TF		Davidson M	12oa	4cl F-MG
45	MG TF		Patton N	13oa	5cl F-MG
47	MG TD		Ward M	14oa	6cl F-MG
65	MG TD		Knoll R	15oa	7cl F-MG
120	MG TD		McConnell R	16oa	8cl F-MG
124	Porsche 356 1300		Geoghegan R	17oa	9cl F
22	MG TC		Quinn R	18oa	9cl F-MG
160	MG TD		Steele M	19oa	10cl F-MG
94	MG TF		Cracraft L	20oa	11cl F-MG
11	Porsche 356 Super		Thompson R		
30	Porsche 356 America		Hassan C		
76	Porsche 356		Burnell R		
148	Porsche 356		Earl J		
183	Porsche 356		Evans H		
10	MG TD		Williamson H		
29	MG TD		Williams J		
51	MG TD		Ward O		
58	MG TD		Gilbert R		
60	MG TD		McNamara J		
73	MG TD		Mills D		
80	MG TD		Ryan J		
86	MG TD		Stoll C		
93	MG TC		Martin D		
96	MG TD		Boardman M		

101	MG TD		Cooper H		
108	MG TD		Durbin G		
109	MG TD		Cooper W		
114	MG TD		Skitarelic D		
116	MG TD Mk II		Shaw C		
117	MG TD		Davis D		
121	MG TD		Lovell R		
125	MG TD		Van Hold J		
129	MG TC		Randell W		
141	MG TD		Davinport F		
156	MG TD		Becker H		
162	MG TD		Constant H		
165	MG TF		Richardson R		
172	MG TD		Brower A		
175	Singer SM 1500		Goodwin B		
181	MG TC		Snowdon J		
186	MG TC		Bakker G		
176	Cooper Mk VII F3		Whitney H	Dnf L11	
179	Formula III		Heneur J	dns	

Buckeye Cup 42 laps	Race distance 148.3 miles	Class Unrestricted	Starters

Race winner's time 1hr 33min 22.8sec		Average speed 96.38mph	

5	Ferrari 375 MM	O364 AM	Kimberly J	1oa	1cl CM
31	Ferrari 375 MM	O372 AM	Walters P	2oa	2cl CM
6	Ferrari 340 AM	O204 A	Lunken E	3oa	3cl CM
68	Cunningham C4R		Johnston S	4oa	1cl BM
12	Jaguar C-type	XKC 030	Katskee L	5oa	4cl CM
67	Cunningham C4R		Cunningham B	6oa	2cl BM
17	Kurtis 500 S Cadillac		Ensley J	7oa	3cl BM
3	Ferrari 225 S	O166 ED	Lloyd W	8oa	1cl DM
73	OSCA MT4 1450	1137	Bott F	9oa	1cl FM
27	Jaguar C-type	XKC 032	Erickson E	10oa	5cl CM
32	Jaguar C-type	XKC 009	Wyllie M	11oa	6cl CM
50	Allard JR Cadillac	3403	Tilley R	12oa	4cl BM
23	OSCA MT4 1350	1114	Linton O	13oa	2cl FM
153	Jaguar C-type		Skillman N	14oa	7cl CM
8	Arnolt Bristol Bolide		Wacker F	15oa	2cl DM
13	Austin-Healey 100S	3504	Cooper J	16oa	3cl DM
79	Jaguar XK 120M		Wallace C	17oa	1cl C
69	Ford Special		Evans R	18oa	8cl CM
62	Austin-Healey 100		Dantone W	19oa	1cl D
168	Triumph TR2		Salzgaber R	20oa	1cl E

87	Uihlein Special		Brocken K		Cl FM
99	Austin-Healey 100		Stiles P		2cl D
113	Triumph TR2		Wilson C		2cl E
173	Triumph TR2		Davis A		3cl E
91	OSCA MT4 1450	1133	Simpson J		Cl FM
157	MG TC		Fergus R		cl F
26	Siata 208 S Spyder	BS 530	Kuhn R		cl GM
140	Austin-Healey 100		King J		Cl D
25	Austin-Healey 100		Glowacks E		Cl D
111	Austin-Healey 100		Goldich R		Cl D
71	Triumph TR2		Brooks J		Cl E
139	Triumph TR2		Cathey G		Cl E
74	Jaguar XK 120		Manting J		Cl C
134	Jaguar XK 120		Palmer D		Cl C
171	Jaguar XK 120		Mason R		Cl C
84	Jaguar XK 120		Kerr T		Cl C
92	Allard J2X		Gray W		Cl BM
130	Kurtis 500 S		Ridgen W		Cl BM
154	Allard J2		Davis W		Cl BM
177	Allard J2		Parker D		Cl BM
187	Allard J2X Cadillac	J2192	Warner F	Dnf	Cl BM
151	Jaguar XK120M		Mull J		Cl CM
49	Ford Special		Larson R		Cl CM
55	Excalibur J		Ullrich H		Cl DM
56	Excalibur J		Gary R		Cl DM
105	Austin-Healey 100M		Fergus J		Cl DM
147	Austin-Healey 100		Earl J		Cl DM
1	Ferrari 375 MM	O382 AM	Spear W	Dnf L1	Cl CM
33	Fageol-Porsche Special		Fageol L		

March AFB 7.1. 1954

Race 1 7 laps	Race distance 24.5 miles	Class F, FM, HM Novice	Starters 24

Race winner's time		Average speed	

67	OSCA MT4		Chapman H	1oa	1cl FM
145	MG Special		Mauser R	2oa	2cl FM
90	Jupiter Special		Stevens M	3oa	3cl FM
118	Porsche 356 Super		Orr J	4oa	1cl F
31	Moretti Coupe		Howard R	5oa	1cl HM
17	MG TD		Hanford H	6oa	4cl FM

50	MG Special		Hughes J	7oa	5cl FM
138	Porsche 356 America		Morlang W	8oa	6cl FM
126	MG TC		Bishop N	9oa	2cl F
180	HRG		Madeira R	10oa	7cl FM
81	MG TD		Youngberg J	11oa	3cl F
179	MG TF		McLean E	12oa	4cl F
210	MG TD		Burhop D	13oa	5cl F
167	MG TD		Brigandi K	14oa	6cl F
172	MG TD		Dair J	15oa	7cl F
199	MG TD		Decker S	16oa	8cl F
33	MG TD		Royer D	17oa	9cl F
158	MG TD		Arnold J	18oa	10cl F
58	MG TF		Meyers R	19oa	11cl F
129	MG TD Mk II		Lawrence J	20oa	8cl FM
159	Simca Offy		Eschrick W	21oa	9cl FM
255	DB Panhard		Manley F	22oa	2cl HM
257	MG Special		Monise F	Dnf L5	
56	Trojan Special		Trevitt G	Dnf L3	

Race 2	7 laps	Race distance 24.5 miles	Class C & Mod Novice	Starters 39

Programme cover for the March AFB event. (Terry O'Neil Collection)

Race winner's time			Average speed		
71	Ferrari 250 MM	0282 MM	Hively H	1oa	1cl DM
132	Morgensen Special		Morgensen R	2oa	1cl CM
174	Powell Special		Hauser E	3oa	1cl BM
153	Kurtis 500 S		Smith R	4oa	2cl BM
195	Jaguar XK120		Miller W	5oa	1cl C
99	Morgensen Mercedes		Crane D	6oa	2cl C
133	Jaguar XK120M		Austin J	7oa	3cl C
154	Jaguar XK120		McGraw H	8oa	4cl C
66	Jaguar XK120		O'Connor A	9oa	5cl C
162	Jaguar XK120		Collins W	10oa	6cl C
105	Jaguar XK120		Eurengy A	11oa	7cl C
189	Jaguar XK120M		Sharp A	12oa	8cl C
59	Jaguar XK120		Furlong D	13oa	9cl C
209	Chevrolet Corvette		Benavides T	14oa	10cl C
157	Jaguar XK120M		Blackwell C	15oa	11cl C
171	Jaguar XK120M		Miller R	16oa	12cl C
42	Jaguar XK120M		Montonen H	17oa	13cl C
69	Jaguar XK120		Weller R	18oa	14cl C
266	Jaguar XK120		Yarter N	19oa	15cl C
94	Chevrolet Corvette		Peterson R	20oa	16cl C
213	Jaguar XK120		Fisher H	21oa	17cl C
110	Jaguar XK120M		Jones H	22oa	18cl C
53	Triumph TR2		Knowe W	23oa	1cl E
39	Triumph TR2		Pierson T	24oa	2cl E
98	Triumph TR2		Rosenthal G	25oa	3cl E
101	Triumph TR2		Utley R	26oa	4cl E
62	Jaguar XK120		Thomas L	27oa	19cl C
78	Triumph TR2		Newton A	28oa	5cl E
265	Jaguar XK120		Spezze R	29oa	20cl C
177	Morgan Plus 4		Caton L	30oa	6cl E
84	Triumph TR2		McRoberts R	31oa	7cl E
51	Triumph TR2		Dettman J	32oa	8cl E
217	Triumph TR2		Phillips M	33oa	9cl E
143	Triumph TR2		Cox T	Dnf L5	
19	Jaguar XK120M		Little J	Dnf L4	
68	Austin-Healey 100		Scholtas R	Dnf L3	
202	Fiberglass Special		Loveland V	Dnf L2	
187	AB Special		Bowles W	Dnf L2	
22	Lincoln Mercury		Driscoll D	Dnf L1	

Race 3.	7 laps	Race distance 24.5 miles	Class MG	Starters 18

Race winner's time 23min 15.8sec		Average speed 63.50mph	
58	MG TD	Meyers R	1oa	1cl F
122	MG TD	Choisser J	2oa	2cl F

161	MG TC	Curland M	3oa	3cl F
210	MG TD	Burhop D	4oa	4cl F
179	MG TF	McClean E	5oa	5cl F
44	MG TD	Barrett C	6oa	6cl F
141	MGTD	Sinclair S	7oa	7cl F
81	MG TD	Youngberg J	8oa	8cl F
126	MG TC	Yeagle C	9oa	9cl F
167	MG TD	Brigandi K	10oa	10cl F
172	MG TD	Dair J	11oa	11cl F
37	MG TD	Reynolds R	12oa	12cl F
18	MG TD	Bradley J	13oa	13cl F
33	MG TD	Royer D	14oa	14cl F
158	MG TD	Arnold J	15oa	15cl F
211	MG TD	Rottman E	16oa	16cl F
199	MG TD	Decker S	Dnf L3	
61	MG TF	Brigham R	Dnf L2	

Race 4 10 laps	Race distance 35 miles	Class C, D, E, F, H	Starters 41

Race winner's time 29min 46.75sec	Average speed 71.28mph

83	Jaguar XK120M	Peterson J	1oa	1cl C
195	Jaguar XK120	Miller W	2oa	2cl C
12	Jaguar XK120M	Katskee L	3oa	3cl C
162	Jaguar XK120	Collins W	4oa	4cl C
82	Jaguar XK120	Teaby G	5oa	5cl C
69	Jaguar XK120	Weller R	6oa	6cl C
28	Jaguar XK120	Garlick W	7oa	7cl C
85	Jaguar XK120M	McGregor J	8oa	8cl C
94	Chevrolet Corvette	Peterson R	9oa	9cl C
118	Porsche 356 Super	Kunstle J	10oa	1cl F
183	Triumph TR2	Owen L	11oa	1cl E
54	Porsche 356 Super	Kieckhefer W	12oa	2cl F
78	Triumph TR2	Turnstall W	13oa	2cl E
256	Porsche 356 Super	Manley F	14oa	3cl F
61	MG TF	Brigham R	15oa	4cl F
58	MG TF	Quimby C	16oa	5cl F
89	Swallow-Doretti	Boyd E	17oa	3cl E
161	MG TC	Curland M	18oa	6cl F
65	DB Panhard	Parker F	19oa	1cl H
123	DB Panhard	St Louis G	20oa	2cl H
79	Triumph TR2	Dilloway T	R	
149	Triumph TR2	Kretz E	R	
63	Jaguar XK120M	Lozano I	Dnf L6	
120	Jaguar XK120M	Borden J	Dnf L6	

122	MG TD	Choisser J	Dnf L6	
180	HRG	Stephenson I	Dnf L4	
41	Singer SM 1500	Sullivan R	Dnf L3	
18	MG TD	Bradley J		
43	Swallow-Doretti	McEachen J Dr		
44	MG TD	Barrett C		
64	Jaguar XK120	Masterson R		
74	MG TF	Trennert R		
84	Triumph TR2	McRoberts R		
87	Jaguar XK120M	Hearn B		
111	Porsche 356	Kieckhefer W		
130	Morgan Plus 4	Thompson C Dr		
131	MG TF	Parkinson J		
158	MG TD	Datig F		
168	Porsche 356	Holbrook R		

Race 5 5 laps	Race distance 17.5 miles	Class Ladies	Starters 19

Race winner's time 16min 57.8sec	Average speed 63.36mph

70	Bu-Ford Special	Balchowsky I	1oa	1cl BM
149	Olds Corvette	Hoppe H Dr	2oa	1cl CM
79	Triumph TR2	Davis M	3oa	1cl E
177	Morgan Plus 4	McBratney J	4oa	1cl D
51	Triumph TR2	Detman B	5oa	2cl E
203	Singer SM 1500	Sawyer P	6oa	1cl F
129	MG TD MkII	Lawrence C	7oa	2cl F
183	Triumph TR2	Owen B	8oa	3cl E
68	Austin-Healey 100	Matthews S	9oa	2cl D
90	Jupiter Special	Stevens J	10oa	3cl F
167	MG TD	Clark C	11oa	4cl F
210	MG TD	Brennen B	12oa	5cl F
80	Singer SM 1500	Day M	13oa	6cl F
98	Triumph TR2	Lachman A	14oa	4cl E
212	Aston Martin DB2	Burkhard J	15oa	3cl D
33	MG TD	Royer J	16oa	7cl F
211	MG TD	Kramer M	17oa	8cl F
126	MG TC	Bishop M	Dnf	
170	Arnolt-Bristol	Grover M	Dnf	

Race 6 15 laps	Race distance 52.5 miles	Class F, FM, GM, HM	Starters 37*

Race winner's time 42min 15.20sec	Average speed 74.73mph

91	OSCA MT4 1450	1133	Simpson J	1oa	1cl FM

125	VW Special		Lovely P	2oa	2cl FM
9	OSCA MT4 1450	1135	David W	3oa	3cl FM
145	MG Special		Playan M	4oa	4cl FM
10	Beavis Offenhauser		Beavis G	5oa	5cl FM
50	MG Special		Gillespie R	6oa	6cl FM
32	Porsche 356 America		Bunker A	7oa	7cl FM
117	OSCA MT4 1350	1127	Leson C	8oa	8cl FM
67	OSCA MT4		Chapman H	9oa	9cl FM
90	Jupiter Special		Thomas W	10oa	10cl FM
118	Porsche 356 Super		Kunstle J	11oa	1cl F
40	MG TD mod		Dalton J	12oa	11cl FM
46	Porsche 356		Dickey D	13oa	12cl FM
17	MG TD		Hanford H	14oa	13cl FM
31	Moretti Coupe		Biehl J	15oa	1cl HM
25	DB Panhard		Peron P	16oa	1cl GM
61	MG TF		Brigham R	17oa	2cl F
58	MG TF		Meyers R	18oa	3cl F
141	MG TD		Sinclair S	19oa	4cl F
255	DB Panhard		Manley F	20oa	2cl HM
44	MG TD		Barrett C	21oa	5cl F
86	MG TD		Twohey L	22oa	14cl FM
37	MG TD Mk II		Reynolds R	23oa	6cl F
65	DB Panhard		Parker F	24oa	2cl GM
123	DB Panhard		St.Louis G	25oa	3cl GM
30	Crosley		Thompson C	26oa	3cl HM
134	MG TD		Solt V	27oa	7cl F
18	MG TD		Bradley J	28oa	8cl F
129	MG TD Mk II		Lawrence J	Dnf L12	
122	MG TD		Choisser J	Dnf L11	
279	MG TC		Mahon D	Dnf L10	
166	OSCA MT4 1450		Stewart P	Dnf L9	
138	Porsche 356		Taylor A	Dnf L8	
1	Lotus-MG		Bell W	Dnf L6	
8	Crosley Special		Cannon J	Dnf L5	
158	MG TD		Arnold J	Dnf L4	
41	Singer SM 1500		Sullivan R	Dnf L3	

- #11, Porsche 550 (550-011) crashed in practice, driven by J von Neumann, and did not race.

Race 7 35 laps	Race distance 122.5 miles	Class C, BM, CM, DM, EM	Starters 41

Race winner's time 1hr 30min 30sec		Average speed 74.4 mph

4	Ferrari 375 MM	0382 AM	Spear W	1oa	1cl CM
2	Ferrari 375 MM	0286 AM	Hill P	2oa	2cl CM
100	Ferrari 375 MM	0372 AM	Johnston S	3oa	3cl CM
26	Ferrari 340 MM	0350 AM	Edwards S	4oa	4cl CM
108	Jaguar C-type	XKC 017	Brero L	5oa	5cl CM
5	Ferrari 375 MM	0364 AM	Kimberly J	6oa	6cl CM
115	Ferrari 340 MM	0322 AM	Irish R	7oa	7cl CM
147	Kurtis 500 S Buick		Murphy W	8oa	8cl CM
104	Mabee Special		Wysong M	9oa	1cl BM
71	Ferrari 250 MM	0282 MM	Hively H	10oa	1cl DM
35	Ferrari 212 Ex	0078 E	Wheeler H	11oa	2cl DM
132	Morgensen Special		Morgensen B	12oa	9cl CM
83	Jaguar XK120M		Peterson J	13oa	1cl C
200	Triumph TR2		Kieckhefer W	14oa	1cl EM
162	Jaguar XK120		Collins W	15oa	2cl C
133	Jaguar XK120M		Austin J	16oa	3cl C
85	Jaguar XK120M		McGregor J	17oa	4cl C
52	MG V8-60		Peldigo P	18oa	3cl DM
149	Chevrolet Corvette		Kretz E	19oa	2cl BM
183	Triumph TR2		Owen L	20oa	2cl EM
174	Powell V8 Special		Powell B	21oa	3cl BM
135	Jaguar XK120		Evans H	Dnf L26	
27	Jaguar C-type		Erickson E	Dnf L25	
99	Morgensen Mercedes		Bird T	Dnf L21	
21	Lincoln Ford		Murphy R	Dnf L20	
3	Jaguar XK120		Mendelson M	Dnf L19	
48	Aston-Martin DB2-4		Steele H	Dnf L19	
70	Bu-Ford Special		Balchowsky M	Dnf L16	
109	Kurtis 500 S		Chatfield T	Dnf L16	
165	Siata 208S Special	BS 537	McAfee E	Dnf L13	
29	Cannon MkIII		Seeley J	Dnf L9	
73	Fageol-Porsche Special		Fageol L	Dnf L7	
101	Triumph TR2		Utley R	Dnf L5	
150	Allard J2X Chrysler	J3208	Barneson J	Dnf L4	
14	Kurtis 500 S Mercury		Buderin A	Dnf L3	
49	Jaguar Special		Drake R	Dnf L2	
34	Jaguar Special		Wilder E	Dnf L2	
6	Ferrari 340 AM	0204 A	Lunken E	Dnf L1	
156	Allard J2X		McHenry T	Dnf L1	
139	Mercedes 300 SL		Orr J	Dnf	
12	Jaguar XK120M		Katskee L	Dnf	

11

SCCA national and regional races at non-SAC military bases 1954

Suffolk ADC, Westhampton, Long Island
9.5.1954 (Regional/ADC)

"Two-litre Maseratis completely dominated the day's racing, taking first and second in one event and first, second, and third in another." **(Road & Track)**

With Bridgehampton now off the race calendar, the New York Region of the SCCA needed to find another venue to fill the void. To find a venue that fulfilled all of the criteria to replace Bridgehampton would have been a pipe dream, so the race committee looked at alternatives with different characteristics. Floyd Bennett Field NAS had been used in 1953, though not by the SCCA – instead titturned to Suffolk Air Defence Command Base, situated some two miles from Westhampton Beach on Long Island, and about 75 miles east of New York City. This alternative venue offered wide open runways with the potential for the SCCA to devise its own course, so they negotiated and reached agreement with the Base Commander for the use of the facility on a similar basis to the SCCA agreement with SAC bases. As a result, the Suffolk County Trophy Race, together with 3 supporting races, was held under the auspices of the New York region of the SCCA. The races were co-sponsored by the Air Force Defence Command of the 519th Air Defence group, with all proceeds from the event going to the Airmen's Living Improvement Fund for better recreational facilities.

Suffolk County Air Force base served as the prime Air Defence Command base responsible for defending the New York metropolitan area against hostile air attack. It must have appeared strange to witness sports cars scurrying down the runways, instead of the usual F-86D all-weather fighter interceptors of the 519th Defence Group.

An admission ticket to the Suffolk County Sports Car Races. (Courtesy Michael Eaton Collection)

Strange to relate is the fact that no two parties that reported the races (and there were only a few of those!) could agree on the length of the circuit measured out on the runways and taxi strips of the airfield. *Speed Age* quotes it as being 2.25 miles long, the *New York Times* as nearly 2 miles long, whilst *Road and Track* assured its readers that it was in fact only 1.55 miles long, with a straightway of 3300ft. Without admission from the race officials, it was more likely that the latter figure was the correct one. With this variance in mind, the official results are in doubt, not so much for the positions that the drivers finished in, more for the times, average speeds, and distance covered in each race. If nothing else, the result of this confusion bore a passing resemblance to the track layout problems encountered at nearby Floyd Bennett Field in 1953, where the track length turned out to be an educated guess.

As an aside, 8 pages of the programme were taken up by Jaguar advertising material. This followed 12 pages of the Andrews AFB programme being used in a similar manner. Max Hoffman, east-coast importer for Jaguar placed the adverts, as he was making a last-ditch attempt to retain his relationship with William Lyons at Jaguar Cars. William Lyons had recently formed Jaguar Cars North America Corporation to give Jaguar greater control over the American operation, and Max Hoffman could envisage his lucrative business dwindling away.

A four-race programme had been arranged at the ADC base, two

Another Jaguar, the driver of which remains unidentified, chases Bob Grossman's Jaguar XK120. Finishing positions are unknown for this race at Suffolk ADC. (Ozzie Lyons, courtesy Pete Lyons Collection)

In the second race, Johnston's OSCA finished in third place. Hansgen's Aston-Martin failed to finish the race. (Courtesy Michael Eaton Collection)

McKenna's Jaguar weaves its way past two MGs in the first race. (Courtesy Michael Eaton Collection)

Frank Ahrens drove his Motto-MG in the third race, but his result is not known. (Courtesy Michael Eaton Collection)

William Wonder prepares for the feature race in his Austin-Healey. (Courtesy Michael Eaton Collection)

events of fifty miles, one feature race of one hundred miles, and the other feature race of one hundred and fifty miles were advertised. However, using the revised track length, the race distance would have been reduced to the figures shown in the result tables.

The first race on the programme was for all Classes of production cars, plus modified cars under 1100cc, and attracted an entry of 40 cars. The race was won by Russ Boss driving a JaguarXK120M, with Walt Hansgen second, and Crusoe third, also driving Jaguars.

Class winners were Fred Allen driving his Austin-Healey in Class

The wide expanse of Suffolk County ADC did not offer much protection from the weather. Warm clothing was the order of the day. (Courtesy Michael Eaton Collection)

D, James Graham in his potent Porsche 356 in Class F, Don Vitale in a Nardi in Class HM, and John Bentley in a Siata in Class GM.

The second race was for modified sports cars over 1500cc and proved an interesting duel between the Maserati A6GCS of Fritz Koster and Proctor, driving McNought's newer Maserati, and the OSCA MT4 owned by Cunningham, but driven by Sherwood Johnston. The three cars were never far apart, but Koster stayed ahead of his rivals to take the chequered flag. He finished ahead of Bill Proctor and Johnston, with Duncan Black in fourth place, driving his modified Lester-MG. Actor Jackie Cooper drove his Austin-Healey 100 to a Class DM victory, though never seriously challenged for overall top places in the race. Interestingly, some of the owners of the larger-engine specials, more frequently seen at Thompson Raceway, made the short journey to Long Island to try their luck. George Rabe brought his Riley-Ford V8, while John Meyer drove his Meyer-Cadillac Special.

The 77.5-mile third race, for under-1500cc production cars, went to James Graham driving his Porsche 356. He finished ahead of John Bentley, who surprisingly broke the dominance of the Porsche 356 models driving a Siata 1100, and, in doing so, won Class GM. Driving in his first race, Emanual Pupulidy finished in third place, just two seconds behind Bentley, while Alfons Koster finished in fourth place. Both of the latter named drivers were driving Porsche 356s. George Schrafft, driving his Palm Beach Crosley, won Class HM, while Mike Hunt was in the first of the MGs to cross the finish line.

The 75-lap feature race, covering some 116 miles, brought the Maseratis and OSCAs together again, and also the modified Jaguars, an Aston-Martin, Frazer-Nash, and Austin-Healeys. Twenty-nine cars lined up for the start; this time, Bill Eager was driving McNought's Maserati and Hansgen had swapped to George Tilp's Aston Martin DB2 Offenhauser. The Jaguars of Wallace and McKenna were first off the line, but in the early stages of the race, Hansgen overtook them and established a lead, followed by Eager in a Maserati. Hansgen held the lead for eight laps, then Eager overtook him. For the next six laps, the two of them passed and re-passed each other, much to the excitement of the 27,000 spectators, until Hansgen was forced to pit, after his car broke a carburetor flange. He returned to the race following repairs, but the mishap cost him eight laps. Meanwhile, Eager drew away from the field with Lloyd, Koster, Johnston, and Boss in pursuit. Further down the field, the Austin-Healeys of Jackie Cooper and Fred Allen were battling against a car making its racing debut in America, the 2.8-litre Pegaso driven by Brete Hannaway, but regrettably, it stripped its gears and had to retire on the nineteenth lap.

At the halfway mark, the Maserati driven by Eager was in the lead, closely followed by Koster, Johnston, and Lloyd. Of the four drivers, Lloyd was the beneficiary, first moving past the OSCA of Johnston, then catching and passing Koster for second place. It ended a remarkable 1-2-3 for the Maseratis, with Johnston's OSCA in fourth place, and first in Class F. Charles Wallace won Class C in his Jaguar XK120, and Fred Allen won Class D in his Austin-Healey 100S, while Class CM was awarded to Walt Hansgen.

The event was deemed as a success, both by the SCCA and Suffolk ADC, as the event filled the gap in the calendar left by the demise of Bridgehampton. However, drivers and spectators alike still yearned for the days when true road racing took place on Long Island, though, in truth, there was little hope of that happening again. A brighter future loomed, though, as plans were in hand to develop a private track at Bridgehampton, but that promise would not be fulfilled until 1957.

Atterbury AFB, Columbus, Indiana
30.5.1954 (Regional/AFB)

"Organisation of the racing programme would put all of the National sports car races to shame." Jerry Coleman, official race starter (Evening Republican, Columbus, Indiana)

Atterbury AFB fell under the control of America's Continental Air Command, and was located near Columbus, Indiana. The event was another fine example of co-operation between the SCCA and the armed services, both groups being quick to capitalise on the potential benefits of holding the races.

The initial idea stemmed from the Commander of the 43rd Hoosier Reserve Wing, based at Atterbury, who was looking around to find some method of stepping up the interest in the Reserve Training Programme. Sponsorship of a race was suggested, and Major Richard Smithson was designated the responsibility of negotiating a deal with the Indianapolis Region of the SCCA. Bob Tappan was their representative, and agreed to form a link, not only with Atterbury AFB, but also the Columbus Junior Chamber of Commerce, who had joint sponsorship of the event. Timing of the event was planned, so that it ran almost concurrently with the Indianapolis 500 – that way, there would be a spin-off of spectators who had travelled to the area for that event on Memorial Day. Plentiful support for the forthcoming races was provided in the local paper *The Evening Republican*, as it gave good pre-race coverage for several days in the build-up to the event. Having organised a race at Stout Field in 1953, the Indianapolis region was looking for an alternative venue for 1954, as Stout Field course had proved to be too short, especially for the

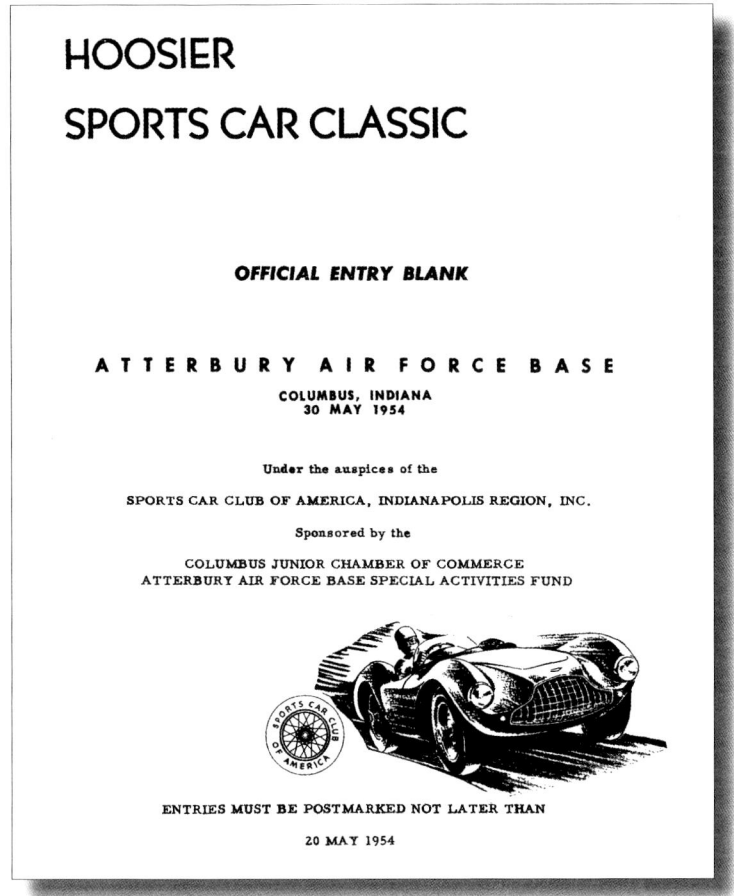

An Official Entry Blank for the event at Atterbury AFB. (Courtesy Bruce Perry Collection)

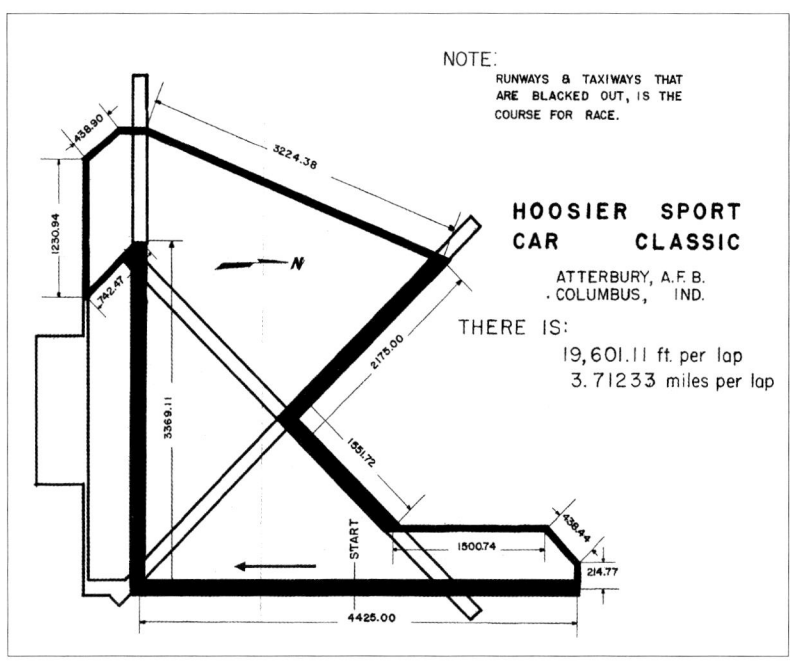

Track layout at Atterbury AFB. (Terry O'Neil Collection)

bigger cars. A much larger facility was required, and Atterbury suited its needs, as a course of 3.7 miles was planned to cover the wide expanse of concrete runways and taxi strips. As part of the agreement between the SCCA and Atterbury AFB, all proceeds raised from the Hoosier Sports Car Classic would be used to equip a new Columbus Youth Centre, and improve airmen's living conditions at Atterbury AFB.

Spectators began arriving at the air base as early as 7am, and, by 10am, 14,460 cars had travelled through the gates into the airbase. Crowds of between 25,000 and 30,000 spectators (depending on which report was accurate) turned up for the event.

There were four races on the programme; the first one, the Jaycee Cup for production cars under 1500cc, started at 10am. With such a diverse mix of cars, the entrants were divided into marque Classes, so there ended up being five races in one. Various Porsche models dominated the front of the grid, and as the flag dropped, Bob Magenheimer's Porsche Super took an early lead, with Bill Pickerel right behind him. Shuck, in another Porsche, made his way into second place on the second lap, with Ralph Durbin moving into third spot in his MG TF, but Pickerel fought back to regain second spot. Meanwhile, Magenheimer was drawing away from the field, and by the time he reached the chequered flag, had managed to lap almost everybody else. Pickerel finished a distant second, and Durbin took a commendable third place in his MG TF. Cole, in his Singer, won the Miscellaneous Class, Crane the Porsche America Class, and Lange the MG TD Class. Having all of these Classes made it a busy time for Miss Edith Mae Krumme ('Miss Sports Car'), as it was her duty to congratulate each of the winners throughout the day.

The Bartholomew County Trophy Dash was a 56-mile event for production cars over 1500cc, and brought together modified and standard production Jaguars, Austin-Healeys, and a new Triumph TR2, which was placed in Class D alongside the Austin-Healeys, as it was the only Class E car present in the race. Much as expected, the Jaguar XK120M cars dominated proceedings from the start; Kilborn jumped into an early lead, as Jess Coleman dropped the flag with Dr Grove right behind, and Attaway pushing him hard. Surprisingly, Salzgaber's TR2 had established an early lead against the Austin-Healeys and was right behind Tom Newcomer in his Jaguar. On the sixth lap, Salzgaber broke a left wheel and slowed the car, allowing Vollmer to take a lead in Class D, which he retained until the end of the race. At the front, Kilborn had a comfortable lead to win the race, with Dr Grove in second place, having seen off the challenge of Attaway. Missing from the race was Jack Ensley,

An unidentified Siata at Atterbury. (Courtesy Bakalar Air Museum)

G and H, which brought to the grid Rubini in his new MG powered Lotus, Bentley with his very potent Siata 1100cc, Arnolt in a Nardi, and MacArthur in a Bandini Crosley. Pre-race favourites were Magenheimer in his Porsche Super, and Durbin in his MG TF.

As in the first race of the day, Magenheimer took an early lead, and at the end of the first lap was followed at a distance by Bentley's Siata and Durbin's MG TF. The smaller engine modified cars were well among the larger Porsche models, MacArthur and Seaverns battling between themselves for fourth place overall. The top three places remained unchanged during the race – only MacArthur and Seaverns were undecided until the very last moment, as they crossed the line together, with MacArthur's Bandini getting the vote for fourth place.

The Columbus Cup attracted a field of 39 cars, and such was the quality of the entrants, any one of them was in contention to take their Class prize, although, when it came to the overall prizes, the options looked somewhat limited. Kimberly had turned up with his all-conquering Ferrari 375MM, and Lunken had thrown down the gauntlet by entering his recently acquired ex-Kimberly Ferrari 340AM. Three other Ferraris were listed to take part, though Lunken's Ferrari 225S, prepared for Hassan to drive, was cannibalised for spare parts to put on Lunken's 4.1 Ferrari and did not start. Up against the Ferraris were a number of Allards, a Kurtis 500, Fageol's twin-engine Porsche, and a Ford Special.

who had originally entered, but had been taken ill prior to the race date. It was hoped he would be well enough to be chief starter for the races, but, come the day, he was absent.

The third race of the day was entitled the Hoosier Reserve Wing Trophy Dash, a 74-mile race for production cars under 1500cc and modified cars under 1100cc. As with the first race of the day, the field was divided into separate Classes, six in all. A fair few cars from the first race re-appeared, though this time challenged by the modified Classes

The grid formed with Lunken on the second row, surrounded by Allards and Jaguars, while Kimberly found himself in eleventh grid slot. Lunken's Ferrari started well and took the lead, followed by Fageol's Porsche, a car that, in the past, had promised much but had delivered little. It took three laps for Kimberly to weave through the field to take the lead, and there he stayed, with Lunken and Fageol behind him. The main fight was for the next three positions, with Rigden in a Kurtis, Skogmo in an Allard, and Ullrich in an Excalibur exchanging positions lap by lap, all of them being hounded by Bill Heldt in a Ferrari 166MM that used to belong to Bill Spear. As the race progressed, the Excalibur dropped of the pace, and it was soon evident that Ullrich was making frequent pit stops, as was Gary in the other Excalibur. This allowed Kilborn, driving a Jaguar, to come into fifth place, but well behind the leaders. Further down the field, the battle for Class honours was intense, Wacker's Arnolt-Bristol leading Heldt's Ferrari in Class EM, with two Siata 208S models in close attendance, Krasburg driving an MG TD leading Class F, and Tom Newcomer leading in the Standard Production Jaguar Class.

The unluckiest driver at the event was Bob Salzgaber. He had

Jim Kimberly, with his Ferrari 375MM, won the feature race at Atterbury. (Courtesy Bakalar Air Museum)

brought an MG Special and a TR2 to race, blew the engine of the MG in the first race, and had a wheel break on his TR2, once in the second race, and again in the feature race. He was the unenviable and undisputed winner of the 'hard-luck trophy' awarded at the Victory banquet.

Rough estimates made by the co-sponsors put the expenses of the event at $22,000, while gate receipts totalled some $27,000, leaving them with a useful profit to share between the Columbus Youth Centre and the Airmen's Living Conditions Improvement Fund. "We think it was a terrific success," said Aldo Tombari, Columbus Jaycee, who served as general chairman of the sports car races. "I don't think we should pass up an opportunity to stage a similar show next year," he added. (*Evening Republican*)

Competitor's plaque for entering the event at Atterbury AFB. (Courtesy Bakalar Air Museum)

General Motors put on a static display of futuristic cars including the 'Firebird.' (Courtesy Bakalar Air Museum)

Westover AFB, Springfield, Massachusetts
12/13.6.1954 (National/AFB)

"The day's smoothly-run schedule of events, and the obvious excitement and enthusiasm of the thousands of spectators, was a satisfying reward for the men of the Air Force Base." Alix Lafontant (Road & Track)

Just one week after the races at Chanute AFB, the eighth national event of 1954, heralded as the New England national Races, was held at Westover AFB. Located on the edge of Springfield, the venue was the first one to hold a SCCA National event in the state of Massachusetts. It was unfortunate that it coincided with the Le Mans 24-hour race, as the Cunningham Team and some of the leading American drivers such as Walters, Spear, Johnston, and Fitch were attending that event, detracting from the quality of the field at Westover AFB.

At the date of the New England National Races in 1954, Westover AFB was not under the control of Strategic Air Command. The transfer did not take effect until 1955, as, until then, the huge Westover installation held a duel role. It was home to the Atlantic Division of the Military Air Transport Services, and also home of the 60th Fighter-Interseptor Squadron. Major General Wetzel and Base Commander Colonel Clinton Wasem were the people who made decisions for the military at Westover, and it was they who the SCCA management needed to negotiate with, to arrange for the use of the Base. It was agreed that if the terms were the same as the terms applicable with the existing SAC bases, then the Base could indeed be used, so proceeds from all ticket

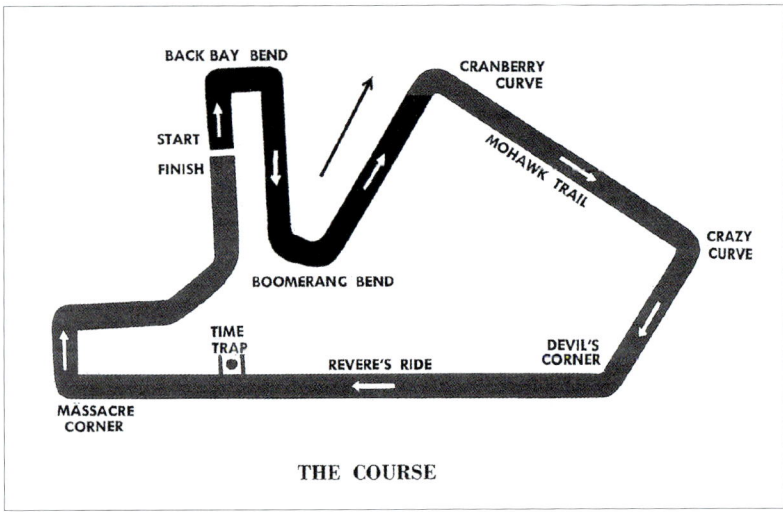

Track layout at Westover AFB. (Terry O'Neil Collection)

sales, programmes, and other items would be donated to the Airmen's Living Improvement Fund at Westover AFB.

The very nature of the operations carried out at Westover AFB by the military meant that the major runways had to be kept clear at all times, but the large airfield still offered plenty of scope to lay out a demanding track on the service runways. The proposed course measured 3.7 miles in length, over concrete and asphalt surfaces 50ft wide, and incorporated six 90-degree bends, a few curves, and a straightway of 4,900ft.

Thanks to the efforts of the public relations personnel at the Westover base, the build up to race day was well covered in the local Springfield newspaper, with articles about the drivers and cars. They also put enormous effort put into ensuring that State Police and National Guard were in position to direct and control the flow of traffic onto the air base on race day, as a sizeable crowd was expected to turn up.

Early morning rain did little to deter the sports car enthusiasts turning up for the 9am start to the race programme, and, by lunchtime, the crowd had swelled to around 30,000 people, now bathed in warm sunshine. The 'Minute Man' race was first to take place, a race for Porsches and under 1100cc modified cars. The modified cars appeared to be able to out-pace the Porsche contingent – a varied selection of them held the top positions as the race unfolded. Makins driving his OSCA took the lead and stayed there, initially pushed by Rudkin in his Bandini. As the race progressed, Makins took control and extended his lead to nearly one whole lap ahead of second placed Rudkin. The little PBX Special of Candy Poole crept up from seventh place to third position, while John Bentley's Siata finished fourth, ahead of the first Porsche to finish, that of John Bye in fifth place.

The Paul Revere Race was run for standard and factory modified Jaguars. One of the best exponents of these cars was Charles Wallace, and he didn't disappoint the crowd. From the time the green flag dropped to the chequered flag, he led the race in Jack Pry's Jaguar XK120M, with only Russ Boss being quick enough to apply any sort of a challenge. Boss finished in second place, ahead of Jack Crusoe and Richard Perrin, all of them driving M specification cars.

The third race, The Clipper Race, was for under three-litre production cars and under two-litre modified cars. Jim Kimberly was in an OSCA borrowed from James Simpson, as Simpson could not be in attendance. Competition to Kimberly's OSCA was provided by the presence of Duncan Black's modified Lester-MG, Koster's Maserati, and a host of Austin-Healeys on the start grid. Excitement grew as the race started, with first Kincheloe in an Austin-Healey 100, then Koster in his Maserati sharing the lead for the first six laps, with Kimberly not far behind. Waiting for the right moment, Kimberly took the lead on the seventh lap, as Koster's Maserati began to slow down, eventually to retire on the eighth lap. Kincheloe hung on to take second place with Schrafft's Siata 208S in third position, and Duncan Black's Lester-MG fourth. Kimberly won Class FM, Kincheloe Class D, and Shrafft Class EM. Of the smaller capacity cars, Rees Makins did best, finishing in sixth place over all, and first in Class GM in his OSCA.

The 45-mile Mayflower race was for MGs competing for National Championship points, together with any Class GM and HM cars that cared to join in and try for a trophy. It would appear to have been more of a show for the spectators than a meaningful race, as only one MG ended up in the top four finish positions. John Bentley led the race

*Conley's Siata in action at Westover AFB.
(Ozzie Lyons, courtesy Pete Lyons Collection)*

take the lead. Having ample time in hand over the second-placed car, he kept the crowd entertained by progressively going quicker through the speed trap, lap after lap, culminating in a speed of 148mph.

Bill Lloyd in his Ferrari held second place some distance behind Kimberly for the entire race, with Duncan Black, maybe unsurprisingly due to the lack of opposition, finishing in third place in his Lester-MG. Charles Wallace headed three Production Class Jaguars into the next three places.

The crowd was undoubtedly entertained throughout the day, but from the SCCA's point of view, the feature event of the day was disappointing, and the quality of entrants did not reflect the effort put into the event by Westover AFB personnel. The victory dinner and presentation of the trophies – the only compensation afforded to the winners in the SCCA – went ahead in the evening to climax the programme.

Fort Worth NGB, Texas

1.8.1954 (regional/NGB)

"Bill Jarnigan leapt from his blazing Allard JR as leaking gas on hot brake drums started a fire. Jarnigan jumped at 40 mph, but was not seriously injured."

(Fort Worth Star Telegram)

*Lloyd's Ferrari 225 finished in second place behind Kimberly in the feature race, the Steve Canyon Classic.
(Courtesy Wolery Collection IMRRC)*

from the start in his quick little Siata, chased by Bob Richardson in his MG TF, the pick of the MGs in this race. He finished second overall, but took maximum championship points, ahead of DiGiacomo's Cisitalia and Kern's Siata. The second MG to finish the race was that of Monroe Davidson in another TF. The one serious accident of the entire event took place in this race when Robert Rodier's MG TC overturned at one of the corners. Luckily, Rodier escaped with cuts and bruises, and a fractured nose – and dented pride.

The feature race of the day was the Steve Canyon Classic run over 175 miles of the track. Coming so soon after the races at Chanute, it has to be said that the participants was not quite as challenging this time. It was difficult to see who was capable of mounting a challenge to Kimberly, as the likes of Spear, Gregory, Edwards, Erickson, and Ensley were all absent. Lou Fageol had brought his unique twin-engine Porsche Special to the meeting, and it was considered that it might present a challenge to Kimberly, but alas, the car spun out early in the race, and was quickly followed by retirement. So the race turned out as predicted, with Kimberly putting on a one-man show for the crowd.

Starting from fourth place in the line-up of cars, Kimberly needed only a mile to prove the supremacy of his car and his acknowledged driving ability. He passed two cars on the first bend, then proceeded to haul in Rutherford's Allard, before overtaking it at Cranberry Curve to

For a reason that is not made apparent in any report, the Texas Region of the SCCA sanctioned and organised the third running of the Guardsman's Trophy Races, held at the Eagle Mountain National Guard Base, a few miles north of Fort Worth. The race meeting was sponsored by the Eagle Mountain National Guard Base, with proceeds of the meeting going to local charities.

The previous two events had been organised by the Foreign Auto and Sports Car Club but the reason for the change of organiser could be that many of the FASCC members were also SCCA members, and, being a larger club, could put more resources into the organisation of the event. Just as annoying is the ambiguity of the race event. While the SCCA referred to it as the 'Guardsman's Trophy Races,' the local papers and *Road & Track* magazine entitled the event the 'Guardsmen's Trophy Races.' While of little significance to many, it was another example of the inconsistency in reporting of that era that makes accuracy very difficult.

The *Road & Track* reporter was not having a good day, as he referred to the track as being 3.8 miles long, whereas the track was the one used

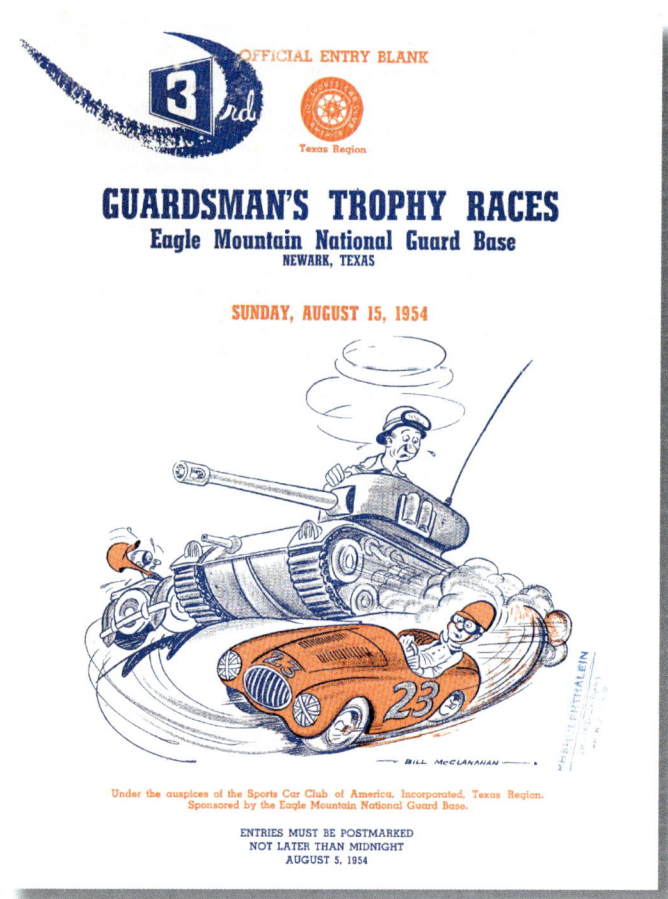

An Official Entry Blank for the event at Fort Worth NGB. (Courtesy Bruce Perry Collection)

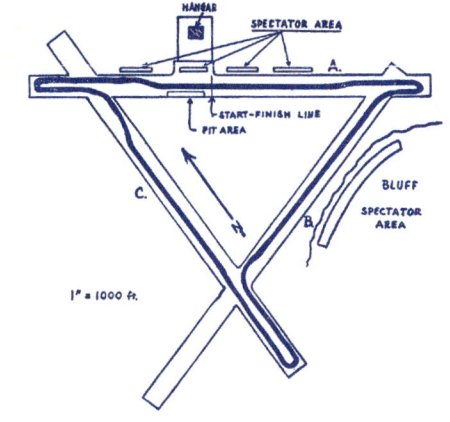

Track layout at Fort Worth NGB. (Terry O'Neil Collection)

in December 1953, and measured only three miles in length. Following on from the successful use of electronic timing devices at Moffett NAS in 1953, the SCCA had two timing devices installed to give straightway speeds of the cars, one on the north-south runway, the other on the northwest-southeast runway. It was anticipated that speeds of over 160mph were attainable on both straightways.

    Five races were scheduled for the programme, starting with a thirty-minute production sports car race for Classes C, D, E, and F cars. The *Fort Worth Star-Telegram* were thoughtful enough to publish a list of entrants for the races, which one can only imagine would have mirrored that printed in the race programme, and while it generally reflected the actual start grids, was far from accurate. Twenty-three cars were down to start the first race, the Eagle Mountain Trophy which featured a Le Mans start in front of a 9000 throng of spectators, all trying to keep cool in temperatures well over 100ºF. Dr Harold Fenner proved to have the most nimble feet, and the fastest car. He was first away from the Le Mans start and jumped into a lead he never relinquished in his dark grey Jaguar XK120. Bob Masterson came from far back in the field to pass both Bob Schroeder and Curtis Attaway, to finish second overall. In Class D, Banes beat Val Scroggie to the flag, both driving Austin-Healeys, while Staley won Class F in his Porsche 356, ahead of Art Bunker, and came fourth overall.

    The twelve-lap Blue Bonnet Cup for modified sports cars was the second race and brought out a number of main-race contenders. Carroll Shelby, driving Roy Cherryhome's Jaguar C-type out-sprinted Jarnigan, driving Tom Davis' newly acquired Allard JR to the first turn, and stayed in the lead for the remainder of the race. It finished with Shelby coasting home, with Koehne and McMullen finishing in that order. Jarnigan spun through a turn midway in the race and came in fourth. The Nash-Healey driven by Parks met a premature end when Parks hit a hay bale course-marker coming out of the first turn of the third lap, resulting in the car overturning, though, luckily, Parks escaped uninjured. Koehne took Class BM honours, while Stuart Harvey won Class DM in an MG

TC V8-60 belonging to Noah Smith, and Norman Scott took Class FM in his Continental-MG.

The third race could be called a sprint race, as it covered just five laps of the circuit and was for production MGs. There were fourteen entries for the race, though the number of starters is unclear. John Goans, driving a TC model, won the race, followed by Roy Heath in a TD MkII, and William Roberts in a TD model.

The fourth race was for Classes FP, FM, and HM, and brought together a varied array of Specials and Porsche models. Norman Scott, driving his Continental-MG Special, a car made up of components from MG and Cooper, easily won the race, ahead of Staley and Bunker in Porsche 356 models and Cherryhomes in his Moretti.

It was an impressive drive by Cherryhomes and warranted his Class HM victory, ahead of Betts driving a Giaur and Robb's Siata.

The main event of the programme was a 75-mile race, covering twenty-five laps of the course. Unfortunately, not all of the entrants made it to the start grid. Charles Brown failed to show with the ex-Phil Hill Ferrari 250MM, and Bob Sommers' Allard J2 Cadillac (ex-Roy Cherryhomes), which Shelby drove to victory in the first Guardsman's meeting, had been given a make-over, but was not made ready in time for the race, either. Because of the exclusions caused by various reasons, it was not a very competitive field that lined up for the Le Mans style start to the race.

Shelby, in Cherryhomes' C-type, had a poor start, and was ninth round the first bend, but rapidly cut through the field of seventeen cars to take the lead by the end of the second lap. An even worse start by McMullen saw him down in sixteenth place, and it took him ten laps to climb up to second position. Meanwhile, things were not going so well for Jarnigan in the Allard JR, as he appeared to spend more time spinning off the track than being on it. One of his excursions must have damaged the fuel line, as coming out of a turn on the fifth lap, leaking fuel ignited against a hot brake drum, causing the car to burst into flames. Jarnigan didn't wait to bring the car to a halt but jumped out while still doing 40mph, managing to escape serious injury. Just as well, as the car went up like a torch, and was virtually destroyed. It would be a sight that new owner Tom Davis didn't enjoy watching. Jarnigan was taken to Harris Hospital, where he was treated for cuts and bruises, then released. Other drivers also had to retire – Riddelle Gregory, the Second Guardsman's Trophy winner, went out of the race with a bent rod in his Jaguar C-type, and Charles Bowen pitted in his MG Special with a valve system that was beyond repair.

Meanwhile, at the front of the race, Shelby had quickly extended his lead, and lap by lap, he was carving his way through the rest of the field. When the chequered flag was shown, he had lapped everyone at least once, with the exception of McMullen, who was also driving a Jaguar C-type in second place, giving Shelby his second victory in the Guardsman's Trophy Race. McMullen crossed the finish line just over two minutes after Shelby, while third place went to Dr Harold Fenner in a Jaguar XK120, making it a clean sweep for the Coventry marque. Class D was won by Dr Val Scroggie driving his Austin-Healey ahead of Tom Bibb, while Robb's Siata was victorious in Class HM, ahead of Samuelson's Nardi.

A Victory banquet and presentation of trophies was held at the National Guard's Base canteen on Sunday evening, where the prizes were awarded to overall and Class winners by the Base commander, Col Burton Lyons.

Start grid for the Blue Bonnet Cup race, Jarnigan's Allard JR alongside the Jaguar C-types of Guy Simons and Riddelle Gregory on the front row. (Courtesy Michael T Lynch)

12

1954 Statistical Review

Suffolk County AFB 9.5.1954

Race 1	25 laps	Race distance 38.75 miles *	Class C, GM, HM	Starters 40

Race winner's time		Average speed	Track assumed to be 1.55 miles*	

21	Jaguar XK120M		Boss R	1oa	1cl C
4	Jaguar XK 120		Hansgen W	2oa	2cl C
33	Jaguar XK120		Crusoe J	3oa	3cl C
44	Nardi Spyder		Vitale D		1cl HM
77	Siata 300BC 750 Spyder	ST 435 BC	Bentley J		1cl GM
48	Porsche 356		Graham J		1cl F
73	Austin-Healey 100S	3504	Allen F		1cl D
2	Bandini Crosley		Raymond A		
6	Giaur		Dominianni F		
7	Jaguar XK120M		Lavac H		
11	Jaguar XK120		Sparacino P		
13	Pegaso 2.8		Hannaway B		
17	Jaguar XK120M		Janis C		
23	Jaguar XK120M		Constantine G		
24	Jaguar XK120		Heller D		
26	Porsche 356 1500		Powell S		
29	MG TD		Zirinsky D		
30	Jaguar XK120M		Wehman R		

Programme cover for the Suffolk ADC event. (Courtesy Bruce Perry Collection)

31	Jaguar XK120M		Scannell J		
32	Jaguar XK120M		Grossman R		
35	Jaguar XK120M		Kaback S		
37	Triumph TR2		Guild S		
38	Crosley		Pickering N		
39	Jaguar XK120M		Blackburn D		

41	Jaguar XK120M		Joseph N		
42	Austin-Healey 100		Simonds H		
43	Fiat Balilla		Herzog V		
45	Porsche 356		Pupulidy E		
46	MG TD		Hunt G		
53	MG TD		Cuomo R		
54	Porsche 356		Wood B		
55	Crosley		Deshon R		
56	Jaguar XK120M		Mull J & E		
57	Jaguar XK120M		Watson R		
58	MG TC		Wolf F		
60	Austin-Healey 100		Buck E		
63	Crosley		Findlay D		
64	Jaguar XK120		Woodbury W		
66	Cisitalia 202		Di Giacomo C		
70	Jaguar XK120M		Kaplan J		
74	Siata 300BC 1100 Spyder		Norwood J		
76	Siata 300BC 1100 Spyder		Kern W		
85	Jaguar XK120				

Race 2 25 laps	Race distance 38.75 miles	Class Unrestricted	Starters

Race winner's time 32min 27.5sec	Average speed 71.53mph

50	Maserati A6 GCS	2039	Koster F	1oa	1cl EM
15	Maserati A6 GCS	2053	Proctor F	2oa	2cl EM
86	OSCA MT4 1450	1137	Johnston S	3oa	1cl FM
4	Lester MG		Black D	4oa	2cl FM
18	Austin-Healey 100S	3504	Cooper J		1cl DM
3	Aston-Martin DB2 Offy		Hansgen W	dnf	
5	MG TD		Rodney M		
10	Jaguar XK120M		McKenna T		
12	Jaguar C-Type		Miller F		
14	OSCA MT4 1450	1139	Moffett G		
20	Bandini Siluro Offy		Pauley J		
25	Veritas		Stickney M		
27	Riley-Ford V8		Rabe G		
28	Ferrari 225 S	0166 ED	Lloyd W		
34	Keift Bristol		Ceresole P		
48	Porsche 356		Graham J		
49	MG Offenhauser		Micheals D		
52	Siata 208S	BS 501	Cicurel R		
59	Allard J2		Haber M		
61	Meyer-Cadillac Special		Meyer J		
62	MG TD		Tsakis H		

65	Keift MG		Underwood J		
68	MG TD mod		Atkins G		
72	MG TD		Parrington G		
75	Austin-Healey 100		Kolaczkowski W		
71	Austin-Healey 100		Wonder W		
8	Austin-Healey 100				
88	OSCA MT4				
60	Austin-Healey 100		Buck E		

Race 3 50 laps	Race distance 77.5 miles	Class F, GM, HM	Starters

Race winner's time 1hr 14min 3sec	Average speed 62.83mph

48	Porsche 356		Graham J	1oa	1cl F
77	Siata 300BC 750 Spyder	ST 435 BC	Bentley J	2oa	1cl GM
45	Porsche 356		Pupulidy E	3oa	2cl F
47	Porsche 356		Koster A	4oa	3cl F
111	Palm Beach Crosley		Schrafft G		1cl HM
46	MG TD		Hunt G		1cl F-MG
2	Bandini Crosley		Raymond A		
6	Giaur		Dominianni F		
22	Siata 300BC 1100 Spyder		Pompeo A		
29	MG TD		Zirinsky D		
38	Crosley		Pickering N		
40	Porsche 356		Braun L		
43	Fiat Balilla		Herzog V		
44	Nardi Spyder		Vitale D		
51	Porsche 356		Meeker D		
53	MG TD		Cuomo R		
54	Porsche 356		Wood B		
55	Crosley		Deshon R		
63	Crosley		Finlay D		
66	Cisitalia 202		Di Giacomo C		
69	Porsche 356		Krinsky R		
74	Siata 300BC 1100 Spyder		Norwood J		
76	Siata 300 BC 1100 Spyder		Kern W		
79	Motto MG		Ahrens F		
80	MG TD		Comito L		

Race 4 75 laps	Race distance 116.25 miles	Class DM, EM, FM, C	Starters 29

Race winner's time 1hr 36min 29sec	Average speed 72.28mph

15	Maserati A6 GCS	2053	Eager W	1oa	1cl EM

	Maserati A6 GCS		Lloyd W	2oa	2cl EM
50	Maserati A6 GCS	2039	Koster F	3oa	3cl EM
86	OSCA MT4 1450	1137	Johnston S	4oa	1cl FM
73	Austin-Healey 100S	3504	Allen F		1cl D
3	Aston-Martin DB2 Offy		Hansgen W		1cl CM
	Jaguar XK120		Wallace C		1cl C
9	Frazer-Nash LM MkII	100/174	Bonadies A		
12	Porsche 356		Miller F		
18	Austin-Healey 100S		Cooper J		2cl D
1	Frazer-Nash		Boss R		
10	Jaguar XK120M		McKenna T		
13	Pegaso 2.8		Hannaway B	Dnf L19	
52	Siata 208S	BS 501	Cicurel R		
4	Lester-MG		Black D		
20	Bandini Siluro Offy		Pauley J		
34	Kieft-Bristol		Ceresole P		
49	MG-Offenhauser		Micheals D		
68	MG TD mod		Atkins G		
71	Austin-Healey 100		Wonder W		
48	Porsche 356		Graham J		

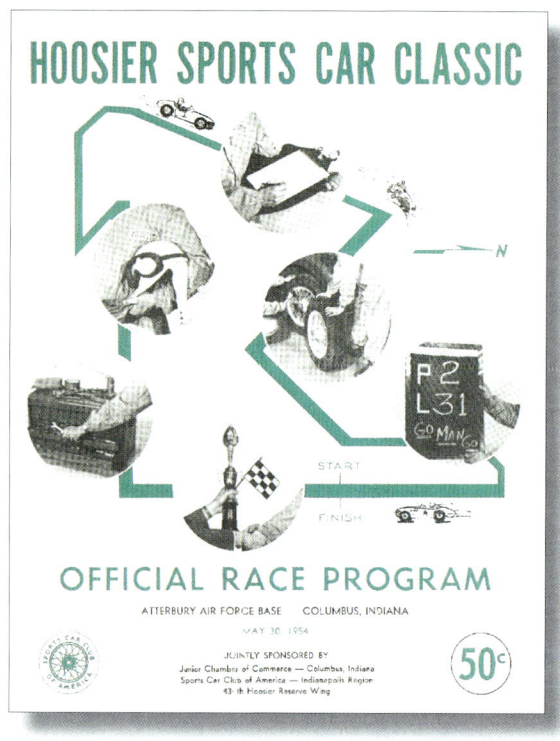

Programme cover for the Atterbury AFB event.
(Terry O'Neil Collection)

Atterbury AFB 30.5.1954

R1 Jaycee Cup 15 laps	Race distance 56 miles	Class F	Starters

Race winner's time 50min 31.2sec	Average speed 66.5mph

77	Porsche 356 Super	Magenheimer R	1oa	1cl F
36	Porsche 356 Super	Pickerel W	2oa	2cl F
85	MG TF	Durbin R	3oa	1cl F TF
73	Porsche 356 Super	McClintock	4oa	3cl F
52	Porsche 356 Super	Shuck W	5oa	4cl F
47	Porsche 356 America	Crane L		1cl F PA
91	Porsche 356 America	Baker R		2cl F PA
54	Porsche 356 America	Tappan R		3cl F PA
48	Porsche 356 America	Brown C		4cl F PA
45	MG TF	Patton N		2cl F TF
89	MG TF	Moxley		3cl F TF
6	Singer SM 1500	Cole P		1cl F misc
71	MG TD MkII	Snowdon J		2cl F misc
64	Porsche 356 1300	Geoghegan R		3cl F misc
87	Volkswagen	Wilder E		4cl F misc
30	Singer SM 1500	Goodman B		5cl F misc

79	MG TD	Lange S		1cl F-TD
100	MG TD	Cooper W		2cl F-TD
42	MG TD	Boardman M		3cl F-TD
94	MG TD	Biggs		4cl F-TD
31	MG TD	Marlett		5cl F-TD
69	MG TD	Mills D		6cl F-TD
41	MG TD	Pettit M	Dnf L5	
23	MG Special	Salzgaber R	Dnf L1	

R2 Bartholomew County Tr 15 laps	Race distance 56 miles	Class C, D	Starters

Race winner's time 48min 16.5sec	Average speed 69.6mph

66	Jaguar XK120M	Kilborn J	1oa	1cl CM
56	Jaguar XK120M	Grove J	2oa	2cl CM
114	Jaguar XK120M	Sclavi F	3oa	3cl CM
34	Jaguar XK120M	Attaway C	4oa	4cl CM
70	Jaguar XK120	Newcomer T	5oa	1cl C
104	Austin-Healey 100	Vollmer P	6oa	1cl D
107	Jaguar XK120M	Lawrence E		5cl CM

#	Car		Driver		Class
32	Jaguar XK120M		Davis W		6cl CM
112	Jaguar XK120		Kopplin K		2cl C
35	Jaguar XK120		Nelson		3cl C
68	Jaguar XK120		Rowell K		4cl C
49	Austin-Healey 100		Tardiff Dr		2cl D
51	Austin-Healey 100		Dukes D		3cl D
75	Austin-Healey 100		Waxelman		4cl D
57	Austin-Healey 100		Stewart P		5cl D
26	Triumph TR2		Salzgaber R	Dnf L6	6cl D*
55	Austin-Healey 100		Earl	Dnf	
105	Austin-Healey 100		Austin A	Dnf	
95	Jaguar XK120M		Woodnorth H	Dnf	
18	Jaguar XK120M		Ensley J	Dns	

*car moved up from class E

Hoosier Res Wing Tr 20 laps	Race distance 74 miles	Class F, GM, HM	Starters

Race winner's time 1hr 9min 0.3sec		Average speed 64.3mph	

#	Car		Driver		Class
77	Porsche 356 1500		Magenheimer R	1oa	1cl F
97	Siata 300BC 1100 Spyder	ST 435 BC	Bentley J	2oa	1cl GM
85	MG TF		Durbin R	3oa	1cl F-TF
88	Bandini Crosley		MacArthur S	4oa	1cl HM
4	Siata 300BC 750 Spyder		Seaverns B	5oa	2cl HM
6	Singer SM 1500		Cole P	6oa	2cl F
54	Porsche 356 America		Allen D	7oa	1cl F-P
48	Porsche 356 America		Brown C		2cl F-PA
91	Porsche 356 America		Baker R		3cl F-PA
45	MG TF		Patton N		2cl F-TF
89	MG TF		Moxley		3cl F-TF
79	MG TD		Lange S		1cl F-TD
43	MG TD		Stoll C		2cl F-TD
94	MG TD		Biggs		3cl F-TD
69	MG TD		Mills D		4cl F-TD
71	MG TD MkII		Snowdon J		3cl F
3	Lotus MkVI-MG	26	Rubini G		2cl GM
109	Fiat Balilla		Forsyth P		3cl GM
37	Bandini-Crosley		Whitlock J		3cl HM
9	Siata 300BC 750 Spyder		Jones		4cl HM
38	Siata 300BC 750 Spyder		Mueller J		5cl HM
83	Crosley Super Sport		Carr		6cl HM
67	Nardi-Crosley		Arnolt S	Dnf L3	
98	Nardi Spyder		Gougleman P	Dnf	

30	Singer 1500 SM		Goodman	Dnf	

Columbus Cup 20 laps	Race distance 74 miles	Class BM, CM, DM, EM, C, D, F	Starters 39

Race winner's time 59min 16.8sec		Average speed 74.9mph	

#	Car		Driver		Class
5	Ferrari 375 MM	0364 AM	Kimberly J	1oa	1cl CM
15	Ferrari 340 AM	0204 A	Lunken E	2oa	2cl CM
33	Fageol-Porsche Special		Fageol L	3oa	3cl CM
1	Kurtis 500 S		Rigden J	4oa	1cl BM
8	Arnolt-Bristol Bolide		Wacker F	5oa	1cl EM
66	Jaguar XK120M		Kilborn J	6oa	1cl C
53	Allard J2X Cadillac	J1859	Gray W		4cl CM
177	Ford Special		Evans		Cl CM
2	Allard J2 Cadillac		Skogmo D		2cl BM
34	Jaguar XK120M		Attaway C		2cl C
56	Jaguar XK120M		Grove J		3cl C
46	Jaguar XK120M		Silkman M		4cl C
107	Jaguar XK120M		Lawrence E		5cl C
39	Jaguar XK120M		Mueller J		6cl C
92	Ferrari 166MM	0054 M	Heldt W		2cl EM
19	Siata 208S Spyder	BS 530	Kuhn R		3cl EM
76	Siata 208S		Ball W		4cl EM
7	Ferrari 166MM	0010 M	Cornett D		5cl EM
24	MD TC s/c		Dietrich C		6cl EM
70	Jaguar XK120		Newcomer T		1cl CP
112	Jaguar XK120		Kopplin K		2cl CP
35	Jaguar XK120		Nelson		3cl CP
110	Excalibur J		Ullrich H		1cl DM
111	Excalibur J		Gary R		2cl DM
93	MG TD		Krasburg R		1cl FM
40	MG TD		Queen J		2cl FM
78	Allard Palm Beach		Wilson C		3cl FM
116	MG TD		Antos		4cl FM
14	MG TD		Rickert C		1cl F-TD
10	MG TD		Andrews F		2cl F-TD
13	MG TD		Holland J		3cl F-TD
11	MG TD		Kriplen D		4cl F-TD
12	MG TD		Eichrodt		5cl F-TD
55	Austin-Healey 100LM		Earle J		1cl D
51	Austin-Healey 100		Dukes D		2cl D
105	Austin-Healey 100		Austin A		3cl D
26	Triumph TR2		Salzgaber R	Dnf L4	
50	MG TC V8-60		Kite H		

	Aston-Martin DB2 Offy		Hansgen W	Dnf
	Ferrari 225S	0220 ED	Hassan C	Dns

Westover AFB 13.6.1954

Minute Man Trophy 12 laps	Race distance 45 miles	Class F, GM, HM	Starters approx. 16

Race winner's time 36min 44sec	Average speed 73.5mph

7	OSCA MT4 1100	1112	Makins R	1oa	1cl GM
3	Bandini Crosley		Rudkin H	2oa	1cl HM
74	PBX Special		Poole C	3oa	2cl HM
77	Siata 300BC 1100 Spyder	ST 435 BC	Bentley J	4oa	2cl GM
54	Porsche 356 Super		Bye J	5oa	1cl F
76	Siata 300BC 1100 Spyder		Kern W	6oa	3cl GM
16	Crosley Super		Stetson H	7oa	3cl HM
47	Porsche 356 Super		Hanna H	8oa	2cl F
34	Porsche 356 Super		Hunt E	9oa	3cl F

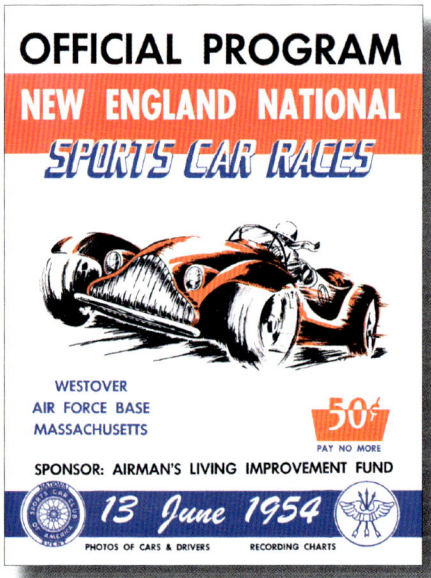

Programme for the Westover AFB event. (Terry O'Neil Collection)

119	Siata 300BC 1100 Spyder		Norwood J	10oa	4cl GM
18	Giaur		Dominianni F	11oa	4cl HM
52	Siata 300BC 750 Spyder	ST 425 BC	Ahr K	Dnf L9	
41	Nardi Spyder		Vitale D	Dnf L8	
56	Cisitalia 202		Di Giacomo C	Dnf L7	
19	Porsche 356 Super		Lilley L	Dnf L5	
99	Crosley		Arnold L	Dnf L5	
48	Porsche 356 Super		Graham J		
55	Siata 300BC 1100 Spyder		Keller R		

Paul Reeve Cup 19 laps	Race distance 75 miles	Class C	Starters

Race winner's time 55min 35.76sec	Average speed 80.94mph

40	Jaguar XK120	Wallace C	1oa	1cl C
1	Jagaur XK120M	Boss R	2oa	2cl C
8	Jaguar XK120M	Crusoe J	3oa	3cl C
9	Jaguar XK120M	Perrin J	4oa	4cl C
23	Jaguar XK120M	McKenna T	5oa	5cl C
64	Jaguar XK120M	Bucher R	6oa	6cl C
29	Jaguar XK120M	Norman J	7oa	7cl C
20	Jaguar XK120M	Fahnestock H	8oa	8cl C
33	Jaguar XK120	Fonda D	9oa	9cl C
57	Jaguar XK120	Ceresole P	10oa	10cl C
88	Jaguar XK120	Randle W	11oa	11cl C
21	Jaguar XK120M	Constantine G	R	
30	Jaguar XK120M	Sadri V		
32	Jaguar XK120M	Appleton F	R	
38	Jaguar XK120	Eager W		
42	Jaguar XK120M	Forno V	Dnf	
46	Jaguar XK120	Kaplan J		
61	Jaguar XK120M	Conrad J		
69	Jaguar XK120	Lawrence E	Dnf	
83	Jaguar XK120	Locarni R	Dnf	

R = raced, no result available

Clipper Cup 18 laps	Race distance 65 miles	Class D, F, FM, GM, HM	Starters

Race winner's time 48min 49.02sec	Average speed 79.89mph

91	OSCA MT4 1450	1133	Kimberly J	1oa	1cl FM

85	Austin-Healey 100		Kincheloe W	2oa	1cl D
93	Siata 208 S	BS 501	Schrafft G	3oa	1cl EM
4	Lester-MG		Black D	4oa	2cl FM
22	Austin-Healey 100S	3505	Allen F	5oa	2cl D
7	OSCA MT4 1100	1112	Makins R	6oa	1cl GM
65	Frazer-Nash		Moran C	7oa	2cl EM
95	Triumph TR2		McConkey R	8oa	3cl D
35	OSCA MT4 1450		Weinman M	9oa	3cl FM
89	Triumph TR2		Robinson J	10oa	4cl D
28	MG TD-Offy		Sinon F & Michaels R		3cl EM
34	Porsche 356 Super		Hunt E		1cl F
47	Porsche 356 Super		Hanna H		2cl F
43	MG TF		Davidson M		3cl F
77	OSCA MT4 1100		Bentley J		2cl GM
76	Siata 300BC 1100 Spyder		Kern W		3cl GM
3	Bandini Crosley		Rudkin H		1cl HM
74	PBX Crosley		Poole C		2cl HM
18	Giaur		Dominianni F		3cl HM
70	Maserati A6 GCS	2039	Koster F	Dnf L8	
2	Frazer-Nash MM		Grey H		
14	Austin-Healey 100S	3504	Cooper J	R*	
16	Crosley Super		Stetson H		
19	Porsche 356 Super		Lilley W		
24	Bandini Siluro-Siata 1500		Merrill R	R	
27	Austin-Healey 100		Simonds H	R	
41	Nardi Spyder		Vitale D		
44	OSCA MT4 1450	1139	Moffett G		
45	Austin-Healey 100		Deane C	R	
48	Porsche 356 Super		Graham J	R	
50	Austin-Healey 100		Miller E	R	
51	MG TD		Cornell R		
53	MG TD		Cuomo R		
59	Austin-Healey 100		Kunz H	R	
62	Siata 300BC 1100 Special		Conley A		
63	OSCA MT4 1450	1138	Brewster W		
78	OSCA MT4 1350	1124	Wessell III H	Dnf	
79	Austin-Healey 100		Jackson-Moore R		
86	Denzel		Toland R		
87	Austin-Healey 100		Livingstone K	Dnf	
90	Austin-Healey 100		Zuver G		
94	Austin-Healey 100		Gilmartin R	R	
119	Siata 300BC 1100 Spyder		Norwood J		

*R = raced, no result available

Mayflower Race 12 laps	Race distance 45 miles	Class F, GM, HM	Starters

Race winner's time 37min 34.38sec		Average speed 71.86mph	

77	Siata 300BC 1100 Spyder	ST 435 BC	Bentley J	1oa	1cl GM
75	MG TF		Richardson R	2oa	1cl F-MG
56	Cisitalia 202		Di Giacomo C	3oa	2cl GM
76	Siata 300BC 1100 Spyder		Kern W	4oa	3cl GM
43	MG TF		Davidson M	5oa	2cl F-MG
47	Porsche 356		Hanna H	6oa	1cl F
72	MG TD		Dager J	7oa	3cl F-MG
11	MG TD		Bastrop L	8oa	4cl F-MG
119	Siata 300BC 1100 Spyder		Norwood J	9oa	4cl GM
98	MG		Boss R	10oa	5cl F-MG
97	MG		Hahn D	11oa	6cl F-MG
58	MG TD		Sterling G	12oa	7cl F-MG
67	MG		Berckemeyer J	13oa	8cl F-MG
16	Crosley		Stetson H	14oa	1cl HM
39	MG TD MkII		Robinson O	15oa	9cl F-MG
12	MG TD		Holbert R	R	
31	MG TD		Ehrman G	R	
51	MG TD		Cornell R		
53	MG TD		Cuomo R		
60	MG TF		Nash R		
7	OSCA MT4 1100	1112	Makins R	Dnf	
68	MG TC		Rodier R	Dnf	
82	MG		Burgess T	R	
84	MG TD		Rodney M	Dnf	
18	Giaur		Dominianni F	Dnf	

R = raced, no result available

Steve Canyon Classic 47 laps	Race distance 175 miles	Class Unrestricted	Starters

Race winner's time 2hr 5min 13.38sec		Average speed 83.85mph	

5	Ferrari 375 MM	0364 AM	Kimberly J	1oa	1cl CM
25	Ferrari 225 S	0166 ED	Lloyd W	2oa	1cl DM
4	Lester-MG		Black D	3oa	1cl FM
40	Jaguar XK120		Wallace C	4oa	1cl C
64	Jaguar XK120		Bucher R	5oa	2cl C
8	Jaguar XK120		Crusoe J	6oa	3cl C
65	Frazer-Nash		Moran C	7oa	2cl DM
42	Jaguar XK120		Forno V	8oa	4cl C
10	Nash-Healey LM		Gray P	9oa	2cl CM

13	Austin-Healey 100S	3504	Cooper J	10oa	3cl DM
71	Allard J2		Keith R		3cl CM
22	Austin-Healey 100S	3505	Allen F		1cl D
14	Austin-Healey 100		Jackson-Moore R		2cl D
89	Triumph TR2		Robinson J		3cl D
81	MG		Licht E		2cl FM
34	Porsche 356		Hunt E		3cl FM
46	Allard J2		Kaplan J	R*	Cl BM
110				R	Cl CM
36	Allard J2X		Rutherford S	Dnf	Cl BM
73	Fageol-Porsche Special		Fageol L	Dnf	Cl CM
6	Ferrari 225S	0220 ED	Lunken E	Dnf	
1	Jaguar XK120M		Boss R		
2	Frazer-Nash LM		Grey H		
7	OSCA MT4 1100	1112	Makins R		
9	Jaguar XK120M		Perrin R		
17	Bandini Siluro Offy		Pauley J	R	
20	Jaguar XK120M		Fahnestock H	R	
23	Jaguar XK120M		McKenna T	R	
24	Bandini Siluro-Siata 1500		Merrill R	R	
26	Allard J2 Cadillac		Carveth R		
27	Austin-Healey 100		Simonds H	R	
28	MG TD Offenhauser		Sinon F		
32	Jaguar XK120M		Appleton F	R	
33	Jaguar XK120		Fonda D		
35	OSCA MT4 1450		Weinman M		
37	Aston-Martin DB2		Hansgen W	R	
44	OSCA MT4 1450	1139	Moffett G		
47	Porsche 356 Super		Hanna H		
50	Austin-Healey 100		Blanchard H		
61	Jaguar XK120M		Conrad J		
63	OSCA MT4 1450	1138	Brewster W		
66	Ford-Riley		Rabe G		
69	Jaguar XK120		Lawrence E		
70	Maserati A6 GCS	2039	Koster F		
78	OSCA MT4 1350	1124	Wessells III H		
80	Pegaso		Fanelli L		
85	Austin-Healey 100		Herson D	R	
86	Denzel		Toland R		
87	Austin-Healey 100		Livingstone M		
88	Jaguar XK120		Randle B		
90	Austin-Healey 100		Zuver G		
91	OSCA MT4 1450	1133	Simpson J		
92	Jaguar XK120		Timmins P		
93	Siata 208 S	BS 501	Schrafft G	R	
94	Austin-Healey 100		Gilmartin R		
95	Triumph TR2		McComkey R	R	
117	Kurtis 500 S Cadillac		Ensley J	DNS	

R = raced, no result available

Fort Worth 15.8.1954

Eagle Mountain Tr	Race distance	Class C, D, E, F	Starters

Race winner's time 30min		Average speed	

3	Jaguar XK120M		Fenner H Dr	1oa	1cl C
10	Jaguar XK120M		Masterson R	2oa	2cl C
46	Jaguar XK120M		Attaway C	3oa	3cl C
39	Porsche 356		Staley I	4oa	1cl F
15	Austin-Healey 100		Banes W		1cl D
4	Austin-Healey 100		Scroggle V Dr		2cl D
	Austin-Healey 100		Bibb T		3cl D
	Porsche 356 Super		Bunker A		2cl F
44	Porsche 356		Rich J		3cl F
51	Jaguar XK120		Schroeder R		4cl C
9	Porsche 356		Richter R		
16	MG		Joerns J		
17	MG		Petersen R		
18	Siata 208S		Rezzaghi C		
19	MG TD MkII		Heath R		
26	Jowett Jupiter		Wright G		
36	Austin-Healey 100		Thomas J		
42	Austin-Healey 100		Cashion A		
48	Jaguar XK120		McGrade E		
49	Austin-Healey 100		Simpson R		
51	Jaguar XK120		Schroeder R		
53	MG TD		Wilson C		
12	Nash-Healey		Parks O		
56	MG TC		Goans J		

Blue Bonnet Cup 12 laps	Race distance 36 miles	Class Unrestricted	Starters

Race winner's time		Average speed	

23	Jaguar C-Type	XKC 020	Shelby C	1oa	1cl CM
	Allard J2 Cadillac		Koehne G	2oa	1cl BM
7	Jaguar C-Type	XKC 034	McMullen L	3oa	2cl CM
1	Allard JR Cadillac	3404	Jarnigan W	4oa	2cl BM

43	MG TC V8-60		Harvey S	5oa	1cl DM
24	Continental-MG Special		Scott N	6oa	1cl FM
11	Moretti		Cherryhomes R	7oa	1cl HM
48	Jaguar XK120		McGrade E		1cl C
21	MG Special		Whitehead B		2cl FM
56	Nardi		Samuelson R		2cl HM
35	Siata 300BC 750 Spyder		Place A		3cl HM
12	Nash Healey		Parks O	Dnf L3	
80	Jaguar C-Type	XKC 033	Gregory R	Dnf	
5	MG mod		Donoghue W		
6	Austin-Healey 100M		Ellison R		
8	Alfa Romeo Disco Volante		Rezzaghi C		
10	Jaguar XK120		Masterson R		
22	MG Special		Saunders J		
27	Siata 300BC 750 Spyder		Robb H		
31	Jaguar C-Type		Simons G		
32	Allard J2X Chrysler	J1732	Duncan D		
34	Giaur		Betts W		
40	MG TC Special		Bowen C		
54	MG TD		Hill P		
109	Allard J2 Cadillac		Rose D		
52	Crosley		Mayfield E		

Oregan Trophy 5 laps | Race distance 15 miles | Class MG | Starters

Race winner's time | Average speed

55	MG TC	Goans J	1oa	1cl F
19	MG TD MkII	Heath R	2oa	2cl F
28	MG TD	Roberts W	3oa	3cl F
16	MG	Joerns R		
17	MG	Peterson R		
29	MG TD	Galbraith G		
30	MG	Fortson K		
33	MG	Boyles W		
38	MG	Jelley J		
41	MG	Gray D		
47	MG	McGrade E		
50	MG	Bowen C		
53	MG TD	Wilson C		

Colonal's Cup 15 laps | Race distance 45 miles | Class F, FM, GM, HM | Starters

Race winner's time | Average speed

24	Continental-MG Special		Scott N	1oa	1cl FM
39	Porsche 356		Staley I	2oa	1cl F
	Porsche 356 Super		Bunker A	3oa	2cl F
11	Moretti		Cherryhomes R	4oa	1cl HM
21	MG Special		Whitehead B	5oa	2cl FM
44	Porsche 356		Rich J	6oa	3cl F
34	Giaur		Betts W		2cl HM
27	Siata 300BC 750 Spyder		Robb H		3cl HM
9	Porsche 356		Richter R		
16	MG		Joerns J		
20	MG TD		Galbraith G		
22	MG		Saunders J		
26	Jowett Jupiter		Wright G		
35	Siata 300BC 750 Spyder		Place A		
54	MG TD		Hill P		
56	MG TC		Goans J		

Guardsman's GP 25 laps | Race distance 75 miles | Class Unrestricted | Starters 17

Race winner's time 55min 5sec | Average speed 80.6mph

23	Jaguar C-Type	XKC 020	Shelby C	1oa	1cl CM
7	Jaguar C-Type	XKC 034	McMullen L	2oa	2cl CM
3	Jaguar XK120M		Fenner H Dr	3oa	1cl C
	Allard J2 Cadillac		Koehne G	4oa	1cl BM
10	Jaguar XK120M		Masterson R	5oa	2cl C
4	Austin-Healey 100		Scroggle V Dr		1cl D
	Austin-Healey 100		Bibb T		2cl D
24	Continental-MG Special		Scott N		1cl FM
46	Jaguar XK120M		Attaway C		3cl C
48	Jaguar XK120M		McGrade E		
51	Jaguar XK120M		Schroeder R		
37	Austin-Healey 100		Reece H		3cl D
27	Siata 300BC 750 Spyder		Robb H		1cl HM
56	Nardi		Samuelson R		2cl HM
40	MG TC Special		Bowen C	Dnf	
1	Allard JR Cadillac	3404	Jarnigan W	Dnf	
80	Jaguar C-Type	XKC 033	Gregory R	Dnf	

13

1954-end of the SCCA/SAC era

An important era of co-operation between the SCCA and Strategic Air Command came to an untimely end in 1954. It was not because of lack of organisation, safety issues or the amounts of funds raised, but because the initial idea had spiralled out of the control of the SCCA and Curtis LeMay. Complaints, real or imagined, had come to the attention of the politicians, or to be more precise, one in particular, Congressman Errett P Scrivner. With his own agenda to fulfil, the chance of getting the better of an opponent who had the potential of being able to wield more influence than himself, was just too good to miss. That opponent was Curtis LeMay.

As in most large organisations, where numerous people are involved in the running of the business, it is impossible to achieve complete harmony within the workforce. So it was with the SCCA/SAC races. From day one, it was a learning curve for all concerned, and, inevitably, mistakes were made. In the main, military discipline won through, though there was always the possibility of disquiet amongst the ranks. This occasionally came to the fore, and when aired publicly, the publicity came to the notice of the chairman of the House Subcommittee of Air Force Appropriations, Errett Power Scrivner.

Complaints based on local issues were generally dealt with by the Base Commander concerned, but the issue that concentrated Scrivner's mind came as a result of a letter sent to the *Tampa Tribune* by two airmen based at MacDill AFB.

The letter, printed on February 28 1954, appeared under the banner headline: "Did MacDill Races Cost Taxpayers $100,000?" and alleged that hundreds of MacDill officers and airmen were coerced into buying tickets, and selling tickets off base as far away as Clearwater. At MacDill, airmen had been utilised to put up spectator stands, which had been trucked to and from the base by the Air Force at a cost of 54 cents a mile, and to dismantle an entire maintenance dock. During this process, most of these men performed no military duties. Airmen were then asked to 'volunteer' labour to staff the races during their recreational time. It was maintained that the event had wasted thousands of hours and $100,000 of tax payers' money because of what they called General LeMay's " … fanatic devotion to sports car racing." The letter concluded, "… except for hot-rod and racing fans, there is no profit, only loss involved. Since when has the Air Force existed to satisfy the whims of one man to the detriment of its primary mission, the establishment of effective air power for the defence of our nation?"

On March 8 1954 during the debate on the military appropriations bill, Scrivner demanded answers from the Air Force to the questions raised in the letter. Scrivner purported to have an open mind on the issues surrounding the sports car races, and stated the following: "It is not that I am opposed to somebody having sports car races or entertaining the public or anything else, but it has many repercussions, and I am opposed to the use of Government property and dollars for that purpose." (*Sports Car.*) Scrivner claimed that his motive in raising the issue at the appropriations bill debate was to give the Air Force ample time to answer the charges, before the imminent SCCA/SAC race at nearby Andrews AFB, which President Eisenhower was expected to attend. What the Air Force was not aware of was that Scrivner had his backroom boys in the General Accounting Office crunching out the 'hidden costs,' such as depreciation on equipment, operating expenses, and loss of proficiency, and training involved in holding the events. Today, that would be termed as 'creative accountancy.'

Scrivner concluded that, "… they (the races) cost Uncle Sam far more than is contributed to the recreational funds of sponsoring bases. It would be far better and cheaper if Congress, upon need shown, appropriated more money, $3 or $4 or $5 per airman, for added comforts, rather than have these races disrupt base operations." (*Kansas City Times*) "It does not appear to be an effective means of improving the living conditions of airmen, particularly in relation to the personal sacrifices and disruptions to business entailed." (*Atchison Globe*.)

Responding to the general points made by congressman Scrivner, Col AJ Beck, commander at Offutt AFB, stated in the Sunday 18 April issue of the *Journal Star* newspaper: "Charges that sports car races at SAC bases might have cost more than they netted were simply not so." Referring specifically to the Offutt race, Beck stated, "Our records are open for inspection by Congressman Scrivner or anyone else, any time. I cordially invite the citizens of Omaha, out State Nebraska, and Iowa to come to the next race on 4 July and see for themselves the manner in which it is conducted, and to inspect the many benefits provided by last year's race."

The Air Force came back to Scrivner to protect their position, giving details of the income and expenditure of the events held so far, stating that net proceeds to date amounted to over $254,000, and that labour, materials, and insurance had been paid for from the gross receipts. They called upon a supporter of the races, Republican Congressman Roman L Hruska, who told the House of Representatives: "This is a meritorious programme. It is well and creditably managed. It is accepted and supported by the public with enthusiasm. It is earnestly hoped that it will continue." (Sports Car)

The answers, though, didn't satisfy Scrivner, as he insisted that, on a financial basis, not everything had been taken into account. He conducted his argument to Congress in such a way that he made it sound as if the nation's taxpayers were, in effect, subsidising the races, while the proceeds were going to the Airman's Living Improvement Fund, and not to the taxpayers, who provided the facilities. He was also unhappy about the aspect of volunteer work carried out by the enlisted men. "There is a difference between the letter and the spirit of how a regulation is enforced," he stated.

In short, Scrivner had already made his mind up, and that was reflected in the manner he presented the case in the House of Representatives (see appendix 1). The realisation of this fact by Curtis LeMay led him to acknowledge that this was a fight he wouldn't win.

"All we wanted to do was to help a bad situation," an unnamed SAC official complained at the time, "… you'd think we were trying to rob a bank."

One awkward question that LeMay had to fend off was why more than forty plane trips had been made in connection with the races. (I don't know the answer to that question, but you can be sure that LeMay didn't admit to flying his team of Allards to some of the races – Author)

Not surprisingly, the SCCA were concerned at the way things were developing, and its President, Charles Moran, and another SCCA official, George Rand, met to confer with Scrivner on May 13 in Scrivner's office at the US Capitol. There, they tried to persuade Scrivner to back down on his position and allow the races to continue. It would appear that their pleas were in vain; the only concession Scrivner was prepared to make was that races arranged for the remainder of the year could go ahead if written contracts were in effect. Assurances of this action came after Scrivner had talked to General Twining, Chief of Staff of the Air Force, and Under Secretary for Air, James Douglas.

In June, the event at Chanute AFB went ahead as originally planned, and according to TK Field, director of national events for the SCCA, the organisation had not been officially advised of the ban. Major General BE Gates, commander at Chanute, took the opportunity to vigorously defend the arrangement between the Air Force and the SCCA. He declared that he would be happy to have the details – and the success – of the races scrutinised by any of the congressmen, or others, that had questioned whether the races should continue. His attempts to help the situation, together with those of Col AJ Beck at Offutt AFB, fell on deaf ears as, when put to the vote, Congress agreed to Scrivner's request for the Air Force to order a cessation of the races.

Finally, the decision to put a stop to the SAC/SCCA programme was announced according to an article published in the *Atchison Globe* on 20 July: "The House was told today that sports car races conducted under Air Force auspices entail 'a great direct and indirect cost to the taxpayers, little of which is accounted for.' 'The average cost per race for military personnel,' Scrivner said in a congressional record statement, 'is estimated by the General Accounting Office at from $23,000 to $115,000. If military labour costs were considered, profits claimed for the races would be turned into a deficit.' The General Accounting Office reported that approximately 100,000 man-hours are expended on each race, of which approximately 20,000 represent regular duty time and 80,000 non-duty, or 'volunteered time.' Other costs not fully accounted for in determining profits from the races include the cost of lumber, canvas, oil and gas, communications and military buses, and tractors."

Scrivner had led a fight in Congress that resulted in cancellation of almost all the races scheduled for the future. As a result of this decision taken by Congress, the races that had not had signed agreements were deleted from the SCCA programme. The end of an era had arrived.

Despite the disappointment felt by the SCCA at the untimely end to the races, they thought it right that they should honour the man who had given them hope for the future. In recognition for his contribution to the SCCA, Curtis LeMay was awarded the Joel Woolf Barnato Award in 1954.

The one redeeming feature from this affair was that people had sat up and taken notice of the success of these races, for they had kept the momentum of sports car racing going at a time when they could so easily have been stopped. They had also prompted individuals and organisations to start investing in new closed circuits throughout America, which would prove the way forward for the sport in the immediate future. Despite the untimely end to these races, they had laid the foundation to a better, safer era in the late 1950s, when other considerations were to concentrate the minds of Clubs and drivers.

The following venues were scheduled by the SCCA for races on a provisional basis, but were subsequently not used for various military operational reasons during 1953.

Castle AFB Meced, California 17-5-1953
Forbes AFB, Topeka, Kansas 21-6-1953
Sherman AFB Fort Leavenworth, Kansas 21-6-1953
Buckley Field NAS, Denver 30-8-1953
Castle AFB Meced, California 4-10-1953

The following venues were cancelled as a result of the ban issued by Congress. At the time of the ban coming into being, agreements between the SAC and the SCCA had not been signed by either one or both parties for use of the locations.

Stewart AFB, Newburgh, New York
Travis AFB, Fairfield, California 26-9-1954
Stead AFB, Reno, Nevada 26-9-1954
Turner AFB, Albany 24-10-1954

Appendix

Transcript of the speech given by Hon Errett P Scrivner in the House Of Representatives on Monday July 19, 1954:

Mr Speaker, during the debate on the military appropriations bill, I discussed the matter of sports car races on Strategic Air Command bases.

This matter has now been looked into from various angles by investigators for the Appropriation Committee and by the General Accounting Office. The GAO report was not available until after the bill had been presented to the House.

In as much as these races have been the subject of magazine and news articles, and editorial comment, parts of the GAO report should be made available to the Congress and to the public, although the question is now moot, inasmuch as the Air Force has ordered all but 3 or 4 future races to be cancelled.

In view of that cancellation, the GAO investigators' work was cut short, but even so, was sufficiently complete to justify the criticism made and to support the action taken by the Air Force.

The introduction and summary of the GAO follows:

Basis for investigation

This investigation was initiated as a result of information received from responsible sources to the effect that sports car races being held from time to time at Air Force bases, particularly bases of the Strategic Air Command, were a serious disruption to normal Air Force business, and provided little, if any, benefit from a financial or moral standpoint. The programme has also been the subject of complaint letters from private citizens and comment in congressional quarters.

Scope of investigation

Investigation included a visit by investigators to MacDill Air Force Base, Florida, in January 1954, while races were being held, development of information from the records at several bases where races previously had been held, and a fairly comprehensive examination of the records and files on the sports car racing programme at Headquarters, Strategic Air Command. Investigation at SAC Headquarters also included interviews with General Curtis E LeMay, Commanding General of SAC, and other Air Force officers connected with the programme.

Summary of findings

The SAC racing programme has taken on the proportions of a major activity. Approximately 100,000 man-hours are expended on each race, of which approximately 20,000 represent regularly scheduled duty time.

SAC regulations provide for reimbursement to the Government for the labour costs of Government-employed civilians, for services furnished, and for Government-owned supplies and materials issued which are not returned to base supply in usable condition. The SAC regulations are at variance with regulations applicable to the Air Force generally in that Air Force regulations also require reimbursement for labour costs of military personnel used on this type of activity. The average labour costs per race for military personnel is estimated at $23,000 for regularly scheduled duty time, and $115,000 overall.

In addition to the cost of military labour, one of the major items of cost for which no reimbursement is made is the use of military equipment, including aircraft. Upwards of 40 trips by airplane have been made between Air Force bases by observer groups in connection with the sports car racing programme.

There appears to be a strong undercurrent of opposition to the racing programme among Air Force personnel, who feel that regular Air Force business operations are seriously disrupted by the general preoccupation of personnel with sports car racing. No substantial evidence was found that military operations were disrupted.

Information developed in the investigation points up a number of legal problems, such as basic legal authority for using military installations for sports car racing, and the legal capacity of the custodian of the Strategic Air Command airmen's living improvement fund to enter into binding agreements with the Sports Car Club of America.

Since the programme brings a net return of hardly more than $5 or $6 per enlisted man per year, it does not appear to be an effective means of improving the living conditions of airmen, particularly in relation to the personal sacrifices and disruptions to business entailed.

By orders of USAF headquarters dated April 28 1954, the scheduling of future sports car races on Air Force bases was prohibited, and races already scheduled, other than those for which binding contracts existed, or for which substantial amounts of funds had been expended, were ordered cancelled. As of the time this report is written, 3 races had been cancelled, 8 races were allowed to remain on schedule, and the fate of 4 races was still under consideration.

Mr Speaker, the report, which supports the above findings, sets out some very interesting points.

Races become major activity

It points out the fact that the SAC races have become a major activity, calling for a 72-page manual of information on how to plan and conduct them. The manual covers layout of course, erection of concession stands, latrines, bleachers, crowd and traffic control, communications, fire fighting, insurance, publicity, and so forth.

Preparations begin three or more months in advance by military personnel at the base, during duty hours for the most part, and, in one or more instances requiring 5 officrs and 6 enlisted men. Surrounding towns are visited – via military transportation – for publicity stories and ticket sales.

Let the report speak for itself:

Work details of enlisted men are used to construct ticket booths, latrines, and food and beverage stands, to erect bleachers and snow fences (for crowd control), and to clean up the base before and after the races. At the Offutt race, five ticket booths were constructed, 16,000ft of snow fence were erected, 14 outdoor latrines were built, nine concessionaire stands were constructed, and borrowed bleacher seats for 25,000 persons were secured, erected, dismantled, stacked, and returned.

Base communications personnel install temporary telephones in race committee headquarters, and provide race day telephone service to the judges' stand, to positions around the track, and to the press box. At Offutt, these services include the installation of switchboard facilities at the judges' stand, which were connected with telephones in the pits, at the starter's position, and at various points around the track. Approximately 11 miles of wire were used in making this installation.

Starting several months before the race day, with a nucleus of key race committee personnel working on a spare-time basis, pre-race activity increases as the date of the race draws near. Three weeks prior to the race, 10 or 15 persons are devoting almost all their duty time to it, with perhaps several hundred working part time. On the day before the race, the day of the race, and the day following, several hundred officers and enlisted men are working full time on the project. One commanding officer estimated that 1100 enlisted men and 72 officers were actively utilised on putting on the race at his base.

The racing event calls for the use of airfield runways, the erection of barricades and markers, requiring the fields to be closed for 2 or 3 days prior to the run, and, of course, the day of the race. Frequently, this calls for the transfer of activities to other nearby bases, such as it did at MacDill, where operations had to be transferred to Tampa Municipal Airport – contact being kept by shuttle bus.

Military manpower required

Crowd control requires many airmen. At Offutt, it is reported that this phase of the race alone called for 10,000 airman hours.

The report states;

No records have been maintained of military man-hours spent on sports car racing.

However, estimates have been made which show that at Turner Air Force Base 18,962 duty hours were expended. The comptroller at Offutt, 1953, estimated 117,239 man-hours were used – duty and non-duty. The average man-hours are in the neighbourhood of 100,000 at a conservative estimate of $1.15 per hour – or $115,000 per race, which far exceeds the gross sales.

The GAO report shows that there is a great direct and indirect cost to the taxpayers, little of which is accounted for.

Although Air Force regulations required reimbursement to the Government for the cost of duty hour activities in events like this, here is what the GAO report says:

Cost to taxpayer

The original SAC regulation on reimbursement to the Government for costs incurred in connection with sports car racing provided that reimbursements would be made "… for any military labour utilised during regularly scheduled duty hours, and for any material furnished by the Government."

The regulations went on to say that material used during the event and returned in undamaged condition would not require reimbursement.

It soon became apparent that reimbursement for military labour would probably turn a race profit into a deficit, and this part of the regulation was never enforced. On April 28 1953, after three SAC races had been run, the regulation was changed to provide for reimbursement to the Government "… for labour utilised on work projects during regularly scheduled duty hours." The effect of this change was to limit reimbursement for military labour to that used on normal base maintenance type construction and repair work. This type of labour has been handled by the services as a "costed" item for many years.

On June 25 1953, shortly before the first Offutt race, and while the local Air Force auditor was pressing for some sort of record keeping on military labour being utilised in the forthcoming Offutt race, the regulation was again changed to provide that reimbursement should be made to the Government "… for civilian employee labour utilised on work projects." The revised regulation went on to say that "… neither reimbursement to the Government for military labour utilised nor the keeping of records thereof is required." The effect of this change was to exempt military labour from reimbursement and to set up a new category of reimbursement, namely, civilian labour, which had not been mentioned in the prior regulations and which is not used to any considerable extent on the sports car races.

How loss turned to profit

Particular attention is called to the GAO statement:

It soon became apparent that reimbursement for military labour would probably turn a race profit into a loss, and this part of the regulation was never enforced.

The report also shows that, although regulations require reimbursement to the Government for civilian labour used, in all except three, there is no record of reimbursement, although it is quite obvious that civilian employees were engaged in these activities – in administration, supervisory, and secretarial work.

Although the Air Force claimed that the duty time was made up by overtime, GAO couldn't find evidence of that, even though it is a known fact that many who were assigned to race duty were given leave or passes with pay.

Little reimbursement

Very little reimbursement was made for material, such as lumber, canvas, wire, film, oil and gas, and so forth, and countless items, which, although small in themselves, eventually run into surprising figures.

No reimbursement is made for use of military vehicles, including planes or the fuel and oil used therein. Neither is there for communication equipment, such as telephones and radio, nor office equipment, tools, and the like.

At Offutt, for instance, reported cost of Government transportation furnished shows that 5-ton tractors were driven 1487 miles, and passenger sedans 2618 miles. However, the reimbursement was just $86.90 for gasoline, and $1.70 for oil.

The GAO reports point out the largest equipment item for which there has been no reimbursement is that of planes used by 'observer groups' who travel under 'temporary duty travel orders.' No per diem was authorised, but all other pay and allowances were received.

Opposition in Air Force

As to the attitude of Air Force personnel, the report shows:

There appears to be a strong undercurrent of opposition to this racing programme among Air Force personnel.

Phone calls which I have received and letters sent to me are convincing proof that this is an understatement.

But let us proceed with the report:

This undercurrent has reached such proportions that many officers have gone out of their way to voluntarily express their feelings to GAO representatives during the course of personal and official conversations. The consensus of the feelings of these officers seems to be that regular Air Force business is seriously disrupted by the general preoccupation of personnel at administrative and supervisory echelons, with the additional responsibilities of the sports car races. Two officers told the investigators that they had successfully objected to having military personnel under their jurisdiction detailed to racing duties on the grounds that their official workloads would not permit the diversion. The inference seemed to be that they had taken this stand at some risk to their Air Force careers, because it would be interpreted as a failure to support command policy.

Military activities interfered with

GAO representatives making an inspection of supply operations at MacDill Air Force Base, at the end of the January 1954 race, found supply office records in a chaotic condition, and the supply division in the process of extensive overhaul. Labour crews, working on special detail from the Warner-Robins air material area, were at work packing and crating hundreds and thousands of dollars worth of excess property that had been generated at the base, apparently due to failure to maintain the necessary paperwork controls over inventories. Nevertheless, on the day following the MacDill races, 22 airmen assigned to the base supply office were away from their jobs, working on a cleanup detail.

In another incident, a representative of the GAO, making arrangements to visit an Air Force base to observe supply operations, was requested by the base command to defer the visit until the following week, because the base was engrossed in getting ready for a sports car race.

The foregoing incidents are typical of the hundreds of disruptions, large and small, that necessarily entail from an operation as extensive as the sports car races. The cost or damage resulting from these disruptions would probably bear no relationship to the vale of the man-hours involved. A few hours of neglect in maintaining supply records can result in hundreds of thousands of dollars lost to the Government.

Were the services volunteered?

The Air Force has stated that most, if not all, of the services rendered were voluntary. My mail reflects an entirely opposite view.

The GAO did not go into this phase of the races. However, their report does show that at MacDill, orders were actually cut detailing officers and men to specific duties in connection with the races. This, according to General LeMay, was a deviation from Air Force policy, yet the Air Force holds that any injury received by military personnel during any of these events will be considered in line of duty.

Although the Air Force also claimed that, contrary to information given to me, leave and passes were not cancelled for a period of time before and after the races.

The report goes into some detail as to the purpose for which expenditures are made, but quite naturally does not raise the question of the attitude of the other military personnel who are on duty on the bases, where funds cannot be so raised and so used.

Repeat performance

The report does show that "… repeat performances are not financially successful" and concludes that the races are not financial successes. The report states:

Turner Air Force Base, first race $47,764, second race $3,964
MacDill Air Force Base, first race $30,746, second race $23,393
Bergstrom Air Force Base, first race $24,337, second race $8,315

Even if the level of return, which has averaged about $28,000 per race up to the present time, could be sustained, it is doubtful that the racing programme could be regarded as a financial success. This return probably represents not more than $5 or $6 per enlisted man a year, a small sum indeed in relation to the effort and personal sacrifice involved on the part of the officers and men in putting on a race, and a drop in the bucket in relation to the overall annual cost to the Government of providing for the housing and welfare of the personnel at any given base.

Effect on morale

While effect on morale was not within the specific orbit of their investigation, the GAO report says:

Also for consideration, of course, is the effectiveness of the programme from the standpoint of morale. SAC Headquarters has taken the position that, apart from the material benefits derived from the programme, a direct morale benefit accrues from airman participation in this type of programme. Against this intangible benefit, there would have to be offset the equally intangible adverse effect on morale of those personnel who do not find the races interesting and whose participation is on something less than a voluntary basis.

Mr Speaker, as I have previously stated, I have no objection to sports car races, as such. However, the use of Government property at the expense to the taxpayer is something to which I do object. I would be derelict in my duty if I did not. It is my purpose to get the greatest amount of defence possible for the lowest number of dollars. Dollars spent for these races are not available for defence.

Personally, I feel that the decision of the Air Force was a proper decision made upon full consideration of all facts, and that such decision, leaving out some rather complex legal questions, is fully justified by the report of the GAO and that of our committee investigators.

(Congressional Record Vol 100 Part 8, pages 10977-10979)

14

SCCA Championship standings

1953

The top 25 places are based on points obtained from 16 Sports Car Club of America National events organised during 1953. It should be noted that of those 16 events, only nine are covered by the text in this book. Drivers were not limited to one car or one class, hence cumulative points for different races at one event could be taken into account. It was a system that faced mounting opposition from the expanding membership, as it was perceived to be biased towards those members having more than one car to compete with. The National Contest Board decided to change the system for the 1954 season.

The ranking for 1953 was as follows:

1 WM Spear 6775 points (Ferrari)
2 RH Makins 6050 points (OSCA)
3 J Kimberly 6000 points (Ferrari)
4 R Fergus 5150 points (MG)
5 K Miles 5000 points (MG Special)
6 JG Benett 4512.5 points (MG, Ferrari)
7 J Ensley 4500 points (Allard)
8 M Gregory 4500 points (Jaguar)
9 P Gougelman 4500 points (Nardi)
10 T Newcomer 4200 points (Jaguar)
11 M Goldman 4150 points (Porsche)

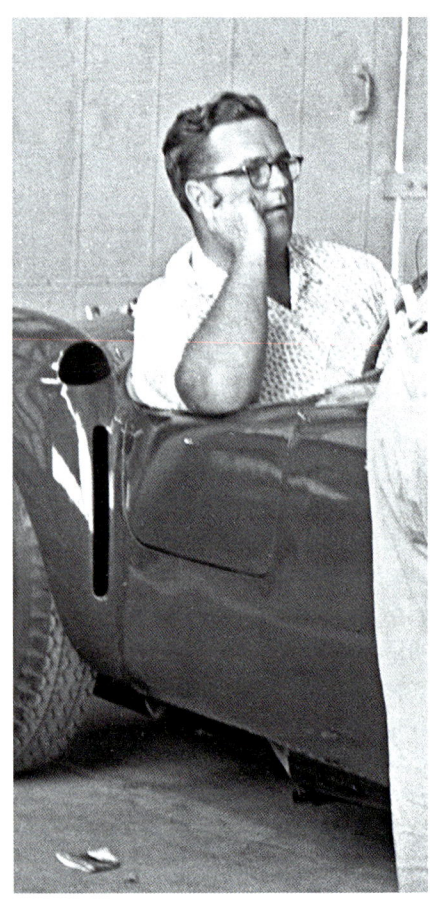

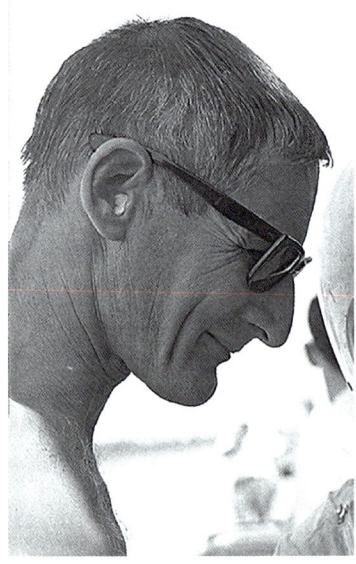

Ken Miles.
(Terry O'Neil Collection)

William Spear.
(Courtesy Wolery Collection IMRRC)

Phil Hill.
(Terry O'Neil Collection)

John Fitch. (left)
(Courtesy Dave Nicholas)

Sherwood Johnston. (in car)
(Courtesy Dave Nicholas)

Jim Kimberly.
(Terry O'Neil Collection)

Briggs Cunningham.
(Courtesy Dave Nicholas)

12 B Cunningham 4075 points (Cunningham, OSCA)
13 J Fitch 4075 points (Cunningham)
14 R Wing 3750 points (Jaguar)
15 P Lovely 3500 points
16 W Lloyd 3400 points (Porsche, Ferrari)
17 P Hill 3300 points (Ferrari, Jaguar)
18 R Bird 3250 points (Jaguar)
19 W Fleming 3250 points (MG)
20 A Coppel 3150 points (OSCA)
21 G Schrafft 3150 points (Crosley)
22 S Johnston 2900 points (Jaguar, OSCA)
23 R Blackwood 2800 points (Jaguar)
24 E Boynton 2750 points (Frazer-Nash)
25 J Cochrane 2750 points (Allard)

1954

A change in the way the SCCA championships were calculated resulted in drivers racing for Class awards, a fairer way of judging a driver on his skill, as opposed to how many cars he could afford to run at any particular event. The change resulted in more entries for races, perhaps because competitors felt that their chance of success had increased significantly.

The top six drivers in Class rankings were as follows:

Class B modified
1 J Ensley 4750 points (Kurtis Kraft)
2 S Johnston 3125 points (Cunningham)
3 W Gray 2500 points (Allard J2X)
4 C Moran 2125 points (Cunningham)
5 P Walters 2000 points (Cunningham)
6 J Meyer 1375 points (Meyer Special)

Class C modified
1 J Kimberly 9500 points (Ferrari)
2 W Spear 4000 points (Ferrari)
3 S Edwards 2750 points (Ferrari)
4 E Erickson 2250 points (Jaguar)
5 J McAfee 2000 points (Ferrari)
6 L Katskee 1875 points (Jaguar)

Class C production
1 C Wallace 6500 points (Jaguar)
2 R Boss 3625 points (Jaguar)
3 E McGrade 2500 points (Jaguar)
4 C Attaway 2000 points (Jaguar)
5 S Weiss 2000 points (Jaguar)
6 W Smith 1625 points (Jaguar)

Class D modified
1 W Lloyd 7000 points (Ferrari)
2 R Lyeth 2500 points (Ferrari)
3 C Hassan 1875 points (Ferrari)
4 W Jarnigan 1500 points (Ferrari)
5 A Melville 1250 points (Ferrari)
6 S Carkhuff 1000 points (Austin-Healey)

Class D production
1 W Kincheloe 3000 points (Austin-Healey)
2 F Allen 2500 points (Austin-Healey)
3 R Jackson-Moore 2000 points (Austin-Healey)

4 G Swift 1750 points (Austin-Healey)
5 L Franke 1375 points (Austin-Healey)
6 W Dantone 1000 points (Austin-Healey)

Class E modified
1 F Wacker 2750 points (Arnolt-Bristol)
2 E Boynton 2750 points (Frazer-Nash)
3 D McNought 2500 points (Maserati)
4 J Lowe 2000 points (Frazer-Nash)
5 J Procter 2000 points (Maserati)
6 W Carpenter 1875 points (Kieft-Bristol)

Class E production
1 R Salzgaber 1875 points (Triumph TR2)
2 F Hern 1000 points (TR2)
3 W Kiekhefer 1000 points (TR2)
4 R McConkey 1000 points (TR2)
5 J Robinson 1000 points (TR2)
6 R Wing 1000 points (TR2)

Class F modified
1 B Cunningham 4375 points (OSCA)
2 P Stewart 2750 points (OSCA)
3 W David 2500 points (OSCA)
4 D Black 2375 points (Lester-MG)
5 G Moffett 2250 points (OSCA)
6 J Von Neumann 2250 points (Porsche)
7 J Simpson 2250 points (OSCA)

Class F production
1 A Bunker 3875 points (Porsche)
2 R Thompson 3875 points (Porsche)
3 R Durbin 2125 points (MG)
4 J Kunstle 1500 points (Porsche)
5 R Pace 1500 points (Porsche)
6 C Lawrence 1375 points (Porsche)
7 P van Antwerpen 1375 points (Porsche)
8 F Proctor 1375 points (Porsche)

Class G modified
1 R Makins 7500 points (OSCA)
2 J Bentley 4000 points (Siata)
3 G Rubini 1750 points (Lotus)
4 A Coppel 1000 points (OSCA)
5 R Keller 1000 points (Siata)
6 C Rutan 875 points (VW Special)

Class H modified
1 C Poole 4000 points (PBX)
2 H Rudkin 2250 points (Bandini)
3 H Everly 2000 points (Crosley)
4 F Crouzet 1500 points (DB)
5 G Schrafft 1500 points (PBC)
6 A Place 1250 points (Siata)

Northeast American Sports Car Races
1950-1959

Terry O'Neil

Hardback • 25x25cm • £100.00 /$200• 432 pages • 499 colour and b&w pictures • ISBN: 978-1-845842-54-3

Focuses on the different aspects that contributed to the emergence of Northeast American sports car racing during the 1950s. Its evolution was neither easy nor uneventful for drivers, clubs or track owners, and the politics, intrigue and tragedy that came to characterise the period are covered here in fascinating detail.

For info on any Veloce book, call +44 (0)1305 260068. email info@veloce.co.uk, or visit us on the web at www.velocebooks.com
• Prices subject to change • P&P extra

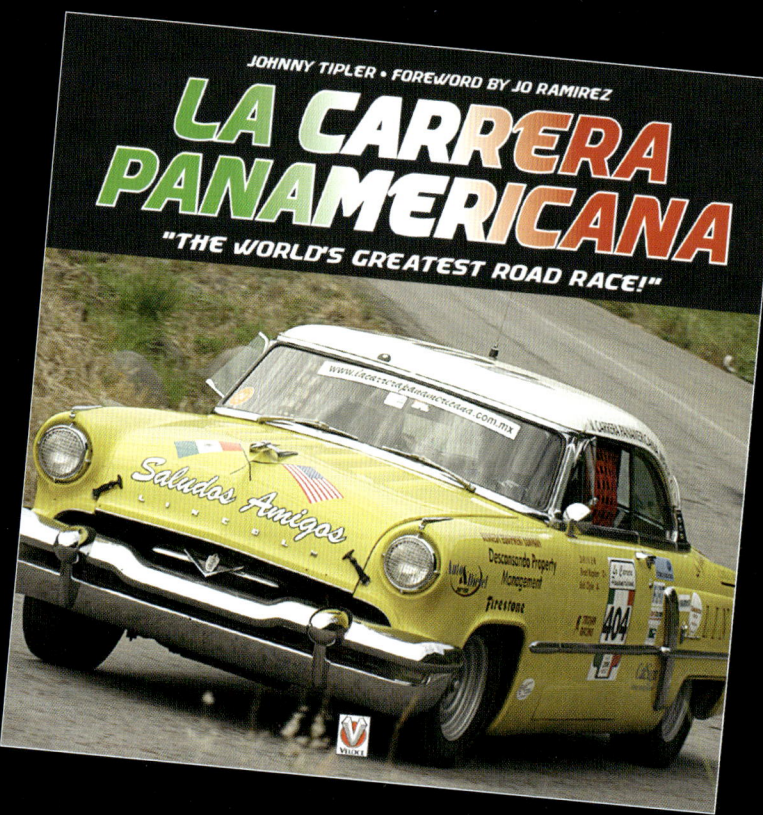

Hardback • 25x25cm • £50.00/$99.95 • 256 pages
• 316 colour and b&w pictures • ISBN: 978-1-845842-46-8

Hardback • 25x25cm • £19.99 • 272 pages
• 429 colour and b&w pictures • ISBN: 978-1-845841-70-6

Following the format of the authors' award-winning The British at Le Mans, this book recounts the history of the Indianapolis 500 race through the eyes and actions of those British-born or British citizens who have driven in it, or been involved in any way – be it as designer, mechanic, or official.

Through photos of the stunning countryside and cities visited en route, action shots and parc fermé, interviews with drivers and key personnel, plus vivid narrative, readers are transported to Mexico for an eye-witness account of the fantastic Carrera Panamericana, "The World's Greatest Road Race." Includes a full history from 1950.

For info on any Veloce book, call +44 (0)1305 260068, email info@veloce.co.uk, or visit us on the web at www.velocebooks.com
• Prices subject to change • P&P extra

Index

Cars

Allard J2 / J2X 37, 54, 84, 86, 98, 109, 111, 128, 138
Allard JR 17, 38, 43, 124-6, 185
Allard K2 19, 21
Allard LM 47, 48, 54
Arnolt-Bristol 180
Aston-Martin DB2 104, 133, 178
Austin-Healey 100 124, 126, 131, 146, 177-8, 184

Bandini 20, 180, 182
Beavis Offenhauser Special 54, 108
Buckler Special 126

Cisitalia 124, 183
Continental-MG Special 98, 111, 185
Cooper F3 47, 147
Crosley 20, 48, 53, 78, 98, 111, 126
Cunningham C2-R 17
Cunningham C3 27, 29
Cunningham C4-R 22, 50, 52, 55, 125, 152
Cunningham C4-RK 22, 127, 141
Cunningham C5-R 50, 52-3, 55

D B Panhard 129
Du Pont Ford Special 86
Dyna-Panhard 97

Excalibur 86, 180

Fageol Special 78-9
Ferrari 166MM 23, 27
Ferrari 212 Ex 27, 97
Ferrari 225 S 22, 27, 43, 86
Ferrari 250 MM 83-4, 124-5, 129
Ferrari 340 AM 23, 27, 48, 97, 111, 138
Ferrari 340 Mexico 27, 32, 43, 45, 53, 103, 105, 129
Ferrari 375 MM 124, 126, 133
Ford Special 33, 47
Frazer-Nash 43, 81, 108

Giaur 48, 129, 185

Glockler-Porsche 20, 33, 76, 83, 85, 126
GMC Aston-Martin 83-4

Hansgen Jaguar Special 104
HRG 126, 153

Jaguar C-type 20, 23, 29, 33, 39, 43-4, 48, 79, 111, 124, 141, 184
Jaguar XK120 / 120M 32, 42-4, 47, 49, 51, 54, 75, 79, 85, 97-9, 108, 126, 128, 146, 177-9, 184
Jaguar XK120 Silverstone 33, 85-6
Jowett 49, 102, 107
Kieft-Bristol 124
Kieft-MG 102
Kurtis 48, 52, 55, 79, 83, 97, 109, 136, 139, 153

Lester-MG 178, 182

Mabee Special 111, 154
Maserati A6 GCS 43, 45, 178

MG TC /TD / TF 10, 12, 20, 33, 42, 47, 51, 54, 75, 80, 83, 98, 102, 108, 124, 126, 138, 180
MG Special 42, 185
Moretti 147, 185
Morgensen –Cadillac Special 97
Motto-MG 176

Nardi 33, 42, 83, 178
Nash-Healey 86, 184

OSCA MT4 20, 23, 27-9, 31, 33, 37, 42, 48, 51, 54, 80, 85, 106, 123, 126, 128, 139, 140, 146, 152, 178, 182

Palm Beach Crosley 124
PBX Crosley Special 131
Porsche 356 41, 49, 54, 78, 85, 128, 131, 139, 146, 153, 177-9
Porsche 356 America 41, 48, 80, 85
Porsche 550 Spyder 48, 130

Riley-Mercury V8 12

Siata 38, 42, 55, 124, 127, 178, 180
Simca 8 Comp Sport 41, 47, 81
Singer 1500 SM 41, 97, 179
Sunbeam Alpine 81

Triumph TR2 153-4, 179, 181

Uihlein Special 138

Volkswagen 107

Whitmore-Fitch Special 27-8, 44

Drivers/Owners
Allen F 177-8
Ash D 101
Attaway C 179, 180

Balchowski M 47
Banta H 47
Barlow R 11
Beavis G 54, 108
Benett J 23, 37, 42, 46, 105-6
Betts W 111, 129, 185
Bird T 97, 108
Black D 178, 182-3
Block C 47-8
Boss R 52, 102, 124, 128, 177
Bott F 138, 151
Bowen C 111
Boynton E 43
Braniff C 130
Briney M 54, 108
Brocken K 32, 138, 147
Brookes J 146
Brown C 23, 37, 185
Byrd R 47, 78

Carsten T 29
Ceresole P 51, 124, 146
Chaney Brown S 32, 38

Chapin S 75-6
Chatfield 47
Cherryhomes R 98, 184-5
Clifford W 98
Cochrane J 47
Cole P 119
Cook F 111
Cooper J 178
Coppel A 48, 80, 83
Cornett D 41
Crawford E 85
Crean J 97
Crouzet F 128
Crusoe J 177
Cunningham B 8, 22-3, 27, 46, 50, 123, 146, 152

Daigh C 81, 108-9
David W 48
Dayton A 39, 98
Demetry T 12
Di Giacomo C 183
Dietrich S 75
Drake R 54, 108
Duncan D 33, 39, 98-9, 139
Durbin R 84, 124, 134-5, 179

Eager W 178
Edwards S 48, 154
Ehrman G 102
Ensley J 21, 33, 37, 51-2, 76, 149, 183
Erickson E 27, 36, 53, 124, 183
Eyerly H 48, 78

Fageol L 79, 85
Fenner H Dr 32, 98, 111, 185
Fergus R 27, 75, 84-5, 134-5, 144
Feuerbacher A 33, 86
Fifield C 78
Fitch J 22-3, 27-8, 50, 125
Fleming W 27, 38

Gardner R 27

Garthwaite A 20, 23
Gegan R 12, 29
Gilchrist J 111
Gillespie W 80
Goldman M 42, 75, 139
Goldschmidt E 102
Gougleman P 33, 42
Graham J 178
Gray W 39, 105
Gregory M 33, 39, 48, 54-5, 103, 105
Gregory R 54, 75, 99, 111, 130, 185
Grier R 11
Grove J Dr 179

Hall J 37
Hamlett J 23
Hannaway B 103
Hansgen W 49, 103-4, 106, 177-8
Hansen R 79
Harrison T 54
Hassan C 20, 85, 102
Heldt W 180
Henderson T 47
Heskall I 42
High T 54
Hill F 39
Hill P 28, 48, 53, 83-4, 97, 153-4
Hively H 153-4
Hoffman M 20
Hopkins R 49
Hudson J 78
Huntoon G 20-1, 23, 28-9, 52, 124

Jarnigan W 111, 130, 185
Jones S 99, 111
Johnston S 28, 33, 51, 178

Katskee L 85, 140, 151
Keller R 51, 124
Kieckhefer W 152, 154
Kilborn J 75, 85, 179

Kimberly J 22, 28, 33, 38, 46, 54, 76, 85, 124-6, 130, 135, 137, 139-41, 149, 151, 180, 183
Kincheloe W 131, 136, 182
Kling K 48
Koehne G 98-9, 109, 184
Koster F 43, 178, 182
Kuhn R 42, 147

Lamoreaux W 97, 102
Larson F 33, 39
Leighton C 33
Leson C 81
Lewis M 23, 39, 76, 151
Lloyd W 37, 52, 102, 106, 135-6, 151, 183
Lovely P 48
Lowe J 81, 108
Lucas T 11
Lunken E 23, 76, 85, 149, 180

Mabee J 98, 111, 154
MacArthur S 85
Magenheimer R 85, 179
Makins R 29, 37, 51, 54, 123, 131, 140, 146, 152, 182
Marsh D 85
McAfee E 55
McAfee J 33, 37, 39, 80, 97
McConkey R 131
McDougall R 48
McMullen L 111, 185
McNought D 136
Menefee R 97, 108
Miles K 54, 80, 83, 97, 108-9
Miller P 102
Moffett G 31, 51, 128
Moore C 41
Moore P 36
Monise F 153
Moran C 62
Morgensen R 97
Murphy R 97

Negley J 48
Newcomer T 36, 39, 75, 180

Pollack W 56, 79
Poole C 51, 106, 131
Proctor F 42, 124, 178

Qvale K 11, 47

Rainwater L 27, 32
Rand G 12
Rigden J 147, 180
Robb H 185
Rodier R 183
Rodney M 102
Rosenberger A 36, 86
Rudkin H 182
Ruttman A 55
Ryberg R 42

Said B 31, 33
Salzgaber R 20, 37, 76, 85, 179, 181
Samuelson R 38, 111
Sands B 53
Sawyer G 48
Schilling D 17, 126
Schott C 103
Scher 47 47
Schrafft G 20, 23, 51, 124, 126, 146, 182
Scott N 98, 111, 135
Scott R 20-1, 32, 50, 52, 111, 124
Shelby C 23, 37, 39, 98-9, 111, 135
Sheppard J 124
Shillam D 108
Simpson J 23, 37-8, 42, 54, 105, 123, 146
Spear W 22-3, 27, 32, 46, 48, 53-4, 56, 103, 105, 124, 126, 135, 138, 141, 149
Steiner R 47
Stiles P 29

Stoll C 42
Stripe M 55, 75-6
Stroppe W 46, 79, 83, 97, 108-9
Swartley K 84
Swift G 47

Thompson R 51, 126, 131, 147
Tilley R 15-17, 34, 36, 52, 124
Trego E 33, 76
Trimble R 47
Trotter D 83-4

Ullrich H 180
Urbas J 39, 76, 85

Van Dyke L 34
Van Hanstein F 48
Vollmer P 179
Von Kreidner E 53
Von Neumann J 11, 33, 48, 97

Wacker F 14-17, 20, 23, 27, 53, 59, 138, 151, 180
Wallace C 47, 86, 102, 137-8
Walters P 27, 50, 52-3, 105, 124, 125, 149
Warner F 27, 37-9
Weiss C 47
Wessells III H 103, 132
Wheeler H 47
Whitmore C 27
Whitney H 147
Williams R 32
Wing R 36, 42-3, 85
Wyllie M Dr 42, 75, 126, 135

Yare R 42
Yates L 97
Yedor C 54

Venues
Andrews AFB 122, 130-137
Atterbury AFB 178-181

Bergstrom AFB 28-34, 128-130
Bridgehampton 12, 34
Broward County Speedway 12
Buchanan Field 11

Chanute AFB 26, 74-76, 122, 137-139

Fort Worth Eagle Mountain NGB 97-99, 110-111, 183-185
Elkhart Lake 12, 20, 75

Floyd Bennett Field NAS 99-106

Golden Gate 34

Hunter AFB 122, 126-128

Janesville 46

Lockbourne AFB 39-45, 141-152
Long Beach NAVSTA / Reeves Field 106-109
Luke AFB 96-97

MacDill AFB 26-28, 123-126
March AFB 53-56, 152-154
Moffett NAS 26, 46, 79-84

Offutt AFB 17, 34-39, 139-141

Paine AFB 26, 40, 76-79
Pebble Beach 12, 34

Reno 46

Sebring 17, 26
Stead AFB 45-48, 151-2
Stout NGB 84-86
Suffolk ADC 175-178

Thompson Raceway 12, 46, 152
Torrey Pines 12
Turner AFB 18-19, 34, 48-53

Watkins Glen 11-12, 18, 152
Westover AFB 140, 181-183

Establishments, organisations, personnel
Airmen's Living Improvement Fund 15, 23, 29, 45, 56, 75, 123, 128, 130-1, 140, 152, 175, 181
American Automobile Association 8, 99, 100
Argetsinger C 12
Automobile Racing Club of America 10-11

Beck A J Col 139, 195

California Sports Car Club 8, 11-12, 53
Collier Baron 10
Collier Miles 10
Collier Sam 10, 12

Dearborn N 20, 23, 35

Eisenhower D President 136-7

Foreign Auto and Sports Car Association 97, 110, 183
Four Cylinder Club of America 8, 11, 53, 96

Gates B Major 74, 76, 138
Grand Prix of Endurance Inc 99, 100

Harris III B 75

LeMay C 14, 16-19, 36, 131, 140, 152, 194-196
Long Beach MG Club 106

MG Car Club 11
Motor Sport Club of America 11

Olds T Commander 18, 23, 34

Puget Sound Sports Car Club 77

Road Racing Register 8

Scrivner E Senator 53, 125, 131, 139, 194-9
Sports Car Club of America 8, 11, 14, 17

Ullman A 26, 99

Williams W 128

Newspapers and magazines
Albany Herald 48
Arizona Republican 96
Atchison Globe 195
Austin American 128
Autosport 48
Car Craft 106
Champaign Urbana Courier 137, 138
Charleston Daily Mail 131, 141
Columbus Dispatch 41, 141, 151
Evening Republican 178
Fort Worth Star-Telegram 97, 110, 183-4
Journal Star 195
Kansas City Times 139, 195
Marion Star 41
Motor Sport World 12
National Speed Sport News 9, 97
News-Gazette Champaign 76
New York Times 99, 176
Nevada State Journal 47
Omaha World Herald 35, 38
Phoenix Gazette 96-7
Reno Evening News 47
Road & Track 53, 74, 76, 79, 123, 130, 175, 181, 183
Speed Age 19, 26, 176
Sports Car 23, 29, 34, 46, 139, 152, 194
Sportswagon 11
Tampa Morning Tribune 123, 125, 194
Time magazine 34, 137
Waukesha Daily Freeman 137